Dialect Writing and the North of England

Dialect Writing and the North of England

Edited by Patrick Honeybone and Warren Maguire

EDINBURGH
University Press

Edinburgh University Press is one of the leading university presses in the UK. We publish academic books and journals in our selected subject areas across the humanities and social sciences, combining cutting-edge scholarship with high editorial and production values to produce academic works of lasting importance. For more information visit our website: edinburghuniversitypress.com

First published in hardback by Edinburgh University Press 2020

Edinburgh University Press Ltd
The Tun – Holyrood Road, 12(2f) Jackson's Entry, Edinburgh EH8 8PJ

Typeset in 11/13pt Adobe Garamond Pro by
Servis Filmsetting Ltd, Stockport, Cheshire,

A CIP record for this book is available from the British Library

ISBN 978 1 4744 4256 5 (hardback)
ISBN 978 1 4744 4259 6 (paperback)
ISBN 978 1 4744 4257 2 (webready PDF)
ISBN 978 1 4744 4258 9 (epub)

Contents

Figures and Tables

Notes on Contributors

Esther Asprey is a Senior Teaching Fellow at the University of Warwick. Her research interests are the dialectology and sociolinguistics of the languages and varieties of the West Midlands of England. She co-authored the first in-depth account of the dialect of the Black Country and is currently researching linguistic change in Herefordshire and Worcestershire.

George Bailey is a Lecturer in the Department of Language and Linguistic Science at the University of York. His research lies at the intersection of sociolinguistics, language change and phonological theory, with a particular focus on the dialects spoken in the North of England.

Joan Beal is Emeritus Professor of English Language at the University of Sheffield. Her research interests are in sociohistorical linguistics and the history and dialectology of English. Publications include 'English in Modern Times 1700–1945' and 'An Introduction to Regional Englishes'.

Natalie Braber is Associate Professor in Linguistics at Nottingham Trent University. She is involved with sociolinguistic research around language variation in the East Midlands and also 'pit talk': the language of miners in the East Midlands. Recent publications include 'East Midlands English' with Jonnie Robinson and 'Sociolinguistics in England' with Sandra Jansen.

Urszula Clark is Professor of English and Linguistics at Aston University in Birmingham. Her most recent publications are 'Staging Language: Place and Identity in the Enactment, Performance and Representation of Regional Dialects' and 'Spake: Dialects and Voices from the West Midlands'.

Paul Cooper is a Lecturer in English Language at the University of Liverpool. His research focuses on regional varieties of English, with a particular emphasis on Yorkshire dialect. He is also interested in the social values associated with a repertoire of 'Yorkshire' features via the processes of indexicality and enregisterment.

Tony Crowley is Professor of English Language at the University of Leeds. He is interested in the politics of language and his publications include 'Standard English and the Politics of Language', 'Wars of Words: The Politics of Language in Ireland 1537–2004' and 'The Liverpool English Dictionary'.

Jack Grieve is a Professorial Fellow in Corpus Linguistics in the Department of English Language and Linguistics at the University of Birmingham. His research interests include quantitative corpus linguistics, dialectology and computational sociolinguistics.

Diansheng Guo is a Professor in the Department of Geography at the University of South Carolina. His research interests include geographical information science, big data analytics and spatial data-mining.

Rod Hermeston is a Lecturer in Linguistics at Leeds Trinity University. His research includes language and identity in dialect song and poetry, and the stylistic analysis of representations of disability.

Jane Hodson is Professor of English Language and Literature at the University of Sheffield. Her current research focuses on the representation of dialect in English literature. In 2013 she completed the AHRC-funded project 'Dialect in British Fiction 1800–1836'. She has published 'Dialect in Literature and Film' and edited 'Dialect and Literature in the Long Nineteenth Century'.

Patrick Honeybone is a Senior Lecturer in the Department of Linguistics and English Language at the University of Edinburgh. He has published widely on phonology, historical phonology and the phonological dialectology of English. He co-edited *The Oxford Handbook of Historical Phonology*, and is an editor of the journal *English Language and Linguistics*.

Marie Møller Jensen is Associate Professor of Modern English Language at Aalborg University, Denmark. Her research interests focus on Tyneside English and include different approaches such as sociocognitive approaches to language variation and change as well as stylistic interpretations of dialect literature.

Warren Maguire is a Senior Lecturer in English Language at the University of Edinburgh. His research focuses on diachronic and synchronic phonological variation in dialects of English and Scots, with a particular concentration on north-east England, southern Scotland and Ulster, and he has published extensively on all of these areas.

Andrea Nini is a Lecturer in the Department of Linguistics and English Language at the University of Manchester. His specialisation is the analysis of linguistic data using computational methods, and his research interests include forensic linguistics, corpus linguistics, computational linguistics and historical authorship attribution.

Ivor Timmis is Emeritus Professor of English Language Teaching at Leeds Beckett University. His research interests are in corpus linguistics for English Language Teaching and historical spoken corpora. He is the author of 'Historical Spoken Language Research', which is based on two small corpora he developed himself: the Mayhew Corpus of 1850s vernacular English, and the Bolton/Worktown Corpus of late-1930s working-class English.

Kevin Watson is an Associate Professor in the Department of Linguistics at the University of Canterbury, New Zealand. He works in the area of sociophonetics. He uses spoken corpora and experimental methodologies to examine language production and perception and phonological change. He has published on the accents of north-west England and New Zealand, and on variation in learning English as a second language.

1

Introduction: What Is Dialect Writing? Where Is the North of England?

Patrick Honeybone and Warren Maguire

1.1. The Rationale for the Volume

How do you write a dialect? This volume addresses this question from a number of different perspectives, considering many of the ways in which people have tried to write dialect (and what that might mean and why they might want to do it), over a number of centuries. All of the examples of texts considered in the book are drawn from one geographical area, for a number of reasons. This is not because this area is necessarily the best place to do it (although a case could be made that, in fact, it *is* the best place to do it, and there are certainly some long traditions of dialect writing in the area[1]). Rather, it is because it can be seen as a coherent part of the English-speaking world – one which has a community of scholars who are interested in it. The area concerned is the North of England. One of the tasks of this Introduction is to explain how we define what this area includes. We do this in Section 1.3. Another task for us here is to explain what we mean by 'dialect writing'. We do this in Section 1.2. As we will see, neither 'the North of England' nor 'dialect writing' is an entirely straightforward thing to define. Our final task in this Introduction is to say something about what each of the remaining chapters in the volume covers and how they fit in with each other. We do that mainly in Section 1.4, although we also refer to chapters where relevant in the other sections of this Introduction (we refer to the volume's chapters using the authors' surnames in SMALL CAPITALS).

The chapters in this volume are interested in dialect writing from a wide range of perspectives – indeed part of the point of the book is to bring together a diverse range of work on the topic, because we expect that we can all learn from each other, even if we are looking at the phenomenon using different analytical methodologies and with different primary goals in mind. The work in this book is interested both in the cultural positioning and impact of the phenomenon of dialect writing *and* in the precise mechanics of how writers produce it. It considers a wide range of types of dialect writing, from eighteenth-century literary texts to twenty-first-century tweeting (so the timeframe that is covered in the volume stretches over the Late Modern and Contemporary periods in the history of English); some contributions are historical while others deal with contemporary material.

Another basic point of this book is to flag up the fact that a large amount of dialect writing exists (and has long existed), produced in a wide range of genres and ways (from poetry to humour to social studies to novels to translations of Standard English texts to locally published pamphlets to handwritten ego-documents to reports of conversations to cartoons to material published in local newspapers to tweets, and much else as well). We hope to raise the profile of dialect writing: there is a lot out there, but much of it is not well-known, and most of it has been very little studied. As the work that we have gathered together here shows, dialect writing is a vastly complex and intricate phenomenon which requires contributions from many disciplines to fully understand. Understanding writers' identities and intentions is crucial, but so is understanding the linguistic structure of the dialects that are being represented, and the nature of the genres that are being written in. Once we broadly understand the phenomenon, we can then see dialect writing texts as linguistic evidence in their own right: evidence of the way in which contemporary dialects are stored and interpreted by speakers (and perceived by readers), and also evidence for earlier stages of dialects (when the texts considered come from an earlier period). Typically, dialect writing is not *intended* to provide evidence to linguists, but it can offer the only evidence that is available for some non-standard varieties at certain points in time.

Given all the above, this book is intended to allow its authors to (i) reflect on some definitional characteristics that define the broad phenomenon of dialect writing, (ii) document what dialect writing exists for certain varieties spoken in the North of England, and (iii) set out some results from the study of specific kinds of dialect writing from the area. It raises (and in part tries to answer) a range of questions, including the following:

- What kinds of genres of dialect writing exist?
- What dialect writing exists for specific dialects at specific periods?
- Who is dialect writing meant for?
- What do writers do when they do dialect writing?
- Why do writers produce dialect writing?
- What attitudes towards dialect does dialect writing reveal?

- How successful is dialect writing in representing dialect variation?
- In what ways can specific repertoires of dialect features become enregistered in dialect writing?
- How useful is dialect writing as linguistic evidence?
- How and to what extent are dialect features represented in dialect writing?
- What kinds of dialect features get represented in dialect writing?
- What types of methodology can we use to investigate dialect writing?

1.2. What Is 'Dialect Writing'?

The defining characteristic of dialect writing is that it intends to represent a non-standard dialect in written form, at least to some degree and in some portion of a text. We should be cautious about assuming that dialect writing is a coherent thing, and that all the texts involved have much in common, however, because there is vast diversity in dialect writing texts. A text could involve a single word or a whole book. A text could involve only small sections of dialect writing (embedded in a text which is otherwise written in Standard English), or the dialect writing could take up the whole text. It is irrelevant whether the attempt at representation of a non-standard dialect is 'successful' or 'accurate' or 'authentic' – the fundamental point is the intention to do so. Dialect writing can simply involve the use of dialect lexis, and/or it might involve the use of dialect morphology and syntax. Very commonly it involves some 'respelling', which involves abandoning the standard spelling of a word or phrase, either in an explicit attempt to represent the fact that the dialect's phonology is different from other dialects, or just to give the impression that the language involved is not intended to be the standard. It is irrelevant whether a text is formally published or not: dialect writing can be anything that involves writing, so it includes messages on Twitter and in emails, and indeed it could include any kind of writing that is written on the internet, as well as handwritten texts that are intended only for a small number of people (or even only for the writer); it also includes short slogans or phrases that have been printed on mugs or tea-towels, and the text in cartoons that might be published in newspapers or books; it can include forms of transcription of the speech of dialect speakers that are not produced by linguists (for example, by folklorists and sociologists); it includes locally published books, pamphlets and poems; and it includes novels and short stories published by national publishers. It is irrelevant whether the intention of a text is humorous or serious, whether it intends to be 'high' literature or 'popular' literature, or whether it has no intention of being 'literature' at all. Dialect writing can be all of these things (and doubtless more). It does need to be written down, of course, so the use of dialect in broadcasting and film only counts if it is included in a script, and plays can feature dialect writing in a play script.

Dialect writing as it is understood here requires some conscious effort to represent non-standard language, and it requires an awareness that the dialect being represented is different from another dialect (typically a standard). Two implications of this are (i) that dialect writing as we mean it is only possible in languages which have a clear standard form, and (ii) that 'naive' spellings, in a language like English, by writers who might not fully know standard spelling, and might simply use graphemes to spell words as they speak them, do not count as dialect writing. We are intrigued by these implications and whether they are the right thing to say. For the moment, we will stick with the definition of 'dialect writing' as it has been set out in this paragraph. In the rest of this section, we consider something of the variation that exists in dialect writing texts, some of the characteristics that are shown by these texts, and some of the issues that we need to engage with in order to understand them. There are a number of traditions of literature that have analysed dialect writing texts, and we also acknowledge what we can of that in this section – it is certainly not the case that all the things that we say here are novel. As just one example of this, we have stressed that an awareness that the dialect being represented is different from another dialect is important, and this echoes both Blake (1981), who writes that 'it is the contrast between one form of language and another … which will categorise one form as non-standard', and Beal (2006), who points out that, once a language has been standardised, it becomes a primary norm against which anything different is judged to be deviant or different and thus viewed as a secondary norm (as, for example, Clark discusses).

There are certainly many different genres of dialect writing, and there are major distinctions to be made about the kinds of texts that fall within our purview. It is clearly the case that texts vary in terms of the amount of dialect lexis that they use (as discussed in this volume, for example, by Braber) and in the amount of respelling that they use (as discussed, for example, by Honeybone), but there are more fundamental issues to discuss if we aim to understand the range of material that falls under our definition of dialect writing. There is considerable variation in terms of how serious or successful dialect writing is in representing a non-standard variety (and indeed in how serious and successful it intends to be). The audience for texts can vary from only the writer themselves to the entire English-reading general public. It is conventional (in part following Shorrocks 1996, who took already existing terms and gave them quite precise definitions) to distinguish between two main types of dialect writing: *literary dialect* and *dialect literature*. 'Literary dialect' refers to the kind of dialect writing that exists in texts which have non-standard forms only in direct speech (for example, in dialogue), with the surrounding text in Standard English, and which are intended for a wide, general audience of readers of English (and which we might expect to be published by national publishers and to be sold throughout the English-speaking world). 'Dialect literature' refers to the kind of dialect writing that exists in texts which use non-standard forms throughout the text, where the text is intended for an audience of speakers of the dialect represented (and which we may therefore expect to be produced and principally available in the area where the dialect is spoken). We use the term 'dialect writing'[2] to cover both of these types of material (and everything in between). We use this term here (although we have not insisted that other authors in the volume do so) in part because this volume includes discussions of both of the kinds of material just mentioned and in part because we recognise that the two-way distinction between 'literary dialect' and 'dialect literature' (while insightful) is too simplistic.

An example of a canonical case of literary dialect can be found in Charles Dickens' (1854) *Hard Times*. This text is relevant to our precise purposes as the novel is set in the North of England (around Coketown, a generic Northern English mill-town). Poussa (1999: 28) reports that it 'arose out of a trip to Preston' in Lancashire. It first appeared serialised in a magazine which was published in London and was aimed at a general non-localised readership. *Hard Times* includes passages like the following, from chapter 10 in 'Book the First':

> He looked at her with some disappointment in his face, but with a respectful and patient conviction that she must be right in whatever she did. The expression was not lost upon her; she laid her hand lightly on his arm a moment, as if to thank him for it.
>
> 'We are such true friends, lad, and such old friends, and getting to be such old folk, now.' 'No, Rachael, thou'rt as young as ever thou wast.' 'One of us would be puzzled how to get old, Stephen, without t'other getting so too, both being alive,' she answered, laughing; 'but, any ways, we're such old friends, that t'hide a word of honest truth fro' one another would be a sin and a pity. 'Tis better not to walk too much together. 'Times, yes! 'Twould be hard, indeed, if 'twas not to be at all,' she said, with a cheerfulness she sought to communicate to him. ''Tis hard, anyways, Rachael.' 'Try to think not; and 'twill seem better.' 'I've tried a long time, and 'ta'nt got better. But thou'rt right; 'tmight mak fok talk, even of thee. Thou hast been that to me, Rachael, through so many year: thou hast done me so much good, and heartened of me in that cheering way, that thy word is a law to me. Ah lass, and a bright good law! Better than some real ones.'

Most of the text of the novel is written in Standard English, as in the first paragraph given here. Where there is direct speech, in quotation marks, however, the speech of some characters is as found in the second paragraph. Much of this is still spelt standardly and is otherwise not different from Standard English, but some dialect lexis is included (e.g. *lad*, *lass*), as is some dialect morphosyntax (e.g. *thou'rt*, *thou wast*) and there is a little respelling which is clearly intended to represent dialect phonology (e.g. *fro'* 'from', *mak* 'make', *fok* 'folk'). Only a few dialect features are represented, although some are very salient (such as the use of *thou*).

Some of the chapters in this volume investigate texts that fit quite clearly into this canonical type of literary dialect. For example, HODSON cites the following passage from one of the texts that she considers – *Letters of a Solitary Wanderer: Volume 2* by Charlotte Smith (1800).

> 'There's noot to be found there, I'll promise you,' said the man, who seemed to shudder at the temerity of my design, while he doubted its motives. 'No, no, there's nothing to be found there; the Priests took care of that. – Some old rubbishy things, indeed, some folks do say, be yet in the old rambling rooms; but, for my part, I'se not go aboot amongst them, special of a night, if there was a bushel of gold to be got as my reward.'
>
> 'But why not? Where is the danger?'
>
> 'Bless you, Master,' cried the peasant, 'it's easy to see you are but a stranger in this country, or you'd never ask such questions. Why, mon, the Abbey is haunted.'

This shows all the characteristics of classical literary dialect, although, as HODSON discusses, it does not necessarily give an accurate representation of Yorkshire English (which it is intended to be). This need not be seen as a 'problem' for literary dialect, if the intention of the use of non-standard forms is simply to represent that the speaker is not speaking Standard English – in principle anything non-standard will do (this point is also discussed by CROWLEY). Much dialect representation in literary dialect can, however, be seen as fundamentally accurate or appropriate in terms of the dialect features represented (Poussa 1999 and Wales 2017 defend Dickens as an observer of dialect, if perhaps of an antiquated form, for example). The issues of the 'accuracy' and 'authenticity' of the representation of a dialect in dialect writing are complicated ones to negotiate, and need to be seen in the light of what a writer intends for a text (see, for example, Hodson and Broadhead 2013 on the ways in which dialects are performed and such performances are perceived by speakers, and HODSON on the notion of 'good' and 'bad' dialect writers).

An example of a canonical case of dialect literature, also from the North of England, is John Collier's (1746) *A View of the Lancashire Dialect* (this is only the first part of the original title of this work, and it has had a range of various subtitles and completely different titles during the many editions in which it has appeared – it is often referred to using the pseudonym that Collier adopted: *Tim Bobbin*).[3] This work is set in South Lancashire, and was first published there, in Manchester (see Alston 1971). At this point, Manchester was a populous Lancashire market town (and what we now think of as 'Manchester English' had not separated itself off from Lancashire English), and as Salveson (1993) explains, Collier was born and raised in villages around it. The text starts in dialect writing (e.g. 'Tim Bobbin enters by his sell, beawt wig; grinning on scratting his nob') and is made up of a set of dialogues written entirely in dialect writing (with only a tiny amount of lines of Standard English in the main text), as below (taken from the 1746 edition, as transcribed and represented in the *Salamanca Corpus of English Dialect Texts*, which is a remarkable resource for finding dialect writing texts up till around 1950 from all over England – see García-Bermejo Giner *et al.* 2011).

> Teh meh word for't, Mearey, nowt's ot's owt con cum on't, when o Mon deeols weh rascotly Fok: Boh os I'r telling the, he neamt a Felley ot wooant obeawt three Mile off on him (boh the Dule forget him, os I done) so I munt gooa back ogen, thro' Rachdaw: so I geet Nip under meh Arm ogen, on bid Justice good neet, weh o heavy Heart theaw mey be shure; on but ot eh thowt eh cou'd ashelt sell hur eh this tother Pleck, it wou'd datinly ha brokk'n.

This is 'canonical' dialect literature, with a very high proportion of respellings and other clearly non-standard forms (we count around two-thirds of the words in this passage as exemplifying non-standard forms), and while the other words in the text are spelt in Standard English spelling it is clear that they are intended as part of the dialect represented (the words belong to the Lancashire dialect represented just as much as they do to Standard English, after all). The text was originally published in the area where the dialect is spoken and it is not intended to be easily comprehensible to all speakers of English. There is no scaffolding text in Standard English that forms part of the text itself. Each of the dialect features represented in the passage (and the other passages included in this Introduction), and the ways in which they are represented, deserve detailed consideration, but we sadly lack the space to give them it here. Suffice it to say that many of the respellings here and elsewhere in the passage, and the dialect grammar and lexis represented, are done insightfully.

Is 'canonical' dialect literature the focus of any chapter in this volume? This already brings up the problem of assuming that there are simply two types of text. HERMESTON and MAGUIRE focus on *The Pitman's Pay*, a long poem from Tyneside (written and published there) by Thomas Wilson from the early nineteenth century. This text features long passages in dialect writing, like the following, which HERMESTON cites:

He grunds the corn te myek wor breed,
  He boils wor soup (yence thought a dream):
Begock! aw's often flay'd te deed
  They'll myek us eat and sleep by steam!

A' this *he* diz wi' parfet ease,
  (The sting o' gallin' labour pouin'):
Then, hinny maisters, if ye please,
  Just let *him* try his hand at hewin'.

This seems more like *Tim Bobbin* than *Hard Times*, but the dialect writing section of the poem is in fact all in quotation marks, and is bookended by lengthy sections that are written in Standard English. Does this mean that the text is not dialect literature? If so, what is it? Literary dialect? (Because the non-standard forms only occur in direct speech?) That would seem like a strange way to classify the text because it has other characteristics that are associated with dialect literature (for example, there is a high level of non-standard forms and the text was first published only in the area where the dialect that it represents is spoken, in a magazine based in Newcastle upon Tyne).

If we consider a few other texts that fall under our definition of dialect writing, we can see something of the breadth of material that it covers. Dialect writing is by no means something that is tied to the distant past. Texts of the two basic types identified above are very much still current: two from the end of the last century, representing Liverpool English, (both discussed by HONEYBONE) are Katie Flynn's (1994) *The Girl from Penny Lane*, which contains canonical literary dialect, and the 'translation' of *Alice's Adventures in Wonderland* (1990), which shows many of the classic characteristics of dialect literature. BRABER discusses contemporary texts of both types from Nottingham. New examples of such texts are always appearing, but so is much else. CLARK discusses some very short texts (of a line or so) that accompany cartoons, and it seems right to say that the text associated with cartoons is one of the most vibrant forms of dialect writing currently being published. *Viz* comic (intended for adults) has a considerable reputation in this area, and has been publishing comic strips featuring several characters which are written to represent a number of different dialects for the past several decades (see Beal 2000 for an analysis of some of this material). One example from the issue of *Viz* that is current as we are writing this Introduction (dated June/ July 2019) is the following dialogue from the characters *The Bacons*, which features a family (Mutha, Fatha and their son Biffa Bacon) from Tyneside. This dialogue features in five panels from the strip (which continues after these panels to deliver a punchline).

Biffa: Reet then, I'm off t'school

Fatha: See yuz, son!
Mutha: Hev a nice day, Biffa!

[At the garden gate]
Fatha: Stop! Wuz're picketin' this fuckin' gate!
Mutha: One oot aall oot!
Biffa: Burra've got t'gan t'school!

Fatha: Not through *this* fuckin' picket line yuz aren't, son.
Mutha: Turn roond an' gan yem or there'll be fuckin' trubble!
Biffa: Eh?!

Mutha: Wuz divven't like *scabs* in this fuckin' family, Biffa!

Biffa: Aalreet… I divven't want nee botha. A'm gannin' back in the hoose.
Mutha: Good lad.

All the text in this comic strip is in dialect writing (the words that are spelt in Standard English spelling are part of the dialect represented just as much as they are part of English), and there is a high level of accuracy in representing several aspects of dialect grammar, lexis and phonology. Such a text seems like it should count as dialect literature, but while *Viz* originated in Newcastle upon Tyne, it has been sold throughout Britain (and abroad) for decades, so the intended audience is not simply a local one who speak the dialect represented.

Furthermore, while all the texts considered so far are examples of fiction (so the descriptions 'literary dialect' and 'dialect literature' are not inappropriate), non-fiction dialect writing also exists, as in Denwood's (1944: 3) 'Editor's notes' to the November 1944 edition of the *Journal of the Lakeland Dialect Society*:

> Weel fwoks, Ah's pleased ta say 'at oor Society hes anudder 'ear ov 'gud gaan' tull its credit. Oor quarterly gedderins hev been varra int'restin, an' we've hed a gey canny lot o' fwolk tull them as weel. Ah missed t' yan at Browton i' Forness, an' wat t' teals Ah've hard aboot it sen, an' t' cracks ov t' gud set – till they hed at tea-time's meead me mooth watter iver sen.

Non-fiction dialect writing also exists in journalism, as in the following extract, which is the first two paragraphs from an article headlined 'Pin Money', from the 13 December 1929 edition of the newspaper *Labour's Northern Voice*. This newspaper was published in Manchester to report on Labour activity in the north, as the local organ of the Independent Labour Party (at the time of this column the ILP was a mainstream organisation, affiliated to the Labour Party, with elected MPs – see, for example, McHugh 2001 – and the newspaper had considerable 'local success', see Cohen 2003). The extract is taken from Salveson (1993), who explains that the author of this piece is Hannah Mitchell, who published regularly in the newspaper under the pseudonym 'Daisy Nook', writing in Lancashire dialect (which she had become familiar with through living in Bolton, even though she grew up in Derbyshire).

> Awih gettin' fed up wi' bein' axed why there's nowt i' th' *Northern Voice* fro' 'Daisy Nook' these days. (Some on us has to wark for our livin'.) Aw towd ye ow were thinkin' o' standin' for th' Council again this last November.
>
> Yo' know th' chaps i' eawr party say they durn't like women candidates because they have to do aw the wark for 'em. Well, that tale met do for the marines, but it won't go deawn wi' any woman as has had a packet. When yo've drafted aw your bills, written yore election address, booked yore speakers, canvassed every afternoon for a fortnight, an' gan eawt a lot o' th' poll cards yo' feel as if yo' were doin' a bit yoreself.

Nini, Bailey, Guo and Grieve's chapter deals with dialect writing texts which are all non-fiction and which are all very recent (from 2014), and very short. They consider a corpus of tweets which are geocoded as coming from the United Kingdom and focus on spellings that represent dialect features from the North of England, such as the one given below.

> Time to gerrup and work out before the derby.

There is a clear piece of dialect writing here: *gerrup* 'get up' spells T-to-R, which is a feature which is fundamentally associated with the North of England (it is also shown in Biffa Bacon's *burra've* 'but I've'), but it is difficult to classify such texts as either one of the two categories that Shorrocks describes.

It has, in fact, long been recognised that this two-way distinction is too simple to encompass all kinds of dialect writing. Hodson (2014: 116) writes, for example, that 'the boundary between dialect literature and literary dialect can be a rather permeable one.' There are many ways in which it does not neatly encompass the kinds of texts that exist. We think that Shorrocks' basic

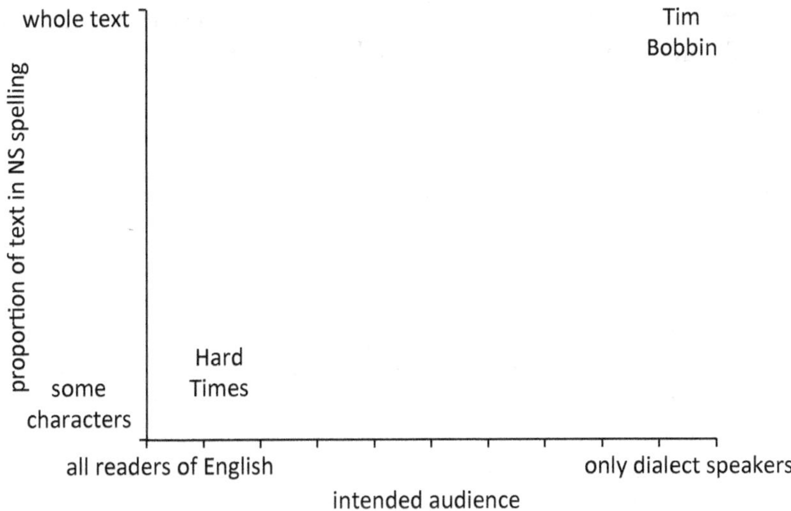

Figure 1.1 The dialect writing space

point is right, but that it might instead be best to think about the distinctions that he describes in terms of two dimensions:

- What is the intended audience of a text?
- What proportion of the text is in non-standard writing?

We can conceive of these two axes as providing a two-dimensional 'dialect writing space', within which we can situate each text, as in Figure 1.1.

On this perspective, literary dialect and dialect literature are not completely distinct categories, but are prototypes of the extremes of difference that is possible given these two clines. They are represented in Figure 1.1 by the texts *Hard Times* and *Tim Bobbin*, which can be seen as exemplifying the two extremes (although, as we have seen above, maybe they don't quite do this perfectly – maybe nothing does?). In principle, we could aim to situate each text in this dialect writing space (although we need to recognise that one text might occupy multiple points in the space if different parts of it pattern differently). In fact, Shorrocks himself is well aware of the fact that the categories that he proposes are complex and that the distinction 'is not absolute' (1996: 386). The way that we have dealt with them here sets them up as strawmen somewhat, and we think that they are still useful concepts (as do many of the chapters in this book, which often use the labels 'literary dialect' and 'dialect literature' – sometimes uncommented, and sometimes pointing out that they are leaky as concepts), as long as they are understood in the way set out here.

There are further complications in understanding the nature of the texts that make up dialect writing. We should in fact likely need to recognise a third dimension if we hope to fully describe the differences that exist among texts:

- How 'published' is a text?

Some texts are only intended for the writer, some for the writer and a small audience of acquaintances and/or directly connected people, while some are informally published in pamphlets or on a website, and still others are professionally published, which will likely involve editing (see MAGUIRE and HONEYBONE for a consideration of the role that editing can play in affecting how a text appears).

Another issue that might affect both the intention of a text and the extent to which it might reflect the dialect features that exist in dialect speakers' minds is the question of whether the writer is a speaker of the dialect themselves or not. Some of the writers mentioned above (for example, Thomas Wilson) are writing in their native dialect, and others are not (for example, Hannah Mitchell). We might expect that a native speaker will represent dialect features accurately, and a non-native speaker might not, but this is not necessarily the case: a native speaker might be a poor observer, or have little insight into how to manipulate spelling conventions (or might even *want* to represent a dialect as a thing to be ridiculed). We might expect the latter more of a non-native writer, but it could equally well be the case that they might be a subtle observer of a dialect and that they care deeply about it (and/or that they are very familiar with previous pieces of dialect writing for a variety). All of this ties in with the extent to which a piece of dialect writing could possibly be seen as 'authentic', or can be used as linguistic evidence for a variety. These are fascinatingly complex issues indeed.

Within the dialect writing space, several more-or-less distinct genres can be recognised, including some of those just exemplified (for example, tweets and non-fiction texts in 'dialect society' publications). 'Generic literary dialect' that simply uses generic features and doesn't make any real attempt to represent a dialect (see the discussion of this in HODSON's chapter, for example) might count as one of these, as might dialect poetry. Another is 'Contemporary Humorous Localised Dialect Literature' (CHLDL), the type exemplified by locally published comic texts that have been in print for the past few decades, and which often have names like *Lern Yerself Scouse* or *Larn Yersel' Geordie* (see Honeybone and Watson 2013 and also ASPREY's, BRABER's, CROWLEY's, WATSON AND JENSEN's and HONEYBONE's chapters in this volume, and also Crowley 2012 specifically on the origins of the *Lern*

Yerself Scouse volume). Another genre could be recognised in texts which conceive of themselves as 'translations' into a dialect, such as the *Gospels in Scouse* and *Alice's Adventchers in Wunderland*, both of which are mentioned in Honeybone's chapter.

Some of these genres have long traditions and established orthographic conventions can emerge to represent specific dialect features in them. Furthermore, specific features can cohere to become 'the features that you use to represent a specific dialect in dialect writing'. Such features can thus develop a high level of indexicality, and it has become common to refer to this process as 'enregisterment', following Agha (2003). Several of the chapters collected here discuss these kinds of issues, including Asprey, Beal, Clark and Cooper, and also Crowley and Honeybone, who sound some cautious notes. Once such features have become enregistered in this way, they can become commodified, which means that short dialect writing texts can be used to sell things like tea-towels, mugs and t-shirts in the area that the dialect is spoken, as discussed in Beal (2009) and Johnstone (2009), for example, and a few chapters in this volume, such as those by Asprey and Braber.

It might even be the case that sets of features could cohere to the extent that we might begin to talk of (aspects of) a standard developing for the writing of particular dialects. The existence of a standard is one of the factors that is often seen as relevant to establishing that a linguistic variety should be recognised as a distinct language (as in, for example, Haugen 1966 and Kloss 1967), and this is a question that is relevant to our purposes. The titles of many CHLDL texts imply that the variety represented is to be seen as a separate language, which needs to be learnt by speakers of Standard English – this is typically meant as a joke, but many of the varieties considered in this volume pass several of the tests that are required to establish 'languagehood', one of which is highly relevant to our purposes: the existence of a tradition of published literature. The linguistic variety (or set of varieties) that these issues are most relevant to in Britain is Scots, which has a fair claim to being a distinct language from English, and – while we explicitly do not consider language in Scotland in this volume – we are clear that we can learn from the discussion of the representation of Scots in writing, in such work as Hagan (2002) and Bann and Corbett (2015). Some of these issues are discussed further by Honeybone.

It is not the case that all of these genres and forms of dialect writing are discussed in this book, but a good number are. The chapters included here discuss novels, cartoons, poems, ego-documents, materials produced by sociologists, 'individual spellings' in texts, a comparison of unedited and edited texts, and much else. Some chapters focus on one type of text (for example, Clark focuses on cartoons, Timmis focuses on sociologically motivated transcription), others consider a range of types of texts (for example, Braber and Asprey, which consider both literary-dialect-type texts and dialect-literature-type texts). Some dialect writing is easily accessible (typically that which tends towards the 'all readers of English' pole of the 'intended audience' axis given in Figure 1.1, and which counts as professionally published). Much other dialect writing, however, is practically hidden from general view. It might just appear in local publications that often don't even make it into local libraries, or in magazines, or publications of dialect societies, or on the internet; very little of this kind of material is indexed or recorded.

Some of the chapters in this volume focus explicitly on the material that exists in the texts considered: Hermeston focuses on a text as literature, considering the use of metaphor; others focus on dialect writing texts as data, investigating methodological issues and considering how linguists might analyse the representation of specific dialect features in the texts; Maguire applies methods of historical phonology; Nini, Bailey, Guo and Grieve apply methods from computational sociolinguistics and geolinguistics; and Watson and Jensen apply methods from corpus linguistics and sociolinguistics, adopting quantitative methods, as does Cooper.

This volume has not appeared in a vacuum. We have referred already in this section to several pieces of previous work which analyse some aspect of dialect writing, but we need to explicitly acknowledge other work, too, as it has shown both much of what might be interesting to consider and also often what kinds of texts exist. Both Blake (1981) and Shorrocks (1996) bemoan the fact that little work has focused on dialect writing, and while this has long been the case, and has not changed very much, there *are* traditions of analysis of dialect writing, including a range of highly insightful material.[4] There are distinct traditions of discussing the use of dialect writing in direct speech in novels, such as Krapp (1926), Ives (1950), Gerson (1967) and Petyt (1970), all of which led to Blake (1981), and has since led to work such as Burkette (2001), Schneider and and Wagner (2006) and Hodson (2014, 2017). There are also traditions of work which have focused on dialect-literature-type material, in part to analyse the material in and of itself, as in Tilling (1972), in part in order to analyse it to gain insight into the structure and/or history of little-described varieties, as in Sixtus (1912) and Klein (1914), and in part to understand its connection to culture, as in Salveson (1993).[5] Dialect writing has thus been assessed in a number of places for its potential as linguistic evidence for the dialects that it represents and their history – further work which does this includes Trudgill (1990), Ihalainen (1994), Wales (2006), and several of the chapters in Taavitsainen *et al.* (1999) and in Hickey (2010). The chapters in these two latter volumes form important collections of work in 'dialect writing studies', as do the relevant pieces gathered in Williamson and Burke (1971), the first six chapters in Heselwood and Upton (2010), and the articles gathered in the (November 2000) special issue of the *Journal of Sociolinguistics* on Non-Standard Orthography – all these are highly relevant to our purposes, especially Wales (2010), which considers dialect writing from northern England, as does Shorrocks (1996, 1999). Other relevant material includes Schneider (1986, 2002) and the considerable amount of work from the Salamanca group, such as Ruano-García *et al.* (2015). Some work which sounds a cautious note is Preston (1982, 1985, 2000) and Macaulay (1991);[6] and there has recently developed a clear strand of work which deals with geographical variation in spelling in social media, such as Eisenstein (2015), Kulkarni *et al.* (2016) and Tatman (2016).

Often previous work has a focus *only* on dialect writing in 'literature', or as evidence for the dialect features from the past, or as evidence for indexicality and enregisterment, or in terms of sociolinguistic variation. We see all of these as vital aspects of dialect writing studies, and it is naturally right that scholars should focus their attention on specific issues, but as we hope is clear from the discussion in this section, we think that the discussion in these traditions needs to be linked, because we can all learn from each other.

1.3. Where Is the 'North of England'?

This question may be easier to address than that considered in Section 1.2, but is also not straightforward – geographically, the fundamental question is: how far south does the North go?

Three of the borders *are* straightforward, at least relatively so. To the north, the border with Scotland represents an unambiguous political boundary, one which has been largely fixed for almost 700 years, though things are not quite so straightforward culturally or linguistically. The town of Berwick-upon-Tweed is a case in point (see Llamas 2010). Although it has been under English control since 1482, this was not completely formalised until the Wales and Berwick Act of 1746, and the town still finds itself having a foot in both countries, as exemplified by the inclusion of Berwick Rangers Football Club in the Scottish leagues. A number of linguistic studies of the Scottish–English border (Glauser 1974; Maguire *et al.* 2010; Maguire 2015; Watt *et al.* 2014) have shown that although the linguistic border between northern England and Scotland more-or-less coincides with the political border, the situation is rather more complex than that with, for example, a fair amount of 'fraying' of isoglosses and something of a transition zone, especially south of the border and at the lowland western and eastern ends (see Figure 1.2).

The sea to the east is a definitive boundary for the North of course, and the same is true of the west coast, though it could be argued that the Isle of Man is partly in the cultural and linguistic 'North' (Barry 1984; Hamer

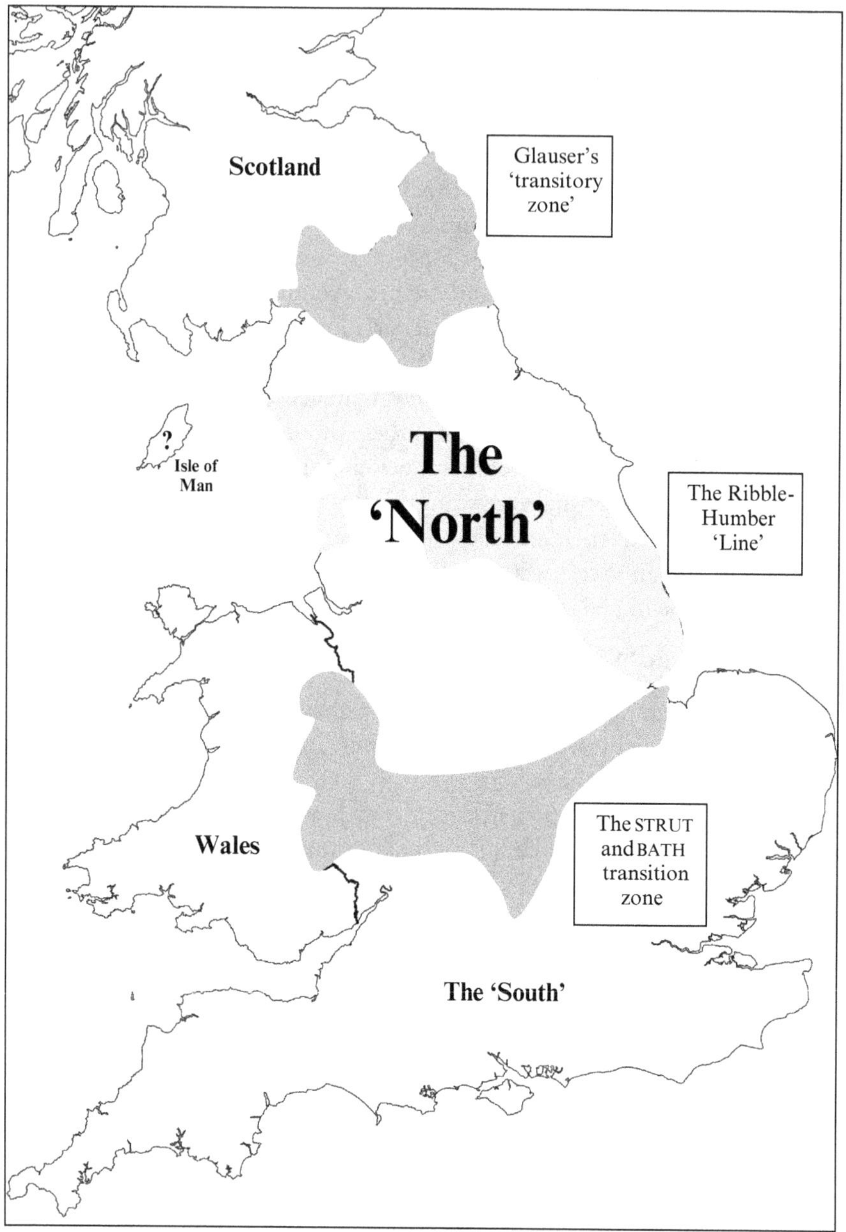

Figure 1.2 The 'North of England'

2007). But once we go south of Merseyside (assuming that the North extends beyond it), the Welsh border takes over the role of defining the boundary of the North of England, although again it doesn't exactly coincide with linguistic and cultural boundaries (Montgomery 2016).

As we mention above, the key question for this section – one which it may be impossible to answer – is where the border lies to the south. That is, where is the North–South divide in England?[7] Answers to this question, in as much as they can be given at all, will vary according to the criteria we consider (and indeed who is doing the considering). Thus the political, economic, cultural, perceptual and linguistic boundaries, even when they can be identified, may not align, and physical geography is of no use to us given the lack of any significant discontinuity in the English landscape. A crucial issue is the position of the English Midlands, and whether they constitute part of the North or are a place (or places) that are completely separate and exist in their own right. Useful analyses of these issues can be found in Wales (2006), Trousdale (2012), Clark and Asprey (2013), Hickey (2015), Montgomery (2015) and Braber and Robinson (2018).

In terms of boundaries based on structural dialect features, different answers are possible depending on the nature of the dialects examined and the features considered. In the traditional dialects of England, as documented in the *Survey of English Dialects* (*SED*; Orton and Dieth 1962–71), there is evidence of a significant divide between 'far northern' dialects and the rest, along a line (actually another transition zone) from the River Ribble in north Lancashire to the River Humber between Yorkshire and Lincolnshire. This now famous 'Ribble–Humber Line' (see Wakelin 1972: 102–4; and also Cooper, this volume, where it is called the 'Humber–Lune/Ribble Line'; and Wales 2006, who also calls it the 'Ribble–(Calder–Aire)–Humber Line'), which involves quite a few phonological isoglosses, appears to be of long standing, but it hardly serves as a useful definition of the limits of the North in England today, distinguishing as it does Cumberland, Durham, north Lancashire, Northumberland, north and east Yorkshire and Westmorland from areas to the south, including most of Lancashire and south Yorkshire, as well as Manchester, Merseyside and the north Midlands.

Two other well-known phonological isoglosses that split northern and southern locations in England are the FOOT–STRUT and TRAP–BATH lines (Chambers and Trudgill 1980: 127–42). The first of these divides locations to the north which have retained a single vowel (e.g. [ʊ]) in both the FOOT and STRUT lexical sets (Wells 1982: 131–3) from those which have a split between [ʊ] in FOOT and [ʌ] in STRUT. The second divides locations to the north which have a short vowel (e.g. [a]) in both the TRAP and BATH lexical sets (Wells 1982: 129–30, 133–5) from those to the south which have a long vowel in

BATH (e.g. [ɑː]). Although these two isoglosses have somewhat different distributions, they both follow a course from the Wash in the east in the south-west Midlands in the west, and group much of the English Midlands with the northern counties. These two features have the advantage that they are still relevant today (many of the isoglosses that defined the Ribble–Humber Line having disappeared with the decline of the traditional features that defined them) and relate to well-recognised shibboleths of Northern English speech (Wales 2006: 29). Figure 1.2 illustrates the distributions of this and the other dialect boundaries discussed above. Of course, relying on small numbers of isoglosses to distinguish the North from the South is potentially misleading, and dialectometrical analyses of large numbers of linguistic features offer a more objective way of addressing the question, albeit one which has not yet revealed an obvious North–South linguistic divide (for examples see Goebl 1997; Maguire *et al.* 2010; Shackleton 2007).

Looking at the North–South divide from a perceptual dialectology perspective gives results which are similar in some ways but which also suggest that the southern limit of the North is imagined differently by different people and may be impossible to define objectively. Montgomery (2015) analyses perceptions in a range of northern locations and finds, perhaps not surprisingly, that participants from northerly locations such as Carlisle and Hexham place the boundary further north than participants from more southerly locations such as Crewe and Hull. Most of Montgomery's participants placed the boundary somewhere between the Ribble–Humber Line in the north and the Wash–Severn Line in the south, though quite a few included parts of East Anglia and the south-east Midlands in the North. It is clear that some people consider the English Midlands to be partly or wholly in the North, and this is consistent with at least some of the linguistic criteria that have been considered by previous researchers (for example, the FOOT–STRUT and TRAP–BATH lines).

Given the uncertainty about the southern boundary of the North, and the inclusion in it, at least under some circumstances, of the Midlands, we take a broad definition of the 'North' of England for the purposes of this volume, as indicated in Figure 1.2,[8] which shows the understanding of 'the North of England' that is adopted in this volume (taking in all or most of the darker-shaded areas and the unshaded area between them, including the 'Humber–Ribble' area, which is included for reference).

Dialects from the area have been the subject of a number of classic studies (for example, Wright 1892; Orton 1933; Hedevind 1967; Shorrocks 1998), and have recently been the subject of considerable academic interest, including a sustained loose collaboration in research involving a substantial group of scholars at universities both in the area and elsewhere in the world.

This is shown by the successful and ongoing series of 'Northern Englishes Workshops', which have been held at the universities of Lancaster (2006), Edinburgh (2007), Salford (2008), Sheffield (2010), Nottingham Trent (2012), Lancaster (2014), Edinburgh (2016) and Newcastle (2018), and by the publication of such volumes as Wales (2006), Hickey (2015) and Beal and Hancil (2017).

1.4. The Contents of the Volume

We considered whether we should organise the chapters in the volume into thematic parts, but we have decided not to. There are many ways in which the chapters relate to each other (in terms of area covered, type of writing covered, aspect of language covered, whether they focus on the effect and intention of the phenomenon overall, or on the specific features represented, or on the extent to which texts can be used as evidence for otherwise unattested stages of a variety, etc.), and any one grouping of the chapters would exaggerate the importance of one of these kinds of links and would downplay the others. We have therefore simply ordered the chapters by alphabetical order of (first-named author's) surname. There are indeed many links between the chapters, and we have tried to flag these up with cross-references at appropriate points in the chapters. All texts were subject to a process of reviewing and cross-reading (involving other authors in the volume), and we hope that this has strengthened the chapters themselves and the links between them.[9] We encourage any reader of any chapter to consider reading other chapters, too.

It is worth being explicit about the areas covered in the book. If we split 'the North' into the sub-areas that are commonly identified, we can say that dialects and dialect writing from the north-east are discussed by BEAL, MAGUIRE, HERMESTON, and in small part by WATSON AND JENSEN; those from Yorkshire are discussed by COOPER and HODSON; those from the north-west are discussed by TIMMIS, CROWLEY, HONEYBONE and in large part WATSON AND JENSEN; those from the East Midlands are discussed by BRABER; and those from the West Midlands are discussed by ASPREY and CLARK; NINI, BAILEY, GUO AND GRIEVE's chapter covers the whole of the North. All of these areas fall into the 'North of England' in its broadest extent, as discussed in Section 1.3, and in a sense this coverage means that all areas of the North are represented in the volume. In a different sense, it would be absurd to say that all areas of the North of England are covered here. For example, the north-west is 'covered' in the volume, but there is a lot on Liverpool and very little on Manchester. This is unfortunate but unavoidable, of course, as no one book could cover every identifiable area in the North of England. The book is not intended as a comprehensive handbook covering everything about dialect writing from all varieties in the North, so there will of necessity be lacunae. We hope that more work will emerge to fill the gaps. In the rest of this section, we say a little about the precise contents of each chapter.

Asprey's chapter describes and discusses several pieces of dialect writing from the Black Country (the area to the immediate west of the City of Birmingham, in the West Midlands), dating from the nineteenth and twentieth centuries, considering both the extent to which certain dialect features are represented in this work and also what this might tell us about the indexicality of these features and the extent to which this indexicality and the features themselves might have changed over time.

Beal's chapter examines evidence of dialect (especially at the lexical level) in the personal writings of the renowned eighteenth-century Tyneside engraver and naturalist, Thomas Bewick. Her analysis of these ego-documents reveals a complex interaction between personal identity and linguistic enregisterment of 'the North' and its relationship with Scotland and Scots, and flags up the importance that ego-documents can have for historical dialectology.

Braber's chapter describes and discusses several pieces of twentieth-century dialect writing (of both the 'literary dialect' and 'dialect literature' type) from Nottingham and the nearby area (in the East Midlands), showing both what kinds of dialect writing exists for this area and whether a wide number of specific dialect features are represented in the texts, and whether different types of texts pattern differently in this regard.

Clark's chapter focuses on dialect writing in late-twentieth-century cartoons from Staffordshire (in the West Midlands), considering a few texts in detail, and focusing on the extent to which such texts can be interpreted through the lens of the Bakhtinian concept of double-voicing, as examples of the burlesque and carnivalesque, and as demonstrations of sociocultural identity, also considering them in connection with the notions of enregisterment and indexicality.

Cooper's chapter examines the process of enregisterment of 'Yorkshire' dialect. Yorkshire is a linguistically diverse county, being split, for example, by the traditional Ribble–Humber isogloss bundle, which might suggest that there is no one 'Yorkshire' dialect. But Cooper finds evidence of ongoing enregisterment of 'Yorkshire' based on shared features and features from the more populous West Riding of the county, indicating a change from nineteenth-century dialect-specific representations which involves 'deregisterment' of traditional local features.

Crowley's chapter focuses closely on the dialect writing that has been produced in Liverpool English (and overtly addresses the extent to which it has been conceived of as 'Scouse'), tracing the beginnings of what can be seen as dialect writing in the variety from the mid to late nineteenth century, considering the development of it in the 1950s and 1960s, and explaining the continuing publication in Scouse in the twenty-first century, focusing on issues of indexicality and enregisterment, and the relationship between dialect writing and 'standard language ideology'.

HERMESTON's chapter looks at metaphor in the early-nineteenth-century Tyneside dialect poem *The Pitman's Pay* by Thomas Wilson. He finds that Wilson uses a wide array of metaphors in the poem, though most of these depend on local knowledge, especially of mining. Hermeston finds Wilson's use of metaphor suggestive of a wider literary context for traditional dialect literature which is frequently both celebratory and self-limiting.

HODSON's chapter focuses on texts from the early nineteenth century that fit well with the definition of 'literary dialect', examining for the first time how a number of novels from this period represent Yorkshire dialects, and considering the extent to which these texts represent dialect features which were found in those varieties versus the extent to which they represent features which are essentially 'generic', 'literary' dialect features which are not actually tied to a specific variety.

HONEYBONE's chapter explores the issues that arise when we consider the extent to which dialect writing can and does represent phonological dialect features, investigating first a set of fundamental issues that constrain dialect writing in general and respellings at the phonological level in particular, and then focusing on extracts from three pieces of dialect writing representing Liverpool English from the second half of the twentieth century, and presenting a quantitative account of the types of respellings found in them and the extent to which they relate to phonological dialect features.

MAGUIRE's chapter illustrates how we might go about using traditional dialect-literature-type texts for understanding the historical phonology of Northern English dialects and the kinds of results that can be achieved from a rigorous analysis of the spellings and rhymes they provide. Examining Thomas Wilson's early-nineteenth-century *The Pitman's Pay* (the same text considered by HERMESTON), he shows that the author has encoded complex aspects of the phonology of Tyneside English in the poem and that these give us a detailed insight into its historical phonology that are not available from later sources.

NINI, BAILEY, GUO AND GRIEVE's chapter analyses non-standard spellings on the social media platform Twitter, examining the geographical pattern of spellings that are indicative of phonological features of Northern English dialects on the basis of a very large set of data (1.8 billion words). Their analysis reveals that users of Twitter employ non-standard spellings to represent their dialects and identities, and that online media provide a vast new source of information for studying dialect variation.

TIMMIS's chapter describes a unique corpus of early-twentieth-century dialect writing from Bolton. This corpus, which was produced as a result of a programme of social observation, consists of descriptions of local events and conversations, often written in dialect writing rather than using Standard English orthography. Timmis discusses some of the key aspects of the dialect represented in the corpus, comparing them to features recorded in later surveys.

WATSON AND JENSEN's chapter focuses on one piece of dialect writing representing Liverpool English from the 1960s (and briefly discusses another which represents Tyneside English), adopting a quantitative methodology which links to the methods and tools used in sociophonetics, and showing how the digitisation of a dialect writing text can in principle allow for the detailed investigation of a set of potential respellings for specific phonological dialect features, and acknowledging that this works insightfully for the Liverpool English text, but throws up complications for the Tyneside text, due to differing respelling practices.

The chapters of the volume have a lot in common, but there are also a lot of differences between them. Some focus on the interpretation of the phenomenon of dialect writing (e.g. CLARK, CROWLEY and HERMESTON), while most of the others focus on interpreting the structural dialect features that are represented in them. Among the latter type of work, some focus on lexis (e.g. BEAL and a good portion of BRABER), some on morphological features (e.g. ASPREY), and several others focus on phonological features (e.g. NINI, BAILEY, GUO AND GRIEVE, HONEYBONE, MAGUIRE, and WATSON AND JENSEN). Some chapters present new or novel corpora or sets of texts (e.g. BEAL, HODSON and TIMMIS); some others present novel analysis of texts that are known from previous work in dialect writing studies.

1.5. Envoi: tara, tata, tarrah, ta-tah, tsarah, taraa, tarrar

One book can't cover *all* types of dialect writing, nor can one book consider all approaches that we need to take in order to understand the phenomenon, nor can one book cover *all* areas of the North of England, but we hope that any reader of this volume who is interested either in dialect writing or in dialects of English from the North of England (or both) will find something of interest in its pages. The chapters gathered here certainly further our knowledge of what kind of dialect writing exists for the varieties considered, and of the ways in which particular pieces of dialect writing go about representing specific dialect features, and of the ways in which such texts can provide sometimes otherwise non-existent evidence for the varieties that they represent. We think that they also advance our understanding of dialect writing as a phenomenon in all of its complicated and multi-faceted glory (as something which can be everything from 'old-fashioned' to 'edgy', as shown in some of the texts exemplified in this Introduction). We hope that this volume will stimulate further work in all the areas that it encompasses, from the understanding of social practice to the structural analysis of texts, and everything in between.

Notes

1. Shorrocks (1996: 390), for example, writes that '[t]he most substantial traditions of writing in non-standard English are those in the North of England'.
2. We do not pretend that we invented the term, of course (see, for example, Krapp 1926; Hagan 2002), but we do think that it is the most useful one to use.
3. This text may, in fact, have stopped being canonical dialect literature quite soon after it was first published, as it was latterly published in editions from London, and various introductions (written in Standard English) and glossaries have been added in the text's many editions, showing that the text was intended for a wide audience, not (just?) those who know the dialect represented. Wales (2017) shows (following Easson 1976) that Dickens, in fact, made use of *Tim Bobbin* when writing the dialect portions of *Hard Times*, which again shows that the text was read by a general audience. In fact, Salveson (1993) argues (perhaps contentiously) that *Tim Bobbin* was never really read by an audience of dialect speakers when it was first published. This flags up the complications in using the canonical definition of 'dialect literature' – a point that we return to below.
4. One immense lacuna in our discussion here is that we do not at all consider work on dialect writing in languages other than English (apart, perhaps, from a few tentative comments about writing in Scots). We know that there is such work, such as Berlinger (1983) and Strand (2019); indeed we suspect that there is a vast amount of it, and we are confident that similar issues to those considered here are discussed in it, and that such cross-linguistically relevant considerations should be brought together. There is also work which takes an explicitly 'English Literature' approach to dialect writing in English, such as Redling (2006). There are clear connections from such work to some of the chapters in this volume, such as those by Clark and Hermeston, but we know that there will be much more work of this type that we could learn from (and vice versa). In addition to this, we are aware that there is work on the psycholinguistics of spelling which is also highly relevant to our purposes, as it can show which spelling conventions are psychologically real for speakers (and thus which conventions might be usable in dialect respelling). We have not been able to interact with such work, but we know that cross-fertilisation with it could prove fruitful. Finally, work on dialect writing should also engage with material that focuses on the system behind English spelling (and its development) in general, such as the material gathered in Cook and Ryan (2016).
5. There is also some work which aims to gather together (early) material which discusses 'dialects of England', including descriptions of pieces of dialect writing, such as Smith (1839), Skeat and Nodal (1877) and Alston (1971).
6. The caution is partly about the use of eye-dialect, especially in cases where non-dialect speakers such as folklorists and sociolinguists are producing written forms

that represent non-standard dialects. The status of eye-dialect in dialect writing is controversial and complex (for a more positive view, see Honeybone's chapter in this volume).

7. This assumes that there is one, of course. Wales (2000, 2006) shows in detail how a wide range of approaches to dividing England into parts (on political, cultural and social lines) do fundamentally recognise this kind of bipartite divide.
8. Base map reproduced from Ordnance Survey map data by permission of the Ordnance Survey © Crown copyright 2001.
9. We are grateful for the many comments that we have received on this Introduction, which have substantially improved it. We do not think that all the authors in the volume would agree with everything that we have written here, however, and any errors in it are, of course, our own.

References

Agha, A. (2003) 'The social life of cultural value', *Language and Communication* 23: 213–73.

Alston, R. (1971) *A Bibliography of the English language from the Invention of Printing to the Year 1800: A Systematic Record of Writings on English, and on Other Languages in English, Based on the Collections of the Principal Libraries of the World, Vol. 9: Non-Standard English, English Dialects, Scottish Dialects, Cant and Vulgar English*, Leeds: E. J. Arnold.

Bann, Jennifer and John Corbett (2015) *Spelling Scots: The Orthography of Literary Scots, 1700–2000*, Edinburgh: Edinburgh University Press.

Barry, Michael (1984) 'Manx English', in Peter Trudgill (ed.), *Language in the British Isles*, Cambridge: Cambridge University Press, pp. 167–77.

Beal, Joan (2000) 'From George Ridley to Viz: popular literature in Tyneside English', *Language and Literature* 9(4): 343–59.

Beal, Joan (2006) *Language and Region*, London: Routledge.

Beal, Joan (2009) 'Enregisterment, commodification, and historical context: "Geordie" versus "Sheffieldish"', *American Speech* 84(2): 138–56.

Beal, Joan and Sylvie Hancil (eds) (2017) *Perspectives on Northern Englishes*, Berlin: De Gruyter.

Berlinger, Joseph (1983) *Das zeitgenössische deutsche Dialektgedicht. Zur Theorie und Praxis der deutschsprachigen Dialektlyrik 1950–1980*, Frankfurt am Main: Peter Lang.

Blake, Norman Francis (1981) *Non-Standard Language in English Literature*, London: Deutsch.

Braber, Natalie and Jonnie Robinson (2018) *East Midlands English*, Boston, Berlin: Walter de Gruyter.

Burkette, A. (2001) 'The use of literary dialect in Uncle Tom's Cabin', *Language and Literature* 10(2): 158–70.

Chambers, J. K. and Peter Trudgill (1980) *Dialectology*, Cambridge: Cambridge University Press.

Clark, Urszula and Esther Asprey (2013) *West Midlands English: Birmingham and the Black Country*, Edinburgh: Edinburgh University Press.

Cohen, Gidon (2003) 'Special note: The Independent Socialist Party', *Dictionary of Labour Biography* 11: 231–8.

Collier, John (1746) *A View of the Lancashire Dialect; by Way of Dialogue between Tummus o'Williams, o'Margit o'Roaphs, and Meary o'Dicks, o'Tummy o'Petty's*
Cook, Vivian and Des Ryan (2016) *The Routledge Handbook of the English Writing System*, Abingdon: Routledge.
Crowley, Tony (2012) *Scouse: A Social and Cultural History*, Liverpool: Liverpool University Press.
Denwood, E. R. (1944) 'Editor's notes', *Journal of the Lakeland Dialect Society* 6, 3.
Eisenstein, Jacob (2015) 'Systematic patterning in phonologically-motivated orthographic variation', *Journal of Sociolinguistics* 19(2): 161–88.
García-Bermejo Giner, Maria F., Pilar Sánchez-García and Javier Ruano-García (2011) *The Salamanca Corpus*. http://www.thesalamancacorpus.com/index.html.
Gerson, S. (1967) *Sound and Symbol in the Dialogue of the Works of Charles Dickens*, Stockholm Studies in English XIX, Acta Universitatis Stockholmiensis, Stockholm: Almqvist & Wiksell.
Glauser, Beat (1974) *The Scottish-English Linguistic Border: Lexical Aspects*, Bern: Francke Verlag.
Goebl, Hans (1997) 'Some dendrographic classifications of the data of CLAE 1 and CLAE 2', in Wolfgang Viereck and Heinrich Ramisch (eds), *Computer Developed Linguistic Atlas of England (CLAE)*, Tübingen: Max Niemeyer Verlag, vol. II, pp. 23–32.
Hagan, Anette (2002) *Urban Scots Dialect Writing*, Oxford: Peter Lang.
Hamer, Andrew (2007) 'English on the Isle of Man', in David Britain (ed.), *Language in the British Isles*, Cambridge: Cambridge University Press, pp. 171–5.
Haugen, Einar (1966) 'Dialect, language, nation', *American Anthropologist* 68: 922–35.
Hedevind, Bertil (1967) *The Dialect of Dentdale in the West Riding of Yorkshire*, Uppsala: Acta Universitatis Upsaliensis.
Heselwood, B. and C. Upton (eds) (2010) *Proceedings of Methods XIII*, Oxford: Peter Lang.
Hickey, Raymond (ed.) (2010) *Varieties of English in Writing: The Written Word as Linguistic Evidence*, Amsterdam: John Benjamins.
Hickey, Raymond (ed.) (2015) *Researching Northern English*, Amsterdam: John Benjamins.
Hodson, Jane (2014) *Dialect in Film and Literature*, Basingstoke: Palgrave Macmillan.
Hodson, Jane (ed.) (2017) *Dialect and Literature in the Long Nineteenth Century*, Abingdon: Routledge.
Hodson, Jane and Alex Broadhead (2013) 'Developments in literary dialect representation in British fiction 1800–1836', *Language and Literature* 22(4): 314–32.
Honeybone, Patrik and Kevin Watson (2013) 'Salience and the sociolinguistics of Scouse spelling: exploring the phonology of the Contemporary Humorous Localised Dialect Literature of Liverpool', *English World-Wide* 34: 305–40.
Ihalainen, Ossi (1994) 'The dialects of England since 1776', in Robert Burchfield (ed.), *The Cambridge History of the English Language, Vol. V: English Language in Britain and Overseas – Origins and Development*, Cambridge: Cambridge University Press, pp. 197–274.
Ives, Sumner (1950) 'A theory of literary dialect', *Tulane Studies in English* 2: 137–82.
Johnstone, Barbara (2009) 'Pittsburghese shirts: commodification and the enregisterment of an urban dialect', *American Speech* 84: 157–75.

Klein, Willy (1914) *Der Dialekt von Stokesley in Yorkshire, North-Riding*, Berlin: Mayer & Müller.

Kloss, Heinz (1967) '"Abstand languages" and "ausbau languages"', *Anthropological Linguistics* 9: 29–41.

Krapp, George (1926) 'The psychology of dialect writing', *The Bookman* 63: 522–7.

Kulkarni, Vivek, Bryan Perozzi and Steven Skiena (2016) 'Freshman or fresher? Quantifying the geographic variation of internet language', in Markus Strohmaier and Krishna P. Gummadi (eds), *Proceedings of the Tenth International AAAI Conference on Web and Social Media (ICWSM 2016)*, Palo Alto, CA: The AAAI Press, pp. 615–18.

Llamas, Carmen (2010) 'Convergence and divergence across a national border', in Carmen Llamas and Dominic Watt (eds), *Language and Identities*, Edinburgh: Edinburgh University Press, pp. 227–36.

Macaulay, Ronald (1991) 'Coz it izny spelt when they say it: displaying dialect in writing', *American Speech* 66: 280–91.

McHugh, Declan (2001) A 'Mass' Party Frustrated? The Development of the Labour Party in Manchester, 1918–31, PhD thesis, University of Salford.

Maguire, Warren (2015) 'The north above the North: Scotland and Northern English', in Raymond Hickey (ed.), *Researching Northern English*, Amsterdam: John Benjamins, pp. 437–57.

Maguire, Warren, April McMahon, Paul Heggarty and Dan Dediu (2010) 'The past, present and future of English dialects: quantifying convergence, divergence and dynamic equilibrium', *Language Variation and Change* 22(1): 1–36.

Montgomery, Chris (2015) 'Borders and boundaries in the North of England', in Raymond Hickey (ed.), *Researching Northern English*, Amsterdam: John Benjamins, pp. 345–68.

Montgomery, Chris (2016) 'The perceptual dialectology of Wales from the border', in Mercedes Durham and Jonathan Morris (eds), *Sociolinguistics in Wales*, Basingstoke: Palgrave, pp. 151–79.

Orton, Harold (1933) *The Phonology of a South Durham Dialect: Descriptive, Historical and Comparative*, London: Kegan Paul, Trench, Trübner & Co.

Orton, Harold and Eugen Dieth (eds) (1962–71) *Survey of English Dialects (B): The Basic Material*, Leeds: Arnold & Son.

Petyt, K. M. (1970) *Emily Bronte and the Haworth Dialect*, A Yorkshire Dialect Society publication, Menston, Yorkshire: Scolar Press.

Poussa, Patricia (1999) 'Dickens as sociolinguist: dialect in David Copperfield', in I. Taavitsainen, G. Melchers and P. Pahta (eds), *Writing in Nonstandard English*, Amsterdam, Philadelphia: J. Benjamins, pp. 27–44.

Preston, Dennis (1982) 'Ritin fowklower daun rong: folklorists' failure in phonology', *Journal of American Folklore* 95: 304–26.

Preston, Dennis (1985) 'The L'il Abner syndrome: written representations of speech', *American Speech* 60: 328–36.

Preston, Dennis (2000) '"Mowr and mowr bayud spellin": confessions of a sociolinguist', *Journal of Sociolinguistics* 4: 614–21.

Redling, Erik (2006) *Speaking of Dialect: Translating Charles W. Chesnutt's Conjure Tales into Postmodern Systems of Signification*, Würzburg: Königshausen & Neumann.

Ruano-García, Javier, María F. Garcia-Bermejo Giner and Pilar Sánchez-García

(2015) 'Northern English historical lexis and spelling', in Raymond Hickey (ed.), *Researching Northern English*, Amsterdam: Benjamins.
Salveson, Paul (1993) 'Region, class, culture: Lancashire dialect literature 1746–1935', PhD thesis, University of Salford.
Schneider, Edgar (1986) ' "How to speak Southern"? An American English dialect stereotyped', *Amerikastudien/American Studies* 31: 425–39.
Schneider, Edgar (2002) 'Investigating variation and change in written documents', in J. K. Chambers, Peter Trudgill and Natalie Schilling-Estes (eds), *The Handbook of Language and Variation and Change*, Oxford: Blackwell, pp. 67–96.
Schneider, Edgar and Christian Wagner (2006) 'The variability of literary dialect as a reflection of panlectal competence: Jamaican Creole in Thelwell's "The Harder They Come" ', *Journal of Pidgin and Creole Languages* 21: 45–95.
Shackleton, Robert G., Jr. (2007) 'Phonetic variation in the traditional English dialects: a computational analysis', *Journal of English Linguistics* 35(1): 30–102.
Shorrocks, Graham (1996) 'Non-standard dialect literature and popular culture', in Juhani Klemola, Merja Kyto and Matti Rissanen (eds), *Speech Past and Present: Studies in English Dialectology in Memory of Ossi Ihalainen*, University of Bamberg Studies in English Linguistics, Frankfurt am Main: Peter Lang, pp. 385–411.
Shorrocks, Graham (1998) *A Grammar of the Dialect of the Bolton Area, Part 1: Introduction – Phonology*, Frankfurt am Main: Peter Lang.
Shorrocks, Graham (1999) 'Working-class literature in working-class language', in A. Hoenselaars and M. Buning (eds), *English Literature and the Other Languages*, Amsterdam: Rodopi.
Sixtus, Johannes (1912) *Der Sprachgebrauch des Dialekt-Schriftstellers Frank Robinson zu Bowness in Westmorland*, Berlin: Mayer & Müller.
Strand, Thea (2019) 'Tradition as innovation: dialect revalorization and maximal orthographic distinction in rural Norwegian writing', *Multilingua* 38(1): 51–68.
Taavitsainen, I., G. Melchers and P. Pahta (1999) *Writing in Nonstandard English*, Amsterdam, Philadelphia: J. Benjamins.
Tatman, Rachael (2016) ' "I'm a spawts guay": comparing the use of sociophonetic variables in speech and Twitter', *University of Pennsylvania Working Papers in Linguistics: Selected Papers from NWAV 44* 22: 160–70.
Tilling, Philip (1972) 'Local dialect and the poet: a comparison of the findings in the Survey of English Dialects with dialect in Tennyson's Lincolnshire poems', in Martyn Wakelin (ed.), *Patterns in the Folk Speech of the British Isles*, London: Athlone Press, pp. 88–108.
Trousdale, Graeme (2012) 'English dialects in the north of England', in Bernd Kortmann and Kerstin Lunkenheimer (eds), *The Mouton World Atlas of Variation in English*, Berlin, Boston: Walter de Gruyter GmbH, pp. 70–7.
Trudgill, Peter (1990) *The Dialects of England*, Oxford: Blackwell.
Wakelin, Martyn (1972) *English Dialects: An Introduction*, London: Athlone Press.
Wales, Katie (2000) 'North and South: an English linguistic divide?' *English Today* 16(1): 4–15.
Wales, Katie (2006) *Northern English a Cultural and Social History*, Cambridge: Cambridge University Press.
Wales, Katie (2010) 'Northern English in writing', in Raymond Hickey (ed.), *Varieties of English in Writing: The Written Word as Linguistic Evidence*, Amsterdam: John Benjamins.

Wales, Katie (2017) 'Dickens and Northern English: stereotyping and "authenticity" re-considered', in Joan Beal and Sylvie Hancil (eds), *Perspectives on Northern Englishes*, Berlin: De Gruyter.

Watt, Dominic, Carmen Llamas, Gerard Docherty, Damien Hall and Jennifer Nycz (2014) 'Language and identity on the Scottish/English border', in Dominic Watt and Carmen Llamas (eds), *Language, Borders and Identity*, Edinburgh: Edinburgh University Press, pp. 8–26.

Wells, John (1982) *Accents of English*, Cambridge: Cambridge University Press.

Williamson, Juanita V. and Virginia M. Burke (1971) *A Various Language: Perspectives on American Dialects*, New York: Holt, Rinehard & Winston.

Wright, Joseph (1892) *A Grammar of the Dialect of Windhill in the West Riding of Yorkshire*, London: Kegan Paul, Trench, Trübner & Co.

2

Black Country Dialect Literature and What It Can Tell Us about Black Country Dialect

Esther Asprey

2.1. Aims of the Chapter

This chapter examines Black Country dialect literature. I look at the small amount of dialect poetry published in the nineteenth century, most of which appeared in local newspapers, and compare it with earlier protest songs from the late eighteenth century, most of which were collected and written down in the 1960s by the folksingers Michael and Jon Raven (in this sense, it is somewhat like Braber, this volume, and a little like Cooper, this volume). I also look at dialect songs circulated in broadsheet form at the annual wakes in the Black Country, some of which were written especially for the event, to examine what we can say about grammatical change both across time in the Black Country and within the Black Country itself. I compare this kind of work to research concerning indexicality and ask how the two approaches can inform each other (in this sense, it is somewhat like Clark, this volume).

2.2. The Black Country Region

The Black Country is an 'imagined community' (Anderson 1983) existing in the minds of its residents, situated within the four Metropolitan Boroughs of Dudley, Sandwell, Walsall and Wolverhampton, to the immediate west of the City of Birmingham. In terms of other areas discussed in this volume, it is closest to the Potteries, discussed in Clark (this volume). It is in the West Midlands, to the west of the area discussed in Braber (this volume). The first nationally known reference to the area now known as the Black Country – though there are earlier highly localised references – came from William Cobbett, author of *Rural Rides*, grammarian, educator and political dissenter. He journeyed through the region and in 1893 referred to it as the

'Iron Country' (Cobbett 1893: 287). In 1838 Hawkes Smith had referred to the region as the South Staffordshire Mining District, while by 1860 one of the first known references in print to the 'Black Country' could be attributed to author Walter White in his 1860 book of travels in the region *All Around the Wrekin*, though the name had appeared locally in print some twenty years previously.

This history of the name reveals the history of the area. The co-occurrence of coal, iron ore and lime were to prove the making of the blackness to which the name 'Black Country' refers. It refers not to the ten-yard coal seam of the South Staffordshire coalfield, but to the heavy air pollution caused by the extreme density of drop forges, smithies and foundries in what was a very small area.

Today the term 'Black Country' has enjoyed a resurgence as an area in heavy post-industrial decline seeks to move forward and attract business and tourism to the area. What was once a stigmatised label for some is now actively employed by borough councils including Sandwell, Dudley and Wolverhampton, by government agencies, and crucially, by residents themselves, in constructing a sense of region and of language. Figure 2.1 shows the Black Country flag, created in 2012 in a competition run by the Black Country Living Museum by twelve-year-old Gracie Sheppard from Stourbridge. The museum's website (https://www.bclm.co.uk/) reports that the flag design

> was inspired by Elihu Burrit, the American Consul to Birmingham who described the region as 'black by day and red by night'. With the chains showing a typical product manufactured in the region. The white symbol in the middle represents the Redhouse glass cone and it's [*sic*] glass making heritage.

It was first used for the inaugural Black Country Festival in 2013, which is now an annual event. The Black Country Society was founded in 1967, and the Black Country Museum in 1978. In 2013 the Black Country Festival was launched, with financial backing from the borough councils of Dudley, Sandwell, Walsall and Wolverhampton. This is a weekend-long summer celebration of the region with activities and entertainments from displays of local industry (glassblowing, chainmaking) to poetry, comedy and spoken-word evenings, and it includes 14 July, which has been declared Black Country Day.

Commodification of the dialect and imagery of the region is also rising. *Black Country T Shirts* launched in Cradley Heath at the end of the 2000s and is now a successful face-to-face and online business in Dudley selling Black Country merchandise in the region and much further afield. Figure 2.2 shows the design on one of their t-shirts.

Figure 2.1 The Black Country flag

Figure 2.2 The Black Country Alphabet (design by Black Country T-shirts Ltd.)

2.3. Overview of Variation in the Black Country Dialect

The dialect associated with the region is a Midlands dialect, viewed by many as conservative, though as Asprey (2007) points out, the area has long had in-migration from other areas of the UK, notably Wales, Ireland, Shropshire and Worcestershire. Current migration from around the UK, as well as Commonwealth countries and the EU, means that the dialect is undergoing change and some levelling. Clark and Asprey (2013) list its major features. Phonologically it is north of what Wells (1982) refers to as the historical FOOT/STRUT split, though many speakers now do have some kind of split, with the STRUT value ranging within the range [ʊ ~ ɤ~ ʌ~ ɒ]. It is definitively north of the BATH/TRAP split, with the Southern value of BATH as [ɑː] parodied as not Black Country. In morphological terms, traces of the [nə] negative marker, yielding forms like [kɒnə] for the negative form of modal *can*, were reported in the *Survey of English Dialects* (Orton and Barry 1971: 1054) but are now moribund. The common negation strategy for auxiliary and modal verbs is younger; it relies on ablaut negation, and is heavily indexicalised, featuring on t-shirts, mugs, tea-towels and used in Facebook groups in stock phrases like 'Black Country ay we' (this is the newer negative form of the verb *be* – 'aren't we', which marks negation using ablaut). The dialect still contains, though at decreasing levels, [n] for present tense verbs (typical of Midlands dialects), [n] for adjectival marking in phrases like 'a boughten cake' for a shop-bought cake, and [n] for noun plurality, in phrases like 'flen' for *fleas* and 'peasen' for *peas*. All three features have been used in the texts I discuss, even though Asprey (2007) shows that in her sample all three are getting rarer in the present-day variety. The present analysis is therefore examining an earlier and, in many ways, more distinct variety, further away from Standard English norms. Such distance and difference can become tools of the dialect literature writer, in that they can add social class, gender, regional and attitudinal information about a character. They also lend themselves to the aims of the producer of indexicalised goods for consumption; a process now closely entwined with the production of dialect literature. The danger for the dialectologist in using such sources as evidence of actual production is clear: presence of a variable in the text is not proof of its presence in the speech community.

The theoretical underpinnings and aims of this chapter are set out in (1) and (2).

(1) I examine the tension between tracking indexicality and enregisterment of features and the use to which features are put by writers for literary effect.

(2) I ask whether there exist theoretical connections between these aims, and who is responsible for indexicalising and enregistering features of a dialect: speakers, or non-speakers who later use the variety for commercial gain.

Sebba (2009) as well as Androutsopoulos and Juffermans (2014) have drawn on terms used by Kloss (1967) to suggest that *Ausbau*, a process whereby linguistically similar varieties diverge as a result of elaborations of functions and resources in society, can be used in a social practice account of spelling. That is, that respelling the Black Country dialect to make it more distinctive could be seen as a choice planned by members of a speech community for various ends – to show distinctions of identity, to differentiate the dialect from another dialect, or simply to make it distinctive as a means of attracting attention (as writers have done) and to make money (as institutions like the Black Country Museum undoubtedly do with the merchandise they sell). We might go further and suggest that an enregisterment of moribund or declining forms remains useful to authors and others marketing the imagined Black Country (museums, musicians, clothing and accessory manufacturers) even when they are no longer a core part of the usage of all the speech community. I demonstrate that some features used in my sample are still in use in the speech community now, and that others feature more consistently than the linguistic record would predict.

2.4. Dialect Literature and Literary Dialect in the Black Country

Shorrocks (1996) makes a crucial distinction between dialect literature and literary dialect (also discussed in several other chapters in this volume, including the Introduction). The first is literature written for an audience which speaks that variety; the second not necessarily so. In the Black Country there is a history of both forms, though the tradition of representing Black Country voices in mainstream literature is not as embedded as it is in many regions, for example, Yorkshire or Lancashire. Ellen Thorneycroft Fowler is the earliest author to represent Black Country voices to a wider audience and used a small amount of literary dialect to do so; though little known now, she was popular during her lifetime (1860–1929). Her novels included *Cupid's Garden* (1897) and *Concerning Isabel Carnaby* (1898), a novel that won wide public acclaim; by 1899 the book was in its fifteenth edition and 40,000 copies had been sold. The novel was translated into French and German and a Braille version was also produced. She also wrote *A Double Thread* (1899), which *The Daily Graphic* named 'The Novel of the Year', and *The Farringdons* (1900). More widely known are works from the second half of the twentieth century by authors such as Meera Syal's *Anita and Me* (1997), Anthony

Cartwright's Cinderheath quartet (Cinderheath being a covername for his native Dudley) (2004, 2010, 2013, 2017), and the novels of Paul McDonald, centred on Walsall (2001, 2004, 2008).

Dialect literature is arguably more consistently represented now in the Black Country than at any other time in the region. Since the term Black Country became more widely popularised in the middle of the nineteenth century, pieces by local poets and writers have appeared in local newspapers at infrequent intervals. At the same time, chroniclers of the region and interested laypeople began collecting broadside songsheets from wakes and fairs. These were written versions of songs, sometimes written to commemorate the wake (festival day) itself. The *English Broadside Ballad Archive* (online) describes their genesis:

> In its heyday of the first half of the seventeenth century, a broadside ballad was a single large sheet of paper printed on one side (hence 'broad-side') with multiple eye-catching illustrations, a popular tune title, and an alluring poem – the latter mostly in black-letter, or what we today call 'gothic,' type.

Although they are mostly written in Standard English, direct speech from the characters is sometimes represented as dialect speech, making these a source of literary dialect. The broadsheet songs often receive a second audience when they are reprinted in local history magazines like the *Blackcountryman* (this being the quarterly, subscription-only journal of the Black Country Society) and the *Black Country Bugle*. This latter is also a local-interest publication, though it combines present-day news with historical interest pieces, old photographs, local recipes and archaeological reports.

The sources used for this study were selected precisely because they feature the use of literary dialect. They come from sources where the authors were more used to writing Standard English (in the case of Bartlett, this poem is his only dialect poem), or used literary dialect for effect (as in the case of Christie Murray, whose narrator thinks in Standard English but whose dialogue is reported in dialect). They do, however, blur the edges between the two categories. The last source, *Summer's End*, has a child narrator whose inner monologue is for the most part robustly Standard English, but segues on occasion into Black Country dialect. The blurring at the edges of the two categories confirms their use but does indicate that some writers' own use of Standard English might not be categorically and cleanly separated from their use of dialect. Indeed, there is much in the very small sample examined here which does not tally with the words of Taavitsainen and Melchers (1999: 14), who assert that

> [in] fiction nonstandard forms are mostly found in dialogues and they are used as powerful tools to reveal character traits or social and regional differences; that is what they 'do' in texts. Thus the function of nonstandard language in literature is to indicate the position and status of the character, and often such features are used for comical purposes to release laughter. It is mostly the low and the rural that are presented as speakers of nonstandard; humorous parts are attributed to minor characters and nonstandard language to side episodes.

This remark is true for some but not all of the data sources, which I now introduce and discuss.

2.5. Data Sources

I have taken texts from time points across the span of three centuries to examine the features that are represented in dialect literature and ask questions about how stable Black Country is as a variety, how it might have changed, and why. I also examine the issues surrounding the use of dialect literature as a source of linguistic knowledge in relation to morphological structure and set down some caveats and challenges for researchers going forward with such research. Data sources are gathered from six different pieces of writing. They span dialogues, songs, poems and novels. Literature written by Black Country authors is sparser than it is in other areas investigated, such as Newcastle upon Tyne and Yorkshire (see, for example, Maguire, this volume; Cooper, this volume). It appears more plentiful, though, than in areas such as the East and North Midlands (see Braber, this volume; Clark, this volume; Hodson, this volume). Dating the literature itself becomes hard when that literature is a song, as I will discuss in the final section of this chapter. Songs can become unmoored from the context and purpose for which they were written. This may lead to a change in content where morphological forms are concerned.

The texts I have chosen span the 1800s–2000s. They are set out in Table 2.1.

Table 2.1 Literature examined for morphological variation

Martin Danvers Heaviside	1817	*Dialogue between a Dudley Man and a Stourbridge Man*	43 words
Anon.	1880	'The Brave Dudley Boys'	143 words
F. R. Bartlett	1886	'The Collier's Story'	456 words
David Christie Murray	1896	*A Capful o' Nails*	*c.* 50,100 words
Anon.	1926	'The Battle of Bilston'	360 words
Archie Hall	1976	*Summer's End*	*c.* 58,460 words

The texts all count as dialect literature. The first text is a four-line dialogue on voting choices which appeared in the *Morning Herald* in 1817. The *Morning Herald* was founded in 1780, and was initially a liberal paper aligned with the Prince of Wales, but later became aligned with the Tories, ceasing publication in 1869 (Oliphant 1892: 228). Martin Danvers Heaviside is a pseudonym of Matthew Davenport Hill, the brother of Reginald Hill, inventor of the Penny Post. He was a regular contributor of satirical content to various newspapers and quarterlies. Born in Birmingham, he later became recorder for that city and a criminal law reformer. The content of the excerpt is satirical and refers to an attempt by the Whig Lord Thomas Foley, contrary to his father's wishes, to stand for parliament in 1816 as MP for Worcestershire against the eventual MP, Henry Beauchamp Lygon (History of Parliament 2018).

The second is a song which was first distributed in the 1820s in broadsheet form following the Corn Laws passing into statute. It is number 1331 in the Roud Folk Song Index, and was recorded by several Midlands artists, including notably Roy Palmer, the West Midlands historian, author and folk musician. It concerns a riot on the Earl of Dudley's estate in which many of his workers ran through Dudley town centre damaging property in protest at inflated corn prices. The version I deal with here was transcribed from the singing of a labourer working at the roadside in Dudley in 1880 by W. H. Duignan, and republished by Jon Raven (1965). Duignan, then, rendered the words into print and can be seen as responsible for orthographical choices and accuracy.

F. R. Bartlett was a Bilston doctor who lived his whole life in the town and would have been witness to the severe deprivation there and the cholera epidemic of 1832. It concerns the death by freezing of a small boy on his way home from school. The story made headline news and is said to have affected Bartlett so badly that he wrote the verse as a reaction to it. The poem is the only one to be written in dialect in a large self-published volume of verse otherwise in Standard English, which he called *Flashes from Forge and Foundry*.

A Capful o' Nails by David Christie Murray is the tale of nailmakers in West Bromwich seeking to escape the truck system whereby they buy raw materials from a ganger or gangmaster and sell the finished nails back to that same gangmaster at a very low and non-negotiable price. Although it was local journalist Christie Murray's first novel, it achieved only limited local success despite having a London publisher. It is dialect literature, being told through the first-person narratorial lens of the protagonist's son, watching his father seek to organise industrial action and ultimately die in the process.

The next source is a verse poem dealing with a cockfight in Bilston (the Prevention of Cruelty to Animals Act in 1849 made cockfighting illegal but it remained hugely popular in the Black Country as elsewhere, and there is an area of Wolverhampton called Fighting Cocks). It was written down in the *Bilston Almanac* in 1923. The *Bilston Almanac* began in 1872 and was a trade directory mixed with songs, poems and local news which appeared for sale annually, but the song dates from some time in the 1830s. It uses many dialect features, though the collector and the person they collected it from are both unknown and so discussing it is problematic.

Perhaps the least canonical of the texts is the last. Archie Hall's writing style does not divide the narratorial voice into Standard English usage and those of characters into dialect usage. Indeed, it is written as a 'coming of age' novel about a boy of thirteen after the Great Depression of the 1930s, contemplating his future in a declining Black Country. He is drawn to life as a bargeman, and spends some time working as a glassblower, but decides to return to school to finish his education on the advice of his friend Gyp, a war veteran and anarchist who spends time in and out of jail and tries to convince the young protagonist that work in the Black Country will no longer be easy to find, and that formal education might offer an escape route. Although the *concentration* of dialect features rises in first-person dialogue, the narrator's own voice is non-standard throughout, and it is not possible to say that the novel is literary dialect.

Buchstaller (2006) reports that covert and overt attitudes to variants differ greatly for quotative *go*. Similarly, informant attitudes in Asprey (2007) to dialect in the Black Country were mismatched. Informants would misreport use/non-use, particularly of variants they considered stigmatised. Thus three informants categorically denied ever using the third-person subject pronoun [əː] but used it at interview many times. Conversely, some informants reported that they used dialect features frequently but did not use these at interview or during discussions with other speakers post-interview. It is worth bearing in mind the caveats that apply to collecting speech in communities whose speech is stigmatised, and worth considering whether singers changed their variety, or whether collectors 'tidied up' speech as they wrote it down.

2.6. Indexicality and Enregisterment

I draw on the related concepts of indexicality (Silverstein 2003) and enregisterment (Agha 2003) to discuss what we can reliably infer about Black Country grammar from historical sources. Silverstein (2003: 194) explains that indexical order is

> the concept necessary to showing us how to relate the micro-social to the macro-social frames of analysis of any sociolinguistic phenomenon. … Such indexical order comes in integral, ordinal degrees, that is, first-order indexicality, second-order indexicality, etc., in the following general schema of dialectic: any n-th order indexical presupposes that the context in which

> it is normatively used has a schematisation of some particular sort, relative to which we can model the 'appropriateness' of its usage in that context. At the same time, there will tend to be a contextual entailment – a 'creative' effect or 'effectiveness' in context – regularly produced by the use of the n-th order indexical token as a direct (causal) consequence of the degree of (institutionalised) ideological engagement users manifest in respect of the n-th order indexical meaningfulness.

Put concisely then, indexical order is the application of a schema to a linguistic form. Should extra meaning be layered onto an existing schema such that the linguistic form accrues a different primary meaning, Silverstein proposes that we call such an order n+1.

Agha uses the term enregisterment to label a 'linguistic repertoire differentiable within a language as a socially recognised register', which has come to index 'speaker status linked to a specific scheme of cultural values' (2006: 231). These related though different theoretical tools help to explain the assignation of meaning to arbitrary forms by speakers and to explain the emergence of a recognisable 'way of speaking' or register which can be associated with a social group. Studies conducted previously both in the UK and elsewhere have argued that the literary language of dialect literature can be a useful source for determining which aspects of a dialect have become enregistered. Beal (2009) examines Geordie and Sheffield dialects. Cooper (2013, 2015) examines Yorkshire. Honeybone and Watson (2013) examine Liverpool, while Clark (2013) examines Black Country and Hermeston (2014) examines Geordie through the performance literature of the music hall. Many other chapters in this volume also address these issues (e.g. Beal, Braber, Clark, Cooper, Crowley and Honeybone).

I present evidence here that there is a Black Country dialect which has become a recognisable register to the people living both inside and outside the Black Country area. I also argue that certain features of the dialect are indexicalised, though the orders at which they are indexicalised vary according to the age and class of speaker, and indeed whether that speaker is inside or outside the Black Country area.

2.7. Variables

The variables chosen for this study were all identified in Asprey (2007), in which I asked informants to respond to a twenty-part questionnaire reporting on usage gleaned from Contemporary Humorous Localised Dialect Literature (CHLDL) books (Honeybone and Watson 2013), literature, poems, recordings and internet glossaries over time. In addition, the features asked about had been attested in previous studies of the Black Country, including Higgs

(2004), Howarth (1988) and Manley (1971). The village of Himley had also been included in the *Survey of English Dialects* because it was on the rural south-western edge of the Black Country. The variables of interest are explained and exemplified in Table 2.2.

Table 2.2 Morphological variants

Variable	Forms	Remarks and examples
Continuous aspect marker	+ ing form	Derives from OE <ōn> prefix *a-running down the road*
Perfective aspect marker	+ ed form	Derives from OE <ge> prefix *had have a-done*
Verbal present tense suffix	<n> ~ <en>	Derives from ME subjunctive [ən] (Wakelin 1972) *Cows they treaden in the muck*
Negative verb DO	Forms with ablaut Forms with more standard negative clitic Forms with [nə]	Ablaut mutation seems newer than more standard clitic AND [nə] forms also known in Shropshire, Staffordshire and Worcestershire (Britton)
Negative verb BE	Forms with ablaut Forms with more standard negative clitic Forms with [nə]	Clitic [nə] forms *I conna go to town today* *He dunna do nothing* *She wunna help you* *We shanna go*
Negative verb HAVE	Forms with ablaut Forms with more standard negative clitic Forms with [nə]	Ablaut mutation *I day see nothing* *I cor see the point* *He doh like it*
Negative verb SHALL	Forms with ablaut Forms with more standard negative clitic Forms with [nə]	*She wo help you* *We share goo*
Negative verb CAN	Forms with ablaut Forms with more standard negative clitic Forms with [nə]	
Adjectival marker	<n> ~ <en>	*boughten cake* = 'shop bought cake' *erden gown* = 'hessian gown'
Noun plural marker	<n> ~ <en>	*flen* 'fleas'
Third person female singular subject pronoun	[əː]	Derives from OE <hēo> *'er's a lovely girl*

In all cases, the chosen written sources were consulted for the presence or absence of these features and the distribution noted. Any alternative possibilities for the variants were also gathered. The results are given and discussed in the next section.

2.8. Results

There are certain remarks we can make about interpreting the data, presented here in Table 2.3. On the face of it, these divide into categories such as time and region. The Black Country dialect has changed over time. The variants that are captured in literature, however, make tracking such changes problematic. The only variant which appears to have fallen out of use in this sample is the perfective marker <a> which derives from OE <ġe->. It is no longer found in the last piece of writing. Comparison with the *SED* (Orton and Barry 1971) suggests that this is also the case among speakers at the time: no instances of this perfective marker were recorded in the locations closest to the Black Country – Hockley Heath (Warwickshire) and Himley (Staffordshire).

The other variants are all attested in the sample and many appear highly stable across time. This indicates one of the problems of doing historical linguistics by examining written sources. Not only is the sample small, but the aims of those writing literature for entertainment may be at direct odds with the aims of descriptive linguists seeking to track variants across time and observe speaker use. The presence of variants in such texts is no guarantee that they are in common use in the speech community at that time. In

Table 2.3 Distribution of morphological variants across literature (grey hashing indicates no variants available)

	1817	1880	1886	1896	1923	1976
Continuous aspect marker		YES	YES	YES	YES	YES
Perfective aspect marker			YES	NO	NO	NO
Verbal present tense suffix		YES	YES	YES	NO	YES
Neg. DO			*dunna*			*doe, dinna, doesn't/don't*
Neg. BE			*binna*	*ain't, isn't*	*binna*	*bay*
Neg. HAVE			*anna*	*ain't*		*ah, ain't, air't*
Neg. SHALL			*shanna*	*shan't*		*s'll not*
Neg. CAN	*caw*					*cor't, can't*
Adjectival marker			YES	YES		YES
Noun plural marker		YES	YES	YES	YES	YES
Third person subject female pronoun		YES	YES	YES	NO	YES

the Black Country this is linked to another issue, which is that variationist linguistics in the UK came late to urban areas affected by migration and thus not 'pure enough' for study. There is a dearth of spoken language to compare features to. Indeed, Taavitsaainen and Melchers capture this well when they refer to the 'dark ages of dialectology' (1999: 14). We can say that the variants used were *known* to the writers of the time and are very possibly intended to represent speech in the region at that time. All of our authors are familiar with the dialect they portray; however, this familiarity may be negotiated given that Hill, for example, was studying law at the time the poem was written, and Bartlett had studied medicine. Nevertheless, both had ties to the region: Hill returned to the family home at Kidderminster after coming down from university and Bartlett returned to live and work in Bilston for the rest of his life. It seems unlikely that they had no contact with speakers of the dialect at all – indeed their professions and domestic life could hardly have precluded contact with some speakers of the dialect. Although Archie Hall left the Black Country to study, his severe depression coupled with his homesickness meant that he later returned to it, and indeed has spoken at length about his relationship with the dialect in a BBC documentary which he filmed in 1974, titled *Archie Comes Home*. Similarly, David Christie Murray, although he went into the army at eighteen and later became a journalist, reporting all over Europe, spent his formative years until eighteen in West Bromwich, and indeed spent much of his journalism career working on local papers like the *Wednesbury Advertiser* and the *Birmingham Morning News*. These authors, then, were professionals who nevertheless had more contact with their home region than many who are educated out of their first variety. It is not possible to say who composed the first versions of *The Brave Dudley Boys*, or indeed *The Battle of Bilston*, but since one concerns local farmers and the other cockfights, it is unlikely that the composers moved in high social circles at all times. In their form, therefore, and their composition as poem and song, these pieces differ from the literature in terms of the speakers who composed them. It is likely that the prose pieces were composed by those whose variety at work was closer to the standard, and that the song was sung and the poem read and recited by those whose first variety was Black Country.

There is also the dimension of class to examine. This is hard to do because some texts allow little interpretation of class. Dudley and Stourbridge in 1817, for example, were both growing towns, though Stourbridge was at the time less industrialised than Dudley. It is hard to make sense of any class comment Danvers Heaviside might be offering, though it is clear that some difference of stance or opinion is implied in his comic couplet:

Dudley Man. 'Oi say, surree, hew dust thee vowt for?'
Stourbridge Man. 'I caw tell – I've not made up my moind.'
Dudley Man. 'Whoysna vowt for –? Thur best feller ee the wurrld; damned his own feyther at foiv' 'ear ode'!

The small sample of older Black Country texts I present here does, I argue, offer us some evidence concerning which features were in use and which are now known to be representative of the region. Even in 1817 the ablaut negative forms of the verb are present in Heaviside's parody text given above. The only texts which allow serious class analysis or indeed any other robust comparison are those with multiple voices and of a greater length. *The Battle of Bilston* has only one narrator, but they give no indication as to their class. There is also only one change from third-person narration to reported speech, though it does encapsulate a change from a more standard negation structure to a less:

Yet that Darlas'on cock was a good 'un,
He was red as a sodger's coat.
And the way he went at the other,
Made the Bils'on men change their note.

For he pecked like a miner a-holin',
And struck clean and straight with his spurs,
'By Christ' said 'Old Bull's Head' 'he's a true un,
And let him say he binna, wot dares.'

But the Bils'on cock warn't yet beaten
He was steel to the very backbone
And with a blow on the head, his opponent
On the turf he dropped dead as a stone.

The change between the more recognisable negation of *warn't* (which is still used in the area today and exists on a cline with [wa:nt ~ wa:, ~wɔ:] and the older [binə] is clear, but from such scant evidence it is hard to say what it can tell us about age or spatial distribution.

Still harder to interrogate is the even older version of *Brave Dudley Boys*, though its structure reveals many now-moribund features of the dialect:

Toims they bin moighty queer, Wo boys! Wo!
Toims they bin moighty queer, Wo boys! Wo!
Toims they bin moighty queer, for the fittle is sa very de-ar,
And it's O! The brave Doodley boys! Wo boys! Wo!

We bin a-marchin up and de-own,
Fur to pull the housen de-own.

The difficulty of comparison is made plain in the lack of opportunity for a negative verb – as a protest song the majority of the verse is about positive (illegal) action and does not contain negative polarity.

Bartlett's *Collier's Story* is a rich source of data, revealing the consistency of the [nə] negative marker, the existence of a-prefixing with the continuous and perfective aspects, and the use of third-person subject female [ə:]:

Well! One day las' Janooary,
Arter trudgin' miles around
Seekin waerk– in' vain as nary
Such a thing sir, c'ud be found,
Tho' fer wicks un wicks tergether
Norra single stroke ah struck
Till ah 'gan a-thinkin w'ether
Fate w'ud ever turn me luck
An ah thus a'bin a'playing orrl the time, right up ter now–
Burras ah were jes' a-sayin
It soo 'appened sir, as 'ow

On that day last Janooary
Ah'd returned wum, tired quite
W'en our little wench there Mary,
W'ot is lookin' thin un w'ite,
Cum a-runnin in a-cryin
Bob's bin sent back from the Schule,
An' ee conna walk – ee's lyin'
On the path be th'owd pit pule.

More useful as a source is Christie Murray, whose novel gives us the nailers and those who finance the nail trade, the merchants. Both groups speak non-standard English, but the merchants live luxurious existences, attending local political events, living in large houses with servants and carriages, and taking up musical instruments for pleasure. One such character is Mr Brambler, a kind and upright merchant who seeks to support the protagonist's father in challenging the corrupt pricing system. His language is more standard than that of Mr Sim the ganger, whom Mr Brambler challenges:

> 'This is a black business' said Mr Brambler, 'and I'm bent at getting at the bottom on it. I suppose you've got some kind of a notion as to whose hand is on it?' … 'may I ask if your ideas pints anywheer in the direction of Quarrymoor?'

Mr Brambler uses non-standard *on* for 'of', has two clear instances of Black Country phonology in the SQUARE and CHOICE sets (*anywheer* and *points*) and uses third-person plural verbal [s] in *pints*. In this he is very different from Mr Sim the ganger, who is only ever represented as using Black Country morphology, and even from the protagonist's morally upright, self-taught father, who aspires to a better life for his children and fellow workers. The narrator is clear that his father can style-shift, and indeed we see this when he starts to talk to workers and suggests a strike:

> 'We'em goin' to get up a bit of a strike.' Father always spoke with a broader accent to men of his own class than he used in talking to educated people like the doctor, or the parson, or the district visitors, who were the only decent people who came our way.
>
> 'We'em goin' to get up a bit of a strike,' he said.
>
> 'Bin you?' said old Blowhard, swinging round to his little anvil, and raining a shower of tinkling blows on the hot iron. 'Then yo' can count me out on it.'
>
> 'I mek bold to say,' said my father, 'as theer's no white men i'the world at this minute as is trod down like we be.'
>
> 'Trew for thee, ode lad,' said Blowhard, wheezing away over his anvil. 'But I'm none for helpin' the thieves to rob us. I'd as lief goo an' play as anybody, but wheer's the grub to come from? I remember the last strike thirty 'ear ago. We'd been at play seven wiks, an' … I'd ha' gi'en all my right o' man for a bit o' tommy.' (1896: 18)

We see here use of verb levelling by the protagonist's father to *em*, use of *we* for object pronoun second-person plural, as well as Black Country relativiser *as* for who. This shift is typical of the narrator's father throughout the novel, and Blowhard's speech typifies all other working men.

A more nuanced source is the multivoiced novel *Summer's End*, which does reveal more about age-related variation, as well as much about class variation. The protagonist gets four weeks' work as an assistant in a glassblowers one summer and befriends the glassblower he is there to assist:

> 'Do we make good glass round here?' I asked. 'Is it well thought on?'
>
> 'The best in the world', he answered, 'bar none. Stourbridge cut glass – Black Country table glass. There comes no better.'
>
> I was pleased.
>
> 'Ah'm glad o' that,' I said sincerely, 'ah really am glad.'
>
> A smile broke his stern face up and made him look years younger.
>
> 'Ah'm pleased that yo'm glad, young 'un,' he answered, 'that's the nicest thing ah've heard said in a long time. Yo' listen to me, – come into glass

> when you leaves school. Thing's will have picked up … come here wi' me and Is'll teach you all that I know. My word's on it.' He took a sandwich from his fittle bag and bit on it. 'Hasn't got any snap with thee?' he asked surprised, 'no fittle to chew on?' He dug into his fittle bag, pulled out a couple of thick wedge sandwiches and handed them to me. 'Get this down thee', he ordered. 'There's enough here for the two on us.' (1976: 72)

This passage shows not only the young narrator's ability to style-shift, but older features of speech. The glassblower uses *thee* forms, second person [s] verb endings in the present tense and the older verb paradigm of *have* [hasnt] before *thee*. Asprey (2007) also found all these forms extant in the speech of the oldest speakers in the Southern Black Country.

2.9. Interpretation of Results

Although the texts vary in length and narrative style and have authors whose immersion in the dialect is likely to have varied across the lifespan, they share a remarkable number of morphological features. This does not in itself imply that the variants are in active use at the time the writers wrote down the texts (with the likely exception of *The Brave Dudley Boys*, which was performed and transcribed). The writers, though, seek to capture something of the dialect, for narrative means and for literary effect. All writers are (as far as they can be traced) well-grounded in their communities and knowledgeable about the dialect, in that their accounts of how it is formed chime well together. In morphological terms the two stand-out suggestions are that the verbal negation system by ablaut which is now so enregistered in the region is variably emergent at best in these sources. Tellingly, it is the Stourbridge man in Danvers Heaviside's early work whose speech is represented as containing ablaut negation, while the Dudley man uses possibly the older strategy of [nə] – the word *whoysna* might be interpreted as *why doesna* (*th*)*a*, though this is extremely ambiguous. Across the rest of the corpus this ablaut negation then remains hidden, restricted only to [nt] and [t] forms, until it surfaces again in Hall (1976). More startling is the continued presence of the older [nə] strategy across time in Bartlett's poem, Christie Murray's novel and the poem about the cockfight in Bilston. Hill does not include it in the youngest piece of literature in 1976, by comparison. At the other end of the scale of stability, the Midlands form of the subject third-person female pronoun is stable across time. So too is the verbal continuous marker. So, for much of the sample, is noun plural [n].

2.10. Dialect Features in Literature

Literature, then, can show us which features are indexically representative of a region, a sub-group of speakers, a gender or a class. It cannot tell us accurately what speakers were actually using at the time the pieces were written, nor what speakers not represented in the literature were doing. If, for example, a woman does not appear in the piece of writing we are examining, it can be no surprise if female pronouns are not present in the text. Similarly, if a variant is not present, we are unwise to claim that it has fallen from use. Prose written in the past tense, for example, may not generate as many perfective forms as prose that refers to events further back in time or completed. Songs may preserve features for metrical reasons.

All pieces contain the female object pronoun [ə:], and indeed this is still in widespread use among speakers today. Unusually though, it seems to be little involved in processes of enregisterment. It was recognised by speakers in Asprey (2007) to be local, judged by many to be overtly stigmatised and local, but is not employed by the new wave of merchandise seeking to use enregisterment as a sales tool. The reasons for this are unclear at this stage since the Black Country is one of the few areas preserving the form, the others being Stoke on Trent (Leach 2018) and Shropshire (Hubbard 1960).

Similarly, if action is completive, past tense forms may be preferred over perfective aspect. This means that tracking perfective marker [ə] is also difficult. Taken together this means a large volume of songs, poems and prose is needed to say anything meaningful about morphological variation existing or not existing. The same, however, is true for collection of morphology in speech of the present day, and so this does not in itself rule out morphology as a subject for examination, and indeed may tell us much about the development and persistence of Black Country morphological forms.

2.11. Indexicality and Enregisterment

As far as the features I discuss here are concerned, it seems that for the authors and singers who rendered these versions, many variables were candidates for being indexicalised as representative of Black Country speakers; however, across time, the ablaut negation form of modal and auxiliary verbs begins to win out for authors against [nə] negation, while forms such as [n] for adjectival marker and [n] for noun plural fall from notice or come to index older speech. As for enregisterment, the second aim of this chapter was to discuss who actually enregisters forms. This is a difficult question indeed. Much work on the subject has relied on written sources where the majority of a population had limited access to literacy and a rich oral culture. Much emphasis is placed in current times on poets and novelists. In the case of the

Black Country, the lives of Bartlett, Christie Murray and Hill teach us that mainstream publishing houses did not value dialect poetry and prose (Hill's other volumes are better-known and sold more; Christie Murray met with no commercial success; and Bartlett did not write in dialect apart from the piece we examine). I would issue a cautious warning against relying on dialect literature or indeed literary dialect to examine indexicality and enregisterment and a plea that more difficult sources be engaged with. In the present time there are newly emergent spaces which allow those whose focus is not Standard English to write and create (see also Nini, Bailey, Guo and Grieve, this volume). Many Facebook groups testify to the fierce pride and interest of residents and speakers in the language and region of the Black Country while revealing that standards of literacy are varying for residents, and that in their writing they reveal much of the Black Country variety as it is today. Similarly the literary output of these communities in the form of jokes, poems, prose and vocabulary lists lends itself to investigation and puts the emphasis on indexicality back into the speech community.

2.12. Discussion and Future Directions for Research

The Black Country contains folk songs which were written after humorous or noted events (at wakes, fairs, bull baitings, cockfights and wife sales (events at which men discontented with their wives would exhibit them in public as a form of disgrace, and often illegally sell them to another man). It also contains songs written for political reasons. It would be prudent to trace different versions of the songs and chart their changing structures and lyrics. By the time of its 1880 rendition, *The Brave Dudley Boys* was a protest song in general terms and no longer an anti-Corn Law song. Golež Kaučič (2005) reminds us that when a song gets taken out of context,

> the process of losing a contextual function is the opposite of its acquisition … During this process, the song's musical image changes as well. The folk song is not a fossilised structure – which is why its wording or dialect can change in the course of transfer from one carrier to another.

In other words, folk songs, learned as they often were 'from the singing' of another, were not always subject to rigid standardisation and might be more representative of the time in which they are sung and observed by song collectors than one imagines. Comparing Raven's 1880 version with the 1967 version collected by Charles Parker confirms this: the [n] verbal ending is gone by 1967.

The Black Country was, as I discussed in my introduction, slower to emerge as a recognised area than some other parts of the country during industrialisation such as Tyneside (see Beal, this volume; Hermeston, this volume). The variety is thus slower to be recognised and labelled (this being a step towards enregisterment) and indexical patterns in dialect literature are harder to remark on until later in the nineteenth century and into the twentieth century (see Clark 2013 for evidence of emergent enregisterment after 1970). Indexicalisation changes over time, and dialect writing is a rich, though complex, source to attest to this. It can be employed in the quest to understand which morphological features symbolise the Black Country at a given moment, but caution must be used when doing so, for all the reasons this chapter has outlined. Similarly, enregisterment and commodification of the variety occurs now at grassroots level, some of it driven by locals keen to see their variety receive recognition for its difference and vibrancy, some by institutions keen to sell merchandise which chimes with the interests of the speech community. This process also can inform us, but the features which are enregistered are by no means the historically most 'Black Country' features, as my analysis has shown.

References

Agha, A., 2003. 'The social life of cultural value'. *Language and Communication* 23, 213–73.

Agha, A., 2006. *Language and social relations*. Cambridge: Cambridge University Press.

Anderson, B., 1983. *Imagined Communities: reflections on the origin and spread of nationalism*. London: Verso.

Androutsopoulos, J. and K. Juffermans, 2014. 'Digital language practices in superdiversity: introduction'. *Discourse, Context and Media* 4–5, 1–6.

Anon., 1850. 'Brave Dudley Boys'. Reproduced in J. Raven and M. Raven, eds. 1965. *Folk out of Focus: being a brief resume of the little known folk lore of the Black Country and Staffordshire*. Wolverhampton: Wolverhampton Folk Song Club.

Anon., 1923. 'The Battle of Bilston'. *Bilston Almanac*, reproduced in J. Raven and M. Raven, eds. 1965. *Folk out of Focus: being a brief resume of the little known folk lore of the Black Country and Staffordshire*. Wolverhampton: Wolverhampton Folk Song Club.

Asprey, E., 2007. 'Black Country English and Black Country identity'. Unpublished doctoral thesis, University of Leeds.

Bartlett, F., 1886. 'The Collier's Story: a tale of hard times'. In *Flashes from Forge and Foundry*. Bilston: Shakspeare Printing Co.

Beal, J., 2009. 'Enregisterment, commodification, and historical context: "Geordie" versus "Sheffieldish"'. *American Speech* 84:2, 138–56.

Buchstaller, I., 2006. 'Social stereotypes, personality traits and regional perception displaced: attitudes towards the "new" quotatives in the U.K.'. *Journal of Sociolinguistics* 10:3, 362–81.

Cartwright, A., 2004. *The Afterglow*. Birmingham: Tindall St Press.

Cartwright, A., 2010. *Heartland*. Birmingham: Tindall St Press.

Cartwright, A., 2013. *How I Killed Margaret Thatcher*. Birmingham: Tindall St Press.

Cartwright, A., 2017. *Iron Towns*. London: Serpent's Tail.

Christie Murray, D., 1896. *A Capful o' Nails*. London: Chatto & Windus.

Clark, U., 2013. '"Er's from off": the indexicalization and enregisterment of Black Country dialect'. *American Speech* 88:4, 441–66.

Clark, U. and E. Asprey, 2013. *West Midlands English: Birmingham and the Black Country*. Edinburgh: Edinburgh University Press.

Cobbett, W., 1893. Rural Rides, vol. 2. London: Dent.

Cooper, P., 2013. 'T'best place in t'world: definite article reduction and the enregisterment of "Yorkshire" dialect'. *Transactions of the Yorkshire Dialect Society*.

Cooper, P., 2015. 'Enregisterment in historical contexts: nineteenth century Yorkshire dialect'. *Dialectologia* 14, 1–16.

English Broadside Ballad Archive, n.d. 'Features'. Available at http://ebba.english.ucsb.edu/page/features. Accessed on 12 June 2019.

Golež Kaučič, M., 2005. 'Folk song today: between function and aesthetics'. *Traditiones* 34:1, 177–89.

Hall, A., 1976. *Summer's End*. London: Shepheard-Walwyn.

Hawkes Smith, W., 1838. *Birmingham and South Staffordshire: or, illustrations of the history, geology, and industrial operations of a mining district*. London: Charles Tilt.

Hermeston, R., 2014. 'Indexing Bob Cranky: social meaning and the voices of pitmen and keelmen in early nineteenth-century Tyneside song'. *Victoriographies* 42, 156–80.

Higgs, L., 2004. *A Description of Grammatical Features and Their Variation in the Black Country Dialect*. Basel: Schwabe Verlag.

History of Parliament, The, 2018. 'Lygon, Henry Beauchamp'. Available at http://www.historyofparliamentonline.org/volume/1820-1832/member/lygon-henry-1784–1863. Accessed on 10 June 2018.

Honeybone, P. and K. Watson, 2013. 'Salience and the sociolinguistics of Scouse spelling: exploring the phonology of the Contemporary Humorous Localised Dialect Literature of Liverpool'. *English World-Wide* 34:3, 305–40.

Howarth, J., 1988. 'The dialect of Walsall in the West Midlands'. Unpublished BA dissertation, Sheffield: University of Sheffield.

Hubbard, W., 1960. 'A grammar of the dialect of Albrighton, North East Shropshire'. Unpublished MA thesis, Leeds: University of Leeds.

Kloss, H., 1967. '"Abstand languages" and "ausbau languages"'. *Anthropological Linguistics* 9:7, 29–41.

Leach, H., 2018. 'Sociophonetic variation in Stoke-on-Trent's pottery industry'. Unpublished PhD thesis, University of Sheffield.

McDonald, P., 2001. *Surviving Sting*. Birmingham: Tindall St Press.

McDonald, P., 2004. *Kiss Me Softly, Amy Turtle*. Birmingham: Tindall St Press.

McDonald, P., 2008. *Do I Love You?* Birmingham: Tindall St Press.

Manley, S., 1971. 'The Black Country dialect in the Cradley Heath area'. Unpublished MA dissertation, Leeds: University of Leeds.

Oliphant, M., 1892. The Victorian Age of English Literature. London: Percival and Co.

Orton, H. and M. Barry, eds. 1971. *Survey of English Dialects B: The Basic Material – Volume 2, Part 3: The West Midland Counties*. Leeds: E. J. Arnold.

Raven, J. and M. Raven, eds. 1965. *Folk out of Focus: being a brief resume of the*

little known folk lore of the Black Country and Staffordshire. Wolverhampton: Wolverhampton Folk Song Club.
Raven, M. and J. Raven, eds. 1966. *Folk-Lore and Songs of the Black Country and West Midlands*, vol. 2. Wolverhampton: Wolverhampton Folk Song Club.
Sebba, M., 2009. *Spelling and Society: The Culture and Politics of Orthography around the World*. Cambridge: Cambridge University Press.
Shorrocks, G., 1996. 'Non-standard dialect literature and popular culture'. In J. Klemola, M. Kytö and M. Rissanen, eds. *Speech Past and Present: studies in English dialectology in memory of Ossi Ihalainen*. Frankfurt am Main: Peter Lang, 385–411.
Silverstein, M., 2003. 'Indexical order and the dialectics of sociolinguistic life'. *Language and Communication* 23, 193–229.
Syal, M., 1997. *Anita and Me*. London: Flamingo.
Taavitsainen, I. and G. Melchers, 1999. 'Writing in nonstandard English: introduction'. In I. Taavitsainen, G. Melchers and P. Pahta, eds. *Writing in Nonstandard English*. Amsterdam: John Benjamins, 1–26.
Thorneycroft Fowler, Ellen, 1897. *Cupid's Garden*. London: Cassell.
Thorneycroft Fowler, Ellen, 1898. *Concerning Isabel Carnaby*. London: Cassell.
Thorneycroft Fowler, Ellen, 1899. *A Double Thread*. London: Cassell.
Thorneycroft Fowler, Ellen, 1900. *The Farringdons*. London: Cassell.
Wakelin, M., 1972. *English Dialects: an introduction*. London: The Athlone Press.
Wells, J. C. 1982. *Accents of English*, 3 vols. Cambridge: Cambridge University Press.
White, W., 1860. *All Round the Wrekin*. London: Chapman and Hall.

3

Dialect and the Construction of Identity in the Ego-documents of Thomas Bewick

Joan Beal

3.1. Introduction

3.1.1. Ego-documents and Historical Sociolinguistics

While the majority of contributions in this volume deal with the use of dialect in literary and popular texts, this chapter investigates the part played by dialect writing in ego-documents. This latter term is not yet listed in the OED but according to the website of the Center for the Study of Egodocuments[1] and History (www.egodocuments.net) it 'refers to autobiographical writings, such as memoirs, letters, diaries and travel accounts' and was 'coined around 1955 by the historian Jacques Presser'. While the origin of the term and of research focused on ego-documents can be attributed to historians, the development of the discipline of historical sociolinguistics in the twenty-first century has been greatly facilitated by the development of corpora of letters and other ego-documents. Nevalainen and Raumolin-Brunberg, reflecting on their experience of compiling the Corpus of Early English Correspondence (CEEC), point out that 'personal correspondence provides the "next best thing" to authentic spoken language and, even with its obvious limitations, makes it possible to extend the variationist paradigm into the more distant past' (2012: 32). Van der Wal and Rutten (2013: 1) note that, in addition to this closeness to speech, ego-documents also have the advantage of filling in the gaps left by more traditional historical studies which have taken their evidence from literary and official texts, and of providing evidence for the language of the middle and lower classes.

Nevalainen and Raumolin-Brunberg's evocation of 'authentic spoken language' as a target to which ego-documents approach and of the 'variationist paradigm' places their work within what Eckert (2012) would term the 'first wave' of sociolinguistics, characterised by studies that discover correlations between linguistic variables and static social categories such as class, gender, ethnic group and so on. Eckert's 'second wave' represents studies which take a more ethnographic approach, concentrating on local rather than global categories and demonstrating the importance of networks in diffusing or resisting innovation, while 'third wave' research considers the active agency of individuals and communities of practice in constructing social meaning via linguistic variation. Eckert describes the third wave as 'in its infancy' (2012: 88) and Conde-Silvestre states that 'historically-oriented approaches within the third wave are, at the moment, scarce' (2016: 46). One reason given by Conde-Silvestre for this relative scarcity of third-wave studies in historical sociolinguistics is the difficulty of reconstructing communities of practice and their dynamics, but ego-documents provide good evidence for the construction of social meaning and especially for the agency of the writer in constructing and representing a persona. The research reported in this chapter therefore takes a third-wave approach, using the framework of indexicality and enregisterment, which is outlined in the following section.

3.1.2. Indexicality, Enregisterment and the Presentation of Self in Ego-documents

The concepts of indexicality and enregisterment were introduced by Silverstein (1976, 2003) and Agha (2003, 2007) and have been used in sociolinguistics (for example, Johnstone *et al.* 2006; Johnstone 2009) and in historical sociolinguistics (Beal 2009, 2017) to explain how linguistic features come to be associated with social meanings and personae and can then be used by speakers or writers to invoke such meanings/personae. There is also discussion of indexicality and enregisterment in Clark, Cooper and Hermeston (all this volume). Silverstein (2003) describes the development of these associations as involving stages of indexicality. At the first, or *n*th stage, there is a correlation between the use of a linguistic feature and some social characteristic which can be observed by outsiders, such as professional linguists, but of which those who use this feature are unaware. When their use of such features is pointed out, speakers are surprised and may deny that they use the feature or, conversely, say they had thought everybody used it. In the Labovian paradigm, such a feature would be described as an *indicator* (Labov 1972: 178–80). At the second, or *n* + 1 stage, the link between the linguistic feature and some social characteristic(s) is rationalised and speakers' use of the feature may vary stylistically according to formality, self-consciousness, etc. Features which are thus used in style-shifting are termed *markers* by Labov. The third or *n* + 1 + 1 level of indexicality is reached when there is evidence of overt awareness of, and metalinguistic comment on, the link between the feature and the social characteristic(s) associated with it. It is at this level that the feature concerned becomes available for social work, as speaker/writer and listener/reader are equally aware of the social meaning of the feature. Labov would describe such a feature as a *stereotype*, but while within the first-wave framework a stereotype is described as a stigmatised feature which will eventually die out, in third-wave research it is recognised that such features have an important role to play in the construction and representation of identity and that speakers and writers have an active part to play in the transmission of the social meanings associated with linguistic features.

Although individual linguistic features such as words or variant pronunciations can thus be associated with and invoke social meanings, social groups or personae are more usually associated with repertoires of features, often referred to by terms such as *accent*, *dialect*, etc. Agha, however, rejects the idea that accents are fixed, objective entities, and prefers the term *register*. He argues that 'the folk-term "accent" does not name a sound pattern alone, but a sound pattern linked to a framework of social identities' (2003: 22). Agha explains the nature of a *register* as follows:

> A register exists as a bounded object only to a degree set by sociohistorical processes of enregisterment, processes whereby its forms and values become differentiable from the rest of language (i.e., recognisable as distinct, linked to typifiable social personae or practices) for a given population of speakers. (2007: 168)

The process of enregisterment involves the creation of a register in Agha's sense via the transmission of messages linking the linguistic repertoire concerned with 'social personae or practices'. Such messages are carried by explicit metalinguistic commentary but also by the use of the repertoire, for example, in literature where its features are associated with characters evoking the social personae concerned. The types of discourse discussed in other chapters in this volume, such as dialect literature (in many chapters), cartoons (in Clark's chapter) and social media (in Nini, Bailey, Guo and Grieve's chapter), all play a part in the process of enregisterment, as do dialect dictionaries and scholarly accounts of varieties, reinforcing as these latter genres do the link between linguistic repertoires and geographical areas.

Of course, in order to be part of an enregistered repertoire, features must be at the third or $n + 1 + 1$ stage of indexicality, but the process of enregisterment further reinforces the link between these features/repertoires and their social meanings. The process is dynamic and speakers or writers do not inevitably use the repertoires associated with their social class, geographical location and so on, but make active use of these to present themselves. In this respect, ego-documents provide an excellent source of historical data: in letters and memoirs, writers are constructing and presenting personae to their correspondents, or to posterity. In this chapter, I examine letters and a memoir written by Thomas Bewick with a view to determining how, within texts otherwise composed in Standard English, Bewick uses elements of a repertoire already enregistered as Northumbrian in dialect literature, dictionaries, etc. to present himself as belonging on Tyneside and as a man in tune with nature and countryside pursuits (in terms of the variety discussed here, the closest other chapters in this volume are those by Hermeston and Maguire; and in terms of conception, this chapter is perhaps closest to that by Nini, Bailey, Guo and Grieve, who consider dialect writing on Twitter and the indexicality of the forms that they find in it). In the next section, I present a brief biography of Thomas Bewick, and an account both of his ego-documents and of biographies of Bewick written by third parties. This should serve to justify the choice of Bewick as a subject for this study.

3.2. Background

3.2.1. Bibliography

In addition to Bewick's own memoir, first published in 1862, and an entry in the *Dictionary of National Biography* (Bain 2004), there are several biographies, including those by Thomson (1882), Dobson (1884), Robinson (1887) and Uglow (2006). The first edition of Bewick's memoir was edited by his daughter Jane and all subsequent editions prior to that edited by Bain (1979) are based on the first edition. As Bain points out, Jane Bewick and the publisher of the first edition made various alterations to the manuscript, so that Bain's edition, which is based on Bewick's original manuscript, is the most reliable. For the purposes of this study, Bain's (1979: 252) explanation of his editorial policy is extremely helpful, as he informs us that he has retained Bewick's marks of emphasis:

> There are numerous underlinings throughout the text which were employed for three purposes, though not always obviously: often for emphasis, sometimes in place of inverted commas round colloquialisms, and often in a tentative manner as an indication of uncertainty of expression. The first two groups have been italicized and the third left in roman.

The editor of Bewick's correspondence with John Dovaston likewise tells the reader that he has represented Bewick's underlinings as italics and his use of double inverted commas by single ones (Williams 1968: 21). In both cases, this editorial practice has enabled me to identify lexical items which Bewick chose to set apart as marked in some way.

Much of Bewick's correspondence survives, but apart from extracts in the biographies and the edition edited by Williams, these are spread across many different archives and libraries from Newcastle upon Tyne to San Marino, California. The late Iain Bain published a checklist of Bewick's correspondence and other papers (1970) and owned a substantial private collection of Bewick's papers, which were acquired by the Wordsworth Trust in 2013. These have since been digitised and the archive can be searched at https://tinyurl.com/ydbpxbxn, but the images themselves are not searchable and no corpus of Bewick's ego-documents exists. The data presented in this chapter have been taken from Bain's edition of the memoir, Williams' edition of the Dovaston correspondence, the archive at the Wordsworth Trust, and the collections held at Newcastle City Library and the Robinson Library, Newcastle University.

3.2.2. Biography

Thomas Bewick (1753–1828) was born in Cherryburn, Northumberland, the eldest son of a tenant farmer who also leased a colliery. After his education, Bewick was apprenticed to the Newcastle engraver Ralph Beilby and eventually became Beilby's partner. Bewick revived the art of woodcut printing, which had hitherto been considered inferior to metal engraving. As well as many commissions for illustrating other authors' works, Bewick published illustrated works on natural history which were extremely well received at the time and have been highly influential ever since: *A General History of Quadrupeds* (1790) and *A History of British Birds* (two volumes, 1797, 1804). His reputation as a naturalist was such that a species of swan was named after him (Bewick's swan).

Bewick's early education got off to a bad start with a master who 'did not spare his Rod' (ed. Bain 1979: 3) and, by his own admission, Bewick frequently played truant, exploring the countryside rather than attending classes. However, a better master was eventually found and, although Bewick recounts having spent much of his time doodling in the margins of his books, he learned 'figures as far as Fractions & Decimals &c', and was then 'put to learn Latin' (ed. Bain 1979: 4). By the time he was apprenticed to Beilby at the age of fourteen, Bewick had therefore had a reasonable elementary education as well as a less formal but, for his career, equally important education in nature. His memoir and correspondence demonstrate that he was capable of writing Standard English, and the account of his library provided by David Gardner-Medwin (www.bewicksociety.org) demonstrates that he was extremely well-read.

Newcastle upon Tyne in the second half of the eighteenth century was an intellectually lively city and an important centre for publishing. As an apprentice engraver, Bewick became acquainted with the many publishers and printers in Newcastle and opportunities for reading were provided by the bookshops and circulating libraries in the city. Uglow tells us that in the early years of his apprenticeship Bewick 'found good friends in the circle that formed around the bookbinder Gilbert Gray' and that 'during winter evenings he worked his way through Gray's bookshelves' (2006: 78–9). Gray had previously worked for the Scottish poet and bookseller Allan Ramsay, an early advocate of Scottish folklore and writing in Scots, whose works were to become popular and influential on both sides of the border. From 1790, Bewick was a member of Swarley's Club, a debating society which met at the Black Boy Inn in the Groat Market, and later became a founder member of the Newcastle Philosophical Society. Among his fellow members of the latter society were John Collier, the son of the dialect writer also called John Collier (better known under his pseudonym Tim Bobbin; see Honeybone and Maguire, this volume, for some discussion of Tim Bobbin's dialect writing), and John Trotter Brockett, the compiler of one of the first dictionaries of Northumbrian dialect (Brockett 1825). We can thus see that he had several friends and acquaintances who took an interest in dialects and dialect writing. (See also Hermeston, this volume, for further discussion of Brockett's glossary.)

Bewick spent almost all of his life on the banks of the Tyne, whether in Cherryburn, Newcastle or, later in his life, Gateshead. He did, however, have a spell in London between September 1776 and June 1777 and a second short visit in 1828. Bewick disliked London and was homesick for Tyneside. In a letter written in November 1776, he wrote of London: 'I like it (or like to live in it) very badly [...] yet would I rather live in both poverty and insecurity in NCastle' (cited in Bain 2004). While in London, Bewick sought out the company of fellow Northerners: according to Uglow 'every Monday night he read the Tyneside papers and met other Newcastle friends at the Hole in the Wall in Fleet Street' (2006: 101). In his memoir and letters, Bewick has nothing good to say about London or the 'Cockneys'. Referring to his first stay in London, he relates 'where ever I went, the ignorant part of the Cockneys called me "Scotchman" ' (ed. Bain 1979: 70). Thirty-one years after the Jacobite rebellion, prejudice against the Scots was common in London, and Bewick's Northumbrian accent would have been indistinguishable from Scots to many Londoners. In a letter to Dovaston in 1828, Bewick, reflecting on his recent trip to London, states that he found the inhabitants as bad as ever.

> The real Cockneys, seem to me to be no way altered in character, since I left them above 51 years ago – they are still fond of high living & talk the in [*sic*]

> way about 'good Wittals' [...] it struck me again, as it had done before, that these little, fat Lumps of the human species, were in the Caterpillar state, & would always remain so. (Ed. Williams 1968: 118)

In an earlier letter, Bewick had taken the opportunity to rail against the ignorance of Londoners after recounting an experience of an order of paper being delayed because it had been sent to 'Newcastle underline' (Newcastle-under-Lyme in Staffordshire).

> I had long known that the generality of Cockney's [*sic*] knew nothing of geography – and that the precincts of London was sufficient for them and I have known one of these very pert Cits, who seemed indeed to be above the common order of them, stoutly affirm that *Philadelphia* was in *Glasgow*. (Ed. Williams 1968: 78)

Apart from these two visits to London, Bewick's travels were confined to the North of England, Scotland and Derbyshire. At the age of twenty-two, he set off on a walking tour, first to Cumbria and then to Scotland. Uglow makes the pertinent comment that this was Bewick's 'Grand Tour – not to Italy or France, but to the west and north of his own country' (2006: 94). His attitude towards Scotland and the Scots was much more positive than that towards London and its citizens. Bewick relates the following anecdote from his time in London, when he met a traveller who had visited Scotland.

> [He] was vociferous in attempting to entertain the company with his account of the filth & dirt he had met with in it – this I could not bear – their kindness was fresh in my memory [...] [I] only told him, that I believed I had travelled on foot, perhaps about 300 miles, through Scotland & had met with no such people there, nor such dirtiness as he described [...] but that I was confident such might be found without going much beyond the street we were in & who in addition to their filthiness, were also the most wretched & abandoned of the human race. (Ed. Bain 1979: 72)

Bewick's account of his visit to Edinburgh in 1823 likewise strikes a positive note.

> Not having seen Edinburgh since August 1776 – I longed to see it again [...] I always thought highly of Edinburgh & its bold & commanding situation – but the new Town (or City of palaces, as it is now sometimes called) had been added to since that time, but all these splendid buildings, are of trivial import, compared with the Mass of intellect & science, which had taken root & been nurtured & grown up to such a height as to rival & perhaps outstrip every other city in the World. (Ed. Bain 1979: 182)

So, at the start and end of his life, Bewick visited both Scotland and London, and was in no doubt about the superiority of the former. His brother John settled more happily in London, and Thomas kept up a correspondence with him in the course of which the brothers exchanged news of Newcastle friends in London and songs in Northumbrian dialect.

This biographical account has been brief, partly for reasons of space, and partly because I wished to highlight the experiences and connections which may have influenced Bewick's awareness of and attitude to dialect. For those who wish to know more about Bewick's life and work, I recommend Uglow's scholarly but highly readable biography (2006). In the next section, I examine in more detail such information we have about Bewick's own language and his knowledge and awareness of his own and other dialects.

3.2.3. Bewick and Dialect

We saw in the previous section that Thomas Bewick spent almost all of his life on Tyneside, and that his brief experiences of London left him with a bad impression of the capital and those he called 'the Cockneys'. His network of friends and acquaintances in Newcastle included several Scots and his view of Scotland, and of Edinburgh in particular, was much more positive. Several of his Newcastle acquaintances and his own brother John took an interest in what were at the time termed 'popular antiquities', including traditional music, song and dialect. We know from Gardner-Medwin's account of Bewick's library that he had a collection of Cumbrian, Northumbrian and Scots songs and poetry, including several volumes of Robert Burns' works and Walter Scott's *Lay of the Last Minstrel.* The Special Collections section of the Robinson Library, Newcastle, holds a copy of a song in Northumbrian dialect in Thomas Bewick's hand, illustrated with a sketch of a mother and child. This was included in a letter to John Bewick dated 9 January 1788, with the note 'it will add one more to your collection', implying that Thomas and John collected and exchanged dialect material. This is the conclusion reached by Robinson:

> Newcastle can boast of many capital songs in the *vulgar tongue,* remarkable for their genuine wit and humour. [...] John Bewick and his friends [...] would often entertain themselves with such ditties on an evening, when the work of the day was over. Though resident in London, Newcastle would ever be fondly remembered. (1887: 92)

Robinson also includes as an appendix two 'tales related by the late Thomas Bewick' (1887: 312), *The Howdy* (midwife) and *The Upgetting* ('the reception held for the recovery of a matron after chilbirth'; Heslop 1892). Robinson tells us that the original manuscripts belonged to John Bell, but we have no further evidence of their provenance. Since there is no clear evidence that Bewick was the author or transcriber of these tales,[2] I have chosen not to analyse these for the purposes of this chapter. Both tales are described as being 'in the teyne seyde dialect one hundred years seyne'. Here, 'teyne seyde' refers not to the modern urban area, but literally to a place on the banks of the Tyne. The dialect represented is more typical of south-west Northumberland than of the city of Newcastle, or even Berwick's birthplace in Cherryburn. Moreover, 'one hundred years seyne' suggests that the dialect represented in the tales was no longer current. This antiquarian view of dialect as something that was dying out was prominent at the time of Robinson's publication. As I have noted elsewhere (Beal 2010: 2–4), dialect dictionaries and glossaries published in the late nineteenth century are routinely prefaced by threnodies lamenting the demise of the dialects catalogued. If 'one hundred years seyne' has its starting point in Bewick's lifetime rather than Robinson's publication, it is an early example of this trend, but the popular antiquities movement of the eighteenth century promoted a similarly nostalgic view of dialect.

The fact that Bewick is said to have related these tales suggests that he was in the habit of 'performing' in dialect, consciously using a repertoire of features to project a persona. Accounts of Bewick's speech provided by his friends suggest that he used a recognisably local variety throughout his life. Of course, these accounts also present the persona recollected by the authors, but they do lend weight to Uglow's assertion that he 'proudly maintained his accent' (2006: 357). John Dovaston's account of Bewick's life, reproduced as an appendix to Williams' (1968) edition of their correspondence, includes representations of, and comments on, Bewick's dialect. One such account bears witness to Bewick's interaction with ragamuffin children in Newcastle.

> He turned to them several times, while he was talking to me, saying 'Get awa', bairns, get awa'; I hae none for ye the day'. As they still kept dogging him, and pulling his coat, he turned into a shop, and throwing down a tester, said in his broad dialect (which he neither affected to conceal, nor pretended to affect), 'Gie me sax penn'orth o' bawbees;' and throwing the copper among the children, said kindly, and with a merry flourish of his cudgel, 'There, chields, fit yourself wi' ballats, and gae hame singing to your mammies'. (Ed. Williams 1968: 134)

This is not necessarily an accurate representation of Bewick's Northumbrian dialect. There are several features here and elsewhere in Dovaston's accounts which are more likely to be Scots ('bawbees', 'gae' rather than Northumbrian 'gan', for instance). Like the Cockneys who mistakenly identified Bewick as a 'Scotchman', Dovaston may well have found it difficult to distinguish between Scots and Northumbrian. There was also much more in the way of precedents for writing Scots in the works of Ramsay and Burns. What is important here is that Dovaston represents Bewick's dialect as 'other' than Standard English, associating this otherness with the persona of Bewick. Dovaston goes on to relate a tale told to him by Bewick, of how he was attacked by a mastiff and 'fetched him, wi' his cudgel, such a hell o' a thwacker owre the lumber vertebrae, that sent him howling into a hovel' (ed. Williams 1968: 134). In both these anecdotes, Dovaston is portraying Bewick as an 'authentic' speaker of his dialect, which he 'neither affected to conceal, nor pretended to affect', and as a strong man who is nevertheless kind to children. Within the framework of enregisterment, we can see this as linking the repertoire of dialect features attributed to Bewick with this persona. Metapragmatic comments by Dovaston explicitly link Bewick's dialect with personal qualities, suggesting that it made his statements more effective. In notes made on a journey to Scotland in 1825, Dovaston comments on a draft of Bewick's memoir. 'The style is nervous, sinewy and broad, like his conversation, a good deal garnished with Northumbrian & Scottish provincialisms, which, in my estimation, particularly when he reads it aloud, strengthen the efficiency' (ed. Williams 1968: 49).

Other witnesses provide evidence that Bewick knowingly used Northumbrian dialect for playful purposes. Uglow gives an account of a story related by Bewick to John Jackson. Although in his own memoir, Bewick stresses how sorry he felt for the wretched state of prostitutes in London, Chatto and Jackson present Bewick's account of how he teased them by playing up to the idea he was a naive country man. He told Jackson how he 'would ask, with an expression of solid gravity, if they knew "Tommy Hummel o' Prudhow, Willy Eltringham o' Hall Yards or Auld Laird Newton o' Mickley"' (Chatto and Jackson 1839: 567, cited in Uglow 2006: 104). A further example of Bewick's humorous use of dialect, related by G. C. Atkinson, is reproduced by Uglow. On one occasion, Bewick's wife criticised him at length for staying out late and for his untidy habits. According to Atkinson,

> all this he endured for some time with much philosophy, till seeing no immediate prospect of a cessation, he began with an enormously long and curiously intoned ejaculation, something like the following 'A-h what a wind there's in our house this morning! Why before I knew you I was a nice, canny, tidy lad – but now I gang about with my coat out at elbows, and taties in my stocking heels! A-h!' This, uttered in a tone of undisturbed good humour and so comic, that his good lady was compelled to desist. (Atkinson 1831, cited in Uglow 2006: 201–2)

Atkinson presents this anecdote as related to him by Bewick, which suggests that Bewick was aware that he could use Northumbrian dialect to do social work: in this case to win over his wife with humour by presenting himself as a lovable rogue. Elsewhere, Atkinson takes issue with Dovaston's representation of Bewick's dialect, referring to 'the difficulty he seems to feel in transcribing the dialect, which he invariably allows to degenerate into low Scotch', when, according to Atkinson, Bewick's dialect was 'a genuine and not offensive Northumbrian, used with the greatest spirit and effect' (Gardner-Medwin 2007: 8).[3] That Dovaston and Atkinson give different representations of Bewick's dialect should come as no surprise, since both were recollecting the anecdotes and Bewick's words. As I have noted above, what is important is that both saw fit to render Bewick's dialect as different from Standard English, and both viewed his use of dialect as effective. In the following sections, after outlining the methodology used, I will explore the ways in which Bewick used dialect to project personae in his ego-documents.

3.3. Analysis

3.3.1. Methodology

As I explained in Section 3.1.1 above, while authoritative editions of Bewick's memoir (ed. Bain 1979) and his correspondence with John Dovaston (ed. Williams 1968) have been published, Bewick's other letters are spread across a number of archives, and no searchable corpus of Bewick's ego-documents exists. It would therefore be very difficult to carry out quantitative research, and even the selection of letters that I have analysed has been chosen according to ease of access[4] rather than any more rigorous criteria. None of the ego-documents examined in this chapter is searchable electronically, so I noted down examples of dialect use as I read through them. Most of these consist of lexical items or phrases, which I entered into the spreadsheet reproduced as Appendix 3.1. I noted whether Bewick highlighted these items by underlining (italic in the published materials) and/or by placing them in inverted commas, and whether Bewick glossed them. While such highlighting on Bewick's part can be taken to imply that he was consciously using terms that he knew to be 'marked' as dialectal, or colloquial, absence of highlighting does not necessarily imply that he was not aware of this.

I looked up each item in four dictionaries: the *Oxford English Dictionary* online (www.oed.com), the online database of Wright's *English Dialect Dictionary* (1896–1905) (www.eddonline-proj.uibk.ac.at), John Trotter Brockett's *A Glossary of North Country Words in Use* (1825) and R. O. Heslop's *Northumberland Words* (1892), the latter two downloaded from www.archive.org. I used these dictionaries to verify the meanings of the dialect words used by Bewick and to determine to what extent they were recorded as exclusively Northumbrian, Northumbrian and Scottish, generally Northern, or more widely used. To a certain extent, this process proved to be circular, as Bewick is cited in these dictionaries, sometimes providing the only citation for the word concerned. We know that Brockett and Bewick were acquainted, and Robinson suggests that Bewick may well have been one of the authorities consulted by Brockett. Robinson cites several instances in the first edition of Brockett's *Glossary* where Bewick's publications are referenced. One of these is *netty* (a toilet).

> *Neddy, Netty,* a certain place that will not bear a written explanation, but which is *depicted to the very life* in a tail-piece in the first edition of Bewick's 'Land Birds' (1797), p. 285. In the second edition a bar is placed against the offending part of this *broad* display of native humour. (Cited in Robinson 1887: 132)

The tail-piece referred to is a vignette entitled 'The Pigstye Netty' in which a man is seen from behind sitting on a toilet in an outhouse next to a pigsty. The OED online also cites Bewick in the entries for *leish, messet, pit heap, parrentory, smout hole* and *strike.* In the case of *strike,* meaning 'a place where salmon are speared', Bewick is the only authority cited by the OED.

Given the input that Bewick and his works have had into some of the dictionaries consulted, I cannot use the dictionaries to 'authenticate' the words concerned, but, within the framework of indexicality and enregisterment, 'authenticity'[5] is beside the point. What matters is that Bewick was aware that these terms were indexed as local, humorous and so forth, that he passed this information on to his readers, and that some of these in turn reproduced it in dictionaries. For example, *netty* is still in use in Tyneside and Northumberland as a humorous term for a toilet, especially an old-fashioned outhouse. Bewick's use of the term and his scatological illustration must have played a part in enregistering the word as local to the north-east of England, and as humorous, while Brockett's inclusion of this and other words cited from Bewick in his *Glossary* would have verified them to his readers as 'north country words'. The process of enregisterment involves, as Agha (2007: 67) explains, a 'speech chain' of messages, transmitted from a sender to receiver, who in turn becomes a sender, and so on. Bewick's use of *netty* in the vignette associates the word with scatological humour and Brockett's entry on the word further transmits this association and affirms the word as 'north country'. Readers of Brockett receive this message and may transmit it further, as do subsequent dialect dictionaries and dialect writings.

In analysing the data selected from Bewick's ego-documents, I have taken a qualitative approach, considering each word or phrase in context in order to determine what indexical meanings Bewick might have intended to convey and how this projects a persona to the reader(s). The words are also discussed according to whether they are highlighted by Bewick, whether they are marked as Northern, Scottish, dialectal, etc. by the dictionaries consulted, and the semantic fields involved (e.g. nature, coal mining, fishing, etc.).

3.3.2. Analysis

Although I have argued in the previous section that we cannot infer from a lack of highlighting that Bewick was unaware that these unmarked words were dialectal, it is worth considering these words as a group. The words marked 'none' in column 3 of Appendix 3.1 are *Auld Cloutie* (first instance), *bairns*, *blaeberry*, *bogglebos*, *brae*, *canny*, *Grandy*, *mall* and *whins*. Apart from *Grandy*, which does not appear in any of the dictionaries consulted, all of these words are marked in these dictionaries as being dialectal, but in use beyond Northumberland: in Scotland, the North of England more generally, or, in the case of *whins*, generally dialectal. Of course, several words highlighted by Bewick were in equally widespread use, but it could be that Bewick was either more aware of this in the case of the words listed above, or, indeed, that he was not aware that they were dialectal at all. The latter is possible especially in the case of *bairns*, which would have been in widespread use throughout the North at the time and is, of course, an everyday, domestic term, as is *Grandy*. *Blaeberry* and *whins* refer to plants which are common in Northumberland, while *brae* denotes a feature of the landscape and *mall* a tool. These would likewise have been everyday words for Bewick, as would *canny* in the sense of pleasant. *Auld Cloutie* and *bogglebos* refer to the supernatural and both are used in correspondence with Dovaston, with whom Bewick shared an interest in Scottish folklore.

When Bewick highlights words or phrases, he is marking them out as different from the Standard English norm of his memoir or emphasising them in some way. Apart from the dialectal words included in Appendix 3.1, Bewick underlines words or phrases which are colloquial rather than dialectal, such as *wild goose chase* (ed. Williams 1968: 69); those in languages other than English, such as the Latin names of species, for example, *Motacilla Sylvia* (ed. Williams 1968: 30); and terms which are used humorously, such as when he refers to his daughters as his *incomparable nurses* (ed. Williams 1968: 77). I included *blarney* and *bare buff* in my selection because I wanted to determine whether these were considered local to the north-east of England at the time, but both are recorded as 'colloquial' in the OED and neither appears in Heslop. *Bare buff* does appear in Brockett, but this may be under Bewick's influence.

In some cases, Bewick glosses the dialect words either directly or in paraphrase as well as or instead of highlighting them, perhaps indicating that his reader(s) might not have known their meanings. These are: *foulploughs*, *Haa houses*, *Hally well*, *howdey*, *lonnings*, *ludge*, *Mimsey*, *parrentory*, *pismires*, *scamps* and *smout hole*. He also glosses *aw is* as 'I am', which in this case is morphologically rather than lexically non-standard. Apart from the term *Mimsey* (mother), all the terms which are glossed appear in the memoir rather than the letters. *Mimsey* appears in a letter from Bewick to Dovaston and is here taken from a children's rhyme. What I have counted as a gloss comes in a summary of the gist of the rhyme's meaning. Bewick writes: 'I have fogot [*sic*] particulars – but the main jet of it amounted to this, that they would enjoy themselves as best they could, while their Mother and their Grandy had trotted off to Church' (ed. Williams 1968: 88). This may not be intended as a gloss, but as a summary of what Bewick could remember of the rhyme. If this is the case, then Bewick's glosses are confined to his memoir, as far as the data selected for this study are concerned. This suggests that he is aware of the potential readership of his memoir being wider than that of his letters. He had conversed with Dovaston many times as well as exchanging letters, so Bewick would have been aware of which words his correspondent would understand. Where the glossed words in the memoir are concerned, Bewick was clearly aware that some of his readers would not understand them, and so his decision to use the dialect terms nonetheless must have been deliberate and intended to have an effect that the Standard English equivalents could not have achieved.

Most of the glossed words refer to local features and customs, or animals. The context in which *smout hole* appears is Bewick's account of a neighbour whose beehives the young Bewick and his friends would visit, crawling through this small hole to the hidden place where the hives were kept (ed. Bain 1979: 27). Using this local term authenticates Bewick's account of his childhood experience, and the attribution of the word *parrentory* (impudent or saucy) to this neighbour, known as 'Tom Howdey' because his mother was a midwife, likewise brings him to life as a local 'character'. *Hally Well* (Holy Well) and *ludge* (a temporary shelter built by miners) both appear in an account of the old men in Bewick's neighbourhood when he was a child (ed. Bain 1979: 30). As with his depiction of 'Tom Howdey', the use of these dialect words authenticates his experience and brings a note of nostalgia. The context in which *lonnings* is used and glossed is a romanticised recollection of the poor people of Cherryburn, who took great care of their gardens in order to be self-sufficient. Bewick relates that 'not a bit of manure was suffered to be wasted away on the *Lonnings* or publick roads' (ed. Bain 1979: 24). Bewick presents these people as the deserving poor, who would 'despise being numbered among the Parish poor' and as 'a bold Pesantry [*sic*], their Country's Pride' (*op. cit.*)

The use of the glossed term *pismires* (ed. Bain 1979: 20) occurs in an account of Bewick's childhood interest in nature and animals and, more precisely, a whole paragraph in which he recounts his impressions of the ants. By the time he wrote the memoir, Bewick's reputation as a naturalist was established. By using dialect terms for the creatures he encountered in his childhood, Bewick demonstrates that his interest in nature was acquired at an early age and that he was largely self-taught. The remaining glossed terms *foulploughs*, *haa houses* and *scamps* likewise occur in contexts involving recollections of Bewick's early life. By using dialect terms and glossing them, Bewick is drawing attention to the difference between his own language and experiences and those of the reader to authenticate the distinctiveness of his experiences.

In fact, almost all of the dialect terms, glossed or not, which appear in the memoir are used in contexts like those discussed above. For example, *jackleg knife*, *kirn supper* and *guiseing*, all of which are highlighted, appear in a vivid account of a childhood experience in which the young Bewick thought he had encountered the Devil, but this had turned out to be a local man in disguise on his way to a local festival (ed. Bain 1979: 18). Much of the later part of the memoir has a very different character, dominated by Bewick's accounts of his political and religious views, and this part of the memoir includes hardly any dialect words. The only exceptions to this are *pought nets* (ed. Bain 1979: 176) and *strike* (ed. Bain 1979: 173), both of which occur in a chapter dedicated to Bewick's views on hunting and fishing. In this context, the use of local fishing terminology authenticates his experience as a fisherman and therefore his credentials as an expert.

In his memoir, Bewick uses dialect sparingly within a text largely composed in Standard English. Dialect terms are used in contexts where Bewick is either recollecting his youth in Cherryburn, or putting forward his views on fishing. Here, dialect words index authentic local knowledge and experience and project to an unknown readership the persona of Bewick as a naturalist, a countryman and a Northumbrian. In his correspondence with friends and family, Bewick likewise uses dialect terms, along with colloquial terms, sparingly, but in this case he is writing to particular individuals whose knowledge of dialect he can gauge, so he does not need to gloss the terms. The vast majority of the letters examined for this chapter were written to John Dovaston (1782–1854), a poet and naturalist with whom Bewick shared an interest in Scottish literature and music as well as natural history. Almost all of the dialect words used by Bewick in his correspondence with Dovaston are highlighted by being either placed in quotation marks or underlined, the exceptions being *canny*, *Grandy*, *bogglebos* and the second occurrence of *Auld Cloutie*, all discussed above. In these letters, Bewick seems to use dialect terms humorously and, especially where the words concerned are or were common to Scots and Northumbrian, to evoke the interest in folklore and Scottish literature shared by the two men. In his letter to Dovaston of 26 November 1824, Bewick uses the phrase 'my Ain Fireside' in quotes, in the context of expressing regret that he is unable to visit Dovaston in Shropshire. Later, he discusses the censorship of an image in Bewick's illustrated edition of Aesop.

> I shall not forget your wishes in regard to 'Auld Cloutie' &c, when only a few copies of the first Ed^{n}. Of Aesop were thrown off, M^{r}. Walker v, with a degree of delicacy which I cannot but think fastidious – banished his satanic majesty & substituted another *block* in his place. (Ed. Williams 1968: 36)

The contrast between the dialectal and familiar 'Auld Cloutie' and the elaborately formal 'his satanic majesty', both referring to the devil, sets Bewick and Dovaston against the 'fastidious' Mr Walker, emphasising the bond between the two correspondents. The second occurrence of 'Auld Cloutie' comes in a humorous anecdote about Bewick's besting of a hell-fire preacher. Bewick relates how he questioned this preacher's warnings about the devil. Bewick argues that the evil in this world is largely carried out by humans, and that the devil should not be blamed and 'might turn out to be a very canny fellow'. Bewick goes on to relate how he gave the preacher 'credit for his being personally acquainted with Auld Cloutie' (ed. Williams 1968: 96). Here, Bewick uses the dialectal terms *canny* and *Auld Cloutie* humorously, bringing a supernatural figure down to earth. In relating this incident to Dovaston, Bewick portrays himself as a man of reason, and invokes the rationalist views that Dovaston shares with him. These examples demonstrate how, in his correspondence, Bewick uses dialect terms humorously, but also to draw on shared ideas and interests, thus cementing the bond of friendship between himself and Dovaston. Bewick is aware of the different readerships of his memoir and his letters and in each case uses dialect to address a particular readership, but in both cases dialect is used to project a persona. As an educated person, Bewick writes mainly in Standard English, and, for the most part, departs from this to achieve particular effects. In the next section, I will place Bewick's use of dialect to do social work in the context of indexicality and enregisterment.

3.4. Discussion

In the previous sections, I have demonstrated how Bewick used dialect words and constructions in texts otherwise written in Standard English to achieve specific effects and to present personae to his readers. In this section, I discuss the chronology of the indexicality and enregisterment of Northumbrian dialect and Bewick's contribution to this process.

According to Johnstone *et al.*, it is at the second order of indexicality that 'regional features become available for social work' and at the third order that such features are used 'to perform local identity, often in ironic, semiserious ways' (2006: 82–3). Reports of Bewick's performance of dialect tales such as *The Howdy* and *The Upgetting*, along with some of the examples of Bewick's humorous uses of dialect discussed in the previous section, indicate that the dialect words and constructions highlighted by Bewick were already indexed at least at the second order.

Johnstone *et al.* propose that the shift from second to third order occurs when there is an ideology of every place having a dialect and when lists of regional forms become available. In Bewick's lifetime, the link between dialect and place was articulated in the contexts of antiquarianism and the Romantic movement, with literature in Scots and some dialects of English, including those of the North, increasingly available. Although academic dialectology begins later in the nineteenth century, some glossaries of (or including) Northern English dialect, such as those of Ray (1674) and Hutton (1781), were already available and, as discussed above, Brockett's (1825) glossary was published in Bewick's lifetime and was influenced by Bewick. These glossaries and collections of Northern songs and tales such as Bell (1814) and Marshall (1818) would have made the link between some non-standard words and constructions and the North of England. As a Northumbrian, Bewick would already have known and used these forms, but exposure to texts such as these would have made explicit to him the indexical link between the linguistic features concerned, the North of England and the social characteristics associated with the North and Northerners.

Awareness of the dialectal nature of one's own usage depends on exposure to other dialects or varieties; in other words, dialect contact. As a child in Cherryburn, Bewick would have had some exposure at least to written Standard English in the classroom, but, as the account of his reactions to London and Londoners in Section 3.2.2 demonstrates, he became aware of the 'otherness' of his dialect when he first moved to London. He was also aware that the Cockneys themselves had a dialect. His reference to 'good Wittals' in the letter to Dovaston of 10 September 1828 highlights what by then was, in Labovian terms, a stereotype of Cockney speech: the pronunciation of <v> as /w/ and vice versa. This had been singled out as a 'fault of the Cockneys' by John Walker (1791: xii–xiii) and was later used to great effect by Dickens. Here, Bewick's use of the Cockney feature in an anecdote recounting the greed and ignorance of Londoners forms a link in the speech chain involved in the enregisterment of Cockney.

During Bewick's lifetime, Northumbrian dialect was in the process of enregisterment. Although Northern dialects of English had been associated with various social characteristics since at least the sixteenth century (Wales 2006; Beal 2017), the enregisterment of more localised dialects within the North, such as Lancashire, Yorkshire and Newcastle ('Geordie'), and the association of these dialects with characteristic personae such as the Lancashire weaver or the Geordie miner, culminated in the nineteenth century, when dialect literature, dialect performance in music halls and dialect dictionaries proliferated. Bewick's use of dialect in his memoir, his letters and in the titles of tail-pieces such as *The Pigstye Netty* both draws on the embryonic enregisterment of Northumbrian in the late eighteenth and early nineteenth centuries and contributes to its ongoing enregisterment. Bewick's fame in his own lifetime, along with his self-representation as a countryman and a Northumbrian, led to him being used as an authority for Northumbrian usage by lexicographers such as Brockett and Heslop, who, in turn, provided the lists of regional forms (Johnstone *et al.* 2006) which seal third-order indexicality.

3.5. Conclusion

Although Thomas Bewick has been the subject of several biographies and a great deal of scholarship in the fields of art history and history more generally, this chapter is, as far as I am aware, the first to address Bewick's use of dialect. The availability of ego-documents such as Bewick's memoir and letters has allowed me to investigate the ways in which Bewick used dialect to evoke the qualities of authenticity and down-to-earth humour associated with Northerners and to project himself as a Northumbrian and an authority on nature and country pursuits. The framework of indexicality and enregisterment emphasises the agency of speakers and writers in drawing on and contributing to the association of linguistic repertoires and characterological personae, so the account provided above demonstrates the part played by Bewick in the enregisterment of Northumbrian English. This account has been limited in scope and qualitative in nature because of the lack of any searchable corpus of Bewick's writings. It is to be hoped that such a corpus can be constructed in order to facilitate more thorough, quantitative analysis.

Appendix 3.1

Word	Meaning	Highlight	Source	OED	Wright	Heslop	Brockett	
Ain	Own	Quotes	Dov.35	18. N.	Var. dial.	No	No	
Auld cloutie	The devil	Quotes	Dov.36	Sc and N	Sc.N	Yes	No	
Auld cloutie	The devil	None	Dov.96	Sc and N	Sc.N	Yes	No	
Aw is	I am	Glossed	Mem. 27		Aw = N	Yes	Yes	
Bairns	Children	None	To Campbell	Bairn 'the Scotch form'	Sc, Ir, N	Yes	Yes	
Bare buff	Topless	Ital + gloss	Mem.57	Colloq	Slang	Yes	No	
Beild	Shelter	Ital	Mem.7/166	Sc and N	Sc.N	Yes	No	
Blaeberry	Blueberry	None	Mem. 205	Sc and N. B. Cited	Sc, Ir, N	Yes	No	
Blarney		Ital	Dov.79	Colloq 1796	Ir, colloq	No	No	
Blarney		Ital	Dov.96	Colloq. 1796	Ir, colloq	No	No	
Boat stower	Boat hook	Ital	Mem.13	Obs ex. Dial. B. Cited	Yks, Lincs	Stower	Stower = stake	
Bogglebos		None	Dov.95	N. This sp.	Sc.N	Yes	Yes	
Brea	Hill	None	Mem.07	Now Sc and N	Sc, Ir, N	Yes	Yes	
Buzzed to death		Ital	Dov.117/119	No marking	None	No	No	
Canny	Good/pleasant	None	Dov.96	N	Sc.N	Yes	Yes	
Clagged	Stuck	Underlined	To Bulmer	Chiefly N	Sc, Ir N var. dial	Yes	Yes	
Cree	Soften	Ital	Mem.09	Dial	N and mid.	To seethe	To seethe	
Fagged	Tired?	Ital	Dov.61	No marking	Sc. N. Other dial		No	
Fairly in for it		Ital	Dov.45	No marking				
Flaid	Afraid	Ital	Mem.26	16cSc(sp)	Sc, Ir, N	Frighten	No	Flaid to death
Foulploughs	Morris or sword dancers	Ital + gloss	Mem.59	'Foolplough'	None	No	No	
Freak	Whim	Ital	Mem.47	'Whim'	Sc,Nbh	Not this sense	No	
Freedrawn		Ital	Dov.103	None	None	No	No	
Fretted	Flustered	Ital	Dov.32	No marking	None	No	Not this sense	
Gills	Narrow valleys	Ital	Mem. 23	n. Counties	Sc and N, K, Sur, Sus	Yes	Yes	
Grandy	Grandmother	None	Dov.88	None	Sc.N	Yes	In a citation	
Grining		Ital	Dov.112	None	None	No	No	
Guiseing	Mumming	Ital	Mem.18	Chiefly Sc and N	Sc.N, Cor	No	Guisers	
Haa houses	Farmers' houses	Ital + gloss	Mem.32	None	None	Yes	No	

Appendix 3.1 (*cont.*)

Word	Meaning	Highlight	Source	OED	Wright	Heslop	Brockett	
Halley Well	Holy Well	Ital + gloss	Mem.30	Sp. in names	Sp. Sc.	Halliday	No	
Hirpled		Ital	Dov.107	Sc and N	Sc. Ir N. Mid	Yes	Yes	
Howdey	Midwife	Glossed + quotes	Mem. 27	Sc and N	None	Yes	Yes	
Jackleg knife	Pocket knife	Ital	Mem.18	None	N.	Yes	Yes	
Kep/-ing	Catch/-ing	None	Mem.124	Sc. & N.	Sc, Ir, N	Yes	Yes	
Kirn supper	Harvest supper	Ital	Mem.18	Sc and N	Sc.N	Yes	Kern baby	
Kocked up	Exhausted	Ital	Dov.105	None	Intoxicated, Nhb	Tipsy	No	
Leish	Lithe	Ital	Mem.63	Dial. B. Cited	Sc.N	Yes	Yes	
Lonnings	Lanes	Ital + gloss	Mem.24	Sc and N	Sc, Ir, N	Yes	No	
Lowsening his skin	?	Ital + quotes	Mem.28	Sp. 18 dial.	Sc.Cum,Yorks*	No	No	*lowsening feast = to celebrate end of apprenticeship.
Ludge	Lodge	Ital + gloss	Mem.30	Sp.Sc	Nhb, Du*	No	No	*temporary shelter for sinkers of mines
Mall	Hammer	None	Mem.09	Now Sc and N	Mall = Sc.	Yes	Mell	
Meldorandum		Ital	Dov.63	None	None	No	No	
Messet dog	Lapdog	None	Mem.18	N. B.cited	N	Yes	Messit	
Mimsey	Mother	Ital + gloss	Dov.88	None	None	No	No	
Ned cakes	Griddle cakes	Ital	Dov.70	None	Nhb 'kneaded'?	Yes	No	
Nice	Exact	Ital	Mem. 173	Now rare	Var. dial.	No	Not this sense	
Nobbit	Only	Ital	Mem.26	Reg. Ch. N.	'Nobbit' Nbh	Yes	Yes	
Parrrentory	Impudent	Ital + quotes+glossed	Mem.27	N. B.cited	None	No	No	
Pell mell		Ital	Dov.92	No marking	None	No	No	
Pismires	Ants	Glossed	Mem.20	Now reg.	Sc and various dial.	No	No	
Pit heap	Spoil heap	Ital	Mem.25	B cited	Heap, var. dial*	Yes	No	*all citations with 'pit' Nhb.
Pought nets	Nets fastened to poles	Ital	Mem. 176	Nb.	None	No	No	
Scamps	Tramps	Ital + gloss	Mem.46/61	Orig. cant	None	No	Yes	
Seddle boards	Boards on top of pit	Ital + quotes	Mem.88	None	None	Yes	No	

Shive	Slice	Ital	Mem.07	Dial	Gen. Dial.	Yes	Yes	
Silkey	Supernatural being	Ital + quotes	Mem.16	None	None	No	No	
Smout hole	Small opening	Ital + gloss	Mem.27	Dial. B. Cited	Smout Nhb. Sc*	Yes	No	*'smout' = fry of a salmon, anything small
Strike	Fisherman's station?	Ital	Mem. 173	Obs. Rare B cited	None	No	No	
The further Ben		Ital + quotes	Dov.44	Sc and N	Sc.N	Yes	No	
Twitter	State of excitement	Ital	Dov.32	Now chiefly dial.	Gen. Dial.	No	Verb	
Whins	Furze	None	Mem.07	Sc and dial.	Gen. Dial.	Yes	Yes	
Will would	(Double modal?)	Ital	Dov.107					
Yen	One	Ital	Mem 26	Sp.	Nhb, Cum	Yensel	Yes	

Notes

1. The spelling 'egodocuments' is used on this website, but as linguists use the hyphenated spelling, I have used this throughout except in quotations.
2. Uglow states that Bewick wrote these two tales (2006: 357), but presents no evidence for this. I am grateful to Nigel Tattersfield for informing me that the two tales had been published by John Grey Bell, the nephew of John Bell, in 1850 and that the copy in the Pease Collection at Newcastle City Library contains a letter by John Grey Bell stating that the two tales were 'in the autograph of Bewick'. Thanks also to Warren Maguire for information about the dialect of these texts.
3. I am grateful to Peter Quinn for alerting me to this comment by Atkinson.
4. I am grateful to the staff of the Heritage Collection at Newcastle City Library and the Special Collections team at the Robinson Library, Newcastle University, for granting me access to letters in their collections.
5. Here and elsewhere, the word 'authentic' and 'authenticity' should be understood as in scare quotes. Given Eckert's (2004) discussion of the notion of 'authenticity' in sociolinguistics, what I intend by these terms is the projection of an 'authentic' persona on the part of the speaker or writer, rather than authenticity by any objective criteria.

References

Agha, Asif (2003), 'The social life of a cultural value', *Language and Communication* 23, 231–73.

Agha, Asif (2007), *Language and Social Relations*, Cambridge: Cambridge University Press.

Atkinson, George Clough (1831), 'Sketch of the life and works of the late Thomas Bewick', *Natural History Society of Northumberland Transactions*, I.

Bain, Iain (1970), 'Thomas Bewick, engraver, of Newcastle, 1753–1828: A checklist of his correspondence and other papers', *The Private Library*, Second series, 3.2, 57–77; 3.3, 124–40.

Bain, Iain (ed.) ([1975] 1979), *A Memoir of Thomas Bewick Written by Himself*, Oxford: Oxford University Press.

Bain, Iain (2004), 'Bewick, Thomas (1753–1828)', *Oxford Dictionary of National Biography*, Oxford: Oxford University Press, online edn. May 2005. http://www.oxforddnb.com.sheffield.idm.oclc.org/view/article/2334. Accessed 26 July 2017.

Beal, Joan C. (2009), 'Enregisterment, commodification and historical context: "Geordie" versus "Sheffieldish"', *American Speech* 84:2, 138–56.

Beal, Joan C. (2010), *An Introduction to Regional Englishes*, Edinburgh: Edinburgh University Press.

Beal, Joan C. (2017), 'Northern English and enregisterment', in Sylvie Hancil and Joan C. Beal (eds), *Perspectives on Northern Englishes*, Berlin: Mouton de Gruyter, 17–39.

Bell, John (1814), *A Right Merry Garland of Northumberland Heroes*, Newcastle upon Tyne: John Bell.

Bewick, Thomas (1790), *A General History of Quadrupeds*, Newcastle upon Tyne: S. Hodgson, R. Beilby and T. Bewick.

Bewick, Thomas (1797), *A History of British Birds, Volume 1*, Newcastle upon Tyne: S. Hodgson, R. Beilby and T. Bewick.

Bewick, Thomas (1804), *A History of British Birds, Volume 2*, Newcastle upon Tyne: S. Hodgson, R. Beilby and T. Bewick.

Bewick, Thomas (1862), *A Memoir of Thomas Bewick, Written by Himself*, Newcastle upon Tyne: Robert Ward for Jane Bewick.

Brockett, John Trotter (1825), *A Glossary of North Country Words in Use*, Newcastle upon Tyne: T. and H. Hodgson for N. Charnley.

Center for the Study of Egodocuments and History: www.egodocuments.net.

Chatto, William Andrew and John Jackson (1839), *A Treatise on Wood Engraving*, London: C. Knight.

Conde-Silvestre, J. Camilo (2016), 'A "third-wave" historical sociolinguistic approach to late Middle English correspondence: evidence from the Stonor letters', in Cinzia Russi (ed.), *Current Trends in Historical Sociolinguistics*, Berlin: de Gruyter, 46–66.

Dobson, Austin (1884), *Thomas Bewick and His Pupils*, London: Chatto & Windus.

Eckert, Penelope (2004), 'Elephants in the room', *Journal of Sociolinguistics* 7:3, 392–7.

Eckert, Penelope (2012), 'Three waves of variation study: the emergence of meaning in the study of variation', *Annual Review of Anthropology* 41, 87–100.

EDDOnline English Dialect Dictionary: www.eddonline-proj.uibk.ac.at.

Gardner-Medwin, David (2007), 'A newly discovered manuscript memoir of Bewick by George Clayton Atkinson', *Cherryburn Times: The Journal of the Bewick Society* 5:3, 1–16.

Gardner-Medwin, David (n.d.), *A Provisional Checklist of the Library of Thomas Bewick*, www.bewicksociety.org. Accessed 11 September 2018.

Heslop, Richard Oliver (1892), *Northumberland Words: A Glossary of Words Used in the County of Northumberland and on the Tyneside*, London: Kegan Paul.

Hutton, John (1781), 'A glossary of old and original words now used in the north of England', in *A Tour to the Caves, in the Environs of Ingelborough and Settle, in the West-Riding of Yorkshire*, London: Richardson and Urquhart and J. Robson; Kendal: W. Pennington.

Johnstone, Barbara (2009), 'Pittsburghese shirts: commodification and the enregisterment of an urban dialect', *American Speech* 84:2, 157–75.

Johnstone, Barbara, Jennifer Andrus and Andrew E. Danielson (2006), 'Mobility, indexicality, and the enregisterment of "Pittsburghese"', *Journal of English Linguistics* 34: 2, 77–104.

Labov, William (1972), *Sociolinguistic Patterns*, Oxford: Blackwell.

Marshall, John (1818), *A Collection of Songs, Comic, Satirical and Descriptive, Chiefly in the Newcastle Dialect*, Newcastle upon Tyne: John Marshall.

Nevalainen, Terttu and Helena Raumolin-Brunberg (2012), 'Historical sociolinguistics: origins, motivations and paradigms', in Juan Manuel Hernandez-Campoy and Juan Camilo Conde-Silvestre (eds), *The Handbook of Historical Sociolinguistics*, Chichester: Wiley Blackwell, 22–40.

Oxford English Dictionary online: www.oed.com.

Ray, John (1674), *A Collection of English Words, Not Generally Used*, London: H. Bruges.

Robinson, Robert (1887), *Thomas Bewick: His Life and Times*, Newcastle upon Tyne: R. Robinson.

Silverstein, Michael (1976), 'Shifters, linguistic categories, and cultural description', in Keith H. Basso and Henry A. Selby (eds), *Meaning in Anthropology*, Albuquerque, NM: University of New Mexico Press, 11–55.
Silverstein, Michael (2003), 'Indexical order and the dialectics of sociolinguistic life', *Language and Communication* 23, 193–229.
Thomson, David Croal (1882), *The Life and Works of Thomas Bewick*, London: "The Art Journal" Office.
Uglow, Jenny (2006), *Nature's Engraver: A Life of Thomas Bewick*, London: Faber and Faber.
Van der Wal, Marijke and Gijsbert Rutten (2013), 'Ego-documents in a sociohistorical perspective', in Marijke Van der Wal and Gijsbert Rutten (eds), *Touching the Past: Studies in the Historical Sociolinguistics of Ego-document*, Amsterdam/Philadelphia: John Benjamins, 1–18.
Wales, Katie (2006), *Northern English: A Social and Cultural History*, Cambridge: Cambridge University Press.
Walker, John (1791), *A Critical Pronouncing Dictionary*, London: G. G. J. and J. Robinson and T. Cadell.
Williams, Gordon (ed.) (1968), *Bewick to Dovaston: Letters 1824–1828*, London: Nattali & Maurice.
Wordsworth Trust Bewick Collection: https://tinyurl.com/ydbpxbxn.

4

Nottingham: City of Literature – Dialect Literature and Literary Dialect

Natalie Braber

4.1. Introduction

Nottingham is a UNESCO City of Literature and can be linked to authors and poets such as Lord Byron, D. H. Lawrence and Alan Sillitoe. Despite this literary heritage, from a linguistic point of view, until recently the city has received scant attention and little was known about the local dialects. These language varieties are not as instantly recognisable as those of Liverpool, Newcastle or Birmingham (see, for example, Asprey, this volume, about the recognisability of English from the Black Country in the West Midlands, and Crowley, this volume, about Liverpool English). Even local people fail to recognise them, as has been highlighted in previous research (Braber 2015), but perhaps this is related to people in Nottingham not having a strong popular cultural notoriety or salience.

The city is located in the East Midlands. Although this region does not have an official capital, Nottingham is treated as such by many, as on the 'Meet England' website, for example,[1] and the city is referred to as *Queen of the Midlands* by John Beckett in his centenary history of Nottingham (Beckett 2006). As such, it is an important centre of the region and although there is language variation within the region, Nottingham English is a good representative dialect for the East Midlands in general (and I define 'Nottingham' quite broadly in this chapter, including nearby and closely related varieties).

The *Survey of English Dialects* of the 1950s is still the most contemporary survey of the region, and more recent descriptions of UK language varieties have not focused on East Midlands dialects. However, new research by the author has shown that there is considerable variation in the region which deserves further investigation (see, for example, Braber and Robinson 2018).

This chapter examines how local language has been represented in 'dialect literature' and in 'literary dialect' (for a similar approach, see Asprey, this volume, and for a somewhat similar approach, see Cooper, this volume). Dialect literature refers to texts, usually short guides, which may include discussions of local language and have considerable portions written in the local dialect, and are often aimed at a local audience (see Honeybone and Watson 2013: 312; see also Honeybone and Maguire, this volume). The language discussed in such publications can be contrasted with that in literary dialect, that is, where authors use non-standard speech for certain characters in fictional work which is otherwise produced in Standard English and aimed at a more general, non-local readership (see Shorrocks 1996). Literary dialect set in Nottingham can be found in stories by local authors such as Lawrence and Sillitoe, but it also emerges from the work of contemporary authors, such as Nicola Monaghan (2007) and Joy James (2008, 2009).

Historically, dialectologists used only 'the authentic speaker' as the subject for their analyses, and saw literary representations of dialect in the nineteenth century as being inauthentic. However, more recently the concept of authentic speakers has come under greater scrutiny, and more attention has been paid to the ways in which dialects are both performed and perceived by ordinary speakers (see Hodson and Broadhead 2013: 316; see also Hodson, this volume, and Cooper, this volume). Preston comments that the examination of 'linguistic caricatures' and 'popular culture' (Preston 1989: 113) also play an important role in the perception of linguistic varieties. Tannen writes that 'literary discourse … rather than being most different from ordinary conversation, is, in fact, most similar to it' (Tannen 1982: 2), although Preston (1982: 304) comments that '[w]riting is a poor, secondary system when compared to speech'. Non-standard linguistic forms can be a very powerful expressive resource and can capture aspects of spoken language and make voices audible where they may usually be unheard (see Jaffe 2000: 498). Hodson, in her work on dialect in film and literature, also discusses the importance of understanding the representation of spoken language in literature. She comments that we can deduce much from the way characters speak (Hodson 2014: 3). In short, dialect has social meaning.

Following a brief description of linguistic features typical of the region in Section 4.2, and of the methodology that I use in Section 4.3, this chapter describes the dialect literature of Nottingham in Sections 4.4 and 4.5. That is followed by a consideration of some examples of literary dialect relevant to Nottingham in Sections 4.6 and 4.7, using authors from the early 1900s to the present day to examine differences and changes in the ways that local language is represented in writing. The analysis focuses on phonetic/phonological, morphosyntactic and lexical features and investigates how closely literary dialect represents the language described in dialect literature or whether there are differences in the representation of local dialect in these two genres.

4.2. Language in Nottingham

As stated, Nottingham is widely regarded as the most important city within the East Midlands. It houses a population of around 308,000 within the official city boundary; including suburbs, the number rises to just over 730,000,[2] and many more work in and visit the city (Beckett 2006: 1). The East Midlands is England's fourth-largest region. Contemporary linguistic studies (such as Britain 2007; Kortmann and Upton 2008) neglect the region, while others only refer to it in passing. Instead, much of what we know about language variation in the region comes from historical work as much research has investigated this variety in relation to the development of Standard English (see, for example Fennell 2001).

UK research in the fields of sociology, politics and linguistics has often discussed the traditional North/South division in England. What makes the East Midlands and Nottingham interesting within this debate is the question of where it fits within the divide. Does Nottingham belong to the North or the South or is it part of a tri-partite division which includes a Midlands in addition to the North and the South (see Upton 2012)? The answer seems anything but straightforward (Trudgill 1999). Linguistically, Nottingham shares features with the North (see, for example, Wells 1982; Kortmann and Upton 2008) such as short [a] in BATH and the unsplit FOOT–STRUT vowel, but there are also shared features with varieties found in the South (Hughes *et al.* 2012), including *l*-vocalisation and *th*-fronting, although these may be spreading throughout the country.

A number of linguistic features can be regarded as characteristic for the region. It can be noted that a low MOUTH vowel, rounded START and PRICE onsets, and HAPPY with [i] and [ɪ] are all present in the variety, as are forms with [ɛ]. Additionally, Nottingham speakers typically use Northern [a] for BATH and [ʊ] for STRUT, but there also exist increasing proportions of accent features traditionally regarded as Southern in origin (*t*-glottalling, *th*-fronting and *l*-vocalisation). This means that the present-day variety can therefore be viewed as a mixture of Northern and Southern forms (for more details, see Braber and Flynn 2015).

Work which has been carried out on the varieties of the East Midlands (see Braber and Robinson 2018) shows that language has changed in the region over the past few decades and can be examined through existing data sets held by the British Library (for example, the recordings and transcripts of *The Survey of English Dialects*, *The Millennium Memory Bank* and *Voices*). One of the authors discussed in the section on literary dialect, Joy James, states that the 'real' old Nottingham accent is slowly dying out but she also states that 'it is a difficult dialect to mimic and of the many TV plays and films based in and around this city, neither actor nor actress has yet managed the pronunciation successfully' (James 2008: 1). Historically, for example, films featuring the Nottingham dialect have not been accurate and have frequently been mocked by critics and lay people alike: for example, Sean Bean's performance in Lawrence's *Lady Chatterley's Lover* and Albert Finney's in Sillitoe's *Saturday Night and Sunday Morning* – both will be looked at in later sections.

Commodification of the local language and subsequent enregisterment is relatively recent in Nottingham and falls behind other varieties in the UK (see, for example, Beal 2000: 347; see also Clark, this volume; Crowley, this volume). However, there is some merchandising available in local shops and one shop, *Dukki*, specialises in products such as mugs, pens and towels with local slogans and words.

4.3. Methodology

For this chapter, examples of dialect literature have been examined and compared to examples of literary dialect. The details of these works and their authors will be discussed in the relevant sections, but in summary, the following books have been used. Dialect literature: *Notts Natter* (Wright 1979); *Ey up Mi Duck* (Scollins and Titford 2000); and Beeton's four volumes entitled *Nottingham as It Is Spoke* (Beeton 1999). Literary dialect: *Forest Folk* (Prior 1907); *Widowing of Mrs Holroyd* (Lawrence 1911); *Lady Chatterley's Lover* (Lawrence 1928); *Penny Lace* (Lewis 1946); *Saturday Night and Sunday Morning* (Sillitoe 1958); *Killing Jar* (Monaghan 2007); *Yo'd Mek a Parson Swear* (James 2008); *Bog all to Swear About!* (James 2009); *Darkness, Darkness* (Harvey 2014); and *Night Raid* (Harvey 2017).

In particular, the use of non-standard spellings, morphosyntactic features, local vocabulary and expressions in these publications has been examined. The fact that spelling and grammar in English are standardised means that any variation authors include can inform us about regional variation, especially what is seen as being 'local'. Furthermore, it can illustrate how such language is different from other varieties in the surrounding region as well as how it is distinguished from Standard English, which can allow writers to be more informal with readers (Androutsopoulos 2000: 515). The decisions authors make can take on social meanings and can be examined in written, as well as spoken, language (Sebba 2012: 1). Other sociolinguistic research has shown that language features can become explicitly linked with certain social values when used by speakers (Cooper 2017: 43). The work in this chapter is preliminary rather than exhaustive. Exact frequencies have not been considered, so this work is qualitative rather than quantitative, which distinguishes it from Honeybone and Watson's (2013) analysis of CHLDL (Contemporary Humorous Localised Dialect Literature), and from Cooper's, Maguire's, Watson and Jensen's and Honeybone's chapters in this volume, and makes it more similar to the qualitative work carried out by Beal in Newcastle (2000, 2009, this volume), and to Asprey's, Clark's and Timmis's chapters in this volume. The focus of this chapter is on which features are considered 'local' by authors and how they are represented within texts. This allows us to establish which features are sociolinguistically salient to these authors, and therefore also to the readers of these works. Working this way, we can also determine which features are enregistered in the dialect (see Agha 2003; Cooper 2017; also discussed by several other authors in this volume). By considering work from the early 1900s to the present day we can also examine changes over time. Preston comments that literary dialect shows that once an author gives a character a linguistic feature, it is likely to occur categorically (Preston 1982: 321).

Due to the length of these works, for some of them, only extracts such as the first 100 pages can be analysed here, but hopefully this contribution will help to bring about future research which deploys a fuller and more thorough examination, using corpus analysis and quantitative methodologies.

4.4. Dialect Literature

Dialect literature (publications written in regional dialect, generally for a local audience) can preserve and record specific dialects (Beal 2009: 140). As such, they can contain considerable metalinguistic commentary. As in other forms of mass communication, the authors have no direct access to their audience and they therefore have an image or ideal (see Bell 1984: 191) to aim their work at. Dialect literature is seen as an acceptable source of data to examine language variation (see Miethaner 2000: 534; Honeybone and Watson 2013: 315). The books used here are contemporary and also have a humorous focus, so they fit in the category of CHLDL suggested by Honeybone and Watson (2013). Hodson states that there is a boundary between dialect literature and literary dialect, where for the first 'much of the pleasure for the readership lies in encountering their own dialect in print, and a significant number of different dialect features may be employed with a high degree of frequency' (Hodson 2014: 116). There has also been other research (Percillier 2017) which has examined to what extent representation in literature differs from real-life language usage, but unfortunately this subject lies outside the scope of this chapter.

The books examined here include *Ey up Mi Duck*, *Notts Natter* and *Nottingham as It Is Spoke*. *Ey up My Duck* (Scollins and Titford 2000) states on the front cover that it is the dialect of Derbyshire and the East Midlands but it is relevant to Nottingham which is the main centre of the East Midlands, so I include it here. Scollins and Titford talk about the importance of preserving the 'fast disappearing dialect of this area' (2000: 9). *Notts Natter* (Wright 1979) focuses specifically on Nottingham. The four slim volumes of *Nottingham as It Is Spoke* (1999) were produced by John Beeton, who states that the purpose of his books is to acquaint people with the language used in Nottingham and to develop skills to use it themselves.

Ey up Mi Duck (EY)

This book was originally published in three parts in 1976 and 1977. In 2000 it was reprinted in a single book version, which includes some additional material. This book is very visual and uses language with a local twist: for example, 'a local gleg at nursery rhymes', where children's nursery rhymes are described using local language (the word *gleg* means 'look'). Scollins and Titford comment in their foreword that one of the distinctive features of language in this region is that it has never had 'the media treatment' (2000: 5) and surprises people outside the region who are unable to imitate it (2000: 14) – any attempt to do so, in TV and film, frequently results in Yorkshire dialects being produced instead.

One of the authors' opinions is that much local language is dying out as much of 'the language associated with wash-day or out-moded agricultural or industrial practices, for instance, is fast disappearing' (2000: 13). This book is possibly the most systematic of all the local dialect literature in the East Midlands and undertakes a systematic (if non-specialist) description of local pronunciation such as monophthongs, diphthongs, consonants and omitted letters – sometimes using linguistic terminology (such as 'diphthongs') and at other times using non-specialist language (such as 'sounds'). For example, they discuss how the letter 'h' 'is never pronounced' (2000: 25) or that T-to-R is found in words such as 'gerrup' and 'is tharall?' (2000: 27). It also includes description of definite article reduction, examples of local pronouns, verbs, prepositions and negations. It includes a glossary, and information on important local aspects of life such as work, weather and children's games, all with a local twist. It finishes with a pictorial local history with examples of local language which include phonetic, morphosyntactic and lexical variation from Standard English. For example, Richard III's proclamation in 1485 at Bosworth of 'A horse, a horse, a kingdom for my horse' is translated as ''Oo's gorra 'oss ter borrer me!' (2000: 113), and a comment on the arrival of Bonnie Prince Charlie in 1745 as 'Tha niver said ote abairt 'em aw wearin' skairts!' (2000: 122).

Notts Natter (NN)

Notts Natter (How It Is Spoke) by Peter Wright is a small handbook produced in 1979. 'Notts' in the title refers to Nottinghamshire. Peter Wright was a *Survey of English Dialects* (Orton and Dieth 1962–71) fieldworker and an academic linguist, so although dialect literature is usually targeted at a popular audience, it still can be informed by credible linguistic research. The introduction to the book examines the history of language in England and Nottingham and explains that this region's language depended heavily on Anglo-Saxon words, as well as many Scandinavian words following occupation by the Danes. Wright also discusses that the varieties used here are different from other Northern varieties, due to features such as 'sen' instead of Northern 'sell' in examples such as 'theirsen' (1979: 4). He explains that language differs throughout the county and, although it may include Yorkshire influence in the North, it sounds very different from Derbyshire. Negative perceptions of this variety are also discussed. Wright states that people claim that Midlanders all mumble (1979: 5) and that Nottingham has a 'wishy-washy nondescript style of speaking' but that this isn't 'reight' (1979: 5). He adds: 'Value judgements are often given about the city's speech. It is branded as having no distinct traits apart from slovenliness' (1979: 28). The book goes through local places names, clothes and body parts, a section on 'wok' – mainly mining – as well as a section on sports and folklore, animals and 't'weather'.

Nottingham as It Is Spoke (JBA = volume 1, JBB = volume 2)

John Beeton has produced four *Nottingham as It Is Spoke* mini-volumes on local language, published in 1999. He comments that the area has long been neglected (JBA: 1) and states:

> From a cursory examination, it may appear that Nottinghamese is a form of slang born out of a lazy or slovenly method of speaking. Closer inspection however will show that it is, in fact, a complete language, containing many unique words and observing a strict grammatical pattern. (JBA: 2)

These books contain word lists, many of which are simply words written together, such as *worreewwee-izzsenn*? ('Was he alone?'), and many of them give information about phonetic and morphosyntactic features: for example, *hissen* ('himself'), or *intitt koad*? ('Isn't it cold?'), which illustrates *l*-vocalisation. Volumes 3 and 4 have additional sections, including children's games and everyday life in the Meadows (a working-class area of Nottingham), but because of space limitations these volumes could not be analysed here.

4.5. Linguistic Features Represented in Dialect Literature

A frequent feature of these books is the semi-phonological spelling (sometimes called 'respelling') used to represent specific features typical of the local dialect (Beal 2000: 343; see also several other chapters in this volume), allowing such features to be 'claimed' by authors as being unique or special to a particular variety (Beal 2009: 138). Such non-standard spellings can clearly index cultural identities (Eisenstein 2015: 162).

4.5.1. Phonetic and Phonological Features: Vowels

In EY, there is an extensive discussion of vowels in the region. It states that these varieties use the *full 'u'* (in FOOT and STRUT words) and the *short 'a'* (for BATH words) (Scollins and Titford 2000: 20) which we would expect in Northern English varieties (using English here to refer to England only). They mention specifically that there are two exceptions to the *short 'a'* rule, as the words *half* and *father* would traditionally be pronounced *ayf* and *fayther*. Also included is a description of other variations on the letter 'a' (2000: 21), where they describe words typically in the FACE lexical set (Wells 1982) and words such as *great* and *make* would be *gret* and *tek* or *ta'e*. Many of these comments are spelling-based rather than phonology-based as most readers will not have an extensive knowledge of linguistics, but will be aware of local pronunciations. Other descriptions can be seen in Table 4.1 which focuses

Table 4.1 Vowels described in Scollins and Titford (2000)

Description in EY	Lexical set (Wells 1982)	Respelling or description in text
full 'u'	STRUT	*bus, sun* (described as 'uh sounds')
short 'a'	BATH	*after, plaster, grass* (described as 'short or flat a')
other variations on 'a'	THOUGHT	*watter* ('water')
	LOT	*wannt* ('want'), *swann* ('swan') but *wesh* ('wash')
	FACE	*mek* ('make'), *tek* ('take')
'e' sounds	FLEECE	*grain* ('green')
	FACE	*reen* ('rain'), *geet* ('gate')
	DRESS	*yit* ('yet') *niver* ('never')
'i' sounds	PRICE	*raight* ('right')
'o' sounds	GOAT	*ova* ('over'), *om* ('home')
		winder ('window'), *goo* ('go')
'er' sounds	NURSE	*bod* ('bird'), *shot* ('shirt')
'or' sounds	THOUGHT	*tote* ('taught'), *dohter* ('daughter')

on monophthongs. From this table we can see that some of the comments describe sounds (but don't change the spelling of words), whereas others are phonologically based and not spelling-based (such as 'grain' for 'green'), so the comments are mixed throughout.

This is a selection of comments made on monophthongs in particular. In the shorter section on diphthongs (Scollins and Titford 2000: 24), the authors mention yod-dropping (which will be discussed in the next section where they say that the first part of diphthongs are dispensed with in words such as *noo* for *new* and *Dooke* for *Duke*), and that words such as *where* and *there* may appear as *wheer* and *theer* and *door* and *floor* as *dooer* and *flooer*. It lists other words with 'newer' pronunciations which are avoided by traditional dialect speakers and may appear as *clo-uz* ('clothes'), *froo-ut* ('fruit') and *cre-um* ('cream') and they comment that speakers add 'additional sounds' to words.

This description of vowels can be compared to the other words used in EY as well as those used in NN and JBA and JBB. In Table 4.2, some examples from these texts are used to illustrate the different findings relating to vowels in these examples of dialect literature.

For words with 'the full u', Scollins and Titford (2000: 20) specifically mention some exceptions, as they state that the words *mother*, *bugger* and *come* may be pronounced *motha*, *bogga* and *com*, particularly in more traditional dialect, but that the alternatives *muther*, *bugger* and *cum* are also possible. In fact, *boggar/bogger/boggered* all appear in Scollins and Titford's book.

In JBA and JBB there is discussion of the HAPPY vowel appearing with a mid-low lax vowel (more like the DRESS vowel) in words such as *Ralleh*, *nebbeh* and *reddeh*. This is a relatively new feature in the region (see Braber and Flynn 2015). None of these books mentions local variation of the LETTER vowel, which is also in a current state of change in the region (with local spellings of *Lestah* for *Leicester* spreading around the region; see also Braber and Robinson 2018).

4.5.2. Phonetic and Phonological Features: Consonants

Previous research has shown that frequent features of non-standard dialect usage in written discourse includes the use of apostrophes to show non-realisation of sounds (Miethaner 2000: 539), also referred to as the 'apologetic apostrophe' in discussions of Scots orthography (Eagle 2008). Another common feature is 'allegro' forms where words are spelled to reflect general processes of connected speech (Preston 1985; Miethaner 2000: 541), such as *wottjowont* for 'what do you want' found in JBA.

In relation to consonants, EY mentions the following features as being typical of local language in the region: *h*-dropping – 'the letter "h" is never pronounced' – and that this occurs in word-initial and word-medial position

Table 4.2 Vowels found in the dialect literature

Lexical set	Spelling found in DL and source	Standard English spelling of word
MOUTH	dairn; rairnd; abaht (EY); aht (JBA); rahnd (JBB) mahth (NN)	down; round; about out; round mouth
GOOSE	dow; te; skewl (EY) boowutts (JBA) bedrowm (NN)	do; to; school boots bedroom
DRESS	git (EY) eead (NN)	get head
STRUT	sum (EY) wunn (JBA); bleddi (JBB) boggar (NN)	some one; bloody bugger
GOAT	goo; guz (EY) omm (JBA) gooin' (NN)	go; goes home going
NURSE	ot; wokkin' (EY) dutti; kottins; shot (JBA); fust (JBB) bod; shot; thoteen (NN)	hurt; working dirty; curtains; shirt; first bird; shirt; thirteen
SQUARE	theer; wheer (EY) theer (NN)	there; where there
FACE	ta'e; sey (EY) mek (JBA) dioo (NN)	take; say; make day
FLEECE	mey; saims (EY) binn (JBB) Manfild; wik (NN)	me; seems been Mansfield; week
THOUGHT	watter (EY)	water
NORTH	fawtnitt (JBB) stooarmy; waam (NN)	fortnight stormy; warm
CLOTH	wesh (JBB) wesh (NN)	wash wash
BATH	cawf (NN)	calf
PALM	fayther (NN)	father
PRICE	reight; tahm (NN)	right; time
HAPPY	Ralleh (JBA); nebbeh (JBB); reddeh (JBB)	Raleigh (bike makers); nebby ('nosy'); ready

(Scollins and Titford 2000: 25). They also comment that it may appear where it is not needed, adding that leaving out the 'h' is not lazy and can actually require more effort as pauses need to be inserted and that this 'characteristic jerky, staccato rhythm' is typical of the region (2000: 25). Other consonants which the writers say can be omitted are 'ce' (i.e. *since* can appear as *sin*), k (*asks* can appear as *asses*) as well as 't', 'd', 'v', th', 'l' 'w' and 'g' (in words ending in *-ing*). Scollins and Titford add that some speakers use Velar Nasal Plus (Wells 1982: 188–9) in this position, as they write that 'far from not pronouncing a g at the end of a word, will sound it very clearly indeed, turning it into a hard g which is stressed' (Scollins and Titford 2000: 26) in words such as *sitting* and *tongue*. Mention is also made of T-to-R, where in words which 'should end in "t" or "s" and is then followed by a vowel, the last letter is often omitted, and an "r" substituted' (Scollins and Titford 2000: 27): for example, *gerrup*, *is tharall?* and *burro worrit?* ('but who was it?'). Table 4.3 shows the consonantal features which occur in the dialect literature.

Table 4.3 Consonantal features in dialect literature

Consonantal feature	Example	**Source**
h-dropping	ere ('here')	EY, NN
	oss ('horse'); omm ('home')	JBA
	omm ('home'); ot ('hot')	NN
k-dropping	ta'e ('take'); ma'e ('make')	EY
yod-dropping	Nooark ('Newark'); Dookeries ('Dukeries')	NN
g-dropping	gooin' ('going'); wokkin' ('working')	EY
	gooin' ('going')	NN
d-deletion	an' ('and')	EY; NN
	annorl ('and all')	JBA
t-deletion	Beeson ('Beeston')	NN
f-deletion	o't'past ('of the past')	EY
v-deletion	o't'brook ('over the brook')	NN
th-deletion	weeya ('with you')	JBA
	wee ('with')	JBB
l-vocalisation	sowjers ('soldiers'); owny ('only')	EY
	koad ('cold'); shoader ('shoulder')	JBA
	cowd ('cold'); aw ('all'); owd ('old')	NN
T-to-R	burrit's ('but it is'); gerrim ('get him')	EY
	gerroff ('get off')	JBA
	ger ('get')	NN
sk → ks	ax ('ask')	EY; NN
r-insertion	terask ('to ask')	JBA

It is clear that most of these features occur across the selected dialect literature. As stated above, many of the features are not unique to the Nottingham region, but the combinations of these features are treated as salient aspects of the local language.

4.5.3. Morphosyntactic Features

It is sometimes difficult to distinguish exactly between phonetic/phonological and morphosyntactic features, and some of the dialect literature includes features of one type in discussion of the other. For example, the word *thee* is discussed in terms of the phonetic realisation of vowel sounds (where *thee* can mean *you*, *there* or *they're*) and definite article reduction is discussed in terms of vowel omissions. Scollins and Titford discuss several morphosyntactic features: definite article reduction, the pronoun system (including demonstrative, possessive, object, relative, reflexive and indefinite) and the use of verbs, negation and prepositions. We also see the occurrence of non-standard agreement of verb and person (*it were*, *we was*) and different variations of modal verbs.

As not all of these can be discussed here in detail, a few examples will be used to illustrate the salient features of Nottingham language. The reflexive pronoun system is seen by the authors as rather distinctive in the region with the use of <sen> for 'self' such as *issen*, *yersen*, *the-selves*, although these forms are found in other varieties of Northern English (Scollins and Titford 2000: 34). This is also alluded to in John Beeton's second volume (JBB: 10) where pronouns are listed as: *missenn*; *yersenn*; *izzsenn*; *ersenn*; *uzzsenns*; *yersenns*; and *thissenns*. Other pronouns are listed as: *mine*; *yorn*; *izzen*; *ern*; *ahn*; *yorn*; and *thearn*.

With regard to verbs, there is mention of verbs which are weak rather than strong as they would appear in Standard English; examples such as *knowed*, *telled* and *growed* are given. Non-standard negations also feature frequently: *manna*, *anna*, *asna*, *didna*, *isna*, *canna*, *nedna*, *willna* and *dossna*, to name but a few, and this can occur when they appear as auxiliary or main verbs. Beeton provides the conjugation of some high-frequency verbs ('to have', 'must', 'have not' and 'to go'), showing the wide variation which can occur.

Many examples of non-standard prepositions are given and it is stated that these are particularly problematic to acquire for 'non-native' speakers. Such prepositions may be omitted altogether (*it belongs me*), additional ones may be added (*gerrup off on it afore yuh fall!*) or changed, with the substitution of 'on' for 'of' being particularly frequent (*sum on 'em's finished*). Table 4.4 illustrates with examples some of these features found in the dialect literature.

Table 4.4 Morphosyntactic features of dialect literature

Feature	Example	Source
Verb negation	dunna ('don't')	EY; NN
	canna ('can't')	EY
	wannt ('won't')	EY
	nedna ('needn't')	EY
	tint ('it isn't')	EY
	ent ('haven't')	JBA
	waint ('won't')	JBB; NN
Non-standard verb form (many of which involve contractions)	y'ay ('you have to')	EY
	genya ('given to you')	JBA
	assal etta ('I shall have to')	JBA
	gennim ('given to him/it')	JBA
	ent'ed ('haven't had')	NN
	dusta ('do you')	NN
	gang ('go')	NN
	catched ('caught')	NN
Non-standard agreement of subject/verb (many of which involve contractions)	silly prairtle were ('silly idiot was')	EY
	ittwerr ('it was')	JBB
Pronoun	thee ('you')	EY
	tha ('you')	NN
Pronoun (reflexive)	is-sen ('himself')	EY
	izzsenn ('himself')	JBA
	missenn ('myself')	JBA
	thissen ('yourself')	NN
Pronoun (possessive)	yourn ('yours')	JBA
	thee ('your')	NN
	thi ('your')	NN
'Our' with family member	aar Annie ('our Annie')	EY
	ahnann ('our grandmother')	JBB
Definite article reduction	int' car ('in the car')	EY
	walk ont' causey ('walk on the pavement')	EY
	i't'nose ('in the nose')	NN
Preposition reduction	i't'nose ('in the nose')	NN
Non-standard preposition	t'bath's full on em ('of them')	NN

There are not examples of all of these categories of morphosyntactic features in each of the dialect literature books. However, morphosyntactic variables are not as common as phonetic variables and so we would not expect a high frequency. It seems that verbs, pronouns and prepositions, as well as definite article reduction, are seen as 'typical' local language features.

4.5.4. Lexical Features

Lexical features are a very important focus of all of these books, representing the local words which are used by speakers in Nottingham ranging from *cob* ('bread roll') to *mardy* ('sulky') and *mashing* ('making tea'), and they also include parts on specific vocabulary related to mining, farming and weather which are treated as local to the region. There are too many examples to list all of them here. To focus on a few, though, there are several different greetings which are enregistered as local, the main one being the term of endearment used for both men and women, *duck*, which can often be found together with the greeting *ey up*. Other forms of greetings are *sorrey* and *youth*. *Ey up Mi Duck* is probably the most typical and distinct Nottingham term (see Braber and Robinson 2018 for more details and images).

There are also Nottingham forms for *anything*, *nothing* and *something*, including *ote* (EY) which is spelled *oat* in Beeton's books, *noat* and *summat* (EY, JBA). Most of the dialect literature gives the term *snap* ('packed lunch'), which is a frequent term used by miners, and many of these books have a focus on 'work' words. For some further examples, see Table 4.5.

Many of the books comment visually on one particular feature by writing words together to emphasise the 'mumbled, fast way of speaking', which the authors suggest can be hard to follow for outsiders. Beeton's work in particular includes entire phrases and sentences run together as one word, something which is a common feature of CHLDL texts, which makes this much more

Table 4.5 Lexical examples in dialect literature

Lexical item	Meaning	Source
wittle	worry	EY
bartled up	clogged up	EY
causey	pavement	EY
flit	move house	EY; JBA
frit	scared	EY
ganzie	pullover	EY; JBB
rammel	rubbish	EY; JBB
gennel/jennel/jitty	alleyways between/behind houses	EY
scraitin'	crying	EY
nesh	feel the cold	EY; JBA; NN
beer-off	off-licence	EY
batchi	foolish	JBA
duddoos	sweets	JBA
tab	ear	JBA
back-end weather	autumnal	NN

inaccessible to outsiders and limits readership to the ingroup who understand this local variety.

In summary, the extensive non-standard variation within the dialect literature ranges from different phonetic/phonological features to morpho-syntactic variation and use of lexical items which are seen as 'local' by these authors. The next section examines to what extent these features are represented in literary work set in Nottingham.

4.6. Literary Dialect

In 'high' literature, local dialect can be used to identify particular local speakers and represent specific local features of language (see also Hodson, this volume; Cooper, this volume). It has been commented (by Honeybone and Watson 2013: 315, for example) that this spelling may be inconsistent as authors are more concerned with artistic effect rather than linguistic accuracy (see also Percillier 2017: 2). Agha notes that such depictions of language in literary works do not just represent realities of language, but 'transform them into more memorable, figuratively rendered forms' (2003: 255). This section will examine some texts written by local authors in which certain characters can be identified as local dialect users. Hodson (2014: 116) comments:

> In the case of literary dialect, the author is more concerned with making the work accessible to a national audience not personally familiar with the dialect in question. As such the dialect representation may be limited both in terms of the range of dialect features represented and the frequency with which they occur.

In order to be perceived as realistic, the author must assume that the audience has sufficient familiarity with the dialect, but in the case of Nottingham, as discussed in Section 4.1, many people are unaware of features of its dialect and therefore rely on the authors for credibility. Although the literature selected for this chapter represents a random sample, much of it is aimed at a national (and international) audience, which is why some more local, autobiographical work aimed at local speakers has also been included. The work considered here includes novels and a play. The general question is whether stereotypical 'generic' grammatical forms, which are seen as non-standard, are used, including multiple negation or lack of verb/noun concordance, and specifically whether and what typically Nottingham features are used. We would assume that the most salient features of local varieties are used (Miethaner 2000: 537; Percillier 2017: 2), but the analysis below will test the accuracy of this assumption.

The following works are examined:

James Prior: Forest Folk (1907) (FF)

Prior was born in 1851 and lived in Bingham, Nottinghamshire. He has been called the Thomas Hardy of the Midlands, but is generally not very well known, although D. H. Lawrence did rate his work and J. M. Barrie was said to have praised it.[3] He is best remembered for *Forest Folk*. Some editions have a glossary for the dialect used. The story is set in the Sherwood Forest area (Blidworth) around the time of the Luddite Frame-Breaking Revolution in the early 1800s. It deals with a titled family, who are all Standard English users, and a farming family who use a non-standard local variety of language.

D. H. Lawrence: The Widowing of Mrs Holroyd (1911) (WMH) and Lady Chatterley's Lover (1928) (LCL)

Lawrence was born in 1885 in Eastwood, Nottinghamshire, where his father was a miner. He won a scholarship to the Nottingham High School but left and trained as a teacher. Much of his writing was banned because of its sexual nature – *Lady Chatterley's Lover* was published in 1928 in Italy but not published openly in the UK until 1960, thirty years after the author's death. The book was notorious for its sexual content, describing the relationship between a working-class man and a married upper-class woman who live in a mining village. *The Widowing of Mrs Holroyd* was published in 1911, with a revised version in 1914, and is a dramatisation of *Odour of Chrysanthemums*, a short story written in 1909 by Lawrence. Of all of the literary dialect works considered in this chapter, Lawrence's novels and poems are the only works which have been the study of linguistic analysis. For example, a study of pronunciation patterns and grammatical patterns with examples from different texts has been produced by Hillier (2008).

Hilda Lewis: Penny Lace (1946) (PL)

Lewis was born in London in 1896. She edited her school and college magazines and taught in London for a time. Married, with one son, she and her husband lived in Nottingham, where she worked at the University of Nottingham. She died in 1974. *Penny Lace* is set in the Nottingham lace industry in the late Victorian period.

Alan Sillitoe: Saturday Night and Sunday Morning (1958) (SNSM)

Sillitoe was born in 1928 and raised in the Lenton and Radford neighbourhoods of Nottingham. He left school at fourteen and worked as a labourer and factory-hand. While serving in the RAF, he developed tuberculosis, and read widely during his convalescence, after which he took up writing, documenting the lives and loves of the working classes. *Saturday Night and Sunday*

Morning was his debut novel and the one he is best known for. Sillitoe died in 2010. Many of his works are based in Nottingham and dialect is used by different characters, this novel focusing on a working-class man who works in the Raleigh Bike Factory.

Nicola Monaghan: Killing Jar (2007) (KJ)

Monaghan was born in 1971 and raised in Nottingham. This novel is her debut work. It is set in Broxtowe, a seedy suburb of Nottingham, where the characters are involved with drugs, prostitution and murder. A review in *The Independent* likens this novel and its characters to an update of Sillitoe's work in *Saturday Night and Sunday Morning.*[4]

Joy James: Yo'd Mek a Parson Swear (2008) (JJ) Bog All to Swear About! (2009) (JJ2)

James was born in the late 1930s in Nottingham and has lived there all her life. She worked as a singer and an entertainer, and later in life started writing her life story. Her different books relate episodes in her life. Much of the dialogue is distinctly local and some of the books start with a vocabulary list and a discussion of local language for the readers.

John Harvey: Darkness, Darkness (2014) (DK)

Harvey was born in London in 1938 and moved to Nottingham in the 1960s; he had spells away from the city but is based there now. He is a Notts County fan and honorary member of its supporters' club. This book is the last case for DI Resnick, who has been dealing with Nottinghamshire murders for twenty-five years.

Clare Harvey: The Night Raid (2017) (NR)

Clare Harvey (date of birth unknown) has lived around the world but is now settled in Nottingham. In this book, world-renowned war artist Dame Laura Knight is commissioned to paint propaganda portraits of factory girls and is sent to the ordnance factories in her hometown of Nottingham.

4.7. Linguistic Features Described in Literary Dialect

4.7.1. Phonetic and Phonological Features in Literary Dialect

Similarly to the dialect literature, there are many words in the text that illustrate local pronunciation and this applies to vowels and consonants. One feature which occurs in the oldest novel, *Forest Folk* (FF), with the only other usage in WMH, is that vowel sounds are sometimes written with diacritics (a diaeresis), for example, *roäd* (road), *beäst* (beast) and *cooät* (coat). The purpose is to emphasise that these are diphthongs in this variety. In this book, only the farming family use non-standard language; the gentry are consistent Standard English users. There are also comments made in the text that the higher-class speakers find the farming family difficult to understand. Table 4.6 shows some of the most common respellings used for vowels found in all the selected works.

Table 4.6 Vowels in literary dialect

Lexical set	Spelling found in LD and source	Standard English spelling of word
MOUTH	faunt (JJ)	found
	dahn (JJ)	down
	nah (JJ) (NR)	now
	abaht (LCL)	about
	showt (PL)	shout
DRESS	yaller (FF)	yellow
	niver (LCL)	never
	iver (PL)	ever
	stiddy (PL)	steady
	ivry (WMH)	every
	whativer (WMH)	whatever
STRUT	coom (FF); cum (SNSM)	come
	commin' (WMH)	coming
	bleddy (JJ) (SNSM)	bloody
	bogger (KJ) (SNSM)	bugger
	bad-un (KJ); un (WMH)	bad-one; one
	munny (LCL) munney (SNSM)	money
	oop (PL)	up
	cump'ny (WMH)	company
GOAT	roäd (FF)	road
	goo (FF) (PL)	go
	cooät (FF)	coat
	oppen (FF)	open
	tomorra (KJ)	tomorrow
	ovver (PL)	over
	hoom (WMH)	home
NURSE	desarved (FF)	deserved
	gel (JJ) (SNSM); gell (KJ)	girl
	sarve (PL)	serve
	wok (SNSM)	work
	eerd (SNSM)	heard
	wor (WMH)	were
SQUARE	somewheer (FF); theer (FF) (PL) (WMH)	somewhere; there
	wheer (LCL) (WMH)	where

Table 4.6 (*cont.*)

Lexical set	Spelling found in LD and source	Standard English spelling of word
FACE	tek (FF) (JJ) (PL) (SNSM)	take
	mek (JJ) (KJ) (PL)	make
	gev (KJ)	gave
	mebbe (PL)	maybe
	grett (SNSM)	great
FLEECE	beäst (FF)	beast
	bin (KJ)	been
	slaip (LCL)	sleep
THOUGHT	watter (FF)	water
	thowt (LCL); thöwt (WMH)	thought
	dowter (PL)	daughter
NORTH	hoss (SNSM)	horse
FORCE	fower (FF)	four
	fer (JJ) (KJ) (PL)	for
CLOTH	weshday (JJ)	washday
BATH	mester (FF) (PL) (WMH)	master
	hafe (FF)	half
TRAP	hev (PL)	have
PALM	feyther (PL)	father
PRICE	ayther (FF)	either
	raight (FF)	right
	oy (FF)	eye
	ah (JJ)	I
	naight (LCL)	night
HAPPY	funneh (JJ)	funny

One difference as compared to dialect literature is that there are no GOOSE vowels listed here. Furthermore, as there are more books discussed in this section, there appears to be more variation in the words found than in the dialect literature. However, there are still some words which feature frequently, such as *somewheer*, *theer*, *mek* and *tek*. The first two only appear in the older texts and not the more modern ones, suggesting that this feature is less common or has disappeared entirely from variation in the region. The HAPPY vowel only occurs in one of the texts, and it is one of the more recent ones. We also see different spellings used to represent the same words (such as different non-standard spellings for *come* and *money*). Similar to the dialect literature, we see more STRUT vowels marked than BATH vowels. Perhaps these authors feel this is such an obvious and salient difference that it does not need to be marked explicitly. Two of the most modern texts (DK and NR) rarely appear here (only *nah* for *now* in NR) or are absent in the non-standard features, a phenomenon that will be discussed later.

The works considered here also contain a large number of consonantal features. Many of these reflect the same features found in the dialect literature. Some of these features are found usually in non-standard variation (such as *g*-dropping in words such as *gooin'* or *somethin'*) but, added together here, they give the flavour of a Nottingham variety. There are many examples of *l*-vocalisation, *h*-dropping and *r*-insertion, but no *th*-fronting and very little yod-dropping is noted. Even in speakers today, this is a feature that speakers are frequently unaware of and therefore may not be represented in the literature. Table 4.7 shows some of the consonantal variation found in the literary dialect texts. As there are so many examples, just a few are provided here to illustrate the features found.

Again, the two most modern novels only appear rarely in this table: NR only once (for *h*-dropping), while the examples used in DK are those which are very generally non-standard (*wi'*, *an'*, *o'*, *'em*, *feller*, *p'r'aps*, to give just a few examples). As well as *g*-dropping in words such as *somethin'* and *gooin'*, we also see this form replaced with a 'k', so we see *nothink* and *somethink* (in WMH and KJ). A few examples of *ask* appear as *ax* or *aks* (FF, LCL, WMH), but only in the older texts, so this also seems to be a feature which has disappeared from the local variety.

4.7.2. Morphosyntactic Features

There are many non-standard morphosyntactic features in the dialect literature and these are the same features which appear in the literary dialect. Examples include definite article reduction, non-standard pronoun usage, non-standard verbs, which are all relatively frequent, and some which feature much less, such as multiple negation which only appears in two of the texts (*that wasn't no way legal* (KJ) and *we didn't mean no harm* (WMH)). The lack of plural marker is also rare: see, for example, *three month* in WMH. There are some other interesting non-standard features, such as *he's none getting wet* in FF, which is clearly an older form no longer in general use.

Some of these non-standard verb forms (such as *munna*, *shonna*, *nedna*) tend to appear only in the older texts, particularly in Lawrence's work, and this suggests they are no longer being used in contemporary language usage. This is also the case for some of the non-standard prepositions, although they do still appear in more recent texts that contain the most non-standard language.

Table 4.7 Consonants in literary dialect

Linguistic feature	Examples
d-deletion	an'all (KJ), annall (JJ) ('and everything'); Lunnen (FF) ('London'); unnerstand (PL) ('understand'); an' (WMH) ('and')
f-deletion	o' (DK; JJ; WMH) ('of'); outta (KJ) ('out of')
h-deletion	eyyin' (JJ) ('having'); oss (JJ) ('horse'); ome (JJ2) ('home'), an't (KJ), aven't (WMH) ('haven't'); ear-ole (KJ) ('ear-hole'); mek-aste (KJ) ('hurry up'); appen (LCL) ('happen'); 'ave (NR) ('have'); issen (SNSM) ('himself'); eerd (SNSM) ('heard'); eartily (FF) ('heartily')
g-dropping	somethin' (DK) ('something'); talkin' (FF) ('talking'); norrin' (JJ) ('nothing'); swiggin' (JJ2) ('swigging'); tryna (KJ) ('trying to'); comin' (PL) ('coming'); smashin' (SNSM) ('smashing'); dancin' (WMH) ('dancing'); takin' (DK) ('taking')
absence of <r>	hoss (FF) ('horse'); gel (JJ) ('girl'); wo'kin' (JJ2) ('working'); wa (KJ) ('were'); Sat'day/Satdy (SNSM) ('Saturday')
s-deletion	i'n't it (DK) ('isn't it'); (KJ) ('in't')
t-deletion	las' (SNSM) ('last'); kep (WMH) ('kept')
th-deletion	wi' (DK;FF;JJ;KJ;WMH) ('with'); em/emselves (DK; WMH); ('them/themselves'); clo'es (FF) ('clothes'); wi'out (KJ;PL) ('without')
v-deletion	hae (FF), ha'e (WMH), ha' (WMH) ('have'); gie (FF); gi' (JJ;SNSM), gen (JJ), gi-me (KJ) ('give'); ner-more (KJ) ('never-more'); gi-yer (KJ) ('give you'); ne'er (PL) ('never')
w-deletion	al'ays (DK) ('always'); up'ards (FF) ('upwards')
l-vocalisation	on'y (FF;JJ;LCL;PL;SNSM) ('only'); oad (FF); owd (JJ;JJ2; KJ;PL;SNSM) ('old'); a'ready (LCL) ('already'); cowd (SNSM) ('cold'); sowjers (SNSM) ('soldiers'); a'most (WMH) ('almost'); a' (WMH) ('all')
schwa	feller (DK) ('fellow'); yer (FF;KJ) ('you'); tomorrer (FF;SNSM), termorrer (JJ) ('tomorrow'); ter (JJ;JJ2;KJ;LCL;PL;SNSM;WMH) ('to'); Meddars (KJ) ('Meadows'); ser (KJ) ('so'); try-ner (KJ) ('trying to'); ter do (LCL) ('to do'); winder (SNSM) ('window'); foller (SNSM) ('follow'); swaller (SNSM) ('swallow')
T-to-R	thar'ris (JJ) ('that is'); gerrit (KJ) ('get it'); lerr-im (KJ) ('let him'); shurrup (SNSM) ('shut up')
t → k	lakely (KJ) ('lately'); lickle (KJ) ('little')

4.7.3. Lexical Features

In relation to vocabulary, the three texts which use most of the regional lexis are the two autobiographical books by Joy James and the book by Monaghan set in a working-class area of Nottingham which deals with drug-taking and

Table 4.8 Morphosyntactic features in literary dialect

Feature	Example	Source
Verb negation	dunna ('don't')	LCL;WMH
	wun't ('wouldn't')	JJ;KJ
	dun't ('don't')	KJ
	shun't ('shouldn't')	KJ
	nedna ('needn't')	LCL
	canna ('can't')	LCL;WMH
	wain't ('won't')	PL;SNSM
	worn't ('won't')	SNSM
	shonna ('shan't')	WMH
	munna ('musn't')	WMH
Non-standard verb form	mun ('must/will') also spelled maun	FF;LCL;WMH
	suld ('should')	FF
	we's'll ('we shall'); s'll	SNSM; WMH
	yer'd ('you would')	SNSM
	han yer ('have you')	WMH
	knowed ('knew')	WMH
	a-gooin' ('going to')	FF
	a-knocking ('knocking')	JJ
	telled ('told')	FF
	gied ('gave'); gien ('give')	FF
Non-standard agreement of subject/verb	the shawl yer sent were right	PL
	th'air were filthy	PL
	it don't	SNSM
	you was	WMH
	he warn't	FF
	I comes	JJ
	it were	JJ2; KJ
	we was	KJ
	is they	KJ
	it wor	LCL
Pronoun	us (used to mean 'me' and 'we')	KJ; PL
	yer ('you'); also yo	PL
	ta ('you')	WMH
	thee ('you')	WMH;LCL
	ter ('you')	WMH
	her's ('she's')	WMH
	thäigh ('you')	WMH
Pronoun (demonstrative)	them times ('those times')	KJ
Pronoun (reflexive)	by's sen ('by himself')	WMH
	oursens ('ourselves')	FF; KJ
	mysen ('myself')	FF;PL
	hissen ('himself'); also issen	FF;PL;WMH;SNSM
	hisself ('himself')	WMH

Table 4.8 (*cont.*)

Feature	Example	Source
	hern ('herself')	PL
	yersen ('yourself'); yoursen	PL;LCL;SNSM
Pronoun (possessive)	me ('my')	KJ
	us own ('our own')	JJ
	yourn ('your')	JJ;FF;PL
	tha ('your')	FF
	thy ('your')	WMH
	theirn ('their')	SNSM
'Our' with family member	our Joy	JJ
Definite article reduction	one or t'other	JJ
	down t'pit	LCL
	th' 'ouse	WMH
	what's use	WMH
Preposition/infinitive reduction	i'th ('in the')	PL
	t'interfere	PL
	nowt t'eat	SNSM
Non-standard preposition	talkin' on ('talking about')	FF
	not so easy gotten rid on ('rid of')	FF
	on them ('of them'); on us ('of us')	JJ;PL
	neither on you ('neither of you')	JJ; SNSM
	so long ('as long')	KJ
	not as Ah know on ('know of')	LCL
	cured you on it ('of it')	SNSM
	every penny on it ('of it')	SNSM
	I know nowt on 'im ('of him')	WMH
	all on us ('all of us')	WMH

crime. Some of these words are also used outside the East Midlands, such as *mam*, *well* for *very*, *naff* and *gone off* for *happened*, but many others add a very local feel. We can also see that some of the terms used in the older books, specifically words to do with agriculture and mining, are no longer used as such practices have disappeared from common usage. Table 4.9 contains some of the more archaic examples, whereas Table 4.10 includes a selection of examples of the most local words, many of which appear across several texts.

We also see non-standard words such as *nowt* and *owt* in the literary dialect but consistently spelled in this way (and not with the variation seen in the dialect literature). The only exception to this is one occurrence of *öwt* in WMH, which is an older text. There is also a frequent occurrence of *summat* found across the literary dialect. The older texts also contain words such as

Table 4.9 Traditional lexical features in literary dialect

Lexical item	Meaning	Source
auve	move left (for horses)	FF
blawt	noise calves make	FF
wetchud	wet shoes	FF
addle	waste	FF
back-end	autumn	FF
fothering	feeding hay for animals	FF
butty	mining term – man in charge of a team	LCL
cage	mine lift	LCL
gadding	go about in a flippant way	LCL
wezzle-brained	foolish	LCL
pettifogging	petty	WMH
snap	packed lunch	WMH
bantle	lift load of men in pit	WMH
stint	mining term for distance worked/shift	WMH
afterdamp	gas in mine	WMH

Table 4.10 Lexical features still found in current usage

Lexical item	Meaning	Source
batchy	someone who is a bit dim	JJ;SNSM
beer-off	off-licence	JJ;JJ2
bogger	bugger	JJ;KJ
clarty	dirty	FF
corsey	pavement	JJ
dobbie/dobby	game of tig	KJ
flit	move house	JJ;FF
frit	be scared	JJ;FF
mash	make tea	SNSM;KJ;NR
nesh	feel the cold	FF;KJ
tabs	ears	JJ;SNSM

allus (always) and *ay* (yes), which do not appear in the more contemporary fictional work.

Some of the most common lexical items are also common in the dialect literature. For example, *duck* or *duckie* as a term of endearment appear in most of the texts, including the very recent ones, and seem to act as an immediate indicator of 'Nottinghamness'. The term *mardy* (grumpy) is also common in these works. In the dialect literature both *gennel/jennel* and *jitty* are used for alleyways between or behind houses, but in the literary dialect only *jitty* is found (in JJ and KJ). For 'grandmother' we see the word *grammar*

(JJ), but *nanar*, which appeared in EY, does not appear here, although it is frequently used in merchandising of Nottingham products.

The very recent NR has very little local vocabulary in it. The only local lexical items are *m'duck* and *duck* and *duckie*, as well as two local characters saying *ey up* and *ey oop* (in fact, the chapter which opens for the first time in Nottingham starts with the words *ey up*, as if to show that we are now in Nottingham), and one character who says *I've not long mashed tea*. These are clearly 'typical' features which flag up that these (working-class) characters are in fact local. This book is aimed at a national audience, so perhaps the author does not want to alienate other readers.

Similar to NR, where the main characters tend to speak in relatively standard ways (even the main character, who is from and has always lived in Nottingham), is the use of language in DK. In this book there are also meta-linguistic comments (see also Percillier 2017: 10). One of the main police officers is originally from Africa and it is said that her Standard English, acquired at school, was 'now given some character after time spent living in the East Midlands', and about another character who has been away from Nottingham for some time: 'Less than twenty-four hours back and you could hear the local accent resurfacing like rusted slippage in his voice.' There are some examples of a local lexicon used by minor characters (*scraightin'* to mean both scratching and crying/moaning, *nan*, *afore*, *owt* and *nowt*, *duck*, *youth*, *flitted*, *mashing tea*, *cobs* and *ginnel*). Another interesting feature is that these minor 'dialect' characters do not seem to use dialect consistently. This book is about the miners' strike and some of the really important dialogue is standard even when the character speaking is one who normally does use non-standard language. Could it be that the author thinks that using local language here would distract the readers?

4.8. Conclusions

The analysis carried out here has shown that there are 'typical' features of the Nottingham dialect which are represented in dialect writing: examples which illustrate how words are pronounced, examples of non-standard morphosyntactic features as well as a wide variety of local lexis. Comparison between the different texts suggests there is a clear correspondence between language usage discussed in dialect literature and the language used in literary dialect. But changes are under way. Some traditional vocabulary and non-standard spellings are being lost. Books aimed at a wider national or international audience do not use these features or simply use non-standard features that occur throughout the country to signal the working-class origins of speakers. Some literary work is clearly aimed at a non-local audience, whereas some of the work, for example by Joy James, would be less accessible to non-locals who are unfamiliar with the language used in Nottingham. Other, newer features, such as changes in the HAPPY or LETTER vowels, are slower to come through in literature.

Some contemporary texts, notably those that are autobiographical in nature or where the focus is much more strongly on the language used by speakers to show that they belong to the lowest working classes, do still use much more significant amounts of non-standard phonology, morphosyntax and lexical items. However, where non-standard orthography is used, authors need to consider this usage carefully as the results must still be comprehensible, particularly for an audience unfamiliar with the language of Nottingham.

Certain features may occur elsewhere in the country, but what is important here is that they are perceived to be local. What is meant here is that certain linguistic features, such as the use of non-standard prepositions, definite article reduction, yod-dropping and the use of certain vowels, may not be distinctive only to Nottingham, but when used in conjunction with one another can be seen to represent a local language usage. The analysis in this chapter has also shown that some forms are much more sociolinguistically salient than others: for example, the Northern BATH vowel and yod-dropping, which are rarely represented by these authors even though they are in widespread use generally but tend to go unnoticed by non-linguists. By comparing language in dialect literature and literary dialect we can chart the progress of enregisterment of certain linguistic features by claiming they are distinctive to that dialect.

Writers may use respelling to represent speech accurately and such respellings can reflect features that are non-standard or unusual, and although this needs to be examined in more detail, non-standard linguistic features can be combined to define the local dialect and symbolise local identity. This is especially important in a city such as Nottingham where it seems as if lay people have a relatively limited exposure to their own linguistic varieties in the media.

Notes

1. See: http://www.meetengland.com/Incentives/Nottingham-and-the-East-Midlands.aspx where it states that 'Nottingham is the capital of the East Midlands'.
2. See Nottingham Population 2018: http://worldpopulationreview.com/world-cities/nottingham-population/.
3. See both http://tonyshaw3.blogspot.com/2008/01/james-prior-forest-folk-and-blidworth.html and https://nottinghamcityofliterature.com/blog/forest-folk for more information.
4. See https://www.independent.co.uk/arts-entertainment/books/reviews/the-killing-jar-by-nicola-monaghan-6104369.html.

References

Agha, Asif (2003), 'The social life of cultural value', *Language & Communication*, 23: 231–73.

Androutsopoulos, Jannis K. (2000), 'Non-standard spelling in media texts: the case of German fanzines', *Journal of Sociolinguistics*, 4(4): 514–33.

Beal, Joan (2000), 'From Geordie Ridley to *Viz*: popular literature in Tyneside English', *Language and Literature*, 9(4): 343–59.

Beal, Joan (2009), 'Enregisterment, commodification, and historical context: "Geordie" versus "Sheffieldish"', *American Speech*, 84(2): 138–56.

Beckett, John (ed.) (2006), *A Centenary History of Nottingham*, Chichester: Phillimore.

Beeton, John (1999), *Nottingham as It Is Spoke*, Nottingham: JB Enterprises.

Bell, Allan (1984), 'Language style as audience design', *Language in Society*, 13: 145–204.

Braber, Natalie (2015), 'Language perception in the East Midlands in England', *English Today*, 31(1): 16–26.

Braber, Natalie and Nicholas Flynn (2015), 'The East Midlands: Nottingham', in R. Hickey (ed.), *Researching Northern Englishes*, Amsterdam: John Benjamins, pp. 369–92.

Braber, Natalie and Jonnie Robinson (2018), *East Midlands English*, Berlin: Mouton de Gruyter.

Britain, David (ed.) (2007), *Language in the British Isles*, Cambridge: Cambridge University Press.

Cooper, Paul (2017), '"Deregisterment" and "fossil forms": the cases of *gan* and *mun* in "Yorkshire" dialect', *English Today*, 129(33/1): 43–52.

Eagle, A. (2008), 'Aw ae wey: written Scots in Scotland and Ulster'. Online: http://www.scots-online.org/articles/contents/AwAeWey.pdf. Accessed 18 June 2019.

Eisenstein, Jacob (2015), 'Systematic patterning in phonologically-motivated orthographic variation', *Journal of Sociolinguistics*, 19(2): 161–88.

Fennell, Barbara (2001), *A History of English: A Sociolinguistic Approach*, Oxford: Blackwell.

Harvey, Clare (2017), *Night Raid*, New York: Simon & Schuster.

Harvey, John (2014), *Darkness, Darkness*, Doncaster: Arrow.

Hillier, Hilary (2008), *Talking Lawrence: Patterns of Eastwood Dialect in the Work of D. H. Lawrence*, Nottingham: Critical, Cultural and Communications Press.

Hodson, Jane (2014), *Dialect in Film and Literature*, London: Palgrave Macmillan.

Hodson, Jane and Alex Broadhead (2013), 'Developments in literary dialect representation in British fiction 1800–1836', *Language and Literature*, 22(4): 315–32.

Honeybone, Patrick and Kevin Watson (2013), 'Salience and the sociolinguistics of Scouse spelling', *English World-Wide*, 34(3): 305–40.

Hughes, Arthur, Peter Trudgill and Dominic Watt (2012), *English Accents and Dialects*, London: Hodder Arnold.

Jaffe, Alexandra (2000), 'Introduction: non-standard orthography and non-standard speech', *Journal of Sociolinguistics*, 4(4): 497–513.

James, Joy (2008), *Yo'd Mek a Parson Swear*, Nottingham: Joy James.

James, Joy (2009), *Bog All to Swear About*, Nottingham: Joy James.

Kortmann, Bernd and Clive Upton (eds) (2008), *Varieties of English 1: The British Isles*, Berlin: Mouton de Gruyter.

Lawrence, D. H. (1911), *The Widowing of Mrs Holroyd*, London: Nick Hern Books.

Lawrence, D. H. (1928), *Lady Chatterley's Lover*, New York: Collin's Classics, republished 2008.

Lewis, Hilda (1946), *Penny Lace*, Nottingham: Bromley House Editions, republished 2010.

Miethaner, Ulrich (2000), 'Orthographic transcriptions of non-standard varieties: the case of earlier African-American English', *Journal of Sociolinguistics*, 4(4): 534–60.

Monaghan, Nicola (2007), *The Killing Jar*, New York: Vintage.

Orton, Harold and Eugen Dieth (eds) (1962–71), *Survey of English dialects (B): The Basic Material*, Leeds: Arnold & Son.

Percillier, Michael (2017), 'Postcolonial literature and World Englishes: a corpus-based approach of modes of representation of the non-standard in writing', *Literary Linguistics*, 6(1): 1–24.

Preston, Dennis R. (1982), 'Ritin' fowklower daun 'rong: folklorists' failures in phonology', *Journal of American Folklore*, 95: 304–26.

Preston, Dennis R. (1985), 'The Li'l Abner syndrome: written representations of speech', *American Speech*, 60(4): 328–36.

Preston, Dennis R. (1989), *Perceptual Dialectology: Nonlinguists' Views of Areal Linguistics*, Dordrecht: Foris Publications.

Prior, James (1907), *Forest Folk*, London: Leen Editions, republished 2017.

Scollins, Richard and John Titford (2000), *Ey up Mi Duck! Dialect of Derbyshire and the East Midlands*, Newbury: Countryside Books.

Sebba, Mark (2012), 'Orthography as social action: scripts, spelling, identity and power', in Alexandra Jaffe, Jannis Androutsopoulos, Mark Sebba and Sally Johnson (eds), *Orthography as Social Action: Scripts, Spelling, Identity and Power*, Berlin: Mouton de Gruyter, pp. 1–19.

Shorrocks, Graham (1996), 'Non-standard dialect literature and popular culture', in Juhani Klemola, Merja Kytö and Matti Rissanen (eds), *Speech Past and Present: Studies in English Dialectology in Memory of Ossi Ihailainen*, Frankfurt am Main: Peter Lang, pp. 385–411.

Sillitoe, Alan (1958), *Saturday Night and Sunday Morning*, New York: HarperCollins, republished 2008.

Tannen, Deborah (1982), 'Oral and literate strategies in spoken and written narratives', *Language*, 58(1): 1–21.

Trudgill, Peter (1999), *The Dialects of England*, 2nd edn, Oxford: Blackwell.

Upton, Clive (2012), 'The importance of being Janus: Midland speakers and the "North–South divide"', in Manfred Markus, Yoko Iyeiri, Reinhard Hemberger and Emil Chamson (eds), *Middle and Modern English Corpus Linguistics*, Amsterdam: John Benjamins, pp. 257–68.

Wells, J. C. (1982), *Accents of English*, Cambridge: Cambridge University Press.

Wright, Peter (1979), *Notts Natter: How It Is Spoke*, Skipton: Dalesman Publishing.

5

Enregistering Dialect Representation in Staffordshire Potteries' Cartoons

Urszula Clark

5.1. Introduction

This chapter discusses a set of cartoons that feature Staffordshire Potteries dialect, the first of which are taken from cartoon booklets written by Alan Povey and Andy Ridler and illustrated by Don Turner in the 1970s, and the second from a local newspaper written and illustrated by Dave Follows from 1985 to 2003. I argue that the use of dialect in writing is an intentional act and can be accounted for theoretically through the concepts of enregisterment and indexicality, Bakhtinian concepts of double-voicing (1981) as well as the burlesque and carnivalesque (1984), and Burke's ([1937] 1959) concepts of frames of acceptance and rejection. Often, writing in dialect juxtaposes the norms and values 'outside' the community with those 'within' it, identifying with a cultural and social normativity which may be at odds with those from 'outside' it. Respellings in dialect thus serve to highlight the *abstand*: that is, the distance between representation of a dialect and the reference variety which serves as the norm (Jaffe 2000). Orthography depicts not only a representation of a sound pattern alone, but also links to a framework of sociocultural identity. Written by 'insiders', dialect representation acknowledges the stigma attached to variation by 'outsiders' while at the same time also mocking that self-same stigma (Clark 2013b).

The chapter moves on to explore both the imaginative and mental dimensions of dialect writing. As Honeybone (2011: 176) says: 'languages exist … mentally, on the grounds of speakers' perceptions. People have conceptions of who speaks the same language as them – that is, of who belongs to their close or extended speech community.' Languages also exist imaginatively, in relation to speakers' and listeners' perceptions. People have/draw upon pre/conceptions of, for example, character, social status, wealth and intelligence triggered by language use. Cartoonists exploit 'us' and 'them' by imaginative representation through visualisation of dialect in respelling. Such respelling can also be thought of as both situational and metaphoric code-switching. Situational, as in conventionalised distribution, and metaphoric in that it 'captures linguistic evocations of localness typically short and often unique' (Androutsopoulos 2010: 748). In this way, the cartoons discussed in this chapter can be said to index spaces and associated social types through double-voicing and stylisation. In turn, they also disrupt or undercut conventionalised framings of acceptance and rejection in relation to social stereotypes by turning them on their heads and subverting dominant linguistic ideologies.

In Section 5.2, I explore the issue of standard versus non-standard in relation to writing, before moving on in Section 5.3 to discuss the twin concepts of enregisterment and indexicality, in 5.4 the Bakhtinian concept of double-voicing and in 5.5 Burke's concepts of frames of acceptance and rejection. Section 5.6 then applies the theoretical framework identified in Sections 5.2 to 5.5 to the analysis of the sample of Staffordshire cartoons, before moving on to the conclusion in 5.7.

5.2. Dialect Writing as an Intentional Act

An important issue to be taken into account when considering writing in dialect is that its use is popularly perceived as standing in opposition to writing in Standard English. Consequently, its reception by the public at large can still be bedevilled by prescriptive notions of linguistic 'correctness' and 'superiority'. Studies such as those of Johnson (2005), Sebba (2007) and Crowley (this volume) establish that, as with accent, dialect writing is always understood with reference to a 'standard' or norm, in this case Standard English. Furthermore, non-standardness is conventionally linked to stigma. This does not mean, however, that non-standard forms cannot simultaneously be used to represent linguistic pride or regional identity, in exactly the same way as stigmatised speech forms can have 'covert' prestige or value in alternative markets. Beal (2006: 531) points out that the representation of accent and dialect in writing becomes an issue once a language has been standardised, and thus becomes a primary norm against which anything different is judged to be deviant or different and thus viewed as a secondary norm. Primary norms are those which govern 'correct' linguistic practice and behaviours, and secondary norms determine the authority to specify and/or to modify the primary norms.

One major way in which dialectal variation from Standard English is indicated is through respelling. Preston (1985) identified three types of respelling: *allegro speech*, *eye dialect* and *dialect respelling*. The first two categories, *allegro speech* and *eye dialect*, describe features that are shared by all dialects but are not at the standard end of the continuum, while dialect respelling marks regionally specialised use. *Allegro speech* attempts to capture the fact that speech is casual, and not necessarily monitored in the same way as Standard English spelling. Such spelling is characteristic of non-standard features shared by other dialects. For example, writing *snice* 'that's nice', *would of* 'would have' and *gonna* 'going to'. Forms which reflect no phonological difference from their standard counterparts are known as *eye dialect*. For example, *wot* for *what*; *sez* for *says* and *enuff* for *enough*. Dialect respelling attempts to capture regional and social features of pronunciation, and, for the purpose of this chapter, includes variation in both phonology and morphosyntax such as the Black Country *mon* 'man', *saft* 'soft' and *yawm* 'you are' (Clark and Asprey 2013; Clark 2013a, 2019). The point here is that in using non-standard spellings to represent either non-standardness in general or a specific dialect, many readers will read in stigma regardless of writers' conscious or unconscious motivations or intentions. However, Androutsopoulos (2010) also makes the distinction between situational and metaphoric code-switching of the kind evident when writing draws upon non-standard orthography. Representation of dialect through orthography post-standardisation – whether as allegro speech, dialect respelling or eye-dialect – can be said to be metaphoric, in that it is a linguistic evocation of localness. The cartoons discussed below illustrate such a metaphoric evocation (and several other chapters in this volume also consider respelling in dialect writing, sometimes from other perspectives, including those by Asprey, Braber, Cooper, Hermeston, Honeybone, Maguire, and Watson and Jensen).

Jaffe (2000) has called attention to the fact that orthography is a tool of what she calls 'abstandssprache': that is, language by distance. Respellings in dialect serve to highlight the *abstand*: the distance between representation of a dialect and the reference variety which serves as the norm. As a result, whether or not such distance reflects negatively or positively upon the dialect and its speakers depends to a certain degree upon whether the text was written by a speaker of the dialect, and thus an 'insider', or whether the view of the dialect is imposed from 'outside'. Just as accent does not name a sound pattern alone, but a sound pattern linked to a framework of social identity (Agha 2003), so too orthography not only depicts a representation of a sound pattern, but also links to a framework of social identity in much the same way. As Jaffe comments, representation of non-standard writing in texts written by 'outsiders' to the community of speakers it purports to represent is thus appropriated by the 'outsider', with no representational control of those who are represented. As a result, 'they are almost always subject to "darker" interpretations based on the well-known stereotypical conventions that link linguistic nonstandardness with stigma' (Jaffe 2000: 509). Such writing, as Jaffe notes, reproduces and continues the notion that non-standardness links to stigma, and goes a long way towards perpetuating stereotypical, generally negative portrayals of social identity.

By contrast, non-standard writing in texts written by 'insiders' draws upon specific, enregistered, double-voiced regional forms to perform local identity in self-conscious, ironic and mocking ways. In an earlier work that considers writing in Black Country dialect (see also Asprey, this volume), places and dialects are essentially linked while also subverting the ways in which social stereotypes are represented by dialect. Furthermore, use of dialect in texts of the kind exemplified in this chapter often juxtaposes the norms and values of those 'outside' the community – in terms of both social class and geographic distance – with those 'within' it, thereby identifying with a cultural and social normativity which may be at odds with those from 'outside' it. They do this in ways which aim to subvert ideologies of social class and linguistic 'correctness', through the use of the very phenomenon which is stigmatised: enregistered forms of the dialect itself (Clark 2019).

Theoretically, conscious use of dialect, whether it be in speech or writing, has been increasingly viewed through the lens of the twin concepts of *indexicality* and *enregisterment* (see Johnstone 2009, 2011; Beal 2009; and also the chapters in this volume by Beal, Braber, Crowley and, with some close connection to issues discussed here, Hermeston), discussed in the next section.

5.3. Indexicality and Enregisterment

The concepts of indexicality and enregisterment have come increasingly to provide ways to account for the complex interaction between linguistic variation and social and geographic mobility. They identify the ways in which speakers and writers draw upon language as belonging to a specific social group in varying degrees of metapragmatic awareness and self-reflexivity ways as well as the linguistic tokens themselves (Adams 2009; Beal 2009; Clark 2013a; Clark and Asprey 2013; Johnstone 2016). Traditionally, dialect use has been perceived in terms of relatively stable sets of linguistic conventions or rules that can be mapped onto social and physical spaces. Dialects map onto geographic space and sociolects onto demographically defined groups that are generally linked at a national, rather than regional, level. Through the range of linguistic features any one of us employs in relation to both dialect and register, we can thus be identified with a specific place and/or group onto which any regional or social dialect maps. However, sociolinguists' work over the past ten years or so, in particular, has led to a greater degree of problematisation. As Johnstone (2013: 290) says:

> We now ask questions about why people use features of one variety or another, rather than assuming that people inevitably speak the way they first learnt to speak, and the answers we arrive at have to do with identity and agency rather than only with geography and demography.

Silverstein (1992, 1993, 2003) and Agha (2003, 2007), drawing upon semiotics and the works of Jakobson and Pierce, have developed a framework that links linguistic choice to social meaning and how sets of linguistic choices can be construed as varieties of linguistic use that relate to both dialect and register. The concept of indexicality as proposed by Silverstein refers to the essential connection between micro-analytic and macro-analytic phenomena and frames of analysis. Micro-analytic phenomena are those identified in specific utterances in speech or lexical/morphosyntactic items in writing, and subsequently analysed in relation to linguistic frameworks associated with conversation/discourse analysis and pragmatics. Macro-analytic phenomena include social categories such as age, ethnicity and gender or social partitioning and associated cultural values such as rich and poor, citizen and alien. The interconnection between the micro- and macro-phenomena is an essential one, in that the micro-order is neither autonomous nor independent of the macro-order but rather embedded within it. The wider sociocultural contexts within which indexicality is marked is as important as the individual or sets of linguistic variables themselves. The contexts in which micro-phenomena occur, while being embedded within the wider macro-order, can be said to be mediated through intermediate or mezzo-analytic contexts and phenomena (Fairclough 1995; Androutsopoulos 2010).

Och's (1992) theory of indexicality, although related specifically to gender, shares many similarities with that of Silverstein. Och writes that the relationship between language and gender 'is constituted and mediated by the relation of language to stances, social acts, social activities and other constructs' (1992: 337). The same can also be said of the relationship between language and any social category, since arguably they are all constituted and mediated in and through discourse. As Och goes on to point out, anthropological and sociological studies of language assume that (a) language across a whole range of social contexts varies in systematic ways that can be studied in relation to their linguistic meaning, and (b) variation is part of the meaning indexed by linguistic structures and gives rise to social meaning. Thus, two or more phonological variants of the same word such as a long /ɑː/ or short /a/ in a word such as *bath* may share the identical referent of the word *bath* but convey different social meanings. In this case, in the UK, the long /ɑː/ has long been associated with being from the South and more 'posh' and middle class than the short /a/, which is associated with being from the North and working class.

Och also says that competent members of any community interpret such meanings unconsciously as part of the processes of socialisation. However, dialect features can also be drawn upon in deliberate, self-conscious ways to enact and evoke particular social meanings, such as in the cartoons discussed in this chapter, that also point to people's acute awareness of socialisation processes. Thus, while earlier sociolinguistic research correlated dialect use with non-linguistic variables such as social class, changes in social organisation and structure from the mid twentieth century onwards have led to this correlation being loosened and weakened. Increased educational opportunity and social mobility have led to a widening of the middle classes and a shrinking of the working classes (Savage *et al.* 2013) and a corresponding dialect levelling across all regions of the UK. At the same time, there is a sense in which people do not wish to lose sight of their working-class backgrounds and regional identity (Clark 2019), and writing in dialect creates a space where this can be done.

Writing in dialect can thus index a geographic place, an industrial working-class family history and a middle-class present at one and the same time. Such indexical use can function to trigger an association with a place, its largely working-class culture and industrial heritage. Enregistered features thus may also stand in place of the dialect as a whole. In this way, an urban working-class identity once manifested through manual labour has, in contemporary post-industrial times, transferred to language instead. The closer to family and home, the greater the use of regional accent and dialect; the further away or more public the context, such as work and work-related functions beyond the immediate region, the less they may feature and disappear altogether, or not (Clark 2019). It is thus no accident that writing in dialect such as that in the Staffordshire Potteries cartoons discussed below is found most in writing that is published locally, by local presses and newspapers for a local audience (see Honeybone and Maguire, this volume, for some further consideration of the localness of dialect writing).

While indexicality refers to general processes and stages of linguistic awareness and reflexivity, Agha's (2005) concept of 'enregisterment' refers to the specific forms used in discourse. Specific regional forms are enregistered to mark a sense of place identity and dislocated from social immobility. Enregistered forms – particularly in writing – are thus drawn from highly codified lists to perform local identity, often drawn upon in comic, mocking, ironic or semi-serious ways to undercut dominant ideologies linked to linguistic and social hierarchies. Often, writing in dialect links dialect to place while also subverting the ways in which the social stereotypes they enact are represented by dialect itself. Furthermore, dialect use often juxtaposes the norms and values of those 'outside' the community – in terms of both social class and geographic distance – with those 'within' it, thereby identifying with a cultural and social normativity which may be at odds with those from 'outside' it. They do this in ways which aim to subvert ideologies of social class and linguistic 'correctness', through the use of the very phenomenon which is stigmatised: enregistered forms of the dialect itself (Clark 2013b, 2019). This phenomenon can be accounted for through the Bakhtinian concept of *double-voicing*, discussed in the next section.

5.4. Bakhtin and the Concept of Double-Voicing

Bakhtin, writing in his essay *The Dialogic Imagination*, makes the point that '[a] common unitary language is a system of linguistic norms. But these norms do not constitute an abstract imperative; they are rather the generative forces of linguistic life' (1981: 61). In other words, the norms that constitute a standard form of a language and its related sociolect such as English, and as discussed above, are not intrinsic to the language itself. Rather, they have developed over a long period of time, supported by mediated hegemonic practices and regulated and reproduced through education, the media, publishing and so on. In contrast to the concept of unitary language, Bakhtin goes on to say that:

> At any given moment in its evolution, language is stratified not only into linguistic dialects in the strictest sense of the word ... but also ... into languages that are socio-ideological: languages of social groups, 'professional' and 'generic' languages; languages of generations and so forth. (1981: 271–2)

Although Bakhtin was concerned with literary representations of language in the novel, his concept of unitary language is a useful one here in that it underlines the ways in which language varieties are associated with different social groups with different ideological perspectives. The term Bakhtin uses for the multiplicity of language varieties is *heteroglossia*. He argues that any language exists in a state of continual tension between the hegemonic forces that promote unity in a language, which he terms *monoglossia*, and the multiplicity of dialects of which it is actually comprised. Regional dialects and sociolects that comprise a language such as English, then, are in a constant interplay of tension of which the performers and writers discussed in the chapters of this book are perfectly aware and which they exploit to the full in their performances and written texts.

Bakhtin also makes the point that utterances may have several *voices*, in so far as there can be a speaker's or writer's voice, the voice of someone referred to within the utterance, the voice of another on whose behalf a message is being relayed and so on. In this way, the voices of any speaker/writer and that of others can be blended in the course of any utterance and become part of the social meaning indexed as part of it. Bakhtin calls this phenomenon *double-voiced discourse*. Although Bakhtin considered this concept in relation to the study of drama and literature, he was also keenly aware of the ways in which double-voiced discourse can also occur in the day-to-day speech of our ordinary lives, and he often related the language of literature to that of everyday speech genres. Double-voicing is thus to do with identifying different semantic intentions uttered by the same speaker or writer, and is to be found within all forms of cultural production whether literate or non-literate, highbrow or popular, verbal and non-verbal.

Double-voicing can thus also be thought of in terms of multi-voicing, since double-voicing implies a binary relationship between two discourses, when in fact Bakhtin's concept of heteroglossia and others such as polyphony point to plural or multi-voiced dimensions of discourse. More relevant, perhaps, is the concept of polyphony in relation to heteroglossia and the power issues implicit therein. Often, writing in dialect draws upon comedy and humour, and cartoons, of course, exemplify this. Again, turning to Bakhtin, and also to Burke ([1937] 1959), provides further theoretical framing for the discussion of dialect use in cartoons.

5.5. Cartoons, Humour, the Burlesque, Carnivalesque and Dialect

In general, writing that draws upon dialect use in the representation of speech such as the cartoons discussed below tend to be dubbed 'working class', in opposition to those where representation of speech is written in Standard English and thus 'middle class'. Such a distinction serves to isolate the dialogue in a text unnecessarily from its broader sociological context, and monologises that which is essentially dialogic. However, speaking or writing in dialect can be viewed as a direct challenge to conventional assumptions about the ways in which Standard English mediates the world. Writing that employs dialect mediates the world in a different way and through a different social lens than that written (or indeed spoken) entirely in Standard English. Rather than dubbing such writing 'working class', it can be viewed in terms of not only Bakhtin's concept of the *carnivalesque* (1984) but also Burke's (1937/1959) notion of *burlesque* and the corresponding *frames* of acceptance and rejection.

One very obvious way in which cartoonists subvert dominant ideologies in their cartoons is through the use of humour. Linguistically oriented theories of humour focus particularly upon ambiguity and bi-sociation. As Goatly (2012: 21) points out, ambiguity has long been recognised as essential for most kinds of humour and bi-sociation stresses the incongruent nature of humour. He cites the work of Attardo (2001) where a situation or an idea is represented and intended to be perceived in two self-consistent but habitually incompatible frames of reference. These frames are also referred to as 'scripts' or 'schemas', in relation to the ways in which we store stereotypical knowledge about events, actions and beliefs in and about the world. Humour more often than not involves telling jokes, the structure of which includes a setup, an incongruity and a resolution, in which a disjunctor or punchline introduces an incongruity (Goatly 2012: 22).

Tsakona (2008) also refers to Attardo in saying that humour results from full or partial overlap of two different and incompatible scripts (discussed further below) being activated in any one cartoon or series of cartoons. In cartoons, humour is constructed linguistically through the opposition created by a jab line and a punchline, both of which serve different functions. Pictorial elements of a cartoon play a supporting role by providing a background to the humorous utterance. In the cartoons that follow the orthography of Standard English in representing speech, linguistic form is taken for granted and assumed to be unproblematic. Drawing upon dialect in the representation of such utterances serves to disrupt reading, in that it makes it far more difficult to decode the utterances. Decoding relies upon and presupposes a knowledge of the cultural and social information both the utterances and pictorial elements in any cartoon exploit, for the production of humour.

The cartoons discussed below also accord with Bakhtin's concept of the carnivalesque about which he wrote in relation to his work on the novelists Rabelais and Dostoevsky. In these works, Bakhtin emphasises the tradition of folk humour in the grotesque aspects of Rabelais' writing which he traces to a 'folk spirit' that is an anti-authoritarian, dissident and subversive strand of medieval and Renaissance culture that found expression in vents like Bacchanalian excess, May Day celebrations and working-class riots. The multi-voicedness Bakhtin attributes to the carnival folk spirit can be seen to run contrary to the monologic discourse of authority that emanates from the standard language of the 'centre of power', whether that be the Church, the Law or, in Bakhtin's case, the excesses of Stalinist political oppression. As Scott (2016: 319) writes: 'Against this official language of the centre arises a Babel-like cacophony of voices and discourses which compete with and feed from each other in a complex and ever-evolving discoursal system.' In Saussurean terms, Scott goes on to say, carnival can be viewed as both a signifier and a signified. It can be the object of representation and, more crucially, its means: the sketch *and* its narrative method.

Drawing attention to dialect, or in literary terms the demotic or vernacular, functions as a direct challenge to conventional assumptions about the ways in which writing in Standard English mediates the world. To dub writing in dialect as 'working class' is to isolate the text unnecessarily from its broader sociological context, and to monologise that which is essentially dialogic. Rather than being perceived as 'working class', such writing can be thought of as carnivalesque. The carnivalesque also pervades the cognitive dimension of any discursive act, most notably in relation to the shared sense of the ways in which discourse is framed between the producer and the receiver. Cartoons, made up of both visual and verbal representations, have the potential to exploit their essentially carnivalesque nature.

Two concepts that are central to the cognitive dimension of discourse analysis are those of 'frame' and 'perspective'. 'Frame' refers to 'the fact that discourse participants need a shared sense of the way in which discourse is framed; i.e., an overall sense of the function not discourse in the social situation' (Ensink and Sauer 2003: 4). 'Perspective' refers to the context of discourse which is necessarily displayed from some point of view. The use of the term *frame* as so defined is thus metaphorical, evoking a spatial context such as the separation of a painting by a literal frame, and also structures time, as where the opening and closing of a curtain or use of music constitutes the frame in which theatrical performance is perceived in time and separated from events that occurred before and after. The concept of frame thus accounts for the human need to set up structural understandings of the ways in which the world functions (Fauconnier and Sweetser 1996).

Ensink and Sauer distinguish between two different kinds of cognitive frames: knowledge and interactive, with perspective adding a third dimension. Knowledge frames are to do with what we already know about the world and how that knowledge is used in our understanding of it. The concept of frame, sometimes also called *schema* or *script*, as Ensink and Sauer say, 'accounts for coherence in knowledge as used for the representation and understanding of the world' (2003: 5). For instance, in the first set of cartoons given below, the flat caps worn by the characters are stereotypical of evocations of (mainly Northern) middle-aged working-class men, as are the curlers worn by the middle-aged female in the last cartoon, of (mainly Northern) working-class females. The visual elements intersect with the verbal, that in turn serve to disrupt our knowledge or schemas, associated with Standard English orthography, where respelling disrupts Sebba's zone of proximal meaning through, for example, splitting words normally spelt as one or depicting what would be two words in Standard English as one.

Interactive frames pertain to our behaviour in different social settings. Participating in interaction requires a shared sense of the kinds of activity in which participants are engaged, such as awareness of personal space, conventions associated with turn-taking, interruption, pauses, forms of address and so on. Such a use of the term frame has been applied to the analysis of interaction in many different situations and is similar to Goffman's (1981) concept of 'footing'. The concept of 'perspective', while similar to that of frame, is different from it in that it is concerned with the literary stylistic perspective of point of view (Simpson 1993). Implicit in any communicative act is the point of view or perspective that is being presented by interlocutors in speech (or authors and their readers in writing). Discoursal or textual aspects that contribute to the analysis of perspective, then, include use of active or passive voice; lexical choices that express different opinions and deixis: that is, the ways speakers and writers fit discourse to the time and place within which it is produced and, in the analysis of narrative, the point of view of the narrator. Concepts such as frame and perspective, then, add a cognitive dimension to the analysis of discourse that complements that of enregisterment.

An author whose work continues in dialogue with Bakhtin and also with the concept of frames is Kenneth Burke (1937/1959), whose work has been particularly influential in film, TV and video studies. Burke discusses how, in order to cope with the injustices of life in particular, people tend to position themselves in relation to the human condition or situation as being either 'friendly' or 'unfriendly'; accepting the universe or protesting against it, as acceptance and rejection. Burke draws upon the work of the American philosopher and psychologist William James, in whose view action and results did not stem from purely utilitarian principles. This is because to choose a lesser evil can be viewed as an act, if such a choice leads to the eventual opportunity to choose an even lesser evil. Burke (Burke 1937/1959: 3–4) writes that:

> In the face of anguish, injustice, disease, and death one adopts policies. One constructs his notion of the universe or history, and shapes attitudes in keeping. Be he poet or scientist, one defines the 'human situation' as amply as his imagination permits; then, with this ample definition in mind, he singles out certain functions or relationships as either friendly or unfriendly. If they are deemed friendly, he prepares himself to welcome them; if they are deemed unfriendly, he weights objective resistances against his own resources, to decide how far he can effectively go in combating them. … [C]all a man a villain, and you have the choice of either attacking or cringing. Call him mistaken, and you invite yourself to attempt setting him right.

Frames construct human perception discursively, as discussed in the section above. However, Burke divides the concept of frames into two, namely those of acceptance and rejection. He defines frames of acceptance as 'the more or less organised system of meanings by which a thinking man gauges the historical situation and adopts a role with relation to it' (1937/1959: 5). Frames of rejection are defined as taking their 'color from an attitude towards some reigning symbol of authority, stressing a *shift in the allegiance* to symbols of authority' (1937/1959: 21). Frames of acceptance correspond to the epic, tragedy and comedy, which includes carnivalesque, while those of rejection include burlesque, elegy, grotesque and satire. Individuals and groups are criticised through the burlesque frame by negatively caricaturing them rather than through challenging their argumentation. Burlesque thus criticises the behaviour of others and in ways that amplify their stupidity. Carnivalesque invites audiences to question established hierarchies; burlesque, by contrast, appears as a rejection of the dominant group's authority. The use of carnivalesque in verbal art releases audience members from communal norms and allows people to resist symbols of authority and power, thereby allowing the audience to think freely about the world; to laugh, and, through laughter, disrupt social order. Thus, while carnivalesque mocks a community as a whole, burlesque targets the individual. However, Burke acknowledges that the comic cannot of itself promote social change, and is thus only ever at heart a 'frame of acceptance'. It can, though, help people to understand or make sense of the modern world, acting as a coping mechanism, a means of understanding the current social order and anyone's individual place in it.

Cartoons that draw upon enregistered, double-voiced dialect serve much the same comic and satiric purposes as films in terms of mocking established hierarchies of social order in particular. The cartoons discussed below illustrate some of the ways in which cartoonists draw upon frames and references in burlesque and carnivalesque ways, subverting dominant ideologies not only through the use of humour, but also that of dialect, to revert and subvert the dominant social order and their underlying ideologies. Jaffe (2012: 221) also makes the point that non-standard spellings have a great deal of communicative potential, in that they operate at a visual graphic level and are indexically associated with sociolinguistic difference. Aligning this visual graphic level with the illustrative backgrounds against which they are set has the potential to be subversive, by calling into question dominant language ideologies and the social hierarchy in which they are embedded.

5.6. The Staffordshire Potteries and Its Cartoons

The Staffordshire Potteries is a region that lies in the north of the West Midlands county of Staffordshire, and thus at the most northern end of the West Midlands. The regional pronunciation of *North Staffordshire* is enregistered in writing as *North Staffy Cher*, where *North* is standard, and *Staffordshire* is split into two words: *Staffy* for *Stafford* and *Cher* for *shire*. The region brings together what were once originally six separate towns, namely Hanley, Fenton, Longton, Burslem, Tunstall and Stoke. These six towns were formed into the single county borough of Stoke-on-Trent in 1910, and awarded city status in 1925. Until the 1970s, the major employment of the region centred on coal mining, steel, the railways and, distinctive to the region, pottery. The creation of the canal network in the nineteenth century meant that china clay could be imported from Cornwall to the potteries founded in the region, most notably for the production of fine 'creamware'. Like many other industrial regions of the UK, since the 1970s the Potteries region has suffered post-industrial decline as a result of the loss of manufacturing. Like many other regions of the West Midlands, it also has its distinctive dialect and accent, which in the Potteries straddles the boundaries between the West Midlands and Northern regions and its isoglosses. Like other Northern dialects, that of the Potteries has a short /a/ in BATH and TRAP (in relation to Wells' 1982 keywords and lexical sets), which indicates that it is a Northern variety, as does the lack of any distinction in the vowel sounds of words such as FOOT and STRUT.

Other features, though, share characteristics of West Midlands dialects, such as <mon> for *man*; the use of <her> for *she* and the use of <-st> ending, as in *thee bist, thee cost, thee hast*. Levitt (1968) has identified other features such as the <oa> in words such as *boat, throat, coal* realised as [ʊ] which can be spelt as *boot, throot, cool*; the vowel sound in *meat, key, seem, piece* is realised as [ei], giving *mate, kaye, same, pace*; the <ou> in tokens such as *about, shout, cloud* is realised as [ai], as in *abite, shite* and *clide*. Conversely, tokens such as *there* or *where* are realised as *theyere* or *weyer* and *door* and *floor* as *dooer* and *flooer*. Such a feature indicates that this dialect is further north in character than those found in other West Midlands regions further south. This is not surprising given that Staffordshire is situated to the north of the West Midlands, but it does indicate the likely boundary of this feature. A further feature also identified by Levitt is the vocalisation of /l/ in words such as *ball*, which is pronounced with the usual GOAT vowel [oʊ], to give *bow*, and *oud* in place of *old*. With the Black Country, the Staffordshire Potteries dialect shares the retention of a back vowel in words such as *mon* (for *man*), *hond* (for *hand*, often with the h dropped to give *_ond*) and *bonk* (for *bank*).

Like dialect writing in other regions in the West Midlands, North Staffy Cher writing in dialect appears mainly in publications printed by local presses and in local newspapers, aimed at a local readership, as in the case of the cartoons discussed below. These cartoons, as with other types of dialect writing such as narrative stories, draw upon the features identified above in their orthographic representation of the Potteries dialect and accent. As cartoons, the verbal elements are given as spoken, and therefore as a form of metaphoric code, and without any kind of situational anchoring that might be found in other kinds of writing, such as a verbal process/reporting verb like *said Jabeez* that might appear in a narrative story. Alan Povey and Andy Ridler wrote a series of cartoon booklets published in the 1970s, illustrated by Don Turner, one of which is called *Arfur Tow Crate in Staffy Cher* (published in 1973). Povey was born in Stoke on Trent in the 1930s, hailing from a Potteries background; Ridler was born in Bristol in the 1950s and began working at BBC Radio Stoke in the 1970s, while Don Turner was also born in Stoke on Trent. The booklet is a glossary of North Staffy Cher dialect, with the glossary appearing on the right-hand page and a cartoon on the left-hand page.

A distinctive feature of dialect representation through orthography in the cartoons is the disruption of what in Standard English appear as either a single lexical item split into two, or two lexical items rolled into one. The title of the book of cartoons, *Arfur Tow Crate in Staffy Cher*, translates in Standard English to *How to Talk Right in Staffordshire. Arfur* is one word when in Standard English it is two, *how to*, but also doubles as the beginning of *tow crate* which is *talk right*, and *Staffy Cher* are two words where in Standard English it would be one: *Staffordshire*. The only item represented in standard orthography is *in*. Sebba (2012: 43) has made the point that variation in the spelling of individual words is subject to linguistic limitations. He illustrates this with the word *dog*. The spelling <dog> has three letters which reflect its pronunciation. However, there are possible variations to this such as <dogg> which still conforms to the conventions of English in surnames such as *Clegg* and *Rigg* and which the rapper Snoop Dogg also uses. One might inject humour into the spelling by calling a German Shepherd <dög>, with the use of the umlaut invoking 'foreignness', particularly Germanness. At some point, however, variants of a word like <dog> become unintelligible. A spelling such as <Dd@gG> would appear to be losing the ability to represent the word *dog* in anything but a highly localised and ecologised context. Sebba uses the concept of the zone of social meaning to explain this phenomenon. As Sebba (2012: 6–7) says:

> The concept of the *zone of social meaning* refers to the fact that in order to be socially meaningful, an item must be different from some element of the repertoire in a specific way, but also be sufficiently similar that it can be *recognised* as a variant of, or alternative to, that thing.

Sebba's concept of the zone of social meaning is similar to that of *abstand*: the distance between representation of a dialect and the reference variety that serves as a norm. In the cartoons, the zone of social meaning is stretched to its limits and beyond, since not only does one need to be familiar with the North Staffordshire dialect to decode the writing in the cartoons, but also be cognisant of the changing of lexical boundaries in and between words in their representation. *Abstand* is thus at as great a distance as it could arguably possibly be. Sebba also points out that where the potential for variation exists, it is usually exploited and forms an increasingly integral part of the linguistic

Figure 5.1 A cartoon from Povey, Ridler and Turner (1973)

landscapes that surround us. Cartoons make it possible for this evocation of a linguistic landscape to intersect and be part of a visual landscape. In the first cartoon considered here, reproduced as Figure 5.1, taken from Povey *et al.* (1973), a typical mid-twentieth-century Stoke on Trent urban landscape is evoked. A busy main road rises uphill, congested with traffic, bridging over a road at ground level, with terraced housing visible on the right, an iconic large Midlands roundabout with signs to a retail park on the left, and the trees representing nearby countryside visible. This scene is in many ways an iconic representation of many an industrial West Midlands town, crowded with buses, lorries, cars, interspersed with large roundabouts (called locally *islands*), with raised roads crossing ones at ground level, terraced houses cheek by jowl with roads and retail parks encroaching on the surrounding countryside. It sets the background for the men that feature in the cartoon, where two are in conversation and one is struggling up the hill with a speech bubble that is indecipherable.

The jab line of *Wonder way eats code th'* ***Dee*** *Road* '(I) wonder why it's called the Day/D Road' of the first speech bubble on the left is met with the punchline: *Dunner rex may! Shoes daz much at* ***nate*** *ozzy tizz owe Dee!* 'Don't ask me! It's used as much at night as it is all day!' The Potteries pronunciation of the letter *D* and the word *day* is the same: [diː]. The pun of the D road being used as much at night as in the day evokes a self-reflexive, self-deprecating humour that is typical of the region. Under the road numbering system in the UK, a D road is a road destination, and also represents the Roman numeral 500. The D road referred to in the cartoon is numbered on maps as the A500, which runs through the Potteries region and continues west to Nantwich in Cheshire. Built in 1962 as a link between Stoke on Trent and the M6 motorway, it is a highly congested route. One also has to have an understanding of the Staffy Cher Potteries dialect, and the vowel sounds characteristic of it, to stand any chance of interpreting the speech bubbles. It thus serves to reverse commonly held beliefs about the nature of literacy, in that only those conversant with the Potteries dialect, rather than with Standard English, are able to stand any chance of decoding it. And in order to do so, one also has to be conversant with the norms of Standard English to stand any chance of decoding. Here, dialect speakers are the 'in group', and Standard English ones the 'out group'.

In total, the two lines comprise 19 lexical items, of which 15 are respelt, with 11 phonologically based respellings and one morphosyntactic dialect form. Only four words are represented in Standard English orthography: *wonder*, *road*, *much*, *at*.

Speaker 1
PHONOLOGY
Dialect respelling

way	'why'
eats	'it's'
code	'called'
dee	'day/D'

Allegro speech

th'	'the'[1]

Speaker 2
MORPHOSYNTAX

dunner	'don't'

SPLITTING WORDS/RUNNING WORDS TOGETHER

shoes	'it's use(d as)'
ozzy	'as i(t)'

PHONOLOGY
Dialect respelling

rex	'ask'

may	'me'
nate	'night'
tizz	'(i)t is'
owe	'all'
dee	'day'
Eye dialect	
daz	'(it's use)d as'

In the second cartoon considered here, given in Figure 5.2, the degree of *abstand* created by the dialect respelling is even greater than in the cartoon discussed above. Here, the municipal sign *Forest Park* indicates the location as Hanley, one of the original six Potteries towns. Forest Park is a large, green open space in the centre of the Stoke region. It was originally one of the deepest coal pits in the North Staffordshire coalfield which, after its closure, was cleared and converted into Hanley Forest Park. The cartoon represents the landscape before it was cleared, with the pit banks (called *bonks*) in the background, and skeletal trees representing a desolate landscape that lends an ironic element to the naming of the area as being both a forest and a park,

Figure 5.2 A cartoon from Povey, Ridler and Turner (1973)

when in fact it is neither. In the foreground, a man in summer dress asks a question of another, older man sitting on a bench.

The jab line: *Are anna bin in theer be fur, feyther. Is thee any whale danny mulls a bite?* 'I haven't been in there before, father. Are there any wild animals about?' is met with the punchline: *Not as are no on ark! Coupler car tosses backer them tray sun erda mine teen shape topath pit bonk!* 'None that are not on the ark! (A) couple of carthorses at the back of those trees and a herd of mountain sheep at the top of the pit bank'.

In this cartoon, there are 36 lexical items, of which all but two are respelt, *in*, *is*, with information values that, taken altogether, are more lexical and morphosyntactic as well as phonological:

Speaker 1
PHONOLOGY
Dialect respelling

are	'I'
bin	'been'
theer	'there'
feythur	'father'
thee	'there'

SPLITTING WORDS/RUNNING WORDS TOGETHER

be fur	'before'
whale danny mulls	'wild animals'
a bite	'about'

MORPHOSYNTAX

anna	'haven't'

Speaker 2
PHONOLOGY
Dialect respelling

shape	'sheep'
bonk	'bank'

SPLITTING WORDS/RUNNING WORDS TOGETHER

coupler	'a couple of'
car tosses	'cart horses'
backer	'at the back of'
tray sun	'trees and'
erda	'a herd of'
mine teen	'mountain'
topath	'at the top of'

MORPHOSYNTAX

them	'those'

In this cartoon, the cartoonists play with the boundaries between morphology, syntax and phonology that serve to create even greater *abstand*: *be fur* is spelt as two separate words, *car tosses* in place of *carthorses*, with the /t/ of *cart* forming the first letter of the second lexical item, rather than the last letter of the first. The same occurs in *mine teen* for *mountain*, where the two lexical items in dialect have very different meanings in Standard English, all of which, taken together, serve to further disrupt reading and decoding. As with the first cartoon, its appeal is to literate speakers who have a working knowledge of the dialect, which places others at a disadvantage and as outsiders, to whom the Staffordshire dialect is rendered incomprehensible. In this way, cartoonists such as Povey and Ridler disrupt the ideological underpinnings of the social status accorded to regional dialects vis-à-vis Standard English.

While Povey, Ridler and Turner's cartoon booklets are no longer in print, another local cartoonist and their contemporary is Dave Follows, who became a professional and celebrated cartoonist. Follows was born in the Staffordshire county town of Stafford in 1941 and lived there all his life. He left school at fifteen and began his career as a cartoonist initially as an amateur, making the transition to professional cartoonist in 1973. His work appeared in newspapers, comics and magazines all over the world, including the *Sunday Times* supplement *Funday Times* and the *Buster* comic. He won a Humorous Comic Cartoonist of the Year award in 1983 for his 'wonder wellies' cartoons that featured in *Buster*. His work also appeared in more than twenty local newspapers, one of which was the *North Staffordshire Evening Sentinel*, for which he wrote a regular series of cartoon strips from 1985 to 2003 (the year he died) called *May un Mar Lady* ('Me and My Lady'), later republished in the same paper in 2004 and again in 2015. He also has a website dedicated to his work: http://www.davefollows.com. The third cartoon considered here, from Follows, in given in Figure 5.3.

Figure 5.3 A cartoon from Dave Follows

Translated, the strip reads:

> It's no good, I can't get to sleep.
> Are you worrying about the rent being three weeks overdue, the final demand for the rates and how we're going to pay next month's car instalment?
> No ... there's a rumour that the Potters Arms is going to close down!

In this strip, which is typical of Follows' work, respellings are made entirely in relation to phonology – unlike Povey and Ridler's cartoons – and thus arguably easier to decode. Again, respelling is largely to mimic vowel sounds as discussed above, such as *neow*, *slayp*, *abite*, *bayin*, *reetes*, *gooin*, *peey*, *cleowse*. The convention of using an apostrophe for missing letters is also used by Follows, which further aids decoding. There is also no lexical/morphosyntactic splitting of the kind found in Povey and Ridler's cartoons, and this makes it more likely to appeal more to the general readership of the newspaper, targeted at a local audience.

The visual elements of the cartoon are of the dark of night, illuminated in the last cartoon by the bedside light that the female half of the couple switches on. Here, stereotypical representation of gender is exemplified through the man and woman lying side by side in bed, with her worries centring upon having enough money to pay household bills and his upon his local public house closing down. Follows' cartoon series thus evokes the domestic side of working-class life, regionalised within the local, Potteries region.

5.7. Conclusion

Povey and Ridler seem to strive to make their representation of utterances in the Potteries dialect as close to their spoken pronunciation as possible through the use of respellings to index regional, Staffy Cher identities. Respellings serve two functions: firstly, they highlight the *abstand*: that is, the distance between representation of a dialect and the reference variety which serves as the norm, and secondly, they represent metaphoric code-switching to capture linguistic evocations of localness, indexing spaces and associated social types through double-voicing and stylisation. In the Povey, Ridler and Turner cartoons, *abstand* is as far as it can possibly be, through the metaphoric code that indexes Staffy Cher men.

It is virtually impossible to decode the utterances in the cartoons without a working knowledge of the North Staffy Cher dialect. In Dave Follows' cartoons, the *abstand* is not so great, with the metaphoric code indexing a stereotypical middle-aged Staffy Cher married couple. Like Povey and Ridler's cartoons, humour in Follows' cartoons is used in enregistered, ironic, carnivalesque ways to evoke regional identities and sympathy on the part of readers to the speakers represented in them, indexing as they do many of the common tropes of working-class life, including the dialect through which they are expressed. The cartoons also frame the experience of working-class life as one of acceptance, where the normally unfriendly frustrations of make-do open spaces, congested roads and making ends meet are rendered, through humour, as friendly. Dialect writing in cartoons, then, is virtually always dialogic, and challenges conventional assumptions about the ways in which Standard English mediates the world. Writing that employs dialect such as in the cartoons discussed here mediates the world in a different way and through a different social lens than those spoken or written entirely in Standard English.

Note

1. In the reviewing process for this chapter, the question arose as to whether this spelling of the definite article as *th'* could be intended to represent Definite Article Reduction, a feature which is widespread in the North of England Reduction (see, for example, Jones 2002), and can involve the realisation of the definite article as [θ], which gets represented as *th'* in dialect writing. Ellis (1889) indicates that there is some DAR in north Staffordshire at the time that he is writing so it is possible that DAR is intended here, but several other linguists familiar with this variety have confirmed that DAR is not a feature that is found there now, and is not enregistered as a feature of the dialect, so it is interpreted as the 'fast speech' deletion of schwa, which is common and widespread in English, giving [ð].

References

Adams, Michael (2009), 'Enregisterment: A special issue', *American Speech*, 84:2, 115–17.

Agha, Asif (2003), 'The social life of cultural value', *Language and Communication*, 23, 231–73.

Agha, Asif (2005), 'Voice, footing, enregisterment', *Journal of Linguistic Anthropology*, 15:1, 1–5.

Agha, Asif (2007), *Language and Social Relations*, Cambridge: Cambridge University Press.

Androutsopoulos, Jannis (2010), 'The study of language and space in media discourse', in Peter Auer and Jürgen E. Schmidt (eds), *Language and Space: An International Handbook of Linguistic Variation, Volume I – Theory and Methods*, Berlin, New York: de Gruyter, pp. 740–58.

Attardo, Salvatore (2001), *Humorous Texts: A Semantic and Pragmatic Analysis*, Berlin: Walter de Gruyter.

Bakhtin, Mikhail (1981), *The Dialogic Imagination*, Austin, TX: University of Texas Press.

Bakhtin, Mikhail (1984), *Problems of Dostoevsky's Poetics*, Minnesota: University of Minnesota Press.

Beal, Joan (2006), *Language and Region*, London: Routledge.

Beal, Joan (2009), 'Enregisterment, commodification and historical context: "Geordie" versus Sheffieldish"', *American Speech*, 84:2, 138–56.

Burke, Kenneth ([1937] 1959), *Attitudes towards History*, Berkeley, CA: University of California Press.

Clark, Urszula (2013a), *Language and Identity in Englishes*, London: Routledge.

Clark, Urszula (2013b), '"'*er's from off*': the indexicalisation and enregisterment of Black Country dialect', *American Speech*, 88:4, 441–66.

Clark, Urszula (2019), *Staging Language: Place and Identity in the Enactment, Performance and Representation of Regional Dialects*, New York, Berlin: Mouton de Gruyter.

Clark, Urszula and Esther Asprey (2013), *West Midlands English: Birmingham and the Black Country*, Edinburgh: Edinburgh University Press.

Ensink, Titus and Christoph Sauer (2003), 'Social-functional and cognitive approaches to discourse interpretation: the role of framing and perspective', in Titus Ensink and Christoph Sauer (eds), *Framing and Perspective in Discourse*, Amsterdam: John Benjamins.

Fairclough, Norman (1995), *Language and Power*, London: Longman.

Fouconnier, Giles and Eve Sweetser (1996), *Spaces, Worlds and Grammar*, Chicago: University of Chicago Press.

Goatly, Andrew (2012), *Meaning and Humour*, Cambridge: Cambridge University Press.

Goffman, Irving (1981), *Forms of Talk*, Oxford. Blackwell.

Honeybone, Patrick (2011), 'Variation and linguistic theory', in Warren Maguire and April McMahon (eds), *Analysing Variation in English*, Cambridge: Cambridge University Press, pp. 151–77.

Jaffe, Alexandra (2000), 'Non-standard orthography and non-standard speech', *Journal of Sociolinguistics*, 4:4, 497–513.

Jaffe, Alexandra (2012), 'Transcription in practice: nonstandard orthography', in Alexandra Jaffe, Jannis Androutsopoulos, Mark Sebba and Sally Johnson (eds), *Orthography as Social Action: Scripts, Spelling, Identity and Power*, Berlin and New York: de Gruyter Mouton, pp 203–224.

Johnson, Sally A. (2005), *Spelling Trouble? Language, Ideology and the Reform of German orthography*, Bristol: Multilingual Matters.

Johnstone, Barbara (2013), 'Ideology and discourse in the enregisterment of regional variation', in Peter Auer, Martin Hilpert, Anja Stockenbrock and Benedikt Szmrecsanyi (eds), *Space in Language and Linguistics: Geographical, Interactional and Cognitive Perspectives*, Berlin: Mouton de Gruyter, pp. 107–27.

Johnstone, Barbara (2016), 'Enregisterment: how linguistic items become linked with ways of speaking', *Language and Linguistics Compass*, 10, 632–43.

Jones, Mark (2002), 'The origin of Definite Article Reduction in northern English dialects: evidence from dialect allomorphy', *English Language and Linguistics*, 6, 325–45.

Levitt, John (1968), *North Staffordshire Speech*, Keele: University of Keele Press.

Och, Elinor (1992), 'Indexing gender', in Alessandro Duranti and Charles Goodwin (eds), *Re-thinking Context: Language as an Interactive Phenomenon*, Cambridge: Cambridge University Press, pp. 335–58.

Povey, Alan, Andy Ridler and Don Turner (1973), *Arfur Tow Crate in Staffy Cher*, Stoke on Trent: Ridler.

Preston, Dennis (1985), 'The Li'l Abner Syndrome: written representations of speech', *American Speech*, 60:1, 328–36.

Savage, M., N. Cunningham, M. Taylor, Y. Li, J. Hjlibrekker, B. Le Roux, S. Friedman and A. Miles (2013), 'A new model of social class? Findings from the BBC's great British class survey', *Sociology*, 47:2, 219–50.

Scott, Jeremy (2016), 'Midlands cadences: narrative voice in the work of Alan Sillitoe', *Language and Literature*, 25:4, 312–27.

Sebba, Mark (2007), *Spelling and Society: The Culture and Politics of Orthography around the World*, Cambridge: Cambridge University Press.

Sebba, Mark (2012), 'Orthography as social action: scripts, spelling, identity and power', in Alexandra Jaffe, Jannis Androutsopoulos, Mark Sebba and Sally Johnson (eds), *Orthography as Social Action: Scripts, Spelling, Identity and Power*, Berlin: Mouton de Gruyter, pp. 1–20.

Silverstein, Michael (1992), 'The indeterminancy of contextualization: when is enough enough?', in P. Auer and A. di Luzio (eds), *The Contextualization of Language*, Amsterdam: John Benjamins, pp. 55–76.

Silverstein, Michael (1993), 'Metapragmatic discourse and metapragmatic function', in J. A. Lucy (ed.), *Reflexive Language: Reported Speech and Metapragmatics*, Cambridge: Cambridge University Press, pp. 33–58.

Silverstein, Michael (2003), 'Indexical order and the dialectics of sociolinguistic life', *Language and Communication*, 23, 193–229.

Simpson, Paul (1993), *Language, Ideology and Point of View*, London: Routledge.

Tsakona, Villy (2008), 'Language and image interaction in cartoons: towards a multimodal theory of humor', *Journal of Pragmatics*, 41, 1171–88.

Turner, Graeme (2011), *Ordinary People and the Media: The Demotic Turn*, London: Sage.

Wells, John C. (1982), *Accents of English*, Cambridge: Cambridge University Press.

6

Russian Dolls and Dialect Literature: The Enregisterment of Nineteenth-Century 'Yorkshire' Dialects

Paul Cooper

6.1. The Enregisterment of 'Yorkshire' Dialect

In an interview with the BBC for their Voices dialect study, William Marshall, then a research student, discussed a perception of the embedded nature of identity and Yorkshire dialect. In discussing the dialects of the historical West Riding[1] (henceforth WR) of Yorkshire, he states: 'It's like a Russian doll – identities within identities. Within England, you're Yorkshire; within Yorkshire, you're West Riding; and within the West Riding you're maybe Bradford or Halifax; and within Halifax you're North Halifax … and it goes on and on!' (BBC 2008)

This notion of embedded regional identities in Yorkshire is also discussed by Beal (2009: 153), who notes that we can observe 'the embedding of a "Sheffield" identity in a broader "Yorkshire" one', and by Cooper (2013: 250) who discusses modern Yorkshire speakers' perception of multiple 'Yorkshire' dialects that are distinct from each other. Beal (2009: 153) goes on to note that, although the two cities of Sheffield in South Yorkshire and Newcastle upon Tyne (henceforth Newcastle) in the north-east have had similar developmental histories, particularly regarding industrialisation over the course of the nineteenth century, the existence of an established 'Yorkshire' variety and the lack of early branding of a 'Sheffield' variety on commodities like coffee mugs and tea towels has meant that while 'Sheffieldish' must share its associations with 'Yorkshire' dialect, 'Geordie' dialect has become explicitly associated with the north-east (see also Beal, this volume). Indeed, because of the explicit links between a repertoire of 'Geordie' dialect features and social values including the geographical location of Newcastle and the north-east, Beal argues that 'Geordie' is enregistered.

Enregisterment refers to the 'processes through which a linguistic repertoire becomes differentiable within a language as a socially recognised register of forms' (Agha 2003: 351). That is, speakers come to link certain language features with explicit social values which can include geographical region, social class, or more abstract concepts like correctness or friendliness. These links are created and maintained via speakers' transmission of ideas about dialects through metapragmatic discourse, or 'talk about talk' (Johnstone and Baumgardt 2004). This kind of discourse can include commentary on the language features of the dialect, where the dialect is spoken and by whom, what the attributes of those speakers are, what an exemplar speaker might look and sound like, and so on (see also Beal 2009; Remlinger 2009; Remlinger *et al.* 2009; Johnstone 2017). In many cases, enregistered repertoires are explicitly associated with a characterological figure or stereotypical identity. The enregistered repertoire of 'Yorkshire' dialect includes Definite Article Reduction (henceforth DAR), *nowt* 'nothing', *owt* 'anything', *summat* 'something', word-initial H-dropping, *reight* 'really', *sen* 'self' and *thee/tha* 'you/your', and has indexical links to social values like authenticity, intransigence, friendliness, sense of humour and the geographical location of Yorkshire along with notions of exemplar 'Yorkshire' speakers (Cooper 2017: 358–9).

Additionally, as Beal (2009: 147) goes on to note, there has been a conception of a 'Yorkshire' dialect since at least the nineteenth century. Cooper (2013: 266) identifies an enregistered 'Yorkshire' repertoire which shares many features with the modern repertoire, consisting of DAR, *sen* 'self', *nowt* 'nothing', *mun* 'must', *owd/oud* 'old', *gan/gang* 'to go' and *owt* 'anything'. This repertoire was identified firstly by analysing historical qualitative commentary from texts including prefatory material in dialect dictionaries and glossaries, travel writing and essays on particular dialects where writers discussed 'Yorkshire' features, their use and 'Yorkshire' dialect speakers. Indeed, Cooper (2013: 257–8) discusses the historical perception of 'Yorkshire' speakers as hospitable and plain-speaking, alongside discourses of authenticity and distinctiveness regarding their dialect. Secondly, dialect literature (henceforth DL), defined by Shorrocks (1996: 386; see also the chapters in this volume by Braber, Honeybone and Maguire, and Maguire) as texts written entirely in dialect and aimed primarily at a local audience, and literary dialect (henceforth LD), which is dialect represented in novels and plays and aimed at a wider audience than DL (Shorrocks 1996: 386), were surveyed to see which features were represented the most frequently and consistently. The repertoire was then validated by asking modern speakers to participate in an online survey (see Cooper 2013, 2016) designed to highlight how well textual material acts as a predictor of enregistered dialect features. The survey required respondents to provide 'Yorkshire' dialect features, then to rate how strongly they associated frequently and consistently occurring features in both the nineteenth-century data and in modern 'Yorkshire' DL and LD with Yorkshire. By comparing the 'Yorkshire' features speakers provided with the frequent and consistent features in the modern corpus data, we are able to see that textual data is a good indicator of which features speakers perceive as 'Yorkshire' dialect. We can therefore use data from the present to explain the past (Labov 1977) and suggest that where 'Yorkshire' features are similarly quantitatively frequent and consistent in historical textual data, those features would have likely been enregistered to nineteenth-century audiences. This analysis highlighted that such features occurred in 50 per cent or more of the corpus texts, where the percentage of tokens occurred in a proportional range of 40:60 and 90:10 DL:LD, and were discussed in 40 percent or more of the qualitative texts (see also Cooper 2015). I make use of these proportions in this chapter in the identification of individual 'Yorkshire' repertoires discussed below. Furthermore, although several of these enregistered 'Yorkshire' features (such as DAR, and non-standard respellings suggesting /l/-vocalisation cf. *owd/oud*) are discussed in Wales's (2010: 68–9) extensive survey of Northern English written forms where she notes their long-standing historical status and acknowledges both inconsistency and variation in written dialect representations, she only states that these features occur in Yorkshire with no additional geographical specificity or consideration of qualitative historical discussion. I argue here that we can observe systematic variation in written representations of nineteenth-century Yorkshire dialect and that this correlates with qualitative discussion of distinct 'Yorkshire' dialects.

We can also see that the 'Russian doll' relationship of 'Yorkshire' identities extends to distinct 'Yorkshire' dialects and that speakers have been aware of distinct enregistered 'Yorkshire' varieties since the nineteenth century. Indeed, Cooper (2013: 120) notes that some nineteenth-century writers explicitly state that the term 'Yorkshire' dialect is insufficient to describe the variation in the region, and there are many nineteenth-century texts which discuss the dialects of very localised areas in Yorkshire, such as Sheffield, Leeds, Whitby, and so on, as well as broader areas like the three historical Yorkshire Ridings (see also Beal and Cooper 2015: 45).

In the following sections I will discuss how dialect variation within Yorkshire was discussed in the nineteenth century and illustrate the ways in which specific dialect areas were defined (in terms of the other chapters in this volume, therefore, this chapter is most like that of Hodson in terms of the area covered). I then turn to a discussion of how these areas were perceived to differ from one another in terms of dialect differences. I address the issues of how individual 'Yorkshire' varieties were enregistered in nineteenth-century dialect writing and how distinct sub-'Yorkshire' repertoires can be identified using the framework for historical enregisterment set out in Cooper (2013). I adopt a quantitative methodology (similar in principle, but different in detail, to the chapters in this volume by Nini, Bailey, Guo and Grieve, and by Watson and Jensen).

6.2. Commentary on Nineteenth-Century 'Yorkshire' Variation

In addition to nineteenth-century texts that focused on a general 'Yorkshire' dialect, there are many examples of texts that sought to represent more localised varieties of 'Yorkshire' dialect. For example, Addy's (1888) *A Glossary of Words Used in the Neighbourhood of Sheffield* explicitly defines the city of Sheffield as an area in which specific words are used when compared to others. This implies that there are certain words that either distinguish Sheffield from other areas in Yorkshire, or that those words are particularly associated with the city. Further examples of this include 'On the Dialect of Cleveland' (Atkinson 1867), where Cleveland is an area in what was the North Riding (henceforth NR) of Yorkshire in the nineteenth century, and *The Folk Speech of East Yorkshire* (Nicholson 1889). Following Honeybone and Watson (2013: 335), who state that such material 'actually promotes the connection between linguistic features and local meaning in the first place', we can see that texts like these are evidence of speakers' explicit linking of language with place.

Many of these texts also provide commentary on the varieties they discuss, such as the anonymous *Dictionary of the Dialect of Batley* (1860: 3), where Batley is a small industrialised town in the WR. The preface to this text demonstrates links between the dialect and certain social values. The author states of Batley dialect that:

> [t]ruly curious and utterly unintelligible to a stranger, are many of the words in vernacular use in our district – but most of them are only curious and unintelligible, because good old English has been gradually driven out of common use by innovations of self-applauded grammarians, and the progress of what in nine cases out of ten, is most preposterously called modern refinement and improvement. We shall occupy a few pages by the exhibition of some of the most remarkable of these distinctive provincialisms, as we think our communications will neither be unamusing nor uninstructive to our readers.

This kind of commentary explicitly illustrates the 'distinctive' nature of the Batley dialect, suggesting that this variety is different to other varieties of English, possibly even other 'Yorkshire' varieties. This is also hinted at in the description of the variety as being 'utterly unintelligible to a stranger', where this could indicate someone who is either not from Yorkshire, or possibly even not from Batley. In other words, this author is directly linking the language features listed in his dictionary with Batley, and imbuing them with the social values of being both 'distinctive' and 'unintelligible' to outsiders. Assuming the text is aimed at local Batley speakers, we can infer a positive view of the dialect from this description based on Johnstone *et al.* (2006: 96), who discuss the role of this kind of metapragmatic discourse in the enregisterment of local dialects, illustrating how they can be associated with regional identity and pride (see also Hermeston, this volume).

6.2.1. Nineteenth-Century 'Yorkshire' Dialect Areas

Although the anonymous writer of the Batley dialect dictionary does not elaborate on the differences between that dialect and others within Yorkshire, Blakeborough (1898: 64–5) notes that 'Yorkshire' dialect is not the same throughout the county:

> Please bear in mind that the North and East Ridings dialectally are the same. Certainly some few words may have been retained or dropped, as the case may be, in each Riding, but the pronunciation is identical, or at least almost so. These remarks, however, do not hold good when applied to the West Riding. Ripon (my native place) and Leeds are not very far distant, only twenty-six miles. Ripon, although in the West Riding, is to all intents dialectically in the North, but by the time you have travelled the twenty-six miles all is changed – you have as it were crossed the line.

Here we can see a distinct demarcation between the north-eastern and south-western parts of Yorkshire, and a divide which bears a resemblance to Wakelin's (1972: 102–3) isogloss bundle which begins 'roughly at the mouth of the Humber and passing (roughly) along the Ouse and Wharfe valleys and out of Lancashire via the Lune and Ribble valleys'. This line, also known as the Humber–Lune/Ribble line has, as Ihalainen (1994: 219) notes, 'until quite recently, been the most important linguistic border in England, separating the north from the rest of the country'. North of this line we may hear older speakers demonstrating pronunciations like '/kuəl/ "coal" and /lɪəf/ "loaf" and /kuː/ "cow"' (Wales 2006: 48). Blakeborough (1898: 477) later goes on to discuss the perceived differences in pronunciation between the NR and WR, giving examples of the same sentence rendered in both 'Yorkshire' varieties:

> The North and West Riding dialects widely differ not only as to vocabulary, but in drawl and intonation; e.g. take the following sentences:–
>
> NORTH RIDING. Noo, mun, wheear's ta gahin' teeah? Ah's gahin' doon t' toon.[2]
>
> WEST RIDING. Nah, lad, whor's ta bahn tew? Ah w' bahn dahn t' tahn.

Some of the specific differences he illustrates here include representations of 'now', 'down' and 'town' which suggest a pronunciation of [uː] in the NR and a pronunciation of [ɑː] in the WR, following Wright's (1892: 220) description of similar pronunciations in his Windhill[3] grammar, where he describes the vowel in 'down' as the same as in 'father' (see also Cooper 2013: 26). This distinction is also noted by Wakelin (1972: 102) as being marked by the Humber–Lune/Ribble line. Moreover, Trudgill (1999: 37) remarks that pronunciations like [kuː] for 'cow' are 'found in Traditional Dialects in northern England' and that 'this particular feature extends just over the river Humber'. Trudgill (2004: 18–19) goes on to state that traditional dialects are characteristically associated with older speakers and traditional Yorkshire pronunciations can include 'long', 'wrong' and 'song' as *lang*, *wrang* and *sang*, whereas 'night', 'light' and 'right' can be *neet*, *leet* and *reet*, as discussed further below. In addition, Beal (2010: 12) draws a parallel between Trudgill's traditional dialects and the dialect areas observed in the nineteenth century by Ellis, thereby suggesting that Blakeborough's representations may well have been recognised as largely accurate to a nineteenth-century audience.

Analysis of these 'commentary' texts illustrated frequent and consistent definition of certain dialect areas within Yorkshire. Several also highlight awareness of individual and specific differences between these areas. These distinctions frequently align with language variation observed in contemporary dialect studies, such as Ellis (1890: 84) who noted that there are nine varieties of Yorkshire dialect in his Eastern North Midland division at Huddersfield, Halifax, Keighley, Bradford, Leeds, Dewsbury, Rotherham, Sheffield and Doncaster. Summarising Ellis's data, we can see that some of the main differences between the 'Yorkshire' varieties in the North Midland division includes Huddersfield and Halifax having *oo* for 'her' where the others have *shoo*. The only exception is Doncaster, which is listed as having *shee*. The Doncaster pronunciation of 'eyes' is given as *aayz*, as opposed to the others, which have either *een* or *in*. In his East Northern division, which Ellis states 'comprises most of the North and East Ridings' of Yorkshire, he notes that there is 'a wonderful uniformity of pronunciation' (1890: 108), particularly when compared with Craven in the northern part of the WR, in his West Northern division. Ellis explains that the pronunciations of 'name', 'clothes', 'home' distinguish between these parts of Yorkshire as in the East Northern division, he gives *ni·ŭm*, *tli·ŭz*, *i·ŭm*, as opposed to *nĭaam*, *klĭaaz*, *hĭaaĭm* in the West Northern. I suggest that 'home' was likely pronounced as [ɪəm] in the former division and either as [hjɑːm] or [hjaːm] in the latter. This is based on Ellis's explanation of his *aa* transcription where he defines several different variants including aa^1, which is described as a pronunciation 'short of a in father'; aa^2 as a 'broader form of aa^1'; and aa^4 which is 'a form of *aa* noted in D31 … lying very near to *aa*[2], but not quite so deep; here it is not generally distinguished from *aa*[1]' (Ellis 1890: xv), where D31 is Ellis's West Northern division. We can therefore see a distinction being made by Ellis here that accounts for differences between the North, East and West Ridings, and between the northern and southern parts of the WR, echoing Blakeborough's comment about Ripon (situated just to the east of the Yorkshire Dales, where Craven is located).

We can also see that within the WR, Sheffield, Leeds and Halifax are among the most frequently and consistently defined and discussed areas. This is likely due to the dramatic increases in population in industrialised areas of Yorkshire over the course of the nineteenth century. Singleton (1970: 45) states that during the Industrial Revolution, areas of the WR like Sheffield evolved from a 'collection of some hundreds of small craft workshops concentrating mainly on cutlery to a group of mammoth companies involved in the manufacture of such products as steel plates, rails and girders'. As a result, urban populations in the WR grew quickly as people moved into the cities to work in these new and rapidly developing industries, and as Wright (1986: 18) states with regard to population numbers in Leeds and Bradford: 'their populations of 172,000 and 104,000, dominated the West Riding textile area'. These increases in population appear to have led to conceptions of localised areas with distinct language varieties, as we can see in commentary on industrialised areas such as Halifax (Crossland 1899) and Sheffield. For example, Addy (1888: viii) discusses the distinct nature of the Sheffield dialect, and states that ten miles 'to the south of Sheffield, and especially to the south-west of that town, the dialect begins to change'. He later stresses the differences between the dialects of Sheffield and Derbyshire when he discusses an example of an old cutler who had moved as a boy from Derbyshire to Crookes in Sheffield and explains that 'he lived there many months before he could converse with people whose dialect differed so essentially from his own' (Addy 1888: viii). Although this gives us no direct insight into the language differences between Sheffield and other areas of Yorkshire, it reinforces the idea that Sheffield had a dialect which was distinctive. Additionally, Banks (1865: iii) states in his Wakefield glossary that several of the words he lists are likely not unique to that area. He notes that speakers from WR towns like 'Barnsley, Ossett, Batley, Leeds, or Bradford' would probably be familiar with them too. However, he delineates a clear divide between the aforementioned areas and locations that were outside the WR such as Whitby, Cleveland, Muker or Hawes, all in the NR, where Banks states that his words would not be understood. This example again illustrates that there was a perceptual divide between the dialects of the three ridings in the nineteenth century. It also illustrates that there was a higher degree of intelligibility between WR varieties than with other areas.

Also illustrated in the data is that the dialect of Craven in the Yorkshire Dales was one of the most frequently defined areas in the nineteenth century. Howson (1850: 107) consistently refers to 'Craven dialect', and distinguishes it from Lancashire dialect. In addition, Carr (1828: vii–viii) notes that the dialect spoken in Craven even varies within that region, stating that there are 'shades of difference in its pronunciation', explaining that 'the true Craven pronunciation of co-al, becomes coil, fo-al, foil'. In the west of the Craven region, he continues, 'the language is strongly impregnated with the Lancashire Dialect', and in the east, he states that pronunciations change so that 'house, is pronounced hoose; and mouse, moose; cow, coo; as in the North and East Ridings of Yorkshire' (Carr 1828: vii–viii). However, the frequent references to the Craven 'language' are evidence of a perception that Craven had a distinct dialect of its own. Repetition of this notion throughout these texts served to strengthen the perceptual links between the language features described above and the geographical location of Craven for nineteenth-century audiences.

Other areas in the north of the WR were the subjects of similar discussions. For instance, Grainge (1863: 223–4) states that the Nidderdale valley, also in the Yorkshire Dales, has its own dialect and that there are 'some peculiarities in the dialect of Nidderdale seldom heard elsewhere'. He illustrates that the dialect of this region is differentiated by the use of the pronoun *ye* as opposed to 'thou' or 'you', and the pronunciation of vowels as 'open': for example, 'dale becomes *daal*', possibly suggesting a pronunciation of [eː] later recorded by Stoddart *et al.* (1999). However, although Grainge (1863: 224) doesn't elaborate extensively on the perceived differences between the dialect of Nidderdale and other Yorkshire areas, he does later describe 'the dialect of Craven' as a separate entity, suggesting that Craven dialect is different from Nidderdale, noting that the main differences are 'in the pronunciation of some of the words'. This kind of commentary can arguably be taken as evidence for a nineteenth-century perception of a general distinction between the northern and southern parts of the WR.

In relation to areas outside the WR, Robinson (1855: vi) notes that previous 'Yorkshire' glossaries have missed 'some of the terms belonging to the North and East Riding of Yorkshire' and that his glossary aims to address this, which suggests perceptions of distinct varieties in the NR and East Riding (henceforth ER). He states that he will focus on Whitby, as 'there is reason to believe that "the North Riding phase of the Yorkshire dialect" exists in its rifest fluency in Whitby and its moorland vicinity' (ibid.: vii). We can see similar discussion in Tweddell's *Poems in the North Yorkshire Dialect* (1878), at the end of which there is a collection of 'opinions of the press' relating to a text written by Tweddell's wife. In one extract (Tweddell 1878:

78) we see the following commentary on the difference between the dialect of Cleveland in the NR and that of the WR:

> Prose and verse are mixed with a master hand; each one is good, either for its humour, its pathos, or the light it throws upon such bits of country life as only well written dialect sketches can illustrate; … A Glossary, written by her husband (the Yorkshire Massey), illustrates the meaning of the dialect words, some of which are puzzling even to a West Riding reader.

We can see further evidence in this example that the Cleveland dialect is distinct from other 'Yorkshire' varieties. It is also explicitly distinguished from the WR dialect and illustrates that varieties of the WR and the NR (and possibly also ER) were markedly different from one another, at least at the level of vocabulary.

Finally, with regard to the ER, Nicholson (1889: 1–2) comments on the disparity in the production of DL between the east and west of the county. He states that there is little written representation of the East Yorkshire dialect, and goes on to note that

> In East Yorkshire there in only one large town, and that, being a sea-port, is cosmopolitan, and contains but a small percentage of dialect-speaking people, so that, scarcity of population, and the absence of 'touch' between current literature and the dialect speakers, may be assigned as probable reasons why there is a dearth of dialect literature.

Nicholson is likely referring to Hull when he talks of a large sea-port town in East Yorkshire, and the 'dearth' of DL he mentions is illustrated by the much smaller number of 'commentary' texts discussing ER dialects (see also Cooper 2013: 84). There were also fewer works of DL seeking to represent the ER available for quantitative analysis, as discussed below.

Nicholson (1889: 2–3) goes on to distinguish the 'Holderness dialect' from the rest of Yorkshire by stating that it has 'no definite article'. This is compared to 'all other parts of Yorkshire', which are described as having either *t'* or *d'*. This suggests a zero-realisation of the definite article as opposed to a glottal stop or alveolar plosive. The possibility of zero-realisations of DAR has also been discussed by Jones (2002: 328), who records this alongside representations of <t'> and <th'> in *A Yorkshire Dialogue* in 1673. Further Holderness-specific variants include *ham*, *yam*, *wom*, *hooam* and *heeam* for 'home' (Nicholson 1889: 2–3), which show representations of pronunciations similar to those noted by Ellis.

The notion of a Holderness dialect area that contained internal variation was also put forward by Ross *et al.* (1877: 9–10). They state that Holderness and the wider ER have distinctive language features that set these areas apart from elsewhere in Yorkshire. This distinction, they argue, is particularly evident at the level of individual words and of particular pronunciations. For example, they include one specific pronunciation which is described as distinguishing Holderness from the rest of the county:

> The peculiar sound of the long *i* before sharps is one of the most striking characteristics of the East (and North) Yorkshire pronunciation; and by this test an East-Riding man may always be distinguished from a native of the West-Riding.

'Sharps' are defined as 'one of the letters *c* (or *s* with a sharp sound), *f*, *k*, *p*, *t*, or the remaining liquid, *r*' (Ross *et al.* 1877: 9–10). Thus, words like 'rice', 'life', 'pike', 'pipe', 'tight' and 'fire' are represented in Glossic as [reys], [leyf], [peyk], [peyp], [teyt] and [feyr] respectively, suggesting a pronunciation of [eɪ] or [ɛɪ]. Cowling (1915: 44) also records this pronunciation at Hackness in East Yorkshire, stating that Middle English /iː/ became [ɛɪ] before voiceless consonants and 'before r'.

This pattern, as found in the *Survey of English Dialects* (SED) data (Orton and Dieth 1962–71), is discussed by Anderson (1987: 40), who attributes it to the fact that, in the North, 'ME /ai/ was reduced to a monophthong at an early date and the evolution of ME /iː/ has been via fronted onsets'. He goes on to state that East Yorkshire dialect will have [ɛɪ] before a voiceless consonant but [aɪ~aː] before a voiced one. The pronunciations discussed by Ross *et al.* above appear to align with these more recent observations, meaning that the [ɛɪ] realisation was likely a distinguishing feature of East Yorkshire dialect in the nineteenth century.

The perception that ER speakers could be differentiated from their fellow Yorkshiremen is further discussed by Morris (1892: 9) in his treatise on the 'folk-talk' of the NR and ER. Some of the features of this 'distinct folk-talk' include a 'softening' of the definite article from *t'* to *d'* and, with regard to reflexive pronouns, Morris lists forms ending in *-en* or *-el*, such as *mysen*, *mysel* for 'myself'. Generally, he notes that the *-en* forms are the more common, although the *-el* forms are 'by no means infrequent, especially in the North Riding' (ibid.: 25). A similar pattern is described for 'into', where *intiv* is given as the East Riding form; *intil* and *intul* 'are more prevalent in the North than in the East Riding' (ibid.: 38). So, despite the commentary regarding the apparent similarities between the NR and ER dialects, we can also observe some discussion of features which distinguish the two.

Overall, we can see that several 'Yorkshire' locations were regularly discussed in the nineteenth century and these tend to focus on the Yorkshire Ridings. Following Johnstone *et al.* (2006: 96), who state that language features begin to 'acquire legitimacy' as they are 'talked about repeatedly in the same or similar ways', we can observe the same process happening here with frequent and consistent definitions of dialect areas within Yorkshire, and that the frequency and consistency of the areas discussed allows for the identification of four general 'Yorkshire' dialect areas in the nineteenth century. These are the WR, which includes the most populated and industrialised areas, West Riding (North) (henceforth WRN) which includes the more northern and rural parts of the WR, the NR and the ER. The alignment of certain texts and discussions with the traditional Yorkshire county boundaries (with the exception of the WRN, which is not referred to explicitly but is indexed by areas like Craven and Nidderdale) appears to be a result of writers 'self-identifying' with these regions. The notion that different ridings within the county had distinct 'Yorkshire' varieties was therefore both created and reinforced by the continued production of dialect texts claiming to represent these varieties. This is similar to Johnstone's (2009) discussion of the influence of commodified dialect on processes of enregisterment. Based on this kind of commentary it is apparent that nineteenth-century writers were aware of systematic differences between these four broad 'Yorkshire' varieties. I will now turn to a discussion of quantitative analysis of DL from these areas which allows for the identification of specific sub-'Yorkshire' repertoires, following Cooper (2013). These repertoires will likely have been enregistered to nineteenth-century audiences, but on a more localised scale than the 'Yorkshire' repertoire Cooper identifies.

6.3. Enregistered Nineteenth-Century 'Yorkshire' Repertoires

In order to identify which features demonstrated frequent and consistent variation in written representations of different 'Yorkshire' varieties, I have analysed 1,000-word samples from eighty-six nineteenth-century DL and LD texts following the methodology of Cooper (2013) described above.[4] All frequency counts were normalised following Biber *et al.* (2006: 263) so as to account for texts where there were fewer than 1,000 words of dialect represented. This came to a total of 82,158 words[5] which were analysed using WordSmith Tools (Scott 2004). As with the 'commentary' texts discussed above, DL and LD texts were selected for sampling if they 'self-identified' as representing a particular area, either in the title of the text, such as many DL texts like Bywater's *The Sheffield Dialect* (1839), or, as in the case of many LD texts, they included some reference to characters being from a particular part of Yorkshire, such as Baring-Gould's (1889) novel *The Pennycomequicks*. One of the main characters in this novel is named Mrs Sidebottom and is stated to be from 'the large Yorkshire village or small town of Mergatroyd[6] in the West Riding of Yorkshire' (Baring-Gould 1889: 7). I should also note that, as Hodson (2016: 31) states, quantitative analysis of historical literary material does not proceed from the assumption that frequent and consistent representations of particular dialect features in writing illustrates 'the real-life use of those features, but does testify to the existence of popular perceptions that those features mark that variety'. Following the arguments of Hodson and of Cooper (2013), I suggest that analysing such material in this way allows us to identify language features that may have been enregistered in historical contexts.

The Yorkshire areas represented by the DL and LD texts patterned in a similar manner to areas described in the 'commentary' texts. That is, we see the same four dialect areas being represented and in similar proportions insofar as there is a much higher number of WR texts and a 'dearth' of ER texts. This resulted in a distribution of 46 WR texts, 13 WRN, 20 NR and 7 ER. There were also systematic differences in the way these 'Yorkshire' varieties were represented by nineteenth-century dialect writers, with some representations being specific to certain areas, although an obvious geographical pattern to the variation in written representations of 'Yorkshire' dialect is not forthcoming when we focus on features that occur in three or more repertoires. Figures 6.1–6.4 illustrate the 'Yorkshire' features in each dialect area that meet the criteria for likely enregisterment set out in Cooper (2013) and highlight several shared features such as DAR, /l/-vocalisation, an [iː]-type vowel in words such as *weel* 'well' and *freeghten* 'frighten', all of which occur in three of the four repertoires. The only feature to occur in all four dialect areas represented here are respellings which suggest a short vowel in certain words in the FACE lexical set, such as *mak* 'make', which I am terming 'short FACE' in an attempt to categorise these respellings as representing a short vowel development in these words. This is distinct from monophthongal FACE where respellings like *maad* suggest a long vowel and a pronunciation like [eː] (see also Maguire, this volume). The short FACE phenomenon is also discussed by Wales (2010: 70), who argues that respellings like *mak* suggest a pronunciation of [a]. However, corpus tokens like *gret* 'great', *med* 'made' and *mek* 'make' suggest a pronunciation of [ɛ], which aligns with the findings of Finnegan (2015: 230), who notes that [ɛ] in some FACE words was recorded in Yorkshire in the SED and has been recorded since the nineteenth century (see also Hodson, this volume). Short FACE was not found in Cooper (2013), although this can be explained firstly by the fact that only general 'Yorkshire' texts were considered in that study, and secondly that the Cooper (2013) corpus was smaller in size and scope.

The features that occur in the majority of repertoires contribute to the notion of a general 'Yorkshire' dialect where certain features can be observed in dialect representations from all over the county. Because of this, it is only when we consider features occurring in only one or two of the four

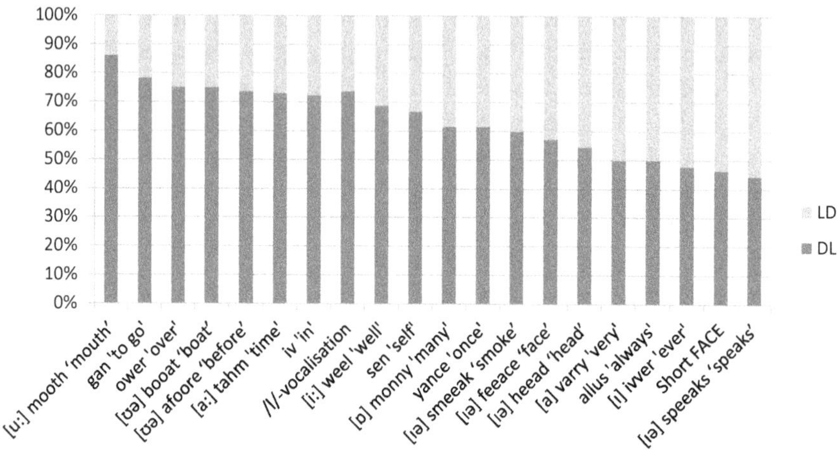

Figure 6.1 Frequent and consistent 'Yorkshire' features in ER texts

repertoires that we start to see geographical distributions of specific sub-'Yorkshire' features that mirror the qualitative commentary discussed above. For instance, we can see examples of respellings suggesting [ɪə] in certain words belonging to the GOAT lexical set with <eea> used in *aleean* 'alone' and *smeeak* 'smoke'. This respelling occurs in ER and NR texts but not those for the WR and WRN. Conversely, we can see *on* 'of', which I am terming 'preposition exchange', predominantly represented in WR texts, but not in the ER and NR. These differences allowed for the identification of four enregistered sub-'Yorkshire' repertoires.

Figures 6.1 and 6.2 highlight that respellings suggesting [u:] in the MOUTH lexical set, as in *mooth* 'mouth', only occur frequently and consistently in the NR and ER.

This pattern is repeated for *gan* 'to go'. Cooper (2016) describes how *gan* has been 'deregistered' as 'Yorkshire' since the nineteenth century, but retains its association with the north-east of England and 'Geordie'. This conclusion is based on a comparison of the historical 'Yorkshire' repertoire and a modern one, both identified in Cooper (2013). The fact that *gan* only appears frequently and consistently in NR and ER texts here goes some way towards explaining its apparent 'deregisterment' as 'Yorkshire'.

Figure 6.2 also illustrates that the distribution of *sel* mirrors that described by Morris above, where *sel* was stated to be more common in the NR, as opposed to *sen* in the ER. Additionally, the NR shares the lexical item *mun* 'must' with only the WRN, as shown in Figures 6.2 and 6.4, further illustrating the perceived 'north–south divide' within the WR in the nineteenth century. As *mun* shows a distinct northern distribution, in that it only appears in

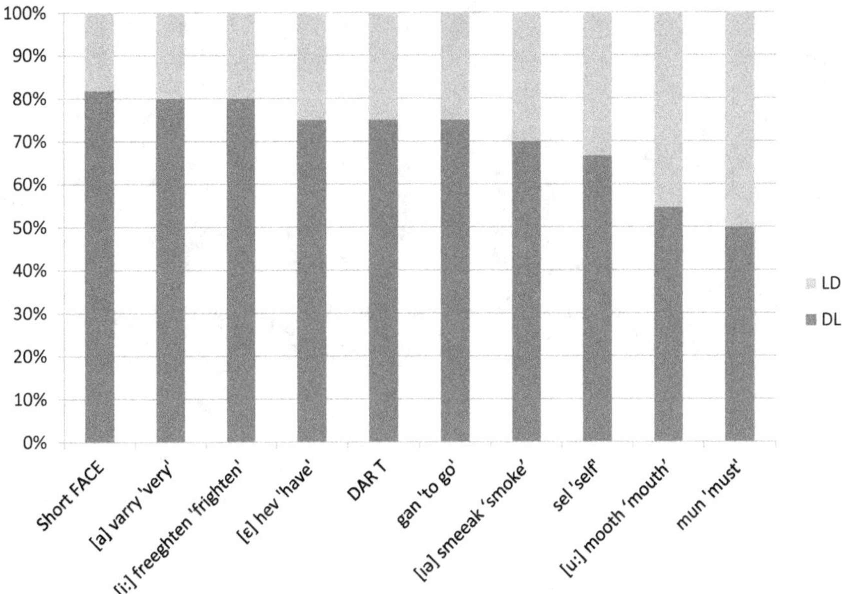

Figure 6.2 Frequent and consistent 'Yorkshire' features in NR texts

the NR and WR (North) repertoires, it is likely that the dominance of WR texts contributed to the 'deregisterment' of *mun* as 'Yorkshire' over the course of the nineteenth century (see also Cooper 2016), as *mun* does not appear in the WR repertoire. Following Haigh (2015), who discusses the possibility of dialect levelling within contemporary Yorkshire and the possibility of a pan-Yorkshire variety forming there, it appears that we can observe a levelling of the 'Yorkshire' repertoires in the direction of the WR variety beginning in the nineteenth century and which has continued to the present day.

In the two WR areas we see the lexical item *nowt* 'nothing' and a suggested pronunciation of [a] in words like *amang* 'among' occurring frequently and consistently, as shown in Figures 6.3 and 6.4. These features do not occur to the same extent in the North and East Ridings, and also appear to be separated by the Humber–Lune/Ribble line.

Similarly, a comparison of Figures 6.1 and 6.4 highlight that the ER and WRN share the features *ower* 'over', the traditionally northern *yan* 'one' and *yance* 'once', which include 'yod-formation' (see also Wales 2006: 170), and a suggested pronunciation of [ɪə] in renderings like *heead* 'head' and in *speeak* 'speak', which are similar to the observations of Ellis.

However, there is a more prevalent tendency in the ER to represent words so that they suggest a pronunciation of [ɪə], as we also observe *smeeak* 'smoke', and *feeace* 'face'. These respellings are not as consistently frequent

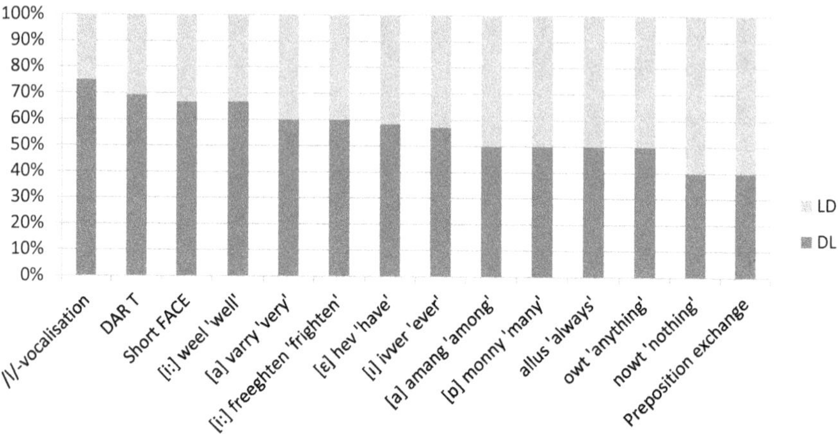

Figure 6.3 Frequent and consistent 'Yorkshire' features in WR texts

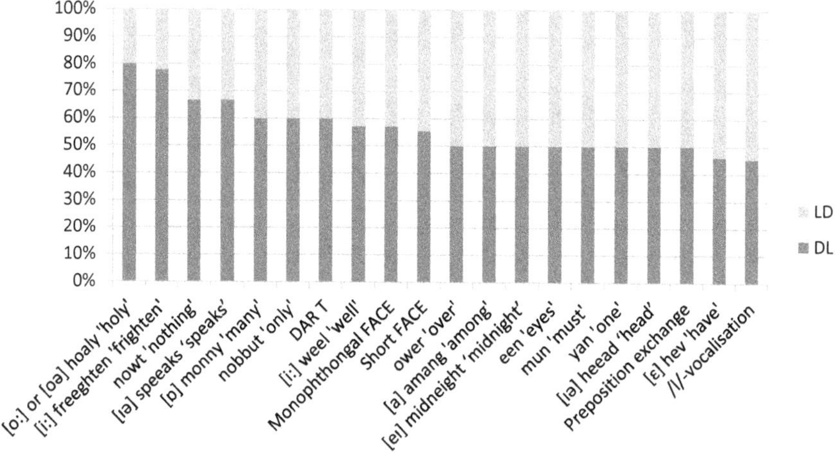

Figure 6.4 Frequent and consistent 'Yorkshire' features in WRN texts

in the other areas as they are in the ER, which reinforces the concept of an ER variety that is distinct from the other areas. Further evidence for this can be seen in the features that only occur frequently and consistently in the ER, as shown in Table 6.1, which illustrates features which are shared between two repertoires and which are unique to individual repertoires. Table 6.1 also includes features such as *iv* 'in', noted by Wales as 'a feature of the nineteenth-century ballads of the North-east and Cumberland' (2006: 170), and a tendency to respell certain words in the PRICE lexical set to suggest a pronunciation of [a:] as in *tahm* 'time', later recorded in Hull by Williams and Kerswill (1999: 146). These features would likely have denoted

Table 6.1 Distinguishing features of 'Yorkshire' dialect areas and enregistered repertoires

Sub-'Yorkshire' repertoire	Feature/suggested pronunciation
WR	[a] *amang* 'among'
WRN	*nowt* 'nothing'
	Preposition exchange
WR	[ɪ] *ivver* 'ever'
ER	*allus* 'always'
WRN	*mun* 'must'
NR	
WRN	[ɪə] *speeaks* 'speaks'
ER	[ɪə] *heead* 'head'
	ower 'over'
	yan, yance 'one', 'once'
ER	[ɪə] *smeeak* 'smoke'
NR	[u:] *mooth* 'mouth'
	gan 'to go'
WR	*owt* 'anything'
WRN	[eɪ] *midneight* 'midnight'
	Monophthongal FACE, e.g. *maad* 'made'
	[oə] or [o:] *hoaly* 'holy'
	een 'eyes'
	nobbut 'only'
ER	[a:] *tahm* 'time'
	[ɪə] *feeace* 'face'
	[ʊə] *afoore* 'before'
	[ʊə] *booat* 'boat'
	iv 'in'
	sen 'self'
NR	*sel* 'self'

ER 'Yorkshire' dialect to nineteenth-century audiences. Indeed, when we compare the features that distinguish between these individual 'Yorkshire' repertoires we can see that the WR repertoire includes features like preposition exchange, *nowt* and *owt*, but not *gan* or the suggested pronunciation of [u:] in *mooth* 'mouth', whereas the ER repertoire would include the latter features but not the former. However, both repertoires include features like DAR, short FACE, etc., discussed above, which are common to all repertoires across the county.

The patterns in the data tell us that enregisterment of nineteenth-century 'Yorkshire' dialect is observably more complex than the 'macro'-level repertoire identified by Cooper (2013), and that a 'Russian doll' effect similar to that described by Marshall above can be seen in relation to sub-'Yorkshire' dialects. The sub-'Yorkshire' repertoires are embedded in a broader 'Yorkshire' one in the same manner described by Beal (2009) with Sheffield. That is, the features enregistered as WR index that specific region as well as simultaneously indexing 'Yorkshire' more broadly. This is reflected in both the qualitative data and the quantitative differences between the repertoires observable in textual sources which purport to represent these individual geographical areas.

6.4. Conclusions

The frequent and consistent definition of distinct 'Yorkshire' dialect areas in the 'commentary' texts suggest that some speakers were aware of the differences between 'Yorkshire' dialects in the nineteenth century. These differences also demonstrate systematic variation in written representations, as illustrated by their occurrence in DL and LD, and the frequency and consistency of the quantitative representations is mirrored in the qualitative discussion of those features and the areas with which they were associated. This suggests that these differences were linked with place by nineteenth-century speakers.

The patterns in the data discussed here also allow us to draw two main conclusions about the enregisterment of 'Yorkshire' dialect. Firstly, the geographical distinction which follows the Humber–Lune/Ribble line illustrated here has implications for discussing language change. For instance, the recession of *gan* in the direction of the north-east and its 'deregisterment' as 'Yorkshire' is logical when we consider that *gan* only ever appeared in significant quantities in the NR and ER texts in the first place. This goes some way towards explaining the differences between the historical and modern repertoires. Secondly, that there were distinct sub-'Yorkshire' repertoires enregistered to nineteenth-century speakers, and that the social values indexed were variable within Yorkshire. Indeed, the same feature may have been used to differentiate one 'Yorkshire' variety from another, while at the same time being enregistered as 'Yorkshire' dialect on a more general level. This highlights that, like the modern 'Yorkshire' identities described by Marshall, enregistered sub-'Yorkshire' repertoires had a 'Russian doll' relationship to a broader 'Yorkshire' one for nineteenth-century audiences and language features could be associated with 'Yorkshire' and more localised areas simultaneously.

Notes

1. Yorkshire was historically divided into three administrative areas called 'ridings', derived 'from a Scandinavian word "third part"' (Wales 2006: 13). See http://www.yorkshireridings.org for a map of the Ridings.
2. 'Now, lad, where are you going to? I'm going down to town' (my 'translation').
3. Where Windhill is an area in the West Riding of Yorkshire, stated to be 'three miles North of Bradford' (Wright 1892: 1).

4. Forty-seven of these texts were originally collected as part of the PhD research conducted for Cooper (2013). See Cooper (2013: 83) for more details.
5. Of which 44,605 came from the Cooper (2013) corpus.
6. This is a fictional town.

References

Addy, Sydney Oldall. (1888). *A Glossary of Words Used in the Neighbourhood of Sheffield Including a Selection of Local Names, and Some Notices of Folk-lore, Games and Customs*. London: Trubner & Co.

Agha, Asif. (2003). 'The social life of cultural value'. *Language & Communication*, 23, 231–73.

Anderson, Peter M. (1987). *A Structural Atlas of the English Dialects*. London: Croom Helm.

Anon. (1860). *Dictionary of the Dialect of Batley, Batley Carr, Dewsbury, Ossett, Lee Fair, Morley, Birstal, Gomersal, Cleckheaton, Hightown, Robert-Town, Little-Town, Mill Bridge, Heckmondwike, Mirfield, and Not Forgetting Thornhill, Gawthorpe, Earlsheaton, Dawgreen, Kilpinhill, and Pudsey*. Batley: J. Fearnsides.

Atkinson, John Christopher. (1848). *A Glossary of the Cleveland Dialect: Explanatory, Derivative and Critical*. London: John Russell Smith.

Atkinson, J. C. (1867). 'On the dialect of Cleveland in the North Riding of Yorkshire'. *Transactions of the Philological Society*, 12, 326–356.

Banks, William Stott. (1865). *A List of Provincial Words in Use at Wakefield in Yorkshire; with Explanations, Including a Few Descriptions of Buildings and Localities*. London: J. Russell Smith.

Baring-Gould, Sabine. (1889). *The Pennycomequicks, a Novel*. London: Spencer Blackett & Hallam.

BBC. (2008). 'The essence of Yorkshireness revealed'. www.bbc.co.uk/bradford/content/articles/2008/10/21/yorkshireness_feature.shtml. Accessed 17 November 2016.

Beal, Joan C. (2009). 'Enregisterment, commodification and historical context: "Geordie" versus "Sheffieldish"'. *American Speech*, 84:2, 138–56.

Beal, Joan C. (2010). *An Introduction to Regional Englishes*. Edinburgh: Edinburgh University Press.

Beal, Joan C. and Paul Cooper. (2015). 'The enregisterment of Northern English', in Raymond Hickey (ed.), *Researching Northern English*. London: John Benjamins, pp. 27–50.

Biber, Douglas, Susan Conrad and Randi Reppen. (2006). *Corpus Linguistics*. Cambridge: Cambridge University Press.

Blakeborough, Richard. (1898). *Wit Character, Folklore & Customs of the North Riding of Yorkshire*. London: Henry Frowde.

Bywater, Abel. (1839). *The Sheffield Dialect*. Sheffield: G. Chaloner.

Carr, William. (1828). *The Dialect of Craven, in the West Riding of the County of York, with a Copious Glossary, Illustrated by Authorities from Ancient English and Scottish Writers, and Exemplified by Two Familiar Dialogues*. London: Wm. Crofts.

Cooper, Paul. (2013). *Enregisterment in Historical Contexts: A Framework*. PhD thesis. Sheffield: University of Sheffield.

Cooper, Paul. (2015). 'Enregisterment in historical contexts: nineteenth century

Yorkshire dialect'. *Dialectologia*, 14, 1–16. http://www.publicacions.ub.edu/revistes/ejecuta_descarga.asp?codigo=1040. Accessed 10 March 2015.

Cooper, Paul. (2016). '"Deregisterment" and "fossil forms": the cases of *gan* and *mun* in "Yorkshire" dialect'. *English Today*, 33:1, 1–10.

Cooper, Paul. (2017). 'Turtlely amazing: the enregisterment of "Yorkshire" dialect and the possibility of GOAT fronting as a newly enregistered feature', in Chris Montgomery and Emma Moore (eds), *Language and a Sense of Place Studies in Language and Region*. Cambridge: Cambridge University Press, pp. 348–67.

Cowling, George H. (1915). *The Dialect of Hackness (North East Yorkshire) with Original Specimens, and a Word-List*. Cambridge: Cambridge University Press.

Crossland, Charles. (1899). 'The vowel sounds and substitutions of the Halifax dialect'. *Transactions of the Yorkshire Dialect Society*, 2, 49–53.

Ellis, Alexander J. (1890). *English Dialects: Their Sounds and Homes*. London: Kegan Paul, Trench, Trubner & Co. Limited.

Finnegan, Katie. (2015). 'Sheffield', in Raymond Hickey (ed.), *Researching Northern English*. Amsterdam, Philadelphia: John Benjamins, pp. 227–50.

Grainge, William. (1863). *Nidderdale*. Pateley Bridge: Thomas Thorpe.

Haigh, Sarah. (2015). *Investigating Regional Speech in Yorkshire: Evidence from the Millennium Memory Bank*. Unpublished MPhil Thesis. University of Sheffield.

Hodson, Jane. (2016). 'Talking like a servant: what nineteenth century novels can tell us about the social history of the language'. *Journal of Historical Sociolinguistics*, 2:1, 27–46.

Honeybone, Patrick and Kevin Watson. (2013). 'Salience and the sociolinguistics of Scouse spelling'. *English World-Wide*, 34:3, 305–40.

Howson, William. (1850). *An Illustrated Guide to the Curiosities of Craven, with a Geological Introduction, Notices of the Dialect, a List of the Fossils, and a Local Flora*. London: Whitaker & Co.

Ihalainen, Ossi. (1994). 'The dialects of England since 1776', in Robert Burchfield (ed.), *The Cambridge History of the English Language*. Cambridge: Cambridge University Press, pp. 197–274. http://dx.doi.org.liverpool.idm.oclc.org/10.1017/CHOL9780521264785. Accessed 24 August 2016.

Johnstone, Barbara. (2009). 'Pittsburghese shirts: commodification and the enregisterment of an urban dialect'. *American Speech*, 84:2, 157–75.

Johnstone, Barbara. (2017). 'Characterological figures and expressive style in the enregisterment of linguistic variety', in Chris Montgomery and Emma Moore (eds), *Language and a Sense of Place Studies in Language and Region*. Cambridge: Cambridge University Press, pp. 283–300.

Johnstone, Barbara and Dan Baumgardt. (2004). '"Pittsburghese" online: vernacular norming in conversation'. *American Speech*, 79:2, 115–45.

Johnstone, Barbara, Jennifer Andrus and Andrew E. Danielson. (2006). 'Mobility, indexicality and the enregisterment of "Pittsburghese"'. *Journal of English Linguistics*, 34:2, 77–104.

Jones, Mark. (2002). 'The origin of Definite Article Reduction in northern English dialects: evidence from dialect allomorphy'. *English Language and Linguistics*, 6:2, 325–45.

Labov, William. (1977). 'On the use of the present to explain the past', in Adam Makkai, Valerie Makkai and L. Heineman (eds), *Linguistics at the Crossroads*. Lake Bluff, IL: Jupiter Press, pp. 226–61.

Morris Marmaduke, Charles F. (1892). *Yorkshire Folk-Talk with Characteristics of Those Who Speak It in the North and East Ridings*. London: Henry Frowde.

Nicholson, John. (1889). *The Folk Speech of East Yorkshire*. London: Simpkin, Marshall, and Co.

Orton, Harold and Wilfred J. Halliday. (1962). *Survey of English Dialects: The Basic Material, Vol. 1: The Six Northern Counties and the Isle of Man, Part 1*. Leeds: E. J. Arnold.

Orton, Harold and Wilfred J. Halliday. (1963). *Survey of English Dialects: The Basic Material, Vol. 1: The Six Northern Counties and the Isle of Man, Part 2*. Leeds: E. J. Arnold.

Remlinger, Kathryn. (2009). 'Everyone up here: enregisterment and identity in Michigan's Keweenaw Peninsula'. *American Speech*, 84: 2, 118–38.

Remlinger, Kathryn, Joseph Salmons and Luanne von Schneidemesser. (2009). 'Revised perceptions: changing dialect perception in Wisconsin and Michigan's Upper Peninsula'. *American Speech*, 84: 2, 176–92.

Robinson, Francis Kildale. (1855). *A Glossary of Yorkshire Words and Phrases, Collected in Whitby and the Neighbourhood, with Examples of Their Colloquial Use, and Allusions to Local Customs and Traditions*. London: John Russell Smith.

Ross, Frederick, Richard Stead and Thomas Holderness. (1877). *A Glossary of Words Used in Holderness in the East-Riding of Yorkshire*. London: Trübner & Co.

Scott, Mike. (2004). *WordSmith Tools Version 6*. Oxford: Oxford University Press.

Shorrocks, Graham. (1996). 'Non-standard dialect literature and popular culture', in Juhani Klemola, Merja Kytö and Matti Rissanen (eds), *Speech Past and Present: Studies in English Dialectology in Memory of Ossi Ihalainen*. Frankfurt am Main: Peter Lang, pp. 385–411.

Singleton, Frederick. (1970). *Industrial Revolution in Yorkshire*. Yorkshire: The Dalesman Publishing Company Ltd.

Stoddart, Jana, Clive Upton and John D. A. Widdowson (1999). 'Sheffield dialect in the 1990s: revisiting the concept of NORMs', in Paul Foulkes and Gerard J. Docherty (eds), *Urban Voices: Accent Studies in the British Isles*. London: Arnold, pp. 72–89.

Trudgill, Peter. (1999). *The Dialects of England*, 2nd edn. Oxford: Blackwell Publishers.

Trudgill, Peter. (2004). *Dialects*, 2nd edn. London and New York: Routledge.

Tweddell, George Markham. (1878). *Poems in the North Yorkshire Dialect by the Late John Castillo, Journeyman Stonemason and Wesleyan Revivalist. Edited, with a Memoir and Glossary*. Stokesley: J. Gould, Printer, Middlesbrough.

Wakelin, Martyn F. (1972). *English Dialects: An Introduction*. London: Athlone Press.

Wales, Katie. (2006). *Northern English: A Cultural and Social History*. Cambridge: Cambridge University Press.

Wales, Katie. (2010). 'Northern English in writing', in Raymond Hickey (ed.), *Varieties of English in Writing: The Written Word as Linguistic Evidence*, Amsterdam: John Benjamins, pp. 61–80.

Williams, Ann and Paul Kerswill. (1999). 'Dialect levelling: change and continuity in Milton Keynes, Reading and Hull', in Paul Foulkes and Gerald J. Docherty (eds), *Urban Voices: Accent Studies in the British Isles*, London and New York: Routledge, pp. 141–62.

Wright, David Gordon. (1986). 'The West Riding textile districts in the mid-nineteenth century', in J. A. Jowitt (ed.), *Model Industrial Communities in Mid-Nineteenth Century Yorkshire*. Bradford: University of Bradford, pp. 17–42.

Wright, Joseph. (1892). *A Grammar of the Dialect of Windhill, in the West Riding of Yorkshire*. London: Kegan Paul, Trench, Trubner & Co.

Yorkshire Ridings Society, The. (2008). 'The Yorkshire Ridings'. http://www.yorkshireridings.org. Accessed 8 June 2018.

7

Representing the Language of Liverpool; or, the (Im)possibility of Dialect Writing

Tony Crowley

7.1. Introduction

The aim of this chapter will be to trace written representations of Liverpool speech from their first appearance in the mid to late nineteenth century through to the present (for further discussion of this variety, see Honeybone, and Watson and Jensen, this volume). In order to do this, it will be important first to give a brief account of the history of language in Liverpool from the mid to late eighteenth century – the point at which it starts to become clear that there is a distinct form of language in the city. It will also be necessary to show how a sensibility towards this form develops in the early to mid twentieth century, largely in the discourse of local newspapers through a series of letters and feature articles. This led to the 'discovery' of Scouse, a term first used in 1950, along with an inaccurate (but still dominant) history of the form, which dates it from the post-Irish Famine period. The 'discovery' of Scouse is significant because it led to the enregisterment of the form over the next two decades in various media – from the first play written in Scouse in 1952, to journalism and popular lexicography (notably the *Lern Yerself Scouse* series). Much of this writing was populist, derivative and repetitive, though it is invaluable in providing access to dialectal lexis and distinctive features of the Liverpool accent. It also prompted the first serious and sustained attempts to represent Liverpool speech, in Frank Shaw's *The Scab*, but more significantly in the work of the Liverpool-Welsh playwright Alun Owen. This new confidence in the Liverpool vernacular carried over to Alan Bleasdale's 'Scully' novels, which in turn prepared the ground for the appearance of a number of contemporary 'Scouse novelists', including Kevin Sampson, Niall Griffiths and Helen Walsh. This chapter will present an analysis of this history and explore the empirical and theoretical questions that it raises. The chapter is structured in the following way. Beginning with a general contextual account of the history of language in Liverpool (in Section 7.2), the analysis continues with evidence of early-twentieth-century local interest in Liverpool speech (7.2.1), followed by the 'discovery of "Scouse"' in the 1950s (7.2.2). The chapter then considers literary representations of Liverpool speech, from the late nineteenth century to the present (7.3), before presenting a critical evaluation of the notions of 'indexicality' and 'enregisterment' in relation to such representations (7.4). The chapter will conclude (7.5) with a reflection on the complexity of representing a specific form of speech, and the very (im)possibility of dialect writing.

7.2. The History of Language in Liverpool

In *Scouse: A Social and Cultural History* (2012), I argued in detail that Thomas Boulton's comic drama, *The Sailor's Farewell; Or, The Guinea Outfit* (1768), published and performed in Liverpool, indicated that even in the mid eighteenth century, there was already an awareness of Liverpool's linguistic distinctiveness (Crowley 2012: 32–5). This is supported by William Moss's comments in *The Liverpool Guide* (1796) regarding unusual Liverpool pronunciations of local place-names: Wavertree, 'pronounced Wa'tree'; Childwall, 'pronounced Childa'; Woolton, 'pronounced Wooton' (Moss 1796: 129–30). In the early nineteenth century, William Shepherd's satire, *The True and Wonderful History of Dick Liver* (1824), offers further evidence that there was a marked sense of distinction between Liverpool and its surrounding area in terms of language. In Shepherd's text, 'Dick Liver', a 'smooth tongued' Dicky Sam (the local name for natives of the city throughout the nineteenth century), constantly outwits a Mancunian cotton spinner, Tom Twist (possibly the first 'woollyback' – Liverpool's derogatory term for non-Liverpudlians). Pointedly, he 'laughed at his Lancashire dialect', including utterances such as: 'Dom the sceawndrill, I'll be deigh'd if I e'er trust him agen' (Shepherd 1824: 7). The demarcation of language was certainly clear by the late nineteenth century. In a comment on Prime Minister Gladstone's accent (Gladstone was raised in Liverpool to Scottish parents), James Picton, the famous Liverpool architect and historian, noted that Gladstone's 'tones and mode of utterance are decidedly of Liverpool origin. We bring our words out "ore rotundo," without the mincing word-clipping of the cockney and equally distant from the rough Tim Bobbin Lancashire dialect' (Picton 1888: 210). The great Lancastrian linguistic divide was already evident: 'the cities of Liverpool and Manchester,' Picton observed, 'only thirty miles apart, differ materially in their dialect' (1888: 210).

Such comments, though indicative, do not offer direct detailed evidence regarding the evolution of a new form of language in Liverpool from the mid to late eighteenth century, but further support for this account can be drawn by inference from Trudgill's account of new dialect formation (Trudgill 1986, 2004). Honeybone's (2007: 112) summation of Trudgill's model is helpful. In stage one,

> [a]dult speakers of established varieties come together, thanks to substantial population movements, in one place. These adults start to accommodate to each other linguistically, to rub off the most extreme differences between their varieties, or to lose features which clearly stand out as minority forms, or which might diminish intelligibility.

The crucial development, however, takes place with the children of these adult speakers, who are either born in the place or move there at an early age. Thus in stage two, these first-generation speakers

> have to come to terms with the various different dialect forms that they hear and are themselves subject to considerable variation because they do not have clear linguistic role models in their peers. They pick up a number of features from their parents and from others around them, in line with the different proportions of the features in the dialects of the speakers who formed the new community, and start the process of koineisation.

This process then leads in time to the formation of the new dialect. It is a model which fits the development of language in Liverpool with precision.

Trudgill's model requires both migration and re-generation of the population and thus, as Honeybone notes, to understand the development of the new linguistic form in Liverpool, 'a study of population movements will be crucial, so population statistics (such as census returns) will be very important' (2007: 111). The population figures for eighteenth-century and nineteenth-century Liverpool are revealing in this respect. From a town of 5,145 in 1700, Liverpool grew to more than 77,653 in 1801, an astonishing rate of increase (more than 1,500 per cent) (Pooley 2006: 175). Evidently such growth, which largely took place on the back of the slave trade, could not have been endogenous and must have drawn people in not only from the immediate hinterland, but also the rest of Britain, and indeed, to a limited extent, from wider afield, usually over developing trade routes. In any case, already by the mid to late eighteenth century, the conditions would have been in place for the formation of a new dialect: massive in-migration to Liverpool, with significant inter-generational population growth.

The patterns established in this period were repeated later: 1801: 77,000; 1821: 118,000; 1841: 286,000; 1851: 376,000; 1861: 462,000; 1901:

684,000. Though not as prodigious as that of the eighteenth century, the population growth rate in the nineteenth century was still remarkable, and again depended on sustained immigration and settlement: 'a continual influx of strangers', as one of Liverpool's first historians described it (Enfield 1773: 28). Another way of putting this point is that over the eighteenth and nineteenth centuries, Liverpool became one of the world's great ports (it was commonly called the 'gateway to Empire') and was a place to which enormous numbers of people moved and settled. In 1841, for example, almost 45 per cent of the total population were immigrants, while in 1861 the total was 49 per cent. Liverpool was thus a locus of language contact and exchange; the immigrants brought with them their own forms of English, or distinct languages (in 1821 Thomas De Quincey referred to 'the many-languaged town of Liverpool'; De Quincey 2000: II, 228), and trade brought its own words. Out of that mix came Liverpool English, a local vernacular subject to many complex influences.

One thing that is clear from this history is that the old account of Liverpool English, or 'Scouse' as it became known, is simply wrong. That version proposed that Liverpool English was in effect an amalgam of Lancashire dialect and the Anglo-Irish of the victims of the Great Famine in Ireland (1845–8). But that cannot be accurate for two reasons. First, it is based on the mistaken belief that Lancashire dialect was still spoken in Liverpool until the 1840s; I have shown how this misperception originated in *Scouse: A Social and Cultural History* (Crowley 2012: 16–24). Second, it reductively supposes that Irish-English was the biggest influence in Liverpool English, whereas recent lexicographical research has shown that American English was more significant (Crowley 2017). In fact, at the level of lexis (and possibly phonology), it is clear that the language of Liverpool has drawn very widely on a range of languages. Liverpool words, in common or specialised use, recorded over the past century-and-a-half, have included: Afrikaans (*scoff*); American English (*ace*); Arabic (*akkers*); Australian English (*not much cop*); Cant (*kecks*); Cornish (*scadge*); Danish (*kip*); Dutch (*mopus*); Fijian pidgin (*bullamacow*); French (*barley*); Gaelic (*kaylied*); Guyanese Creole (*tonka*); Hindi (*dekko*); Irish (*gom*); Irish English (*left-footer*); Italian (*carzy*); Lancashire dialect (*cob*); Latin (*cental*); Latvian (*scouse*); Manx (*tanroagan*); Persian (*bukshee*); Polari (*tusheroon*); Portuguese (*bacalhoa*); Romani (*dixie*); Scots (*ming*); Spanish (*alicant*); Turkish (*burgoo*); Urdu (*custy*); Welsh (*bad breath*); Yiddish (*nosh*) (Crowley 2017).

7.2.1. Early Interest in the Language of Liverpool

Interest in the local Liverpool vernacular is evident from a sustained series of letters and feature articles in the city's newspapers between the 1930s and the 1950s. The correspondence indicates a significant sensibility, indeed self-reflexivity, about the city's linguistic culture, as in Edmund Burke's letter drawing attention to the words *nix* ('to keep watch'), *ek, ek* (a warning), and *do a jowl* (run off) ('Postman' 1931a: 2). Or an anonymous correspondent's ('Postman' 1931b: 2) correction of a previous letter (corrections were commonplace, particularly with regard to etymologies):

> A 'dodger' is a glass of beer containing less than a half-pint and more than a 'pony' or quarter pint. There is a regulation glass for the 'dodger', but until recently few public-houses stocked it, and regarded the measure in the same light as the 'pony' – with contempt … The 'dodger' is known locally as a 'Peter Hudson'.

Pony had been used since the early eighteenth century (it is classed as 'regional' by the *OED*), though *dodger* and *Peter Hudson* are unrecorded. On a general level, the letters are interesting not simply because they reveal dialect vocabulary (there were many interpretations of the Liverpool words for alleyway – *jigger* and *jowler*), but also for their identification of the specificity of usage in spatial terms within the city. Thus T. Jones (1935: 5), writing on 'Liverpool slang', refers to words which were 'purely "Liverpool" and were commonly used when I was a boy living forty years ago in the south-end of the city' (*south-ender* and *north-ender* are still common Liverpool parlance):

> 'Eck-eck!' And 'Hey-up', both with similar meanings, 'Look-out'; the latter also meaning 'Get out of the way'. 'Fudge', farthing. 'Meg', halfpenny. 'Win', penny. 'Joey', threepenny piece. 'Snitch', 'Don't snitch', Don't tell, or Don't give me away. 'Clat', a tell-tale or a gossip. 'Scuffer', policeman. 'Jack', plain clothes policeman. 'Sag', truant.

Jones added a series of very local south-end place-names: *Bully* 'Princes Rd. Boulevard'; *Monkey Rack* 'the boardwalk in Sefton Park'; *Seven Hedges* 'the top of Dingle Lane'; *Greasy Fields* 'Ullet Road playground'; *Cazzy* 'the Cast Iron Shore'; *Cinder Walk* 'a walk overlooking the Herculanaeum dock'; *the Spiky* 'a short cut between Dingle Lane and the shore' (1935: 5). The connection between language and place was also demonstrated by two anonymous correspondents, the first of whom writes for 'those interested in the survival of vernacular speech', citing the 'homely and racy Lancashire colloquialism' 'moss nor sand' (meaning 'no sense' – as in 'couldn't get moss nor sand out of the witness') (Anon. 1933a: 7). To which the second letter adds the important gloss that the phrase was 'unknown in Liverpool, but in districts only three or four miles outside it has long been known … and not merely by people of the poorer classes' (Anon. 1933b: 7). The social and geographic delimitation of language in and around Liverpool was extremely precise (and remained so until its recent spread).

The correspondence in the local newspapers was sustained and was testament to an enduring interest in the connection between Liverpool and its language which intensified after the Second World War (the war's effect on the perceived relation between language and forms of Englishness is a much-neglected topic). An exemplum of this concern can be found in two seminal feature pieces in the *Liverpool Daily Post* in 1950 by a local schoolmaster, John Farrell: *About That Liverpool Accent (or Dialect)* (whose aim was to define 'Liverpool's vernacular not as an accent but as a dialect') (Farrell 1950a: 4) and *This Half-Secret Tongue of Liverpool* (Farrell 1950b: 4). Farrell's texts are fascinating not least because they pre-empt many of the later debates around Liverpool speech, some of which remain current. For example, defending its specificity against 'BBC producers and others [who] represent the local speech-form as "Lancashire", or as the speech of 'a person suffering from chronic obstruction of the nasal passages', Farrell draws attention to the fact that Liverpool vernacular was (as it still is) treated as the subject of comedy or contempt (Farrell 1950a: 4). Likewise, arguing that 'the native speech of Liverpool should strictly be defined as a dialect' (defined as a form 'with differences in vowel quality, in vowel formation and distribution, in consonant quality and distribution, in idiom, vocabulary and speech melody'), Farrell reluctantly admits that the form was (as, again, it largely still is) usually treated reductively as an accent ('the term "accent" is in such widespread and common use that it is pointless not to accept it') (1950a: 4). Notwithstanding the confusion, Farrell nonetheless launches an impressive defence of local speech forms: 'dialect is not of itself bad speech' and 'the tendency to regard dialect as a free source of laughter is to be deplored'. Those 'intelligent people who look on any speaker of dialect as ill-bred and uneducated', he adds, 'should have more sense' (1950a: 4).

Apart from his attack on linguistic prejudice, Farrell's most important achievement in his two essays was to draw attention to specific features of Liverpool speech. For example, though he lacks accurate phonetic terminology, Farrell identifies the Liverpudlian use of Northern /ʊ/ and short /a/ and the occurrence of HAPPY-tensing /i/ ('some differences are shared with other parts of the North of England, for example, the vowel sound in "bun" and the two vowel sounds in "valley"') (1950a: 4). Likewise, he refers to 'the treatment of the sounds in "fair" and "fur"', or what is now known as the NURSE–SQUARE merger, with examples such as 'a fur-hurred lady in a fair coat' and 'Thiid retiin, hamilto Squur'. He also notes the replacement in specific contexts of schwa /ə/ by /ɛ/: 'the Liverpool speaker uses "e" (as in "let") instead [of schwa]: and "dock-worker" becomes "dock-wiike"'. Other observations include TH-stopping ('"dese" for "these"', assimilation '"Norris Kreen" for "Norris Green"', the pronunciation of '"neighbourhood" as two syllables ("neighbrood")', and 'tay' for 'tea'. At the level of lexis, Farrell was also original in his recording of Liverpool terms. In *About That Liverpool Accent (or Dialect)*, he notes *whacker* (the common term used by Liverpudlians to each other until the 1970s); *la* ('lad'); *our* (usually with reference to family – *our Joe*); *kid* ('sister or brother' – *our kid*); *speck* ('place/viewing point'); *skip* ('take a free ride'); *leccy* ('electric tram' – hence *skip a leccy*); *jump* ('board' – a tram, not applied to buses, Farrell notes, though it is now used to refer to any form of transport – *jump a taxi/bus/train/boat*); and *car* ('tram'). He also gives three examples of that dominant, and again under-researched, feature of Liverpool speech, hypocorism: *savvy* and *issavvy* ('this afternoon'); *Lanny* ('Landing Stage'); *Scottie* ('Scotland Road'); and the aforementioned *leccy*. Hence: *He skipped a leccy isavvy down Scottie to get to the Lanny* (1950a: 4). In *This Half-Secret Tongue of Liverpool* Farrell provided another treasure-trove of lexical items and features of Liverpool speech. The common use of hyperbole, for example, was noted in *wringin' soppin wet* ('wet through'), *drownded* ('soaked'), and *murder*, *half-murder*, *paralyse*, *marmalise* and *stiffen* (all of which meant 'to scold severely' or possibly 'to beat') (Farrell 1950b: 4). Other lexical items were also recorded: *to be eaten* ('beaten soundly at sport'); *feller* (non-specific 'man', or used in relation to trades – *bread feller*, *coal feller*, *insurance feller*); *me feller* ('boyfriend, husband'); *old feller/owld feller/owl feller* ('father'); *queer feller/quare feller* ('feckless man'); *clubman* ('insurance agent'); *barney* ('argument'); *chuck* ('jilt'). While others included: *old lady/old woman/old girl* (respectful for 'mother' – as opposed to the disrespectful *owld one/owl one*); *judy* or *girl* ('girlfriend' or 'wife'); *the lads* ('male friends'); *scoff* ('food'); *wet Nellie/wet Neller* ('Nelson cake'); *lunch* (not the mid-day meal but a 'packet of sandwiches prepared at home to be consumed round about mid-morning'); *dinner* or *carrying out* ('sandwiches to be eaten at midday'); *dinner* ('lunch'); *cocoa rooms* ('café'); *off bad* ('absent through illness'); *very bad* ('very ill'); *sweat on* ('await anxiously'); *sweat cobs* ('sweat excessively'); *have a cob on* ('to be moody'); *cob of chuck* ('piece of bread or meat'); *the gear/gear* (excellent'); *meg* ('halfpenny'); *win* ('penny'); *money* ('wages'); *scuffer* ('policeman'); *jigger* and *jowler* ('alleyway'); *cherry-wobs* ('cherrystones' – used for marbles); *to be away for slates* ('to leave in a hurry'); *parapet* ('kerb'). There is one last term: '"scouse", the local stew, gave to native members of the armed Forces (N.C.O.s and men) the name "Scousers"'; Farrell notes that 'this term is hardly ever used as a mark of affection'. Of the use of *scouse* to refer to the language of Liverpool, there is no mention.

7.2.2. *The 'Discovery' of Scouse*

The 'discovery' of Scouse in the 1950s is largely attributable to Frank Shaw, a customs officer on Liverpool docks-cum-linguist/folklorist (Shaw described himself as the founder of 'the Scouse industry'; Shaw 1971: 237). Indeed, it was Shaw who appears to have coined the use of 'Scouse' to refer to language in an article in the *Liverpool Echo* in 1950: 'Scouse Lingo – How It All Began' (Shaw 1950: 4). Previously, as Farrell indicated, *scouse* had meant either a type of stew (from the eighteenth century) or a native of Liverpool (from the late nineteenth century, though this usage was only popularised during the Second World War) (Crowley 2017: *s.v. scouse* n.). Shaw's project, to gain recognition for the language of Liverpool as a linguistic form in its own right, was sustained through a great number of publications in local and national newspapers. It also took the form of a series of attempts to produce a glossary of Scouse: first for the Liverpool Festival (part of the Festival of Britain in 1951), then when it looked as though Britain would join the European Common Market in the early 1960s (as a guide for the hordes of European tourists), and then finally for the visitors to the World Cup games held in Liverpool in 1966. Published as *Lern Yerself Scouse: How to Talk Proper in Liverpool, A Teach-Yourself Phrase Book* (1966), Shaw's text was a phenomenal success, though sales were mostly confined to Liverpudlians and Liverpudlian ex-pats (as opposed to the few Bulgarians, North Koreans and Brazilians who might have made their team's games at Goodison). In fact, so popular was *Lern Yerself Scouse* that four other best-selling volumes, by various authors, were later published by the Scouse Press: *The ABZ of Scouse by Linacre Lane, B.Sc. (Bachelor of Scouse)* (1966); *Wersia Sensa Yuma?* (1972); *The Language of Laura Norder* (1989); and *Scouse International: The Liverpool Dialect in Five Languages* (2000). It was the first volume, *Lern Yerself Scouse*, however, that proved to be the most enduringly popular (though copies of various volumes can still be found on sale at the Museum of Liverpool Life and local bookshops); it is further considered in the chapters in this volume by Honeybone and by Watson and Jensen.

Shaw's interest in Scouse apparently derived mainly from his working contacts with Liverpool dockers, who were designated as the repositories of 'real' Liverpudlian life and linguistic culture. Their role was all the more important given that at the very moment of its discovery, Scouse was (like most dialects) thought to be dying. Thus in an interview with the *Liverpool Daily Post* (Anon. 1955: 6), headlined 'A Proper Jangle in Scouser Lingo', Shaw is quoted as claiming that

> [i]t is in Liverpool docks … that Liverpoolese is maintained and nourished to-day. Like other dialects it is dying; but it is nurtured in lusty health still

by the dockers, who often keep themselves cut off from the world of the Oxford accent.

The idea of Liverpool dockers having to remove themselves deliberately from the realm of Oxford accents in order to preserve Scouse is amusing, but it seems to have been a necessary sacrifice (Shaw 1959a: 6):

> Liverpoolese will never die as long as the port has dockers ... The lingo came from dockland in the first place ... It is dying in most parts of the city but still lives along Liverpool's thirty-eight miles of quay space. And those who hate uniformity will say let it live.

There are two notable features about Shaw's comments. The first is the death of the dialect theme, a recurrent trope since the end of the nineteenth century when railways and education were held to be the culprits (in 1950s Liverpool it was slum clearance, today it is globalisation). The second is the focus on the exclusively male dockers as the preservers of Liverpool English – a masculinist emphasis that runs throughout the history of traditional dialect studies.

As noted above, Shaw's major achievement is to have promoted Scouse in newspaper articles, and other forms of popular culture, often in a light-hearted or comic manner. He was also, however, probably the first person to have attempted a serious piece of writing in Scouse: *The Scab* (1952). The topic of this 'one-act play of Liverpool working-class life written, largely, in Liverpoolese' (the use of *Liverpoolese* reveals that *Scouse*, to refer to language, had not yet caught on) was the impact of the 1926 General Strike on the family of a Liverpool docker. Performed in 1953 at Liverpool's left-wing Unity Theatre, the Manchester Free Trade Hall and as part of the National Drama Festival at Liverpool's David Lewis theatre, the play had the distinction of being censored by the Lord Chamberlain's Office for the use of the word *sod* (Shaw 1952: n.p.). *The Scab* opens thus:

> Polly: Ere y'are, Jud, you may as well ave summit. Want a bit of bread? (He shakes his head). Nowt else. If dis ole strike goes on I spose we won't even ave de tea.
>
> Jud: Aye, it's a terrible thing. (He takes his tea from saucer).
>
> Polly: Ow many times ave I eard Barny say there never wud be a general strike?
>
> Jud: Well, we've got one now. Nine days of it.
>
> Polly: Will it never end? An what good comes of it? We'll all be worse off at the end of it all.
>
> Jud: Don't worry, the strikers is not stopping any essenshul services. The food'll come through anyway.

The scene continues:

> Barney: (Flopping into chair). Begob, I thought me own last our ad come today on the tram. Me old corns givn me jip an all.
>
> Jud: Is the trams runnin then?
>
> Barny: Wunnertwo. University students and cotton clurks an all like that as drivers and conductors. Me eart was in me mouth. Not on'y did we keep stopping an startin a way'd make a real driver cut is throat, but along comes a crowd a strikers. That put the top at on it. They pelted the driver an conductor wit cobs er muck an tried to push the tram over.
>
> Polly: God bless us. Are ye all right?
>
> Barny: Oh, they didden do it. But I adter get off an walk from Brunswick Road. The driver an conductor wus away for slates down Moss Street; dey was faster than their oul tram ad been. I could do wit a cup of tea after all that.

In an important and historically significant addendum, Shaw gives a gloss for the play's non-Liverpudlian actors and producers: *Notes on the Liverpool Way of Speaking*, in which he notes that Scouse 'is spoken with a nasal accent (i.e. the nose is not properly used)' and 'owes much in tone to Dublin but has a slight Welsh sing-song; many of its words are Anglo-Irish. Lancashire influence is inconsiderable' (Shaw 1952: n.p.). Shaw's emphasis on the Irish influence testifies to his role as the first propagator of the false history of Liverpool English as having been produced by a combination of Lancashire dialect and the Irish English of those fleeing the Famine in the mid nineteenth century. This account was based on Shaw's mis-reading of Robert Syers's *History of Everton* (1830) (Crowley 2012: 16–23), and his determination to put the Irish dimension back into the history of Liverpool (the city has a long and conflictual sectarian past). Nevertheless, it does not detract from his observations on Liverpool speech, specifically his direction that older characters in the play should be 'more Irish', including the use of features such as '*youse* (plural of you), *ye* (you), *minnit* (minute), *childer* (children), *dis, dat, ting, wit', t'morra*' (Shaw 1952: n.p.), as well as 'Begob' and 'oul' (as in the extract above). Like Farrell, Shaw also identifies a series of Liverpool speech characteristics, though unlike Farrell, Shaw's explanation is prescriptive: 'the speech is lazy' and subject to 'curtailing, catechrism [*sic*], elision, slurred consonants, wrong vowel usage, and of course, the dropped aspirate' (Shaw 1952: n.p.).

This odd mix of enthusiasm for the speech form and prejudice towards it is typical of the ambivalence towards Scouse that is found in many of its early representations. Nonetheless, Shaw's gloss does furnish important historical examples of features of some forms of Liverpool speech, albeit, as with Farrell, in non-technical language. These comprised the observation that 'some final consonants are over-stressed ("tired" becomes "tiredt")', and a series of what he calls 'fairly constant' 'mispronunciations'. These included: 'i for o in words like "work" (*wirk*)'; 'ew for oo in words like "book", "you" (*bewk, tew*)'; 'u for ai in words like "fairy", "Mary" (*furry, Murry*)'; 'e for i in words like "shirk" (*sherk*)'; 'dee for "-day" in "Sunday" etc'; '*pleece* for "police"'; '*alwis* for "always"'; '*awr* for "our"'; 'i for e in words like "bosses", "pickets", "insurance" (*bossis, pickits, insurince*)'; '*t* for "to", *the* for "they" (so *ave t'* for "have to", *avin the* for "haven't they", which can become *after* and *avindee*'; 'a guttural sound for the final syllable in words like "worker" occurs in (*wirkuh, felluh*)' (Shaw 1952: n.p.). Such material is historically significant, as is Shaw's small glossary for the non-Liverpudlian actors and producers of the play. It contained '*whack, la* (mate)'; '*the gear* (excellent)'; '*chuck* (bread)'; '*scouse* (stew)'; '*scoff* (food)'; '*butty* (piece of bread)'; '*awr kid* (brother or sister, any age)'; '*jigger* (back lane between houses)'; '*scuffer* (policeman)'; '*cob* (piece, as in "a cob er muck")'; '*bevvy* (drink)'; '*blocker* (bowler hat)'; '*judy* (girl)'; '*sag* (truant)'; '*clubman* (insurance collector)'; '*luch* (drink)'; '*Me dream's out* (talk of the devil)'; '*away for slates* (moving swiftly)'; '*talk like a penny book* (speak foolishly)'; '*unmerciful hiding* (a smack: typical hyperbole)'; '*the Twelft* (nothing to do with grouse; it is the 12th July, Battle of the Boyne, Orangeman's Day)'; '*put the top hat on it* (the last straw)'; '*tara* (goodbye)' (Shaw 1952: n.p.).

Evidently, Shaw undertook work that was innovative and significant and his achievements include serious contributions such as *Scouse Talks* (1957), a set of recordings, texts and 'translations'; *Dialect of a Seaport*, a series of articles for the *Journal of the Lancashire Dialect Society* (1958–60); the TV documentary *Morning in the Streets* (1958), in collaboration with Dennis Mitchell, the renowned film-maker of 'everyday life'; and *You Know Me Anty Nelly* (1969), a study of children's rhymes and games in Liverpool that was hailed by the British folklorist Peter Opie. But it must be said that much of Shaw's output in the popular media was less successful and marked by simple prejudice. In 'Liverpoolese, Yes, But I Don't Like Scouse', for example, he declared: 'I was for Liverpoolese. I still am. But I don't see how anyone with two ears and a moderate education can like what has come to be known as Scouse.' 'I am in no way proud of our mispronunciations', he continued, asserting that after returning to Liverpool from a trip away and hearing 'that catarrhal, adenoidal, singsong, containing the worst of Welsh, English and Irish English, I wince' (Shaw 1962: 8). The women of Liverpool were specifically targeted. In the same piece, which cited a headline from an earlier article – 'Model Girls … Until You Hear Them Speak' – Shaw observed: 'I feel at times that Liverpool girls would be lovely if one could not hear' (1962: 8). Such prejudices were hardly atypical, but more importantly, from a linguistic point of view, they undermined the attempt to take Liverpool's language seriously. Indeed, in many respects they simply contributed to representations of Liverpool speech within popular culture as, in Farrell's words, 'bad speech' and 'a free source of laughter'.

7.3. Representations of Liverpool Speech

Negative assessments of Liverpool speech in literature were hardly unusual. In William Tirebuck's *Dorrie* (1891), for example, a stage impresario dismisses a Liverpool character because 'he didn't like the common Liverpool twang about her pronunciation' (Tirebuck 1891: 189). J. B. Priestley's *English Journey* (1934) noted simply that Liverpool 'people – or at least the uneducated among them – have an accent of their own; a thick, adenoidy, cold-in-the-head accent, very unpleasant to hear' (Priestley 1934: 200). And in the Liverpool novelist John Brophy's *City of Departures* (1946: 21), one of the characters reflects on an exchange with a paper-seller in Lime Street:

> The words, emerging as a sustained shrill note between scarcely moving lips, at first were unintelligible to him, meaningless, hardly recognizable as human speech. He had forgotten the ugliness of the Liverpool accent: his ears were not attuned to its adenoidal whine, its flat vowel sounds and slurred consonants, its monotonous rhythms compounded of distant memories of Dublin slums and Welsh villages, but all debased, forced through nasal and oral passages chronically afflicted with catarrh. Liverpool had the ugliest English accent in the world, unless the Bowery in New York or the Cicero district of Chicago could produce something more repulsive. Thorneycroft wondered if his own speech had ever marked him as Liverpool-born. He hoped not.

More interesting for present purposes, however, is the history of literary representation of Liverpool speech, particularly in books set in Liverpool. An early example, which side-steps the question, is William Maginn's *John Manesty, the Liverpool Merchant* (1844), a family drama involving slave-trading set in Liverpool in 1760. From a linguistic point of view, there is little of significance in this text, apart from an explicit refusal to transcribe the dialect used by certain characters identified as specifically Lancastrian (rather than Liverpudlian):

> We know enough of the *lingua Lancastriensis* to render us scrupulous of attempting an imitation, which we are conscious would be a failure. It is a good, solid, dialective variation of the Anglo-Saxon, which should not be spoiled by the mimicry of an intruder ... In not more, but less vernacular English, we shall proceed to tell our tale. (Maginn 1844: I, 136)

If regionality wasn't to be attempted, the already established generic features used in the representation of class speech (Agha 2003: 255-9; see also Hodson, this volume) enabled William Wilson to present a scene in *The Melvilles* (1852), in which the sister of a working-class Liverpudlian woman dying of cholera tells a doctor:

> She's very bad, Sir, awful bad; she wouldn't look at the tea after I took it to her ... I've been obliged to lay her down on the old sofa in the back kitchen, for there isn't a place in the house but what we need ourselves ... poor thing, she lives no place regular. She's like a lost creature, my poor sister; many's the sore heart we've had with her, and I doubt it's coming to an end. (Wilson 1852: 119–20)

Again, there is little that is particularly noteworthy here, unlike Silas Hocking's *Her Benny* (1879), the text which all Liverpool schoolchildren used to read (and then weep over). In this text, there is a clear distinction drawn between urban (Liverpudlian) and non-city speech:

> Just then he heard a countryman inquiring the way to Lime Street station, of a man who stood near him.
>
> 'Here's a chance,' [Benny] thought; and stepping forward, he said, 'I'll show you the way, sir, if yer likes.'
>
> 'Dost thee know th' way thysel', lad?' inquired the man. (Hocking 1966: 143)

The main linguistic interest in *Her Benny*, however, centres on the representation of the speech of the Liverpudlian street children, Nelly and Benny. On the opening page, for example, Nelly declares: 'I'm glad as how they're lighting the lamps, anyhow. It'll make it feel a bit warmer, I reckon ... for it's terrible cold' (1966: 1). A little later, Benny, her brother, exclaims, 'Be jabbers, it's a thripny ... Oh, glory! ... if't ain't haaf a bob ... If he'd a-catched me, I'd got a walloping, an no mistake' (1966: 14). In fact, however, the children's speech is largely composed of the familiar generic conventions for the representation of regionality and class that had been enregistered within the English novel (see Hodson, this volume). Even so, Benny's moral journey from violence, poverty and degradation (he is falsely accused of stealing) to his final status as an upright, Christian hero is ultimately confirmed by his mastery of the social codes of correctness, including language. '"And he has the bearing of a gentleman, too," remarked Miss Munroe. "I expected we were going to be highly amused at his behaviour and his dialect, and so on; but he really speaks quite correctly"' (1966: 181).

The use of recognised conventions continues in Tirebuck's *Dorrie*, a text in which the phrase 'Liverpudlian English' is first used (Tirebuck 1891: 290).

In this case the conventions are those used to represent the criminal class (epitomised in Dickens's characterisation of Fagin in *Oliver Twist*). In one scene in this wonderfully melodramatic text, Dorrie, having been kidnapped, pretends to be dead and becomes the subject of a conversation among her captors:

> 'We've been too long over her' … 'She's clemmed her – that's it'.
> 'She hasn't!' … You can't keep anyone going as *won't* go! She spilt what *I* gave her. She's had her chance and hasn't took it. I suppose if she'd tried it on with *your* throat, you'd have fed her with a spoon – wouldn't you?'
> 'Well, if the blue Peters scent it, this catch isn't mine – that's all'. (Tirebuck 1891: 266)

Across a wide range of Liverpool literature – from James Haigh's *Sir Galahad of the Slums* (1907) to John Owens' *The Cotton Broker* (1921), James Hanley's magnificent five-volume history of the Furys (1935–58) and Alexander Baird's *The Mickey Hunters* (1957) – there are in fact relatively few attempts to represent Liverpool speech. Indeed, even at the very moment when Scouse was being discovered, H. J. Cross's *No Language But a Cry* (1951) relied on features that, with the exception of the use of the word *moke* (Liverpool English for horse or donkey, and by extension an insult), were more familiar from depictions of Cockney dialect:

> 'Nah then, clever,' began the biggest tough, 'nah then, wot about it?' … Stamp on me bleedin' fingers, would yer?' …
> 'I ain't 'andin' over nothink' …
> 'Wot's the trouble, Mick? These mokes pickin' on you?' (Cross 1951: 8–9)

The turning point in literary representations of Liverpool speech is perhaps predictably, but for obvious reasons, found in drama. As noted earlier, Shaw's *The Scab* was an important landmark, though perhaps the first serious, sustained and successful attempt was found in the work of the Liverpool-Welsh playwright Alun Owen: *No Trains to Lime Street* (1959), *After the Funeral* (1961) and *Lena, Oh my Lena* (1960) (all of which were TV dramas). The opening of *No Trains to Lime Street*, a drama of 'three sailors searching for themselves' (Owen 1961: n.p.), sets the tone:

> CASS. Isn't it marvellous, eh! She's like a wink from a fancy woman! Liverpool … the Garden of Eden of the North … (*looking at his watch*) Eh up … musn't keep you waiting love (*He blows a kiss out to the city*) …
> BILLY (*almost dressed, opening the door*). Oh, for God's sake, Cass – you're like a big, soft kid! … Some people have to work, like, for their living, y'know! …
> CASS. Anyroad, forget your work, Billy, we're home! (Owen 1961: 15)

Owen's use of Liverpool accents and dialect in this play was met with considerable criticism, against which he defended himself confidently:

> I have fought for two years now to get plays performed in the Liverpool accent. I've had a battle to get a love scene played in the dialect. I was told the accent was ridiculous, comical, absurd and very ugly. But I believe it is a very lovely accent. People get married, live and die using the Liverpool accent, so I see no reason why they should not make love in the Liverpool accent. I could quite easily have set this play in some never-never land of the north with everybody talking like Grace Fields. (Coles 1993: 203)

Owen's assuredness about Liverpool speech pre-empted its recognition within popular culture in the 1960s (often reductively attributed to the success of the Beatles, though Liverpool had been an important centre for music, comedy and fashion since the late 1950s). Indeed, such was its prestige that an article in the *Liverpool Echo* (Frank 1966: 8), headlined 'That Scouser Accent... It's an ASSET Now', declared that

> the Scouser has arrived; the Liverpool accent is now an asset rather than a liability. They even try to ape it at fashionable parties – with disastrous results, for it is, in the most literal sense, inimitable ... A London firm of consultants told me: ... 'In certain fields a Liverpool accent could be a positive help, implying a toughness and determination to get on with the job'.

This confidence in the Liverpool vernacular carried over to its use in many television dramas (and again the medium is significant): *Z-Cars*, through *Softly Softly*, *The Liver Birds*, *A Family at War*, *The Wackers*, *Boys from the Blackstuff*, *Bread*, *Merseybeat* and (for twenty-one years) *Brookside*. Its most important deployment in novelistic discourse, however, was in Alan Bleasdale's 'Scully novels' (based on radio dramas): *Scully* (1977) and *Scully and Mooey* (1984). These texts prepared the ground for the recent appearance of a number of 'Scouse' novels, including Kevin Sampson's *Awaydays* (1999), *Outlaws* (2001), *Clubland* (2002) and *The Killing Pool* (2013); Niall Griffiths's *Kelly + Victor* (2002), *Stump* (2003) and *Wreckage* (2005); and Helen Walsh's *Brass* (2004).

These 'Scouse' texts constitute a significant innovation in that they are constituted by extended interior monologues, interspersed with dialogue, written entirely in the vernacular, as in Griffiths's *Stump* (which is further considered in Honeybone, this volume), as in this extract (2003: 13):

> – Yeh. Fuck me, am starving.
>
> – Are yeh?

– Yeh. Pure fuckin Hank.
– We'll stop at a place just over the border well an get summin to eat. There's a postie a wanner check out anyway, see if it's screwable.
– Can't wait that long. I could eat a scabby head.
– Well, yill fuckin well have to fuckin wait.

These texts are not only interesting for their experiments in representing Liverpool speech, but also for their self-reflexivity about the form itself. Thus in Sampson's *Outlaws* (2001: 24–5), the central character reflects on spatial and racial linguistic variation within Liverpool:

> People in the North End try to say the Dingle lads have our own way of talking, but that's shite, really. We do have sayings and that, to be fair – the lads at the match used to slaughter us for the way we'd say 'a accident' or 'a escort' and that. What we'd do to properly wind them up is we'd drop an aitch an all, too. A amburger and that. A atchet. But we don't talk no different to any other cunt, in fairness. That's the Tocky lads. It's the Granby firm's got the patter, all the black boys and that, all the lads with race, if you will. Now them lads have got their own thing going on. The black lads that we grew up with round the South End, once they got to a certain age they did all start talking that bit more Yardie, to be fair. They'd be saying 'I axed him' and that instead of 'I asked him'. Perfectly A-OK saying 'I asked him' the year before, but once they started getting older it was all the other thing. 'Ah axthed 'im for thum thkunk.' Putting on a lisp, by the way. Oh yis. *Pretending* to have a speech defect. That was just a handful of them, to be fair – Granby Street and round there. Lisps and Jamaican accents.

This confident and self-reflexive representation of the vernacular is a long way from the use of hackneyed literary conventions established in the nineteenth century to signal class and regionality, and can be viewed as the culmination of an interest in specific features of Liverpool's spoken language that can be traced back to those letters in the local press in the 1930s and 1940s. But this mode of representation also presents a series of problems, to which I will turn by way of conclusion.

7.4. Indexicality, Enregisterment, Representation

How can we make sense of the discrepancy between an apparent awareness of linguistic difference between Liverpool and its surrounding hinterland dating from the late eighteenth century, and the fact that recognition of a distinct form of Liverpool speech dates only from the 1950s (with its representation in writing following thereafter)? The theoretical explanation has to begin with Gal and Irvine's claim concerning the historical 'construction of linguistic contrast and difference', or, in other words, following Silverstein, Woolard and Schieffelin, with language ideology (Gal and Irvine 1995: 970–1; Silverstein 1979; Woolard and Schieffelin 1994). Language ideology in this context refers to the set of processes by which both observers (for example, linguists, folk-linguists, historians, novelists and journalists) and speakers and writers within a sociolinguistic field map and thereby construct a form of language (in the case in question, 'Liverpudlian English' as Tirebuck called it, or 'Scouse', as Shaw named it). Evidently such construction is historically variable and uneven, since there may be, as in the case of Liverpudlian English, a long-standing sense of linguistic distinction, without that awareness carrying developed 'social value' (in this case, a sense of identity based on an understood relation between language and place). In order to achieve what Silverstein calls 'cultural locality', or in other words, precisely the link between language, place and people (Liverpudlian English/Scouse-Liverpool-Liverpudlians/Scousers), specific linguistic features, say particular pronunciations or lexical items, have to be identified as distinctively 'belonging to' that place and those people (Silverstein 1998: 405). Once constructed as indexes, such features then have to be enregistered discursively and repeatedly across a wide variety of contexts in order to consolidate their 'social value' or 'social meaning' (Agha 2003) (see Clark, this volume, and several other chapters, for discussion of enregisterment in relation to dialect literature).

The model appears to work well in relation to the appearance of Liverpool English and Scouse since, as noted in the historical account presented above, although there seems to have been a clear sense of the distinctiveness of language in Liverpool for a considerable period, the indexicality of specific features only develops at a specific historical moment – in effect from the 1950s. The reason for this cultural development at that precise point is unclear, but it was probably related to two principal economic factors: the incipient decline of the docks as part of the general running down of Liverpool as a centre of trade, and the need to reconstruct the city physically and spatially (and therefore culturally) after the widespread damage of the Second World War. The creation of the city's cultural identity then seems closely linked to a sense of both decline and the promise of re-formation, to which of course has to be added the development of Liverpool as an important locus of the mass popular culture that emerged from the late 1950s. Whatever the causes, and they are clearly complex, it is evident that from the 1950s on, the social value of Scouse was enregistered across a wide variety of media and established as the dominant mode through which Liverpool is understood both within and beyond the city.

Indexicality and enregisterment then are helpful in understanding the appearance and consolidation of Scouse as a linguistic and cultural form. But there are also problems with these concepts, which recent Scouse dialect literature brings to the fore. The first issue is the ontological status of the specific features used in indexicality. Consider these passages from Sampson's *Outlaws* and Griffiths's *Kelly + Victor*:

> His fucking biceps are like ten-pin balls, now he's close up, all covered in weird voodoo tatts, the beaut. And them hands of his *are* yowge, by the way. He's got his fists up proper, like he knows how to box, and he's going to take his time and pick Moby off. Good plan. I deck him. (Sampson 2002: 200)

> An then we're out in the city again an then in another pub an then another an then the cathedral so massive is blockin out the stars an I'm off me face in Chinatown, standin beneath them yowge gates thee built in Shanghai an shipped all the way from there to here. (Griffiths 2002: 320)

The question that arises is what status the word *yowge* has in these texts? Is it an indexical form of the Standard written English form *huge*? Or, given that it is in some sense a representation of speech, is this an indexical form of a variant of so-called Standard spoken English /hjuːdʒ/ (to use the *OED*'s transcription)? In this regard, Agha claims that 'novelistic depictions of accent do not merely represent the realities of social life, they amplify and transform them into more memorable, figuratively rendered forms' (Agha 2003: 255). But in what sense does *yowge*, or indeed *tatts*, *an*, *blockin* and so on, 'represent the realities of social life'? Which and whose linguistic realities do these forms represent (albeit in amplified and figuratively rendered form)? Of course, it could be argued that the function of the indexicality and enregisterment of linguistic features in written texts is simply to mark difference (in terms of class, regionality, gender, ethnicity and so forth). In which case, linguists may simply be re-running arguments about realism as a style that have a long history in literary debates. But there is a more important question that remains, which is that if indexicality and enregisterment are ways of understanding the recording of variation, then where does that leave the question of Standard written English and its relation to so-called Standard spoken English? In other words, if a form like *yowge* indexes a dialectal speech form, then what does the Standard written English form *huge* index? For if indexicality and enregisterment apply to written variation, why do they not also apply to Standard English?

7.5. Conclusion

Despite their utility in aiding our understanding of written variation, the problem with the concepts of indexicality and enregisterment is that they leave standard language ideology firmly in place (for a discussion of standard language ideology, see Crowley 2003; Milroy 2001). The same can be said of representations of local vernaculars in dialect literature itself, since it is both helpful as a way of signalling cultural difference, but also highly problematic in that it reinforces the notion that Standard written English is in some peculiar sense a form that represents a particular type of Standard English speech. To put the point succinctly, if *laff* represents dialectal or working-class speech, then whose speech does *laugh* represent? It is this issue of representation that leads to the conclusion that dialect literature is a highly complex form in that it is potentially both politically radical, but also deeply conservative – possible and impossible as a form of cultural representation at one and the same time.

References

Agha, Asif (2003) 'The social life of cultural value', *Language and Communication*, 23, 231–71.

Anon. (1933a) 'Day to day', *Liverpool Post and Mercury*, 4 April, 7.

Anon. (1933b) 'Moss nor sand', *Liverpool Post and Mercury*, 5 April, 7.

Anon. (1955) 'A proper jangle in Scouser lingo', *Liverpool Daily Post*, 1 July, 6.

Baird, Alexander (1957) *The Mickey Hunters*, London: Heinemann.

Bleasdale, Alan (1977) *Scully*, London: Arrow.

Bleasdale, Alan (1984) *Scully and Mooey*, London: Corgi.

Brophy, John (1946) *City of Departures*, London: Collins.

Coles, Gladys Mary (1993) *Both Sides of the River: Merseyside in Poetry and Prose*, West Kirby: Headland.

Cross, H. J. (1951) *No Language but a Cry*, London: John Murray.

Crowley, Tony (2003) *Standard English and the Politics of Language*, London: Palgrave.

Crowley, Tony (2012) *Scouse: A Social and Cultural History*, Liverpool: Liverpool University Press.

Crowley, Tony (2017) *The Liverpool English Dictionary*, Liverpool: Liverpool University Press.

De Quincey, Thomas (2000) 'Confessions of an Opium Eater' (1821, 1856), in *The Works of Thomas De Quincey*, ed. Barry Symonds *et al.*, gen. introd. Grevel Lindop, 21 vols, London: Pickering & Chatto, 2000–3, vol. II, 47, 223.

Enfield, William (1773) *An Essay Towards the History of Leverpool*, Warrington.

Farrell, John (1950a) 'About that Liverpool accent (or dialect)', *Liverpool Daily Post*, 9 August, 4.

Farrell, John (1950b) 'This half-secret tongue of Liverpool', *Liverpool Daily Post*, 24 August, 4.

Frank, Robert (1966) 'That Scouser accent… it's an ASSET now', *Liverpool Echo*, 2 March, 8.

Gal, Susan and Judith T. Irvine (1995) 'The boundaries of languages and disciplines: how ideologies construct difference', *Social Research*, vol. 62, no. 4, pp. 967–1001.

Griffiths, Niall (2002) *Kelly + Victor*, London: Jonathan Cape.

Griffiths, Niall (2003) *Stump*, London: Jonathan Cape.

Griffiths, Niall (2005) *Wreckage*, London: Jonathan Cape.
Haigh, J. L. (1907) *Sir Galahad of the Slums*, Liverpool: The Liverpool Booksellers.
Hanley, James (1935) *The Furys*, London: Chatto & Windus.
Hanley, James (1936) *The Secret Journey*, London: Chatto & Windus.
Hanley, James (1940) *Our Time Is Gone*, London: Bodley Head.
Hanley, James (1950) *Winter Song*, London: Phoenix House.
Hanley, James (1958) *An End and a Beginning*, London: MacDonald.
Hocking, Silas ([1879] 1966) *Her Benny*, Liverpool: Gallery Press.
Honeybone, Patrick (2007) 'New dialect formation in nineteenth-century Liverpool: a brief history of Scouse', in Anthony Grant and Clive Grey (eds), *The Mersey Sound: Liverpool's Language, People and Places*, Ormskirk: Open House Press.
Jones, T. (1935) 'Liverpool slang', *Liverpool Post and Mercury*, 15 June, 5.
Maginn, William (1844) *John Manesty, the Liverpool Merchant*, 2 vols, London: Mortimer.
Milroy, James (2001) 'Language ideologies and the consequences of standardisation', *Journal of Sociolinguistics* 5/4, 530–55.
Moss, William (1796) *The Liverpool Guide*, Liverpool: Crane & Jones.
Owen, Alun (1961) *Three TV Plays*, London: Jonathan Cape.
Owens, John (1921) *The Cotton Broker*, London: Hodder & Stoughton.
Picton, J. A. (1888) 'Does Mr. Gladstone speak with a provincial accent', *Notes and Queries*, 7th Series, vol. 6, 210–11.
Pooley, Colin (2006) 'Living in Liverpool: the modern city', in John Belchem (ed.), *Liverpool 800: Culture, Character and History*, Liverpool: Liverpool University Press.
'Postman' (1931a) 'Nix', *Liverpool Post and Mercury*, 20 October, 2.
'Postman' (1931b) 'The artful dodger', *Liverpool Post and Mercury*, 27 November, 2.
Priestley, J. B. (1934) *An English Journey; Being a Rambling but Truthful Account of What One Man Saw and Heard and Felt and Thought during a Journey Through England during the Autumn of the Year 1933*, London: Heinemann.
Sampson, Kevin (1999) *Awaydays*, London: Vintage.
Sampson, Kevin (2001) *Outlaws*, London: Vintage.
Sampson, Kevin (2002) *Clubland*, London: Vintage.
Sampson, Kevin (2013) *The Killing Pool*, London: Jonathan Cape.
Shaw, Frank (1950) 'Scouse lingo – how it all began', *Liverpool Echo*, 8 December, 4.
Shaw, Frank (1952) *The Scab: A One Act Play Set in Liverpool during the General Strike, 1926. With a Note on the Liverpool Way of Talking*, typescript (author's personal copy), Liverpool Record Office.
Shaw, Frank (1957) *Scouse Talks* (text, with translations, of tape sound recordings made in Liverpool City Library), Liverpool Record Office.
Shaw, Frank (1958) 'Dialect of a seaport I: Dicky Sam, Frisby Dyke, Scouse', *Journal of the Lancashire Dialect Society*, 8, 12–19.
Shaw, Frank (1958) 'The talking streets of Liverpool', *Liverpool Echo*, 25 October, 6.
Shaw, Frank (1959a) 'The strange charm of the lingo of Liverpool's Dockland', *Liverpool Echo*, 30 July, 6.
Shaw, Frank (1959b) 'Dialect of a seaport II [no subtitle]', *Journal of the Lancashire Dialect Society*, 9, 32–41.
Shaw, Frank (1960) 'Dialect of a seaport III: rhymes, games, pub names', *Journal of the Lancashire Dialect Society*, 10, 30–42.

Shaw, Frank (1962) 'Liverpoolese, yes, but I don't like scouse', *Liverpool Echo*, 14 June, 8.

Shaw, Frank (1969) *You Know Me Anty Nelly? Liverpool Children's Rhymes. Compiled with Notes on Kids' Games and Liverpool Life*, Liverpool: Gear Press.

Shaw, Frank (1971) *My Liverpool*, London: Wolfe.

Shaw, Frank, with Fritz Spiegl and Stan Kelly (1966) *Lern Yerself Scouse: How to Talk Proper in Liverpool, A Teach-Yourself Phrase Book By Frank Shaw. Edited with Notes and Translations by Fritz Spiegl and a Scouse Poem by Stan Kelly*, Liverpool: Scouse Press.

Shepherd, William [Timothy Touchstone pseud.] (1824) *The True and Wonderful History of Dick Liver*, Liverpool: Rushton and Melling.

Silverstein, M. (1979) 'Language structure and linguistic ideology', in P. Clyne, W. Hanks and C. Hofbauer (eds), *The Elements: Parasession on Units and Levels*, Chicago: Chicago Linguistic Society, pp. 193–248.

Silverstein, M. (1998) 'Contemporary transformations of local linguistic communities', *Annual Review of Anthropology*, 27, 401–26.

Tirebuck, William (1891) *Dorrie: A Novel*, London: Longmans, Green and Co.

Trudgill, Peter (1986) *Dialects in Contact*, Oxford: Blackwell.

Trudgill, Peter (2004) *New Dialect Formation: The Inevitability of Colonial Englishes*, Edinburgh: Edinburgh University Press.

Walsh, Helen (2004) *Brass*, London: Canongate.

Wilson, William (1852) *The Melvilles*, 3 vols. London: Bentley.

Woolard, Kathryn and Bambi Schieffelin (1994) 'Language ideology', *Annual Review of Anthropology*, 23(1), 55–82.

8

Metaphor and Indexicality in *The Pitman's Pay*: The Ambivalence of Dialect

Rod Hermeston

8.1. Introduction

This chapter explores links between metaphorical expression in Thomas Wilson's extensive Tyneside dialect poem *The Pitman's Pay* and the interaction of this with social meaning in the non-standard dialect. Central concerns are the expectations about the use to which non-standard dialect should be put, and the status afforded to it in the nineteenth century as a consequence of using it for literary purposes.

Set in Tyneside, an area of north-east England, *The Pitman's Pay* is dominated by the voices of coalminers and also, to a lesser extent, their wives (the poem is also discussed by Maguire this volume, and the dialect is close to that discussed by Beal, this volume). It first appeared in periodicals between 1826 and 1830 in *Mitchell's Magazine* (Wilson 1843: xiv). It was subsequently published with other poems in 1843 and later, in 1874, following Wilson's death in 1858. Its author, who was himself a former coalminer but became a schoolmaster and subsequently a businessman prior to writing the piece, was famed as a local poet, and *The Pitman's Pay* gained a local and national reputation (Anon. 1874: xv, xviii, xix–xx). Wilson was also alderman of Gateshead between 1835 and 1853 (Anon. 1874: xxi).

A debate surrounds the historical status of Northern dialects and Northern dialect literature more broadly. This impinges on our understanding of *The Pitman's Pay* and beliefs about the uses to which the Tyneside dialect should be put. I will deal with this shortly. Nevertheless, to understand the cultural context of *The Pitman's Pay* we also need to consider the historical emergence of concepts of a standard language and literary English.

It is well known that through a gradual process beginning in the late medieval period a form of London English became the standard. It was selected for use in the court, and by lawmakers. It became the dominant form in literature and was subsequently codified (Hodson 2014: 24). The first citation for the term 'standard English' in the *Oxford English Dictionary* (*OED*) is 1836.

There is certainly a strong perceived link between the idea of standardisation and literariness. Halliwel in 1847 refers to the 'essential distinction between the language of literature and that of the natives of a country' (cited in Crowley 2003: 90). Joseph Wright in his preface to the *English Dialect Dictionary* contrasts regional dialects with 'the literary language' and 'literary English' (Wright 1898–1905: I, v; cf. Skeat 1912: 1, cited in Crowley 2003: 83). It is true that Crowley (2003: 98–9; and see also Crowley, this volume) argues that the notion of a standard literary English tied to a clearly defined literary canon is the product of linguistic and literary efforts in the 1850s and 1860s. Nevertheless, the number of texts proclaiming themselves to be written in Tyneside dialect in the first half of the nineteenth century clearly indicates a perceived contrast with what they are not, including a standardised or codified literary English. In addition, it is useful to consider the introductory section of the Standard English frame of *The Pitman's Pay* itself (see also Maguire, this volume). This, when contrasted to the bulk of the poem, written in Tyneside dialect, suggests that Wilson sets up a distinction at least between the language of literary epic tradition and the Tyneside dialect that he will give his pitmen:

I sing not here of warriors bold,
  Of battles lost or victories won,
Of cities sack'd or nations sold,
  Or cruel deeds by tyrants done.

I sing the pitmen's plagues and cares,
  Their labour hard and lowly lot,
Their homely joys and humble fares,
  Their pay-night o'er a foaming pot.

(Wilson 1843: 2)

Thus, the Tyneside dialect appears to be more appropriate here to the subject matter that Wilson says he will address and may have more restricted literary functions in this respect.

The poem, despite these points, does contain a great deal of what are historically, traditionally and popularly regarded as literary features – namely metaphors. I will deal with theories which challenge this popular view shortly, but it is important to retain the distinction between theory and a traditional popular view extending back to Aristotle that metaphor is indeed a quintessentially poetic, rhetorical or literary device (see Lakoff and Johnson [1980] 2003: 3; Lakoff and Turner 1989: 138, 215; Semino and Swindlehurst 1996: 146; Underhill 2011: 28, 31, 39). There was, of course, an emerging literary impetus in the eighteenth and nineteenth centuries through the Romantic tradition to valorise the 'authentic' speech of peasants, along with antiquarian and philological interest (Beal 2000: 344; Wales 2006: 129). As Wales says, an image was created of the 'labourer or peasant … as uncorrupted, close to "primitive" nature' (Wales 2004: 34). Nevertheless, building on the evidence given so far, it does seem that both the standard and metaphor were associated unavoidably with literature at or around the time when *The Pitman's Pay* was written. Questions then arise as to the impact of using metaphor in a poem written in the Tyneside dialect in terms of what social and ideological meanings this might construct. We now need to consider the status of that dialect.

8.2. The Status of Northern and Tyneside English

Hodson (2014: 25) argues that the standardisation process also entails a de-standardisation process and attribution of ideas of inferiority for those varieties not selected to act as a standard. Wales (2010: 65–6) nevertheless has questioned the impact of standardisation in the North of England up to the end of the nineteenth century. She also takes issue with notions of devaluation of Northern dialects. Thus, while Görlach (1999: 460) argues that the historical process of standardisation 'almost automatically' devalues writing in local forms, Wales (2010: 66) counters this:

> Devalued to whom? To London publishers and the literati perhaps; and to later, modern compilers of histories of English literature and language and editors of the *OED*; but not to the many writers from the regions themselves, proud of their local identity and heritage. Just as Northern English continued to be a living speech used by both the working and middle classes, so dialect literature, as distinct from administrative or non-literary documents, continued to be written and published throughout the period to 1900, and in ever greater diversity of genres, and by a wider social spectrum of writers, as rates of literacy increased and printing became cheaper.

Wales (2010: 67) argues that such literature should be judged on its own terms. There is no doubt that dialect literature and other forms of written expression in dialect can carry positive social meaning and construct local belonging (see also the chapters by Beal and by Cooper in this volume). Scholars commenting on Northern dialect literature have repeatedly claimed that it and the dialects in which it is written relate to some or all of the following: regional or local identities, populism, labouring-class values of decency, hard work, homeliness, self-help, community and common sense, and so on (see Beal 2000: 353–4, 2017: 28–9; Joyce 1991: 331; Russell 2004: 120, 123, 125; Wales 2006: 132, 2010: 67). These are values in which labouring people could take much pride. Nevertheless, I find it difficult to agree with the suggestion that there is no subordinate status attached to local dialects in Northern dialect literature by those writing and reading it. Beal (2017: 17–20) notes the impact of education and dialect contact in causing nineteenth-century concerns about dialect loss and later discussion of dialect levelling. She acknowledges that the conditions leading to a burgeoning of dialect literature can be the same conditions which actually threaten dialects (Beal 2017: 17–20, 28–9). Wales acknowledges that much dialect writing is viewed as entertainment and is comic, while frequently writers would '"code-switch": reserving standard English for solemn, philosophical or moralizing modes' (Wales 2010: 67). This suggests to me that there is a sense of appropriacy based upon dialect hierarchy in relation to the perceived seriousness of a given register.

I have argued elsewhere that much of the pleasure taken by audiences of early-nineteenth-century Tyneside song emerges from a dialogue with notions of 'correctness' of language and behaviour (Hermeston 2014; see also Clark, this volume, for a discussion of related issues, connected to the representation of a different variety). This might result in a sense of self-celebration among pitmen and keelmen of their frequently comic, unruly and coarse behaviour in songs along with the dialect they are represented using (Hermeston 2014). However, for other local audiences of, for instance, clerks or artisans, who could feel marginally superior and more knowledgeable than these groups, the response to the same songs might stem from a sense of satirical mockery (Hermeston 2014). The dialect is subject to very subtle interpretation depending on audience make-up, based on their knowledge of 'correct' behaviour and language (Hermeston 2014).

In addition, there is ample evidence that local intellectuals, songwriters, songbook editors and journalists perceived dialect hierarchies to exist and could spread that message. Brockett in his dictionary of 1829, *A Glossary of North Country Words*, is an exponent of Northern dialects but hopes that readers will 'no longer hastily pronounce to be *vulgarisms* what are in reality *archaisms*' (Brockett 1829: vii). The Fordyces (1842: iii), in an edition of songs in 1842, apologise to the 'fastidious reader' in case 'an occasional coarseness of expression' meets the eye, but insist 'elegance of language' would be out of place in such material. The dialect songwriter Robson (*c.*1849: v), editor of a collection of songs by himself and others, apologises for

> presenting the public with a book of Songs of a description which may be termed by the fastidious reader to be vulgar and decidedly ungenteel. – The somewhat coarse dialect of Northumbria as spoken by the lower classes of its population, has been stigmatised as a 'bastard Scotch – a mongrel compound of high dried Welsh, scented with Gaelic Rappee.'

Unfortunately, Robson does not give a source for the quotation that he has included here. Clearly, the Fordyces and Robson are being somewhat disingenuous. They and other readers obviously enjoy dialect songs and the rather coarse antics within them. Brockett, as noted, is a defender of Northern dialect. Nevertheless, setting aside stigma related to perceived dialect history, there is clearly a knowledge on Tyneside among exponents of the dialect that potentially it can be considered 'coarse', 'vulgar' and 'ungenteel'. I am not suggesting that these attributions are applied deliberately in *The Pitman's Pay*. Nevertheless, the poem must negotiate these potential imputations.

Crowley, discussing historical attitudes to 'proper English', has observed that central concerns often have been not simply what is proper English, but relate to who are the proper English, and what sets of cultural practices are 'privileged as correct, standard and central' (Crowley 1991: 2). Despite the interest among the Romantics and local middle-class intellectuals in non-standard dialect, and in labourers or peasants as uncorrupted and their voices authentic (Beal 2000: 344; Wales 2004: 34, 2006: 129), the users of non-standard dialects and their behaviour frequently do not fall within definitions such as those set out by Crowley (see also Hodson's chapter in this volume). In relation to accent, Mugglestone (1997: 311) contends that throughout the nineteenth century,

> Sunday schools, elementary schools, training academies for teachers, private schools … all embraced the theory that teaching the 'proper' accent was to form a vital part of educational provision, and that, by such means, regional modes of utterance, regularly construed in works on education as 'evils', 'vices', 'defects', 'faults', and 'peculiarities', were to be eliminated.

Thus, dominant views are difficult to avoid in the nineteenth century even among speakers who continue to use non-standard dialect and write in it. While Joyce (1991: 210, 279) argues that dialect in the nineteenth century is a central symbol of Northern people's culture, and could be used to assert superiority over the centres of power and high culture, it seems wise to acknowledge another point that he makes, namely that the attack on the values of the poor was so persistent it would be a surprise if some of it was not absorbed by them. Wilson, who had gained an education, certainly was not poor, but he had grown up amid such people.

My own view is that for literate people of Tyneside in the nineteenth century, exposed to strong emerging attitudes in education, the non-standard dialect, regardless of the subject matter and uses to which it is put, is highly likely to be judged against a perceived 'correct' form and perceived 'correct' behaviour. Even though it can be used to symbolise regional identity and positive values, on balance it is viewed as subordinate to the emerging standard. In other words, there is an ambivalence towards the dialect. This implies the creation of complex social and ideological meanings for the non-standard dialect. The concept of indexicality is a useful means of describing these and it is to this that I now turn.

8.3. Indexicality and Dialogism

The sociolinguistic concept of indexicality, according to Bucholtz and Hall (2005: 594), 'involves the creation of semiotic links between linguistic forms and social meanings ... In identity formation, indexicality relies heavily on ... ideologies – about the sorts of speakers who (can or should) produce particular sorts of language'. Indexicality here is a result of practice, a process of construction whereby linguistic features aquire social meanings through association with behaviour (Ochs 1992, 1993). For Eckert, linguistic choices 'index attitudes, stances [and] activities that are in turn associated with categories of people' (Eckert 2005: 21–2). Speech style is a 'practice' and constructs personae or 'social types that are quite explicitly located in the social order' (Eckert 2005: 17; cf. Eckert 2008: 456). In other words, speech style can index character, which builds into larger group associations. We can extend the notion of indexicality to orthographic representation of accent and to dialect in writing more broadly. The concept is of great use in dealing specifically with the representation of non-standard dialect in literature. It can encompass social and cultural meanings and ideologies constructed or activated by the text, and also brought to the text by audiences (cf. Hodson 2016: 423–6). Theoretical support for this position is found in the work of Bakhtin, who claims that the meaning of an utterance arises from a *dialogue* as it brushes up against 'thousands of living dialogic threads'; and thus the utterance 'is understood against the background of other concrete utterances on the same theme, a background made up of contradictory opinions, points of view and value judgements' (Bakhtin [1934–5] 1981: 276, 281; cf. Bakhtin 1986: 88–92; Billig 1996: 17–18, 206–7). Ochs (1992: 338) points out that the influence of Bakhtin's notion of *dialogism* on work on the social meaning of language has been considerable. The implication of his thinking is that the 'voices of [the] speaker/writer and others may be blended in the course of the message and become part of the social meanings indexed within the message' (Ochs 1992: 338).

Again, then, I return to the idea that for literate people especially, written dialect that does not adhere to taught literacy conventions and that is used to depict non-refined or lowly characters or the language they use is always likely to be in dialogue with ideas of a correct, proper or standard language and 'correct' or 'refined' behaviour. It is also likely to be in dialogue with notions of a 'literary' standard. This is relevant when I consider the traditional view of metaphor as a literary device. It is important to ask whether this view of metaphor affects social meaning in the non-standard dialect when metaphor is used.

8.4. Metaphor, World-View and Literariness

Metaphor is traditionally viewed as a literary or poetic device (Lakoff and Johnson [1980] 2003: 3; Lakoff and Turner 1989: 215; Semino and Swindlehurst 1996: 146; Underhill 2011: 28, 31, 39). It is important to retain the idea that long-standing popular perceptions do regard metaphor in this way. Nevertheless, for Lakoff and Turner (1989: 50), much metaphor is conceptual and is primarily situated in thought, its linguistic expression being secondary. Metaphor involves mappings between a source domain and a target domain creating new understandings of the target (Lakoff and Turner 1989: 38–9). It occurs in everyday language, not just literary language. It includes simile, since similes, like metaphor, are ways of comprehending a particular concept through other concepts (Lakoff and Turner 1989: 133; cf. Semino and Swindlehurst 1996: 152). In addition, for Lakoff and Turner (1989: 51), because much metaphor is basic and conceptual, we depend on conceptual metaphor to permit shared understanding within our cultures of a very large number of words and idioms that occur in everday speech. Finally, metaphor is said to have a major role in shaping 'world-view' – the way we think and understand reality (Lakoff and Johnson [1980] 2003: 6, 145–6; Lakoff and Turner 1989: 214; cf. Underhill 2011: 13). This, as we shall see shortly, has implications equally for literary representations.

Lakoff and Johnson state that conceptual metaphor is the product of experience and the metaphors we have depend on 'the nature of our bodies, our interactions in the physical environment, and our social and cultural practices' (Lakoff and Johnson [1980] 2003: 247; cf. Kövecses esp. 2005: 231–45). Kövecses (2005: 89–111) looks at within-culture variation in metaphor and lists a set of dimensions along which metaphors may vary. The most relevant dimensions here are the social, regional, subcultural, stylistic and individual. But he notes, 'these dimensions merge in most cases' (Kövecses 2005: 111). He says, 'if it is true that metaphors reveal and, in some cases, constitute human experience … then we should expect metaphors, both of the conceptual and of the linguistic kind, to vary according to these social divisions' (Kövecses 2005: 88).

Pitmen, through their experience as individuals within industrial and local groups, might be expected to display distinctive patterns of metaphor. It is possible that Wilson to some degree recognises actual tendencies of metaphor use among pitmen. However, it is clear on reading *The Pitman's Pay* that Wilson often goes well beyond everyday speech in his representation of metaphor and my focus here is on the relationship between metaphor, world-view and dialect indexicalities in literature. World-view and associated terms refer to well-established areas of study in literary stylistics, and, as we shall see, study of metaphor has been an important aspect of this. Fowler explains the concept of world-view as arising from the accumulation of recognisable linguistic patterns in fiction: 'Cumulatively, consistent structural options, agreeing in cutting the presented world to one pattern or another, give rise to an impression of a world-view, what I shall call a "mind-style"' (Fowler 1977: 76). He sees this as the representation of the 'consciousness' of, for instance, a character or narrator (Fowler 1977: 76). Much has been written subsequently about fine distinctions in terminology and types of representation in relation to mind-style, world-view and so on in literature (Semino and Swindlehurst 1996: 146; Semino 2002: 97, 2007: 168–70). I shall simply retain the term 'world-view' to capture manifestations of thoughts and consciousness including beliefs and attitudes and so on that may to varying degrees be shared by others, along with more individual mental functions, as these are all unavoidably linked (cf. Semino 2007: 169–70). Given that metaphor is seen as revealing world-view in everyday existence it should be no surprise that this can extend into literature and be manipulated by writers. Semino and Steen (2008: 235–7) note that conceptual metaphor often underlies our basic shared understanding of metaphor in literature, though they note that literary metaphor frequently goes beyond this in its originality. Nevertheless, they give a useful overview of studies which examine the revelation of world-view through metaphor in literature and they note the influence of imputed experience on the selection of source domains (Semino and Steen 2008: 240–1). This latter point seems crucial to me and allows us to relate metaphor choice in *The Pitman's Pay* to imputed local or labouring-class experience.

The concepts of world-view and indexicality are in fact cross-cutting and mutually influencing in that they both capture notions of ideology, attitudes, beliefs and so on conveyed through or related to language choice. Put simply, both can give insights into character construction. Indeed, Fowler (1996: 188) clearly believes that use of dialect variation between characters and narrators in literature facilitates the expression of contrasting world-views.

Nevertheless, the notion of indexicality to deal specifically with dialect is a useful one because of its recognised sociolinguistic underpinnings. I therefore retain the two distinct terms.

There is rich use of metaphors in *The Pitman's Pay*. As will become apparent, many give the impression of everyday language, while others are extended and show great literary creativity. As noted, despite the now accepted point that metaphor is not unique to literature, metaphor *is* traditionally regarded as a literary and poetic device (Lakoff and Johnson [1980] 2003: 3; Lakoff and Turner 1989: 215). This then begs a further question as to whether the poem in any way subverts the status of Standard or 'literary' English by virtue of its heavy use of metaphor or whether the metaphors within it are such that they convey world-views which reinforce pre-existing indexical relations and the status of the regional dialect. With these issues at the fore, I now turn to an analysis of metaphor in the poem.

8.5. Metaphor in *The Pitman's Pay*

In *The Pitman's Pay* most of the poem is given over to the dialect voices of pitmen and to two wives of pitmen. Some characters engage in conversation about their present lives, while one miner, Willy, gives an extended account of his life from childhood to old age.

My intention is to consider the types of metaphors used in the poem with a particular focus on source domains. I will take into account idioms, similes, more extended literary metaphors and personification. I will not seek to identify basic underlying conceptual metaphors, quantify use of metaphors or indeed attempt systematically to separate the idiomatic from more elaborate metaphors in my analysis. I prefer instead to give an overall impression of metaphors deployed and the overall impact of Wilson's choice in language on world-view and indexicality. Nevertheless, given my interest in metaphor as a literary device I will draw particular attention to extended metaphors where necessary during my discussion. Where definitions of words are not central to the discussion they are given to the right of the text and are taken directly or adapted from the glossary of Wilson's 1843 edition (pp. xvii–xxiv) and from Heslop (1892–4).

A range of source domains are used in the poem. Prominent among these are coal-mining or work more generally, animals, gambling, slavery and hell and purgatory. The metaphors range from those which are brief and probably idiomatic or near idiomatic, to extended metaphors stretching across verses. There is also personification, whereby concepts are understood through human imagery (see Lakoff and Turner 1989: 72).

One of the most striking points is the number of metaphors and similes which have coalmining or work more generally as source domains. Thus,

Will, an unhappily married pitman (not to be confused with the dominant speaker Willy), complains to his wife:

> Thy tongue runs like wor pully wheel, — *our*
> And dirls my lug like wor smith's hammer. — *vibrates deafiningly, ear*
> (Wilson 1843: 8)

Here he complains of the noise of his wife's 'tongue', comparing it to the noise of mining machinery or equipment. Subsequently, he complains to his friends:

> Aw toil maw byens, till through maw clay — *bones*
> They peep, to please maw dowly kavel ... — *miserable*
> (Wilson 1843: 9)

The word 'clay' here is an idiom for the body (*OED*), a point to which I will return later. The word 'kavel' or 'kyevel' means a lot, a working position in a coalmine allocated by drawing lots but is used also metaphorically for 'one's lot in life' (Heslop 1892–4: 414, 433). Here, of course, it is used as a metaphor for a wife. Will further complains to his friends, comparing the behaviour of a prospective bride to masters prior to employment:

> Just like wor maisters when we're bun,
> If men and lads be varry scant,
> They wheedle us wi' yel and fun, — *ale*
> And coax us into what they want.
>
> But myek yor mark, then snuffs and sneers
> suin stop yor gob and lay yor braggin': — *mouth*
> When yence yor feet are i' the geers, — *once*
> Maw soul! they keep yor painches waggin'.
> (Wilson 1843: 9)

Here the claim is that courtship is like a negotiation for employment (a binding) when the pitman is 'bun' or bound (Wilson 1843: xix; Heslop 1892–4: 112), that marriage is like a binding too, and akin to being tied to the machinery of incessant work. The notion of keeping the 'painches waggin'' arises from the 'shaking of the bowels during excessive exertion' (Heslop 1892–4: 521).

The character who uses mining or work metaphors most is Willy (not to be confused with Will above). After holding forth on the need to ease the lives of pitmen, he says '[i]ts dry wark, varry, moralizin'' (Wilson 1843: 35). Further, talking of his success in asking the parents of his prospective bride for permission to marry her, he says the rest of the terms of agreement were easy or 'caff and sand te mine' (Wilson 1843: 51). Clearly, 'caff' or *chaff* (Wilson 1843: xix) and sand are easier to excavate than stone and coal. Willy then describes his joy at the agreement in terms of being united in a joint working plot, referring to the time when 'SALL was for maw kyevel drawn' (Wilson 1843: 52). Here *kyevel* is equivalent to *kavel* above. Willy, discussing the success of his marriage, also describes it in terms of machinery working correctly:

> But we hev a'ways yet been yable — *able*
> Te keep the wheelband i' the nick
>
> (Wilson 1843: 36)

The impression from these mining or work-related metaphors, some of them probably idiomatic, is of individuals and a community immersed in their working environment, to the extent that it might shape their world-view and outlook on life, and hence their characters. This seems to be no accident. I will discuss extended metaphors related to pit work shortly. However, I wish to discuss a range of other source domains first.

Animals, usually domesticated, but sometimes unsavoury, play an important role as source domains. Willy, the main speaker, recalling his childish excitement at getting out of bed for his first day of work, says:

> Aw lap up, nimmel as a flea — *leapt*
> Or lop, amang wor blankets spangin' — also a *flea, jumping*
>
> (Wilson 1843: 24)

Here Willy is clearly comparing his vigorous enthusiasm as he leapt up to that of the parasites that he experienced jumping about in his bed. There are numerous instances of the word 'dog' being used either as an insult or as an expression of sympathy. In addition, the pitman in an unhappy marriage, Will, says he is 'call'd a henpeck'd, pluckless calf' by workmates (Wilson 1843: 11), while the main speaker, Willy, recalls his younger days below ground in a pit and among the insults hearing the command not to stand 'squeekin' like a half-ring'd hog!' (Wilson 1843: 26). Clearly, these instances are idiomatic but the source domains used remain relevant. Willy later discusses his early manhood finery and his efforts to draw the attention of the local females:

> Like ony chicken efter moot, — *moult*
> When its awd coat it fairly casses, — *casts*
> Aw swagger'd then …
>
> (Wilson 1843: 43)

Here then he describes himself as a chicken after moulting, having cast off its previous coat for a new one. Still later, discussing the growth of his own sons, he proudly tells a friend that they began to 'thrive like trouts' (Wilson 1843: 58). Wilson is creating a sense through source domains of characters whose outlook is limited, modelled in large degree on experience and impressions of lower animals, of the semi-rural, or an older farm-labouring tradition.

There is also a less common but noticeable tendency to use gambling as a source domain. Again, these instances may be more or less idiomatic. Willy refers to goose meat as 'the yess' or *ace* of 'trumps' (Wilson 1843: 25, xxxiv). Discussing slavery, he wonders whether slaves have harder 'cairds than wors te play' (Wilson 1843: 31). Here 'cairds' represents *cards* (Wilson 1843: xix). Willy also wonders, when seeking permission from Sall's parents to marry her,

> if the odds were less or mair,
> That SALL at last maw rib wad be.
>
> (Wilson 1843: 48)

In addition, of Sall's father once permission has been granted, he says the elder man laughs and jokes like 'a cairder wi' the yess' (Wilson 1843: 52). The word 'cairder' is *carder* and 'yess' again *ace* (Wilson 1843: xix, xxxiv). Again, this appears to be based on imputed experience, or at least inherited terms based on such experience, that in some quarters would be deemed non-respectable.

Thus far I have emphasised world-views that seem somewhat limited. Nevertheless, Wilson often presents his characters with great sympathy. The main speaker Willy is also permitted to conceive of his work and life as full of pain and care and this is done also through metaphor. He highlights the slavery of Africans which abolitionists have

> lang been ringin' i' wor ears; *our*
> But let them tyek a luik at wors, *take, look, ours*
> And tell us which the warst appears. *worst*
>
> (Wilson 1843: 31)

Pitwork is also conceived of as a 'purgatory' and, elsewhere, hellish torture invented by the Devil (Wilson 1843: 24, 30, 33). Pitwork then can feel like slavery, torture and punishment, and Willy is able to articulate this idiomatically or through conventional metaphorical terms and imputed experience of moral and religious discourse.

There is also the sense that this main speaker's world-view embraces the benefits of education and self-help, as he conceptualises his own learning as a 'lether' or *ladder*, but he is also wary of 'this new leet' or *light* of education eroding old ways (Wilson 1843: 57, 55). We have some highly conventional metaphors here.

The wider poem also makes clear that there are distinctions between more and less respectable and educated pitmen and their families, and setting discussion of metaphor aside for the moment, one passage especially through the voice of a pitman's wife emphasises the centrality of domestic pleasures and virtues (Wilson 1843: 15–16). Thus, it is important to acknowledge that the indexical associations of dialect articulated and constructed in *The Pitman's Pay* may be lowly but they can reflect decency and domestic virtue.

However, I have focused on metaphor for several reasons. Metaphor is said by scholars to convey world-view in everyday life. It may well be that Wilson has captured some of that in his poem, and I think it certain that he attempts to do so and hence give insight into character. Nevertheless, despite the now accepted point that metaphor is not unique to literature, metaphor, as I have stressed, is traditionally regarded as primarily a literary and poetic device (Lakoff and Johnson [1980] 2003: 3; Lakoff and Turner 1989: 215; Semino and Swindlehurst 1996: 146; Underhill 2011: 28, 31, 39). I am interested in what it means to have metaphor occurring so frequently in language that is heavy in non-standard orthography and vocabulary, and the impact of extended metaphors in this linguistic context.

In this respect, there are examples of extended metaphors that merit close examination. These are based like other metaphors on coalmining, but here Wilson through the voice of Willy clearly shows some literary virtuosity. Hence Willy describes old-style christening celebration meals among the pitmen in coalmining terms. He refers to a dumpling like a 'sma'' or *small* coal-heap and gives an account of its vigorous consumption (Wilson 1843: 58, xxx). Hence, we are told,

This was the kind o' belly-timmer,
  For myekin' pitmen strang and tuiff;   *making, strong, tough*
But now they run them up far slimmer,
  Wi' tea, and other weshy stuff.

Splash gan the spuins amang the kyell –   *go, spoons, broth*
  De'il tyek the hinmost! on they drive –   *take*
Through and through the bowl they wyell –   *pick out*
  For raisins, how they stritch and strive!   *stretch*

This ower, wi' sharp and shinin' gear   *over*
  They now begin their narrow workin' …

(Wilson 1843: 58–9)

The term 'belly-timmer' means *food* but according to *OED* is dialectal by the end of the seventeenth century (cf. Wilson 1843: xviii). Nevertheless, 'timber' can be used as a support in either buildings or a coalmine (Heslop 1892–4: 734; Stukely Gresley 1883: 254). While idiomatic, it is possible that it therefore has some enhanced salience in terms of local labouring-class experience. The same might be said of the term 'blaw-out' used elsewhere to describe drinking sessions or celebrations (Wilson 1843: 56, 58). This sense of the term is general, but again it can have explosive mining associations (*OED*; Greenwell 1888: 81). Regardless of these points, the rest of the passage is certainly mining-related. In the second of these verses, in 'on they drive', the word 'drive' means *excavate* (Heslop 1892–4: 253). As for 'narrow workin'' in the next verse, this refers to excavation of three yards' width or less (Greenwell 1888: 59). In the subsequent verse the hard work continues:

> Though still they're i' the <u>hyell</u> <u>a'</u> <u>hewin'</u>, *whole coal, all, digging*
> Afore they close the glorious day,
> They jenkin <u>a'</u> the pillars <u>doon</u>, *all, down*
> And efter tyek the stooks away.
>
> (Wilson 1843: 59)

Consumption of food is here compared to 'hewin'', *working* or *digging* 'hyell' or *whole coal*, as opposed to that which has been partly worked already (see Heslop 1892–4: 374, 396). The final two of these lines, whereby the miners 'jenkin a' the pillars doon', refers to a process of reducing supporting pillars of coal, leaving 'stooks' which are subsequently removed, after which the roof collapses (Heslop 1892–4: 407, 536–7). Of course, this is actually a metaphorical account of food being demolished.

The next verse refers to coal trade regulations:

> They were nut hamper'd then wi' vends,
> The *torns* were ready – <u>nyen</u> need wait: *none*
> A customer ne <u>suiner</u> sends, *sooner*
> Than back retorns the loaded plate.
>
> (Wilson 1843: 59)

The 'vends' refer to systems of regulation that limit each colliery's coal sales, while the 'torns' or *turns*, meanwhile, refer to the order in which ships can be loaded with coal on the River Tyne (Heslop 1892–4: 759, 479). The idea conveyed here is of unrestricted generosity with the food and unhindered enjoyment of it. More broadly the rest of the metaphor is used to describe energetic consumption through the vigour conveyed in a detailed account of coal mining.

In a further passage, Willy discusses death and the afterlife through an extended metaphor using mining again as the source domain:

And when life's last *stook's* tyen away, — *taken*
And nowt but *wyest* and *ruin* near –
When *creep* comes ower wor *wrought-out* clay,
And all's *laid-in* for iver here – — *ever*

May we a' hyell be won agyen, — *all, whole, again*
Ayont yon dark and druvy river– — *beyond, dirty*
Torn out a *high-main*, bet by nyen, — *turn, beaten, none*
And, without fyellin', *gan* for iver. — *failing, go, ever*

(Wilson 1843: 60)

Death is the removal of the stook (discussed above), leaving the old workings as 'wyest' or *waste* (Heslop 1892–4: 537, 771). At this point 'creep' may set in, whereby there is not enough coal left to support the roof of the mine (Wilson 1843: xx). Meanwhile, being 'wrought-out' refers to a pit being worn or worked out (Wilson 1843: xx, xxxiv; Heslop 1892–4: 799). Heslop (1892–4: 436; cf. Wilson 1843: xxv) suggests that a pit being 'laid-in', the state of a mine when no longer working, is the source of 'laid-in' as an idiom for death. The afterlife is seen in terms of being 'won again', *winning* meaning to arrive at new coal beds (Heslop 1892–4: 790). Meanwhile, the 'high main' refers to the best coal seam on the river Tyne (Wilson 1843: xxiv).

In these passages, using such extended metaphors, Wilson indulges in displays of virtuosity and dexterity. This is clearly literary use of metaphor in Tyneside dialect and in a technical/industrial register. Nevertheless, the source domain thus gives an impression of a world-view immersed in local industrial experience. Indeed, as Wilson acknowledges (1843: x), the industrial terminology would be difficult for readers who lack specialist knowledge. While it is easy to imagine literate miners themselves taking pleasure in seeing their technical language used in such creative ways, cumulatively, there is a limit to the overall world-view conveyed.

It should be noted also that this extended metaphor for death incorporates a highly idiomatic use of the word 'clay' for the human body which has strong analogies in religious contexts (*OED*). We have seen this elsewhere when Will, the unhappily married coalminer, refers to his bones showing through his 'clay' (Wilson 1843: 9). Another miner, Neddy, refers to sleep coming over his 'weary clay' (Wilson 1843: 13). A noteworthy use of clay is the sense of drinking as giving moisture to clay. This use is not restricted to Tyneside and is noted in *OED* as a humorous usage. Nevertheless, Willy recalls the tradition among coalminers of celebrating a workmate's return to work after a wedding with a 'moistenin' o' the clay' (Wilson 1843: 56). Furthermore, this usage is found on five other occasions in the collection from which *The Pitman's Pay* is taken (Wilson 1843). As noted, the use of clay for the body is not restricted to Tyneside. Nevertheless, it may be that among coalminers, accustomed to working in the earth, 'clay' seems to be particularly salient. Hence, returning to the long passage above, the aged body is described by Willy as '*wrought-out* clay' using the mining term to suggest exhausted earth. The impression remains of language reflecting lowly, unsophisticated or localised world-views.

The same could be said of instances of personification found in the poem. Lakoff and Turner (1989: 72) state that personification is metaphor through which we comprehend other things as people, applying our knowledge about human behaviour to understand occurrences, abstractions, natural forces and non-living things. We should therefore expect it to emerge from and reflect world-views. We see this in the personification of 'steam':

He grunds the corn te myek wor breed,	*grinds, make, our, bread*
He boils wor soup (yence thought a dream):	*once*
Begock! aw's often flay'd te deed	*I am*
They'll myek us eat and sleep by steam!	*make*
A' this *he* diz wi' parfet ease,	*all, does, perfect*
(The sting o' gallin' labour pouin'):	*pulling*
Then, hinny maisters, if ye please,	
Just let *him* try his hand at hewin'.	

(Wilson 1843: 35)

This is somewhat comic, conveying a sense of bewildered awe along with some optimism at the versatility of the personified figure of 'steam'. With the mild exclamation 'Begock!' Willy is 'flaid te deed' or *frightened to death* that 'steam' will take over his life (see Wilson 1843: xviii; Heslop 1892–4: 289). Yet with the use of an iconic dialect endearment 'hinny', directed to the masters of the industry, he suggests 'steam' should be allowed to try 'hewin'' – *working or digging coal* (see Heslop 1892–4: 376–7, 374). Again, 'steam's' activities are related to the experience and wishes of the pitman. We also see personification used to describe the freedom from 'labour' and 'care' that comes with a Saturday. At that point 'labour' gives workers respite from punishing duties and 'stays his iron airm awhile' (Wilson 1843: 45). Likewise, 'Care … unyokes his plough', thus releasing his 'nags' from work (Wilson 1843: 46). However, he is condemned along with his 'blear-e'ed titty Grief' (Wilson 1843: 46). Punishing work and pain are thus characterised as labouring people, and 'Grief' as the bleary-eyed 'titty' or *sister* of 'Care' in familial dialect terms (see Wilson 1843: xxxi). The overall effect is a depiction of abstractions in familiar human terms. This, as noted, can be humorous and this is certainly the case with the highly conventional personification of 'time'. The pitman, Willy, describes his impatience at the slow progress of 'time' as he awaits his wedding: 'oft aw thowt he'd dropt asleep' (Wilson 1843: 53). Again, then, the impact is one of a sense of wit and versatility on the part of the poet, but the world-views are homely and unsophisticated and reflect everyday labouring-class experience.

Bailey says that originality in 'vernacular writing never came so close to threatening the hegemony of southern English and of literary tradition as in the nineteenth century' (Bailey 1996: 280). The obvious question is, does the use of metaphor within *The Pitman's Pay* constitute part of any such threat or challenge? At the very least it is worth asking how Wilson has negotiated the concept of literary worth in the poem. These issues, returning to the idea of indexicality and ideology, need to be understood as part of a process constructing social and cultural meaning in language and orthography. This process is facilitated through practice and the association of linguistic features or systems with particular behaviour, functions, individuals and sets of individuals.

The overall impression is that metaphor is central to characterisation and the depiction of a local culture in the poem. Wilson depicts a thriving and varied culture in rich, sympathetic detail. He depicts characters in terms of their lives, work, domestic and local concerns, and leisure pursuits. The world-view of these characters presented heavily through metaphor supports him in this task. Wilson gains a ready readership primarily among local people. This is surely his main literary purpose. The social meaning of the dialect writing in this sense has value to local readers. The poem is very dense in metaphors that are intended to convey a sense of everyday local and labouring-class concerns, and, certainly, some of them are idiomatic, enhancing that impression.

8.6. Conclusion

There is no doubt that Wilson, in his sometimes highly creative deployment of metaphor, allows the Tyneside dialect to accrue connotations of versatility, a certain degree of 'literariness', particularly in the extended metaphors. Nevertheless, these metaphors rely heavily on features of source domains which reflect local, work-related world-views or highly conventional everyday concerns.

The use of metaphor in *The Pitman's Pay* is rich but its functions are restricted. We are permitted to hear ideologies which articulate grievances and pain and virtues of self-help in part through more widespread conventional metaphors. And, of course, more generally Tynesiders clearly enjoyed the characterisations within the poem, which could afford a sense of local identity. Nevertheless, horizons remain limited. I would argue that this impacts on or sustains pre-existing social meanings of the Tyneside dialect and the non-standard orthorgraphy and vocabulary. They are subordinate to ideas of a 'literary' language and this affects notions about the purposes for which the dialect is appropriate.

The poem was enjoyed on its own merits in the nineteenth century but operated within a larger cultural milieu that had already placed the non-standard in a subordinate status. Thus, Tynesiders may apportion value to the dialect and the literature written in it. Nevertheless, literate Tynesiders were aware of a hierarchy of value within which the local dialect took a subordinate place.

More broadly, the findings support the idea that Northern dialect writing is seen as subordinate to ideas of a standard language. As mentioned earlier, Hodson (2014: 25) argues that the process of standardisation creates the notion that other dialects are inferior to the emerging standard. It is worth noting some final and powerful evidence that dialect writers and their audiences in the North of England were quite aware of and influenced by this notion. The dialect writer Clegg (cited in Vicinus 1974: 226), for instance, writes against Lancashire dialect being taught in schools merely for its preservation. Likewise, Joyce (1991: 201) acknowledges the presence of advertisements in dialect books for guides on how to speak and write in the '"correct"' manner. Non-standard dialect, even as it is promoted, is viewed with ambivalence.

There is undeniable literary potential in dialect writing. However, the standard is used for wider literary purposes and its acquisition offers opportunities in actual life which the non-standard is not permitted to yield. Wilson, like many other dialect writers in the North of England, tends to restrict the uses of the dialect, in this case through topic choice and specifically the source domains utilised in metaphor, despite demonstrating skills perceived as literary. This is part of a process of restricting and limiting that which is non-standard even while celebrating it.

References

Anon. (1874), 'A memoir of the life of the late Mr. Thomas Wilson of Gateshead Fell', in Thomas Wilson, *The Pitman's Pay and Other Poems*, London: George Routledge and Sons, pp. xv–xxii.

Bailey, Richard W. (1996), *Nineteenth-Century English*, Ann Arbor: University of Michigan Press.

Bakhtin, M. M. ([1934–5] 1981), 'Discourse in the novel', in Michael Holquist (ed.), *The Dialogic Imagination: Four Essays by M. M. Bakhtin*, Austin: University of Texas Press, pp. 259–422.

Bakhtin, M. M. (1986), 'The problem of speech genres', in Caryl Emerson and Michael Holquist (eds), *Speech Genres and Other Late Essays: M. M. Bakhtin*, Austin: University of Texas Press, pp. 60–102.

Beal, Joan C. (2000), 'From Geordie Ridley to Viz: popular literature in Tyneside English', *Language and Literature*, 9:4, 343–59.

Beal, Joan (2017), 'Nineteenth-century dialect literature and the enregisterment of urban vernaculars', in Jane Hodson (ed.), *Dialect and Literature in the Long Nineteenth Century*, Abingdon: Routledge, pp. 17–33.

Billig, Michael (1996), *Arguing and Thinking: A Rhetorical Approach to Social Psychology*, 2nd edn, Cambridge: Cambridge University Press.

Brockett, John Trotter (1829), *A Glossary of North Country Words, in Use; With Their Etymology, and Occasional Notices of Local Customs and Popular Superstitions*, Newcastle upon Tyne: Emerson Charnley; London: Baldwin and Craddock.

Bucholtz, Mary and Kira Hall (2005), 'Identity and interaction: a sociocultural linguistic approach', *Discourse Studies*, 7:4–5, 585–614.

Crowley, Tony (1991), *Proper English: Readings in Language, History and Cultural Identity*, London and New York: Routledge.

Crowley, Tony (2003), *Standard English and the Politics of Language*, London: Palgrave Macmillan.

Eckert, Penelope (2005), 'Variation, convention, and social meaning', paper presented to the *Annual Meeting of the Linguistic Society of America*. Oakland, CA, 7 January 2005. http://lingo.stanford.edu/sag/L204/EckertLSA2005.pdf. Accessed 9 June 2019.

Eckert, Penelope (2008), 'Variation and the indexical field', *Journal of Sociolinguistics*, 12:4, 453–76.

Fordyce, W. and T. Fordyce (1842), 'Introduction', in W. Fordyce and T. Fordyce (eds), *The Newcastle Song Book; Or, Tyne-side Songster*, Newcastle upon Tyne: W. and T. Fordyce, p. iii.

Fowler, Roger (1977), *Linguistics and the Novel*, London: Methuen.

Fowler, Roger (1996), *Linguistic Criticism*, 2nd edn, Oxford: Oxford University Press.

Görlach, M. (1999), 'Regional and social variation', in Roger Lass (ed.), *The Cambridge History of the English Language, vol. 3: 1476–1776*, Cambridge: Cambridge University Press, pp. 459–538.

Greenwell, G. C. (1888), *A Glossary of Terms Used in the Coal Trade of Northumberland and Durham*, 3rd edn, London: Bemrose and Sons.

Hermeston, Rod (2014), 'Indexing Bob Cranky: social meaning and the voices of pitmen and keelmen in early nineteenth-century Tyneside song', *Victoriographies*, 4:2, 156–80.

Heslop, Richard Oliver (1892–4), *Northumberland Words: A Glossary of Words Used in the County of Northumberland and on the Tyneside*, 2 vols, London: English Dialect Society.

Hodson, Jane (2014), *Dialect in Film and Literature*, Basingstoke: Palgrave Macmillan.

Hodson, Jane (2016), 'Dialect in literature', in Violeta Sotirova (ed.), *The Bloomsbury Companion to Stylistics*, London: Bloomsbury Publishing, pp. 416–29.

Joyce, Patrick (1991), *Visions of the People: Industrial England and the Question of Class 1848–1914*, Cambridge: Cambridge University Press.

Kövecses, Zoltán (2005), *Metaphor in Culture: Universality and Variation*, Cambridge: Cambridge University Press, Kindle edn.

Lakoff, George and Mark Johnson ([1980] 2003), *Metaphors We Live by*, Chicago: University of Chicago Press, Kindle edn.

Lakoff, George and Mark Turner (1989), *More than Cool Reason: A Field Guide to Poetic Metaphor*, Chicago: University of Chicago Press.

Mugglestone, Lynda (1997), *'Talking Proper': The Rise of Accent as Social Symbol*, Oxford: Clarendon Press.

Ochs, Elinor (1992), 'Indexing gender', in Alessandro Duranti and Charles Goodwin (eds), *Rethinking Context: Language as an Interactive Phenomenon*, Cambridge: Cambridge University Press, pp. 335–58.

Ochs, Elinor (1993), 'Constructing social identity: a language socialization perspective', *Research on Language and Social Interaction*, 26:3, 287–306.

Oxford English Dictionary Online. http://www.oed.com/. Accessed 13 June 2018.

Robson, J. P. (*c.* 1849), 'A few words from the editor', in J. P. Robson (ed.), *Songs of the Bards of the Tyne*, Newcastle: France & Co, pp. v–vii.

Russell, Dave (2004), *Looking North: Northern England and the National Imagination*, Manchester and New York: Manchester University Press.

Semino, Elena (2002), 'A cognitive stylistic approach to mind style in narrative fiction', in Elena Seminio and Jonathan Culpeper (eds), *Cognitive Stylistics: Language and Cognition in Text Analysis*, Amsterdam: John Benjamins, pp. 95–122.

Semino, Elena (2007), 'Mind style twenty-five years on', *Style*, 41:2, 153–73.

Semino, Elena and Gerard Steen (2008), 'Metaphor in literature', in Raymond W. Gibbs Jr (ed.), *The Cambridge Handbook of Metaphor and Thought*, Cambridge: Cambridge University Press, pp. 232–46.

Semino, Elena and Kate Swindlehurst (1996), 'Metaphor and mind style in Ken Kesey's *One Flew over the Cuckoo's Nest*', *Style*, 30:1, 143–66.

Stukely Gresley, William (1883), *A Glossary of Terms Used in Coalmining*, London: E. & F. N. Spon.

Underhill, James W. (2011), *Creating Worldviews: Metaphor, Ideology and Language*, Edinburgh: Edinburgh University Press.

Vicinus, Martha (1974), *The Industrial Muse: A Study of Nineteenth-Century British Working-Class Literature*, London: Croom Helm.

Wales, Katie (2004), 'North of the Trent: images of northern-ness and northern English in the eighteenth century', in Helen Berry and Jeremy Gregory (eds), *Creating and Consuming Culture in North-East England, 1660–1830*, Aldershot: Ashgate, pp. 24–36.

Wales, Katie (2006), *Northern English: A Cultural and Social History*, Cambridge: Cambridge University Press.

Wales, Katie (2010), 'Northern English in writing', in Raymond Hickey (ed.), *Varieties of English in Writing: The Written Word as Linguistic Evidence*, Amsterdam: John Benjamins, pp. 61–80.

Wilson, Thomas (1843), *The Pitman's Pay and Other Poems*, Gateshead: William Douglas.

Wright, Joseph (1898–1905), 'Preface', in J. Wright (ed.), *The English Dialect Dictionary*, 7 vols, London and New York: Henry Frowde, vol. I, pp. v–viii.

9

'Did She Say Dinner, Betsey, at This Taam o'Day?': Representing Yorkshire Voices and Characters in Novels 1800–1836

Jane Hodson

9.1. Introduction

The *Dialect in British Fiction 1800–1836* project (*DBF*) investigated the representation of dialect-speaking characters in novels during the key period between the 1800 publication of William Wordsworth's influential *Preface to the Lyrical Ballads* and the 1836 publication of Charles Dickens's first novel, *The Pickwick Papers.*[1] While individual novels within this period have received attention for their dialect representation, including those of Walter Scott, Maria Edgeworth and James Hogg, this project was the first attempt to understand the treatment of non-standard language in fiction within the period more holistically. In quantitative terms, the project found that the percentage of novels making use of dialect representation roughly doubled across this period, from around 15 per cent at the start of the century, to 30 per cent by the 1830s. In qualitative terms, it found a shift from dialect speakers being primarily used in isolation for comic effect, to dialect speakers (at least sometimes) being situated within dialect-speaking communities and given more serious roles. These developments were led primarily by Scots, a variety which, due to its history as a national language, had a well-established set of written conventions (Hodson and Broadhead 2013).

In this chapter I examine the representation of Yorkshire English in sixteen novels published between 1800 and 1836. Unlike Scots, Yorkshire English was never a national language and there was no substantial body of existing textual representation to draw on, although a small number of texts published before 1800 suggest that there was at least some shared understanding of Yorkshire English as a distinct variety. John Russell Smith's *Bibliographical List of the Works That Have Been Published, Towards Illustrating the Provincial*

Dialects lists seven pre-1800 texts as illustrative of the Yorkshire dialect, starting with *A Yorkshire Dialogue* in 1683 (Smith 1839). The Salamanca Corpus (2011) lists ten texts, including a short farce by Joseph Reed, *Margery and Gulwell* (1761), which was performed at the Theatre Royal on Drury Lane prior to its London publication. This farce features the character of Margery, whose speeches showcase a number of broadly 'Yorkshire' features: 'Odsbeed! says she, my Lass, I'll gang wi thee ti't Warld's End – An away we come in good yearnest' (Reed 1761). In this case, the presence of definite article reduction, non-standard pronoun *thee* and vocabulary item *gang* represent features that are attested forms in Yorkshire English and would emerge as fully enregistered Yorkshire features in the nineteenth century (see Cooper, this volume).

The existence of a scattering of texts with some recognisably 'Yorkshire' features does not, however, provide evidence that the wider reading and writing public had a clearly defined sense of Yorkshire English at the time the text was written. As Cooper has demonstrated through his work on the historical enregisterment of the variety, Yorkshire English was a fluid and developing construct throughout the nineteenth century (Cooper 2013; Cooper, this volume). But what was its status among general readers and writers at the start of the century? My approach to this question is different from, and complementary to, that adopted by Cooper. Where he selects texts on the basis that they contain dialect representation and then investigates the linguistic features they make use of, I use the *DBF* database to focus on a specific literary genre and period of time and ask what – if any – evidence there is for a consistent understanding of Yorkshire English across these novels. Furthermore, where he examines both dialect literature and literary dialect in order to identify the differences between them, my own focus is on literary dialect; that is, texts which are written primarily in Standard English with only short passages of dialect representation, typically in direct speech (for a discussion of dialect literature versus literary dialect, see Shorrocks 1996; in this volume, see also Braber, Cooper, Honeybone, and especially Honeybone and Maguire).

In taking this approach, I have a key methodological concern. Modern readers who have spent any time reading recent British fiction are likely to be broadly familiar with present-day enregistered Yorkshire forms and their fictional functions. But, as a number of scholars have demonstrated, it is important to recognise our position as readers at a particular point in time working within a particular understanding of what 'dialect' is. Alex Broadhead, for example, analyses the ways in which the paratextual framing of the poetry of Josiah Relph changed across the eighteenth and early nineteenth centuries, demonstrating that Relph is 'a writer who at different times in his textual history has and has not been a dialect poet' (Broadhead 2017). Horgan discusses the hugely influential *A View of the Lancashire Dialect* (1746) by 'Tim Bobbin' (pseud. John Collier). He argues that when originally published, Collier's use of dialect as a 'mask' was 'hard-edged and subversive', but that this element was lost when Bobbin was claimed by later dialect writers, who reframed his text in terms of their own concerns with 'the value and the honourable traditions of their community' (Horgan 1997: 328). Rod Hermeston explores the social meaning of non-standard language in nineteenth-century Tyneside song, writing that '[c]urrent scholarship tends to emphasise the role of dialect literature in general (and northern material in particular) in fostering solidarity at the levels of locality, region, community or a "working-class"', but that nevertheless 'contemporary discourse shows that Tyneside dialect song of the early nineteenth century is regarded frequently as satirizing these groups' (Hermeston 2009: 265–6). In each case, later framings of the material constitute a significant reorientation of its original purpose.

What each of these studies point towards is the importance of not assuming that either dialect literature or literary dialect are timeless constructs, equally available for everybody to read and derive the same meaning. Just as we now understand dialects themselves to be cultural constructs, so too are categories such as 'dialect literature', 'literary dialect' and 'dialect-speaking characters'. The meanings and boundaries of these categories shift with time and place and have different meanings for different audiences (Johnstone 2011). When individual texts are selected to stand for the development of dialect writing at a specific point in time, much is gained in terms of enabling researchers to focus on the language of that text. But something is also lost: a sense of how these texts might have appeared in their original literary context. Timothy Machan has argued that 'when utterances, speech acts, or the representation of varieties serve the mimetic aspirations of a work's fictional world, they succeed or fail in accordance with how well they reproduce the linguistic semiotics of the reader's social world' (Machan 2005: 17). It is not, of course, possible to go back in time and read dialect-speaking characters in the same way that an early-nineteenth-century reader would have done, and in any case there never was a single representative 'nineteenth-century reader'. But I propose that by reading widely across the novels of the period, rather than focusing only on exceptional cases, we can begin to develop an understanding of the broader set of linguistic semiotics that individual texts functioned within. As such, I am interested not just in texts that contain extensive representation of Yorkshire English, but also those which invoke it briefly and badly.

In this chapter I begin by introducing the *Dialect in British Fiction* database. I then survey each of the thirteen novels recorded as representing

Yorkshire English in that database, as well as three additional novels that I became aware of through an alternative route. I consider the ways in which Yorkshire speech is represented in these texts and the functions that the Yorkshire-speaking characters serve. In conclusion, I consider what these novels reveal about popular understandings of 'Yorkshire English' in the early part of the nineteenth century.

9.2. Dialect in British Fiction

The belief that brief and bad dialect representation can be just as interesting as more detailed representations underpinned the *Dialect in British Fiction* project from the outset. Until that point, histories of fictional representations of dialect (for example, Blake 1981) took as their starting point novelists who were already celebrated for their representations of non-standard language. While such approaches are both understandable and valuable, they ensured that the histories that were told were ones of exceptionalism and innovation: the story that emerges is one of steady improvement as each generation of writers edged closer to what linguists understand to be 'good' dialect representation. In order to provide an account of the wider environment within which that innovation took place, the *DBF* project examined all novels written every four years between 1800 and 1836 (so, 1800, 1804, 1808, etc.) and identified those novels which contained some dialect representation, finally choosing ten novels for each target year (100 novels in total) to describe in greater detail for the *DBF* database.

There are some disadvantages to the methodology we adopted of skimming all the novels every four years and then selecting ten for more detailed analysis. First, because the project was only able to read the novels from every four years, the findings are representative of the period rather than exhaustive: there will be many brilliant dialect novels that did not fall in the target years. Second, the project is still susceptible to charges of exceptionalism: while the net was cast much more widely, the database ultimately chose ten novels per year to focus on (although our notes relating to the original novel reading mean that we are also able to identify novels that did not make it into the database). Finally, in skim-reading 769 novels over a twelve-month period, it is perhaps inevitable that some subjectivity and reader error may have crept in, and this should be acknowledged.

Despite these disadvantages, the *DBF* database provides a wide-ranging insight into the ways in which non-standard language was being used by novelists during this period. In the case of Yorkshire English, the *DBF* database provides a list of thirteen novels which contain some representation of Yorkshire English, and none, as far as I am aware, had previously been discussed in this context.

Alongside the thirteen *DBF* novels, I also include three novels that came to my attention via a different route. In 2017 I was invited by Professor April London to write entries on these novels for her forthcoming *Cambridge Guide to the Eighteenth-Century Novel, 1660–1820* (*CGECN*), an ambitious project which will provide a 1,000-word 'comprehensive listing and critical summary' for each of the 2,600 novels published during the specified period. As all three of the novels I was asked to summarise were published in years outside the target years of the *DBF* project, they were not ones I had encountered before, but each proved to contain a significant amount of Yorkshire English, and would have been obvious candidates to include in a version of the *DBF* database that incorporated the years in which they were published. The question I want to ask by comparing these two sets of novels is: how different are the stories we end up telling about the emergence of fictional Yorkshire English depending on the methods we use to find our representative texts?

9.3. Survey of the Novels

As will become apparent in the discussion that follows, it is difficult to generalise across these novels. As a key aim is to treat each novel on its own terms while also bringing out some broader patterns, I discuss each novel in turn before drawing together some observations across the set.

Robert Bisset, Douglas; or, The Highlander *(1800) and* Modern Literature *(1804)*

Bisset's novels (discussed together because their treatment of Yorkshire English is consistent) contain multiple instances of dialect representation for lower-class characters, including speakers of Scots, Cockney and Yorkshire English. The representations of Yorkshire English are only a few lines, and in each case the character seems intended to be a comic 'type' and the dialect used is both stereotyped and stereotyping. In the case of *Douglas*, a servant in Yorkshire reveals the real identity of another servant who has been passing himself off as a captain:

> [T]he servant espying the Captain, ran up to him, took him very cordially by the hand, calling 'Ned, how dost? I hope hast secured the pleace.' Ned looked confused and made no answer. This his friend observing, and at the same time, espying the cockade, 'what has't lost the pleace and art listed?' Ned slunk away. 'So then,' said our hero to the fellow, 'this person is not a Captain?' 'A Captain,' replied the other, laughing, 'no, no, he was my fellow sarvant, and the 'Squire got him an exciseman's pleace at Northallerton; but I suppose he has been up to some of his old tricks, and got into a scrape,

> he looks so glum. He often used to get measter's clothes and go a courting, and, as he is a hell of a coward, often got licked. Measter missing several things of value, found him out to hae ta'en 'um, and so, Sir, he turned Ned off; but as he knows a thing or two of measter, the 'Squire gave him a good character and got him the place as I mentioned.' (1800, vol. 1: 237–8)

Most of the non-standard features are generic. By this I mean features which are widely used to signal non-standard speech, rather than being specific to Yorkshire. These generic features here include a-prefixing with *a courting*, a general Northern and Scots respelling of *hae* for *have*, a traditional poetic contraction of *ta'en* for *taken* and archaic grammar with *has't lost* and *art listed.* The respelling of *servant* as *sarvant* indicates a pronunciation which is common to most traditional dialects of English; the *DBF* records it as being most commonly used for Irish speakers during the period, although it also crops up in the speech of characters from Scotland, Wales, Lincolnshire and Gloucestershire. One feature that Bisset is very insistent about across both novels is using the <ea> spelling in *pleace* and *measter.* In the case of *pleace* this may be an attempt to represent an [ɪə] diphthong, found in some traditional Yorkshire dialects in many words with RP [eɪ]. The same spelling practice is found in Ronald M'Chronicle's representation of Yorkshire dialect and in *A Tale, for Gentle and Simple*, both discussed below. However, Blake notes that this use of <ea> for words spelt with <a> can be found in a number of texts in the seventeenth and eighteenth centuries to indicate a range of rustic dialects (1981: 107, 116). Overall, the impression of Bisset's representation of Yorkshire is that he is attempting a generic 'rustic' accent rather than anything more specific.

Catherine Selden, Serena: A Novel *(1800)*

This novel tells the story of a woman who has been tricked into a false marriage and finds herself pregnant and abandoned. When she is tracked down to her retreat in Skipton, Yorkshire, a local gossip provides the hero with plot information in a short speech:

> 'He,' continued the gossip, 'as comes here so often to visit the forin lady: I supposes 'tis a Doctor, for poor young thing! she bees just at the down-lying. See, Miss, there's his horse fastened to rail of the little court.' (1800, vol. 1: 125)

As with Bisset, the sense is of a writer who would like to provide a little Yorkshire colour to the speech but has no immediate repertoire for doing so, and so falls back on generic non-standard features, including allegro speech such as *'tis* and *there's.* The respelling *forin* seems to be eye dialect; that is, it looks non-standard on the page but is phonologically empty when spoken out loud compared to the standard spelling (see Hodson 2014: 95–8, for a full discussion of eye dialect, and also the comments in other chapters in this volume, such as those by Braber, Clark, Honeybone, and Watson and Jensen). I can find no evidence that *bees* is a Yorkshire feature, and it only appears in two other texts in the *DBF*: once in the speech of a geographically unspecified peasant, and once in the speech of an Irish peasant. On an initial reading, I was tempted to see definite article reduction in *fastened to Ø rail*, but this would require a more detailed knowledge of the Yorkshire dialect than is otherwise evident, and is rendered further implausible by the fact that *the* occurs three times in its full form.

One unexpected feature of the novel is that, despite the writer's inability to create a distinctive Yorkshire voice, there is a scene where Serena's guardian inveighs against regional English accents, declaring that the Irish accent is 'infinitely preferable to the provincial jargon of many English counties; because the language is always good, though the pronunciation may be faulty'. He goes on to proclaim that he has 'no patience with the arrogant absurdity one so often meets with in Novels, where the author criticises and ridicules the language of the Irish, in a broad Yorkshire, or West country dialect' (1800: 152–7). It is difficult to understand what either the novelist or the character is getting at here: I cannot think of any novels from the period where the narrator writes in 'a broad Yorkshire dialect'. It does, however, indicate an ingrained hostility to Yorkshire English, which is also to be found in other novels considered here.

Charlotte Smith, Letters of a Solitary Wanderer, *Vol. 1 (1800)*

In contrast to both Bisset and Selden, Smith demonstrates a more detailed touch in Volume 1 of her anthology of novellas, *Letters of a Solitary Wanderer*. In the framing narrative that introduces a new story in each volume, the eponymous 'solitary wanderer' writes to his friends and tells them of his travels. In Volume 1 he is near Robin Hood's Bay when he stops and asks for directions:

> 'Aboot three moiles an end,' answered the man in his Yorkshire dialect. …
>
> 'And which, friend, is the way to the ancient house? Can I reach it by following the path I saw you in, that leads through the woods?'
>
> 'Why, you would not go there?'
>
> 'Not go there? Why should I not?'
>
> 'And to-night?'
>
> 'Aye, to-night, or any other night, why not?'
>
> 'There's noot to be found there, I'll promise you,' said the man, who

> seemed to shudder at the temerity of my design, while he doubted its motives. 'No, no, there's nothing to be found there; the Priests took care of that. – Some old rubbishy things, indeed, some folks do say, be yet in the old rambling rooms; but, for my part, I'se not go aboot amongst them, special of a night, if there was a bushel of gold to be got as my reward.'
>
> 'But why not? Where is the danger?'
>
> 'Bless you, Master,' cried the peasant, 'it's easy to see you are but a stranger in this country, or you'd never ask such questions. Why, mon, the Abbey is haunted.' (1800, vol. 1: 19–20)

This contains several items which map onto features that Cooper finds to be in the process of becoming enregistered as Yorkshire in the course of the nineteenth century, including *noot* as a form of *nowt* (although the realisation *noot* is not identified as a variant by Cooper), <a> being realised as <o> in *mon* and *I'se* for *I am*, a feature which Cooper discusses in relation to its appearance in Anne's Brontë's *Agnes Grey*. He notes that 'this feature is not consistently found in either the dialect literature or the dialect commentary', but that 'many of the Yorkshire locations recorded in the *[Survey of English Dialects]* list [az] for "I am"' (Cooper 2013: 132–3).

The respelling of *about* as *aboot* (and, indeed, *nowt* as *noot*) is nowadays perhaps not immediately recognisable as a Yorkshire form. Across the texts of the *DBF* it is most commonly found in Scots, although in dialectological terms it would also work well for the north-east of England, including the traditional north Yorkshire area (see also Cooper, this volume, for examples of such spellings from Yorkshire). *Moiles* for *miles* is harder to interpret/place. Blake notes that Smollett uses *moind* for *mind* when representing Cockney (Blake 1981: 116), although this kind of spelling is also used by Barbara Hofland in her representation of Yorkshire speech, as noted below. The fact that Smith inserts 'in his Yorkshire accent' after the man's first speech, and also has her speaker quietly gloss *noot* as 'nothing', may indicate that she was not entirely confident that her readers would immediately understand what her respellings are intended to indicate.

This character appears only very briefly and – like the gossip in *Serena* – the author's decision to mark out his speech as dialect seems to be prompted by a desire to provide a little local colour for a character who provides local information. Later in the novel, there is a much more extensive representation of several servant characters who have, presumably, been born and brought up in the local area but do not replicate the features that mark the man:

> 'To blame, Miss?' replied the girl. 'Why, it was my fault for leaving of the doors open, contrary to the orders both of Mrs. Gournay, Mr. Camus, and Father Galezza. – 'Twas my carelessness, to be sure; and oh, blessed Jesu!

> what a fright I was in when I found, upon coming to make your bed, that you was gone out!' (1800, vol. 1: 86)

Here there is non-standard concordance of *you was gone out* and some allegro speech in *'Twas,* but these seem to signal her identity as an uneducated servant, rather than as a Yorkshire woman. The discourse marker *to be sure* is unexpected given that the novels in the *DBF* database otherwise assign it to Irish speakers, but perhaps occurs (along with *oh, blessed Jesu!*) to signal that this is a Catholic household, which is an important plot point within the novel.

Samuel William Ryley, The Itinerant *(1808)*

This fictionalised autobiography tells the life of the son of a London grocer who travels widely around the British Isles during his career as an actor and theatrical manager. By the nature of the text, the hero encounters speakers from different parts of the country. The extract of Yorkshire English is relatively short, and is used to voice a drunken man who is tricked into fighting a bear by a stranger:

> 'No, no,' replied the stranger, 'I don't like Yorkshire fighting; hugging, biting, and kicking, does not suit me; but I have a friend without, who is used to them there things; if you like I'll fetch him in.'
>
> 'Aye, aye, *dom* him, *fot* him in, I'll fight *ony mon* ith' country.' The Belward repair'd to the pigsty, and brought forth Bruin, who, from a large siz'd quadruped, was chang'd instantly to a most tremendous biped. In this erect posture, he enter'd the house, and as it was now nearly dark, the intoxicated countryman was the more easily impos'd upon— '*Dom* thee,' he said, 'I'll fight a better *mon nor* thee, either *up* or *down*,' and made an attempt to seize him round the middle, but feeling the roughness of his hide, he exclaim'd— 'come come, I'll *tak* no advantage, *poo* off thy top coat, and I'll fight thee for a crown.' (1808, vol. 1: 98)

Even more than Smith, Ryley seems to be tapping into some cultural knowledge about Yorkshire English. There is respelling of <a> as <o> in *dom*, *ony* and *mon*, definite article reduction on *ith' country* and liberal use of *thee* as a second person pronoun. *Tak* for *take* is suggestive of a short vowel, which might in more recent dialect writing be realised as *tek*; *poo* for *pull* may indicate Northern (including Yorkshire) and Scots historical /l/-vocalisation after short back vowels. The word *fot* is harder to place: the italicisation suggest that Ryley intends it to be taken as a dialect feature, although quite what it indicates is hard to determine.

Ryley's biography (see Sorrell 2004) offers some suggestions as to why Ryley may have been better placed than other authors to access such cultural knowledge about Yorkshire English. First and foremost, he was an actor who would have been familiar with stock Yorkshire characters (see Cooper 2013; Davis 2007). Second, he had personally travelled and lived in various parts of the North of England, and while it is evidently a mistake to assume that personal familiarity with a variety leads directly to the ability to use a conventional set of features to represent it, it certainly increases the opportunity to become familiar with local conventions. Third, the nature of the text means that it is a piece of travel literature, and as I have already suggested, in-text travel seems to inspire writers to provide 'local colour'. In the same novel Ryley provides a much more extensive – and, from a dialect point of view, rather more detailed – passage for a Lancashire character, suggesting that dialect writing was an ongoing interest.

John Brewster, Yorkshire Characters *(1810) (identified via* CGECN*)*

This novel is striking for the quantity and quality of dialect included for the character of William Staveley. As such, like *The Itinerant*, it testifies to the fact that there was an existing repertoire of Yorkshire English that some writers could tap into:

> 'An heark ye, maister Milner, as for t'cattle an sich-like, which ye say hes broken down into yer corn, whya the fences is noan o'mine – their yer own, an' ye should keep 'em in better repair. A'd'niver occasion to come to ye o'sich an errand, 'cause a tak care to ha' my fences, an sich-like tight an snug as they aught to be. But, howsoever, as I doant wish onny man to lose aught by me, a'll pay ye for what ye say ye've lost by it.' (1810, vol. 1: 24–5)

Recognisably 'Yorkshire' features include <oa> spelling in *noan* and *doant*, <o> for <a> in *onny*, definite article reduction for *t'cattle*, as well as some more generic features, including allegro speech processes and the respelling of *such* as *sich*, which is found in *DBF* for a range of characters including Irish, Nottingham and London as well as Yorkshire. Alongside this relatively detailed depiction of Yorkshire English it is notable that Brewster takes care to establish Staveley as an intelligent and positive character a few pages before he opens his mouth:

> At first sight, his appearance and strong provincial dialect operated very strongly against him – but the improvement on acquaintance was so rapid, that I question whether he would have succeeded so well in his claims on your esteem as a polished man of letters. (1810, vol. 1: 16)

The narrator thus demonstrates an awareness of the kinds of hostile, stereotyping responses to a Yorkshire accent witnessed in *Serena*, and attempts to forestall it by asserting Staveley's morality and giving a practical example of his worthiness by recounting his refusal to raise prices to the poor during a scarcity of corn. The novel thus appears to be in advance of the prevailing trends identified in my trawl of the *DBF*, but it is worth making two points. First, despite the fact that the novel is entitled *Yorkshire Characters*, William Staveley is the only character who speaks with a notable Yorkshire accent, and he disappears from the narrative relatively early on. Second, John Brewster was an antiquarian from the North of England, concerned with publishing dialect verse (Sutton and Sweet 2009). As such, like Ryley, he is a liminal figure, with a foot in dialect literature but writing for a national audience.

Anonymous, Adventures of an Ostrich Feather of Quality *(1812)*

Adventures of an Ostrich Feather of Quality tracks the history of a talking ostrich feather as it passes through the hands of various owners. The novel offers various stereotyped characters, including this brief description of a Yorkshire shopkeeper who makes his fortune:

> He walked out of a remote town in Yorkshire, and was taken into the shop of Mr. — to do what he could; and so ignorant was he, I assure you, madam, that when he was asked, what country he belonged to, his reply was, Why, Ize Yorkshire, but Ize honest. He is now a great man. (1812: 85)

This representation is firmly in the realm of comic stereotype, and the character does not exist beyond his ignorance and his repeated use of 'Ize'. As I noted in my discussion of Smith's *Letters*, however, 'I'se' does seem to have some status both as a semi-enregistered form across the nineteenth century and as a Yorkshire feature recorded in the *Survey of English Dialects* (Orton and Dieth 1962–71). As such, the anonymous author may well be drawing on a scrap of cultural knowledge here to provide an appropriate voice for her 'so ignorant' character.

Daniel George, The Adventures of Dick Distich *(1812)*

Dick Distich shares some similarities with *The Itinerant* in that it follows a young man who travels around the British Isles, and who for at least some of the time works as an actor. Unlike *The Itinerant*, however, there is no evidence that it is based on real life (Lee and Haigh 2007). Again, a Yorkshire character appears only briefly and as a figure of fun, but the scene is worth quoting at length for the metalinguistic commentary it includes:

> A young fellow who gave out that he came from Doncaster, made his appearance before the manager to offer himself for a performer. This new candidate for fame spoke any language but english; his dialect being a barbarous mixture of all the provincial jargons: yet he represented himself

> to have been teacher at a school, and a perfect adept in the art of speaking correctly.
>
> The manager, who loved a joke, seemed to approve him, and desired to know his cast of characters. The stage-struck hero declared that they must be all from *Shikespur, Howay,* or *Driedurn*; for instance, he was very great in *Omlet, Mockbeeth, Cryhollanus, Jaffire* and *Willowroy*. The other, willing to carry on the jest, desired to have a specimen of his abilities, and chose the dagger-scene in Macbeth. The young fellow having started, or rather leaped, three yards backwards, began the soliloquy in an accent, tone, and gesture, perfectly original.
>
> [The young man is sent away.]
>
> No sooner had he disappeared, than the manager burst into a loud laugh, and asked Distich how he liked his tragedian? – 'I suppose,' cried he, 'the fellow is some Yorkshire bullock-driver; the effrontery of these clowns exceeds every thing. – A blockhead, who knows no more of grammar than a hottentot, who has no better voice than a raven, and as much elegance as a Russian bear, will come and pester me with his ridiculous offers.' (1812, vol. 3: 97–100)

Although there is *h*-dropping on *Omlet* for *Hamlet* and <o> replaces <a> in *Omlet* and *Mockbeeth*, the primary aim of these respellings is to create amusing names rather than render them via recognisable Yorkshire features. Indeed, the fact that the speaker is specified to be from Doncaster but is said by the narrator to speak 'a barbarous mixture of all the provincial jargons' perhaps hints at a writer who has no defined repertoire of Yorkshire features to draw on. What is noticeable, however, is that this text again expresses hostility to a speaker of Yorkshire English, who is repeatedly described as lacking any expertise in his native language: he speaks 'any language but English' and 'knows no more grammar than a hottentot'. Above all what seems to offend the narrator is that someone with a Yorkshire accent could possibly consider themselves to speak correctly or to be worthy of acting in tragedy.

Barbara Hofland, Says She to Her Neighbour, What? *(1812)*

The attitude to Yorkshire English found in Barbara Hofland's novel, published in the same year, stands in very sharp contrast to the hostility of *Dick Distich*. The novel tells the story of four generations of a Yorkshire family, the Sedgewoods, and in doing so provides a range of minor characters who speak with some degree of Yorkshire English, including this waggoner:

> 'Why, madam,' said the man, addressing Miss Sedgewood, whom he knew, 'he be the queerest man I ever seed; he's quoite a tatterdemalion loike , and still he's soa genteel somehaw, he sets a body all of a wonder: I fun him

walkin ont road last niet, an I offer'd him a lift, for I thout he looked as thof he'd seen better days; an I fun he'd just cum frae Russy , which is a grit way off; and he'd noa monny but queer shillins like this'n, an they wodn't take it this marnin for pay for's breakfast, an monstrous mad I wor; but I tuke care he didn't want for all that.' (1812, vol. 2: 10)

This speech contains a good number of features which appear in other texts in this collection and might therefore be considered to be emergent Yorkshire enregistered forms, including definite article reduction in *ont*, the respelling of <o> to <oa> to represent a monophthong in *noa* and *soa* and the respelling of *come* to *cum*, presumably in order to indicate [ʊ] rather than [ʌ]. There are also some more generic features, including non-standard grammar *he be* and *I wor*, *sich* for *such*, '*g*-dropping' on *marnin* and the <oi> for <i> respelling on *quoite* that was also observed in *Letters of a Solitary Wanderer*. Although a very minor character, his dialect representation is used to situate the character within his local community and to present him in a positive light as someone who looks after a stranger in distress and refuses to be reimbursed for his trouble. As such, it stands with *Yorkshire Characters* as another novel apparently concerned to find the virtue in its regional characters. It is striking that the author is Barbara Hofland who was originally from Sheffield, and was apparently enmeshed in local print culture, writing poems for the local newspaper *The Iris* (Butts 2004).

Anonymous, A Tale, for Gentle and Simple *(1815) (found via* CGECF*)*

This is a fascinating novel about a family who discover an abandoned baby and bring her up alongside their own children, nevertheless being careful to observe distinctions of rank so that the low-born child will be able to find a place in society as an adult. Questions of identity and status are thus at the heart of the novel, and the author makes use of a range of different degrees of Yorkshire English to signal this:

'I canna' think, an' please your honors, as it belongs to any o' they,' said Thomas; 'I'se warrant their canno' be such a good for nought baggage i't' village, seeing o't' pains Madam tacks wi' their morality, as to leave her poor helpless babe to t' waide world loike, i' that fashion; and wi' scarce a rag o' cloaths on, to seave it fro' t' clemency o' t' weather, pratty cratur!' (1815: 4)

The preface to the novel explicitly acknowledges the debt it owes to the novels of Maria Edgeworth, and it is also possible to see the influence of Elizabeth Hamilton's *Cottagers of Glenburnie* (1808), in which an affluent family take a patriarchal and pedagogical interest in improving the lives of dialect-speaking peasants. As such it can be read as an attempt to 'Yorkshireise' a form already established in Scots and Irish English.

As the novel was published anonymously it is impossible to comment on whether any specific aspects of the author's background would have provided access to Yorkshire English. It is, however, worth observing the negative review that the novel received:

> We cannot help wishing that the scene of this story had not been laid in Yorkshire. The barbarous dialect of the West riding would mar the effect of the most pathetic tale that ever was invented [...] The ejaculations of Callum Beg are smooth reading compared to the *beloike's – noa – noa's – and soa's – coorne's and meanwhile's* of the plebeians of the piece. (*Augustan Review*, vol. 1: 248, May–December 1815)

Callum Beg is a character from Scott's *Waverley*, confirming my suggestion that these experiments with Yorkshire English may have been read by contemporary readers in the context of Scots- and Irish-set novels. It also points to the fact that what might, to modern readers, seem like a broadly positive use of Yorkshire English to emphasise themes of identity and belonging could engender considerable resistance from some readers.

Edmond Temple, Memoirs of Myself, by Pill Garlick *(1816)*

This is another novel that tracks the adventures of a young man through different places and social groups, using dialect representation to sketch in a range of characters. Again, the Yorkshire representation is brief and (like *The Itinerant*) posits the speaker as humorously slow on the uptake, failing to recognise that one of his fellow sailors is a girl:

> Jemmy, a Yorkshire youth, solicitous about the health of his messmate, poked his head down the hatchway, and sung out, 'I say, Molly! you're not hurt none, are ye, boy?' At this critical moment Molly had just pulled his wet shirt over his head; but, being in too violent a hurry, he forgot beforehand to un-button the wristbands, and from this neglect, Molly of course became so entangled in the sleeves, as to leave his naked person exposed to the curious eye of his messmate, Jemmy. 'Lord, O Lord, Molly! what great breasts thee have got! – My Stars!!! – Why, Molly, they be for all the world like the breasts of a maid!'
>
> Jemmy uttered this in the true Yorkshire accent, and then scampered to tell Tom, Tom told Bill, Bill told Ben, Ben told Jack. (1816: 249–50)

The use of *thee* could be considered a Yorkshire features, although the intrasentential switch from *you* to *ye* seems unmotivated and hints at a generally slapdash approach to non-standard pronouns. Furthermore, the absence of any other features suggests that this is another representation that seeks to mark the speaker as generically 'rustic' rather than placing him more specifically. Indeed, the observation that he spoke 'in the true Yorkshire accent' implies that the onus is on the reader to imagine the variety.

Anonymous, Normanburn *(1819) (found via* CGECN*)*

Normanburn narrates the childhood and adolescence of Mabella Normanburn. It is set in and around Yorkshire, and it is something of a mishmash of different story lines, featuring a stolen inheritance, a sentimental love story and an abduction. A small number of lower-class characters are marked as speaking Yorkshire English, including Molly, the maid who is responsible for caring for Mabella during her early years:

> [S]he inquired of Molly, why papa did not run up the hill? 'Nay, honey! That's what I moan't tell, I reckon!' says Molly: 'but, I warn'd it, master'll never lug up 't hill.'
>
> 'Why, Molly?' asked Mabella, 'I saw a hare run up.' 'Aye, aye, honey,' said Molly, 'bud may be 't hare could not see 'tauld hoose!' (1819, vol. 1: 38–9)

Again there is a familiar set of conventions for representing Yorkshire English, including definite article reduction (*'t hill, 'tauld hoose*), *old* respelled as *auld* (which Cooper identifies as an enregistered Yorkshire feature in the nineteenth century), and *house* respelled as *hoose* (which was also observed in *Letters of a Solitary Wanderer*). Compared to *Yorkshire Characters* and *A Tale, for Gentle and Simple* this is a less detailed representation of the Yorkshire dialect, although it is still striking as one of the few novels I have encountered from the period that uses dialect to mark speakers as belonging to a particular community.

Anonymous, Tales of My Landlord, New Series, Containing Pontefract Castle *(1820)*

Cheekily exploiting the popularity of Sir Walter Scott's *Tales of My Landlord* series, this novel makes use of many of the same conventions as Scott but sets the action in Yorkshire. As such, like *A Tale, for Gentle and Simple*, it represents an attempt to port a genre that made extensive use of Scots into Yorkshire, and it represents Yorkshire English in the speech of several characters, most notably Mr Turnbull, who is assistant to a cleric:

> 'Get up, master Turnbull, or I will baste you with your own ladle.'
>
> 'Ise going to give tid' colonel a bit of someit in excalpitation like,' quoth master Turnbull.

> 'Hold your Yorkshire tongue, and let me hear what the colonel says.'
> 'Quite amincable, like, I assure thee: dommit, mun! can't thee be civil to a body.' (1820, vol. 1: 98)

Turnbull uses *Ise*, *thee* and *someit* (a version of *summat*), while <o> or <u> for <a> respellings in words such as *dommit* and *mun* provide some conventionalised indications of his Yorkshire accent. He also attempts but mangles some latinate words (*excalpitation* and *amincable*), marking him out as a speaker of greater ambition than any of the Yorkshire characters so far discussed.

Amelia Beauclerc, Order and Disorder *(1820)*

The brief representation of a garrulous Yorkshire gardener in *Order and Disorder* is highly generic:

> 'Lor! sir!' rejoined the gardener, 'Miss did so hug up that nanny-goat man so, and then, sir, you would guide Miss through the labyrinth. I knew how it would be, sir! and nobody could help laughing. Why, if I had not marks, I should never find my way out of it: I have known Mr. Austin keep a gentleman hunting his way for hours to get out of this here labyrinth; and here a bear leaped at him, and there a snake hissed at him, and then a vulture flapped at him. Lor! it was rare fun, to be sartain; but some did na take to it. Master had a grand *quarle* with one gentleman; they talked of fighting about it; but then 'twur made up 'mongst some on um – but —'. (1820, vol. 3: 83–4)

Beauclerc makes use of allegro features (*'twur, 'mongst*), generic 'rustic' respelling (*sartain, quarle*) and non-standard negation (*did na*). As such, the gardener's speech marks his position with the social hierarchy rather than specifically placing him in Yorkshire.

Ronald M'Chronicle (pseudonym), Legends of Scotland, Third Series *(1828)*

This rambling set of intertwined stories contains a large number of different dialects, including extensive Scots and London English, and a smattering of Irish, Spanish and Yorkshire English. The Yorkshire character, Tom, appears briefly as a young man who is startled into believing that his sweetheart, Lucy, is a ghost:

> 'Lauk, Lucy,' said he, 'how glad I be to see you! If ever I meak geam o' a ghost again!'
> So saying his threw his arms round her neck, and kissed her; for which she gave him a smart box on the ear. – 'So you took me for a spirit, master Thomas?' said the indignant damsel.

> 'Ifackins, you've raither too much o' the spirit about you, madam Lucy,' replied Tom, holding his face. 'I only wanted to try whether you were flesh and blud, or no. But I say, Mrs. Lucy, I didn't think such a pretty little hand as yourn could hit so hard.'
>
> 'Would you like me to try again?' retorted she.
>
> 'Noa, noa,' said he; 'we'll be friends. You came here to see me, you know.' (1828, vol. 2: 126–7)

The pronoun *yourn* and discourse markers *lauk* and *ifackins* are generic (Blake notes that *ifacks* is used by provincial characters in Henry Fielding) and there is some marking of allegro speech (*o'* and *didn't*). Other features, however, appear rather more specifically Yorkshire, including the <oa> respelling of *no* to indicate a monopthong and the <u> respelling of *blood*, presumably to indicate [ʊ] as opposed to [ʌ]. It is particularly interesting to note that the <ea> spelling in *make* and *game* occurs again here, suggesting either that it has some status as an enregistered feature of Yorkshire English, or that it continued to be used to mark generic 'rustic' speech.

Thomas Crofton Croker, The Adventures of Barney Mahoney *(1832)*

This novel focuses on the life of Barney Mahoney, a young man from Ireland who is offered the opportunity to work in England and comes to make his fortune, moving between employers in search of his own advantage. The novel represents Irish English very extensively throughout to voice the lead character and his family. Towards the end of the novel, however, it introduces two Yorkshire characters who come to visit the London family he is working for. What stands out about this representation is that, while the characters are highly comic, the comedy runs both ways: the Pearson sisters are countrified figures of fun, but they also puncture the pretensions of their London hosts. Indeed, the very fact that there are two of them allows Croker to represent conversations between them where they reflect on the oddities of polite London society, as in the quotation I have used in my title where the sisters are appalled by the time at which they are expected to eat *dinner*. This cultural relativism, suggesting that the Yorkshire characters may be operating within a coherent set of social conventions, is not to be found in any of the other novels.

The narrator also explicitly expresses some concern with representing their speech accurately, offering a few paragraphs to provide 'some insight into the peculiarity of their *patoîs,* which it is my intention to write as nearly as I may according to the pronunciation'. The representation of their speech is replete with recognisable features of Yorkshire English, and Croker is the first novelist I have come across to use *agh* for *I* (presumably in order to represent monophthongisation). In the scene below, one of the London family attempts to elicit an appropriately impressed reaction from the Pearsons about their experience of London theatre, and is disappointed to find her cousin is very matter-of-fact:

> 'Aye, agh'm glad we've been, it's be some'at to talk on i' Swaledale.'
>
> 'You must have found the theatre more large and splendid than you had calculated upon?'
>
> 'Aye, it's a huge spot, bud agh reckon there's more folks here than there is i' Yorkshire.'
>
> 'The scenery is magnificent.'
>
> 'Aye! t' hoos is rare and faan; bud t' music dung through magh head saw, agh was fain ti get oot.'
>
> 'What thought you of our far-famed tragic actress?'
>
> 'Her in t' green, or t' other wi' a hat on.'
>
> 'Oh, no; those were mere accesseraries. The heroine was in white and silver.'
>
> 'Aw, aye, there was one, agh maand noo, 'at went rampawging aboot, and shooted, and seemed quite i' grief about sommut, agh naw n't what, nut agh. Hev' you browt doon magh nettin', Betsey, lass?' she continued, turning to her sister, 'for agh reckon cuzzen Jones's wawn't want to be thralin' t' streets t' morn, sae agh'll git a bit of wark dun.' (1832: 261–2)

There are relatively few generic features here: most of what is non-standard is doing specific work in terms of representing Yorkshire English. Alongside the respelling of *I* as *agh* there is the parallel respelling of *my* as *magh*. There is consistent respelling of sounds which are [aʊ] in RP as <oo> in *t'hoos*, *noo* and *doon*, and [əʊ] as <aw> in *saw* and *naw*. The respelling of *cousin* as *cuzzen* is suggestive of the vowel [ʊ] as opposed to [ʌ], as has been noted in other texts. Definite article reduction is present in *t'hoos* and *t'music*. The lexical item *summat* appears, spelled both *some'at* and *sommut*.

The novel received positive notices in several leading reviews, and *The Spectator* singled out the representation of the Pearsons for particular approbation: 'There are the adventures also of two Yorkshire ladies, who come to visit their cousins in London; strong, and perhaps somewhat overdrawn pictures, but still clever, and truly Yorkshire. The dialect is perfect in its coarseness' (vol. 1, May–December 1832). In seeking to account for this rich treatment of Yorkshire English, it is noticeable that it takes place in a novel which already had a central character whose speech was strongly marked as Irish English, and also that Crofton Croker was an antiquary who helped to establish the Percy Society, dedicated to publishing rare ballads and poems (McCormack 2006).

9.4. Summary and Discussion

In terms of features, in line with Cooper's findings, there is evidence of a nascent set of enregistered features here. The most prominent two are definite article reduction and <oa> for <o> respellings, each of which occur in six novels, and interestingly in the same set of novels (*Yorkshire Characters*, *A Tale*, *She Says*, *Normanburn*, *Legends*, *Barney Mahoney*). There is a further set that appears more spasmodically: <o> for <a> in words such as *ony* appears five times, a version of *Ise* appears four times, a version of *tack* for *take* appears three times, respellings which indicate [ʊ] rather than [ʌ] appear three times. But overall the picture is highly inconsistent, and there are a number of features which recur across texts but whose status as 'Yorkshire' features must be considered questionable. When faced with such uneven material it is important to bear in mind Philip Leigh's warning that

> literary histories which attempt to delineate differences between literary dialect texts, genres, and periods based on authorial interest and skill in authentic representation of speech have not realised the constitutive role their own imaginations have played in the drawing of those lines. (Leigh 2011: 8)

Related to the question of how literary histories are brought into being, it is worth considering what can be learned by comparing the two sets of novels investigated here from a methodological point of view. When I agreed to take on the three *Cambridge Guide* novels, I asked April how she came to assign these novels to me. She replied that she broadly tried to fit contributor interests and expertise to the novels, and being aware of my interests in representations of Yorkshire and dialect, she offered me two novels with 'Yorkshire' in the title, and one novel where a contemporary review had specifically lamented its use of the 'barbarous dialect' of Yorkshire. The selection of these three novels thus runs directly counter to the principles of selection for *DBF*, being picked precisely because external factors suggested that they had a high likelihood of containing literary dialect. It is worth reflecting on the rather different impressions of the state of Yorkshire English in the popular imagination that might be arrived at by looking at these three pre-selected novels, as opposed to the thirteen novels in the *DBF* database. If these three novels are taken as representative, then the quality and quantity of literary Yorkshire English available to novel readers in the early nineteenth century appears consistently high. Seen in the broader context of the findings of the *DBF* project, the picture looks rather different.

To state the obvious looking across the whole set: there is just not very much Yorkshire English being represented in these novels. Although it is true that some of the more sophisticated treatments (such as *Barney Mahoney*) occur later in the period, there is no evidence that there was a significant increase in Yorkshire English appearing in novels as there was with Scots and Irish (see Hodson and Broadhead 2013). The fourteen novels identified by the *DBF* project as containing some representation of Yorkshire speech (the thirteen discussed here, plus one additional novel which was not chosen for inclusion in the database) constitute under 2 per cent of the 789 novels investigated by the project. To put this into context: in a recent chapter on representations of American English, I used the *DBF* database to identify six novels which contained some representation of American English (Hodson 2017). When it is taken into account that the concept of 'American English' was only just beginning to take shape in the popular imagination, and that the first novel featuring a speaker of 'American English' does not appear in the *DBF* until 1824, the comparison becomes even more striking: in the target years between 1824 and 1836, the *DBF* project has identified six novels that represent American English, but only three that represent Yorkshire English. By contrast, of the 789 novels investigated, the *DBF* project identified sixty-two (8 per cent) that feature Scots, and forty-seven (6 per cent) that feature Irish English. In short, a novel reader between 1800 and 1836 would have extensive access to literary representations of Scots or Irish English, but comparatively little to Yorkshire English.

Furthermore, there is considerable variability in the quality of these representations. Some writers, such as Bisset, Temple and Beauclerc, feature characters who are described as being from Yorkshire but whose speech is only marked with generic 'rustic' features. Other writers, including Smith, Ryley and Hofland, are working within a more specific but limited repertoire. Croker perhaps stands alone with a linguistically insightful representation. It is important not to turn this observation into a moral judgement on 'good' and 'bad' dialect writers, but instead to ask why these differences may occur. A number of possible explanations present themselves for the failure of some writers to use recognisable 'Yorkshire' features. Perhaps the most obvious is that Yorkshire English is not yet strongly enregistered for all writers and readers, and that those writers who do not use specific 'Yorkshire' features either do not have access to such a repertoire, and/or they do not, in Machan's terms, judge the repertoire to be part of 'the linguistic semiotics of the reader's social world'. For these writers, Yorkshire English exists only as a particular instantiation of the more general 'rustic' character type and can satisfactorily be presented as such.

An alternative potential explanation is that the specificity with which writers present Yorkshire English depends to some degree on the genre they are working within, and the function the character serves. Across these novels,

Yorkshire English tends to come to the fore either when the character is the butt of a comic episode, or when they fulfil a role which pivots on their local knowledge. This might suggest that they have origins as the stock characters of comic plays, or as local informants in travel writing. There is also some evidence to suggest that novels which attempt to resituate genres that had been established with Scots or Irish characters into a Yorkshire setting have a particular motivation for representing Yorkshire English, as in the case the of *A Tale, for Gentle and Simple* and the anonymous *Tales of My Landlord.*

Shifting attention to those writers who do show a more nuanced engagement with the emergent register of Yorkshire English, it is easy to see why several of these writers had access to this register: Ryley was a travelling actor; Hofland lived in Sheffield and participated in local print culture; Croker was an antiquarian. These observations suggest that future research may want to examine the role of such intermediary figures, who have access to local dialect writing but at the same time write for national literary audiences.

Finally, it is worth paying attention to the incomprehension and hostility which is expressed towards speakers of Yorkshire English in several of these texts. This is an aspect that is easy to overlook from the comfortable perspective of the twenty-first century when, as Hermeston points out, we are accustomed to see dialect writing framed in terms of solidarity, community and local identity. Many of these novels present their Yorkshire speakers as both isolated and comically stupid; *Dick Distich* presents the would-be Doncaster actor as no better than a foreigner; and even *Barney Mahoney*, which is singular for the degree to which it presents speakers of Yorkshire English as having a viewpoint of their own, frames their introduction with an anecdote about the incomprehensibility of Yorkshire English:

> I recollect once seeing an accomplished and learned gentleman totally nonplused by a sentence which fell from the lips of a young Yorkshireman. He had been to call upon a person whom he did not find at home, and coming suddenly back, said to his friend,–
>
> 'They's no pessen i' t' hoos,' literally translated, 'There's no person in the house.' The gentleman looked at the speaker, and gravely inquired, 'Pray what countryman is this; I have travelled all over Europe and America but do not at all recognize *the language*.' (Croker 1832: 226)

This is the context within which some writers were attempting to present a broader and more sympathetic range of Yorkshire English speakers.

Note

1. Acknowledgement: This work was supported by the Arts and Humanities Research Council, grant number AH/FO19157/1.

Novels Analysed

Anon. 1812. *The Adventures of an Ostrich Feather of Quality.* London: Sherwood, Neely, and Jones.

Anon. 1815. *A Tale, for Gentle and Simple.* London: Rowland Hunter.

Anon. 1819. *Normanburn; or, the History of a Yorkshire Family: A Novel.* London: Sherwood, Neely, and Jones.

Anon. 1820. *Tales of My Landlord, New Series, Containing Pontefract Castle.* London: William Fearman.

Beauclerc, Amelia. 1820. *Disorder and Order: A Novel.* London: A. K. Newman and Co.

Bisset, Robert. 1800. *Douglas; or, the Highlander: A Novel.* London: The Anti-Jacobin Press.

Bisset, Robert. 1804. *Modern Literature: A Novel.* London: T. N. Longman and O. Rees.

Brewster, John. 1810. *Yorkshire Characters: A Novel.* London: J. F. Hughes.

Croker, Thomas Crofton. 1832. *The Adventures of Barney Mahoney.* London: Fisher, Son, and Jackson.

Daniel, George. 1812. *The Adventures of Dick Distich.* London: Effingham Wilson.

Hofland, Barbara. 1812. *Says She to Her Neighbour, What?* London: Minerva Press.

M'Chronicle, Ronald (pseudonym). 1828. *Legends of Scotland, Third Series.* London: A. K. Newman & Co.

Ryley, Samuel William. 1808. *The Itinerant, or Memoirs of an Actor.* London: Taylor and Hessey.

Selden, Catharine. 1800. *Serena: A Novel.* London: William Lane.

Smith, Charlotte. 1800. *The Letters of a Solitary Wanderer: Containing Narratives of Various Description.* Vol. 2. London: Sampson Low.

Temple, Edmond. 1816. *Memoirs of Myself, by Pill Garlick.* London: John Miller.

References

Blake, Norman Francis. 1981. *Non-Standard Language in English Literature.* London: Deutsch.

Broadhead, Alex. 2017. 'The Textual History of Josiah Relph's Cumberland Poems: Inventing Dialect Literature in the Long Nineteenth Century'. In *Dialect and Literature in the Long Nineteenth Century*, ed. by Jane Hodson, 67–88. Abingdon: Routledge.

Butts, Dennis. 2004. 'Hofland [Née Wreaks], Barbara (Bap. 1770, d. 1844), Children's Writer and Novelist'. Oxford University Press. https://doi.org/10.1093/ref:odnb/13457.

Cooper, Paul Stephen. 2013. 'Enregisterment in Historical Contexts: A Framework'. University of Sheffield.

Davis, Jim. 2007. 'The Sublime of Tragedy in Low Life'. *European Romantic Review* 18(2): 159–67. https://doi.org/10.1080/10509580701297885.

Hermeston, Rod. 2009. 'Linguistic Identity in Nineteenth-Century Tyneside Dialect Songs'. Unpublished PhD Thesis. University of Leeds.

Hodson, Jane. 2014. *Dialect in Film and Literature.* Basingstoke: Palgrave Macmillan.

Hodson, Jane. 2017. '"I Expect That I Prefer Them Horses Considerable beyond the Oxen": American English in British Fiction 1800–1836'. In *Dialect and Literature in the Long Nineteenth Century*, ed. by Jane Hodson. Aldershot: Ashgate.

Hodson, Jane and Alex Broadhead. 2013. 'Developments in Literary Dialect Representation in British Fiction 1800–1836'. *Language and Literature* 22(4): 314–32.

Hodson, Jane, Alex Broadhead, Julie Millward, Katherine Rogers and Michael Pidd. 2014. 'Dialect in British Fiction 1800–1836'. November. http://www.dialect-fiction.org.

Horgan, D. M. 1997. 'Popular Protest in the Eighteenth Century: John Collier (Tim Bobbin), 1708–1786'. *The Review of English Studies* 48(191): 310–31. http://www.jstor.org/stable/517600.

Johnstone, Barbara. 2011. 'Dialect Enregisterment in Performance'. *Journal of Sociolinguistics* 15(5): 657–79. https://doi.org/10.1111/j.1467-9841.2011.00512.x.

Lee, Sidney and John D. Haigh. 2007. 'Daniel, George [Pseud. P— P—] (1789–1864), Writer and Book Collector'. Oxford University Press. https://doi.org/10.1093/ref:odnb/7115.

Leigh, Philip John. 2011. 'A Game of Confidence: Literary Dialect, Linguistics and Authenticity'. PhD Thesis, University of Texas at Austin.

McCormack, W. J. 2006. 'Croker, Thomas Crofton (1798–1854), Antiquary'. Oxford University Press. https://doi.org/10.1093/ref:odnb/6741.

Machan, Tim William. 2005. *English in the Middle Ages*. Oxford: Oxford University Press.

Orton, Harold and Eugen Dieth, eds. 1962–71. *Survey of English Dialects (B): The Basic Material*. Leeds: Arnold and Son.

Reed, Joseph. 1761. *Margery and Gulwell*. Scene I, Act I. The Register Office. London: T. Davies: 10–13. http://www.thesalamancacorpus.com/dl_n_yks_d_1700-1799_joseph-reed_margery-and-gulwell-_1761.html, produced by María F. García-Bermejo Giner. Salamanca: © 2011-DING, The Salamanca Corpus, University of Salamanca.

Shorrocks, Graham. 1996. 'Non-Standard Dialect Literature and Popular Culture'. In *Speech Past and Present: Studies in English Dialectology in Memory of Ossi Ihalainen*, ed. by Juhani Klemola, Merja Kyto and Matti Rissanen, 385–411. University of Bamberg Studies in English Linguistics. Frankfurt am Main: Peter Lang.

Smith, John Russell. 1839. *A Bibliographical List of the Works That Have Been Published: Towards Illustrating the Provincial Dialects of England*. London: John Russell Smith.

Sorrell, Mark. 2004. 'Ryley [Formerly Romney], Samuel William (1759–1837), Actor and Author'. Oxford University Press. https://doi.org/10.1093/ref:odnb/24422.

Sutton, C. W. and R. H. Sweet. 2009. 'Brewster, John (1754–1842), Church of England Clergyman and Antiquary'. Oxford University Press. https://doi.org/10.1093/ref:odnb/3373.

Wales, Katie. 2017. 'Dickens and Northern English, Stereotyping and "Authenticity" Reconsidered'. In *Perspectives on Northern English*, ed. by Joan C. Beal and Sylvie Hancil. Berlin and Boston: De Gruyter Mouton.

10

Which Phonological Features Get Represented in Dialect Writing? Answers and Questions from Three Types of Liverpool English Texts

Patrick Honeybone

10.1. Introduction

One of the (many) reasons why linguists are interested in dialect writing is because it might offer an insight into which phonological dialect features are salient to speakers of specific dialects – this can then connect to the complex and little-considered (but quite fundamental) question of what we might mean by 'dialect feature' in the first place: what limits are there on what can count as a dialect feature? How psychologically real are dialect features? Are the dialect features that linguists discuss the same things (or, even, *the same kind of things*) that speakers might discuss? Engaging with these kinds of question connects to some of the ideas that are studied in perceptual dialectology (which might allow us to understand which dialects are recognised by speakers as relevant to themselves) and also to our understanding of linguistic change: we might expect certain types of change only in features which are salient (and others in features which are not). Understanding this aspect of dialect writing thus can in principle offer us much, but also requires much of us. One of the things that it requires is a deep understanding of the kinds of 'respellings' that are typically used in dialect writing to represent phonological dialect features: which respellings actually represent dialect features? How often are they used in texts? Why are some respellings used which *don't* represent dialect features?

One chapter like this cannot hope to answer all these questions, or even to engage with all of these issues, but I list them here because they all shape the lens through which I investigate dialect writing in this chapter, and some of what I consider addresses some of them directly.[1] It strikes me that many of these points are quite poorly understood. The specific question of this chapter's title (which connects to many of the broader issues just mentioned) is: which dialect features get represented in dialect writing? If we can understand this, we can hope to move towards answering some of the other questions just mentioned. I pursue it at the phonological level. Some of the issues that crop up here no doubt also affect the representation of dialect features at other linguistic levels (lexis, morphology, syntax, pragmatics, etc.), but there are also doubtless level-specific issues which are not relevant to the interaction of dialect writing and phonology. I do not engage with them here. We will have enough to deal with even if we focus only on phonology. A substantial separate (but related) goal of this chapter is to work towards an understanding of the whole notion of 'respelling' in dialect writing. We will see that both phonological and non-phonological (and dialectological and non-dialectological) issues constrain and motivate the use of respelling. All of this adds up to make dialect writing an immensely complex and multifaceted phenomenon.

I focus on dialect writing that has been produced to represent one variety of English. The variety in question ranks high in terms of its dialectal salience in Britain, and is notable because it has a number of phonological dialect features which set it apart from many other varieties, including those which are spoken in the same area of the country (I discuss both of these points briefly below). The variety in question is Liverpool English (LE). I have worked to describe aspects of the phonology of LE for around twenty years, and the knowledge of the variety that I have developed over this period will prove to be important below. It can be crucial that a reader knows a variety well in order to fully understand the spellings that might be used to represent it.

In Section 10.2 of this chapter, I consider some basics of dialect writing (of the types that I investigate), and then focus on some of the general constraints that affect its ability to reflect the phonology of non-standard varieties – this discussion is intended to be one of the main contributions of this chapter, as such issues are rarely discussed in detail and are in part quite poorly understood. Section 10.3 introduces the kinds of dialect writing that exists in Liverpool English, and Section 10.4 then considers how respelling is used and which phonological features are represented in a corpus of LE dialect writing texts. I take an inductive, systematic and quantitative approach, noting each occasion of a respelled word in three texts, and allocating them to distinct dialect features (or to eye dialect) as appropriate, thus generating a set of dialect features which are represented in the texts (and which are thus at least some of those that can be represented in dialect writing for LE). This is discussed in the light of some of the issues raised in Section 10.2, and is intended as the other main contribution of this chapter. Section 10.5

concludes, although I should admit from the outset that this chapter is only a small step on the way to understanding the issues that it engages with (both in general terms, as part of 'dialect writing studies', and specifically in terms of understanding LE dialect writing), and part of its intention is simply to set out the issues clearly, and to show what else we need to understand.

10.2. Dialect Writing

The broad spectrum of dialect writing (as discussed in Honeybone and Maguire, this volume) includes a vast variety of types of text, from ephemeral electronic ego-documents (as discussed in Nini *et al.*, this volume) to locally published comic material (as discussed in Clark, this volume) to 'serious' novels (as discussed in Hodson, this volume). I focus on three types of text here, all of which aim to represent Liverpool English in at least part of their text. As further discussed in Honeybone and Maguire (this volume), and as is well recognised (in part following Shorrocks 1996), dialect writing can vary in its intentions along a number of axes, including: the proportion of a text which aims to represent dialect (is it the whole text, or only parts of direct speech, or some other specific parts of the text?); the audience (is the text intended for a general audience of anyone who can read English, or is it intended primarily for readers who speak the dialect represented?); and the seriousness of the attempt to represent the dialect (is the author really attempting to represent the precise dialect features associated with the variety, or doesn't it really matter to the author, as long as the relevant part of the text is seen to be 'non-standard'?). The main texts that I consider in this chapter vary somewhat along these axes, as I discuss when I describe them in Section 10.3, although all of them, I argue, make a serious (and to a non-negligible degree successful) attempt to represent LE. They are all written by people who have a considerable knowledge of LE (which is, of course, not always the case in dialect writing).

10.2.1. Respellings and Representing Phonology in Dialect Writing

The key tool that authors use to represent phonological dialect features is to 'respell' words, whereby words are consciously spelt in a way that is different from their standard spelling – indeed, the use of respelling is one of the most obvious signs that a text is intended to be dialect writing. In part, however, the respelling involved in dialect writing may simply be used to indicate that the text is intended to represent a non-standard variety and may not be intended to represent a dialect feature – this is entirely rational and works straightforwardly: it involves the use of non-standard spelling to represent non-standard dialect. Such respellings may simply be alternative representations of the phonology of a word which does not diverge from the phonology of a reference variety. This can be very productive in English as many words have the same underlying representation in many dialects (or at least involve phonological units which correspond in a one-to-one relationship across dialects), and English orthography involves many graphemes, so that most phonological segments can be written in several ways. Such spellings are often called 'eye dialect', a term that I adopt here. For example, the word *people* (which arguably has the underlying form /pipl/ in most dialects, with the final consonant realised as syllabic) could just as well be spelt *peepul*, as <ee> is a common representation of the tense vowel, and <ul> represents the syllabic /l/ well. Equally, *cow* could be *respelled* as *kow*, which simply makes use of the fact that both <c> and <k> can spell /k/ in English when they occur initially before a back vowel. The spelling out of General English 'weak forms' is also typically seen as eye dialect, as it would also work just as well for Standard English as for a particular non-standard dialect. Thus *was*, which is commonly realised as [wəz] in English, could be spelt as *wuz*, which removes the ambiguity of the spelling of the final fricative and uses <u> to spell schwa (as in *focus*, *rectum*, *syrup*). The use of eye dialect in dialect writing is sometimes disparaged (as in, for example, Preston 1982, 1985). While important points are made in such work (about the representation of non-standard language by non-speakers of the dialect concerned), I argue below that there can also be reasons to view the use of eye dialect in positive ways.

Most dialect writing does not simply rely on eye dialect to mark a text as non-standard, however. The point of interest in this chapter is that many respellings in such texts are intended to represent phonological dialect features. This point is at the same time very obvious and also very poorly understood. There is a fair amount of previous work on the interpretation of what authors are doing when they use respellings to represent dialect phonology in dialect writing, and certain principles are well established, but there is very little work which really goes into the phenomenon in detail, either to understand the processes involved or to consider precisely what specific writers (or sets of writers) have done in representing specific varieties. For example, Beal (2000) aims to document that certain recognised dialect features are represented in certain specific texts, and Honeybone and Watson (2013) focus on a small set of predetermined features to determine how robustly they are represented in texts. Such work typically restricts the number of dialect features that are considered while investigating a text (which is a perfectly sensible thing to do in order to be able to investigate the representation of those specific features). In this chapter, I aim to do the opposite. As I explain in Section 10.4, I aim to consider all of the types of respellings that are used in a number of texts, in order to (begin to) investigate which (types of) dialect features get represented at all in dialect writing.

Given that I am aiming to understand how the dialect features in speakers' phonologies can be represented in dialect writing, it will be important to be clear about some fundamental issues that affect the basic processes involved. I consider them in the remainder of this section. I am not aware of much previous detailed work on these issues, and some of the points discussed here begin from a quite basic level.

Firstly, what *are* dialect features? As I understand it, a 'dialect feature' is a specific structural characteristic of language where a particular non-standard dialect differs from a standard or reference variety (in what follows, I talk of Standard English (StE) when referring to morphology, lexis or syntax, and Reference English, or RefE, when referring to phonology, on the assumption that there is not really a *standard* pronunciation – to most intents and purposes, RefE is something like RP). Defined in this way, many 'features of a particular dialect' will be shared widely with many other dialects – only a few are fundamentally unique to one dialect area – but that does not mean that they are not dialect features of the particular dialect under consideration. For example, just because LE shares an absence of a FOOT–STRUT split with other dialects from the North of England does not mean that 'the absence of a FOOT–STRUT split' is not a dialect feature of LE. On the other hand, dialect features which are *not* shared with other varieties (such as the widespread lenition of stops in LE, for example) might be expected to differ in the extent to which they are salient to speakers (whether they do differ in salience in this way is a moot point – Honeybone and Watson 2013 and Honeybone *et al.* 2017 argue that things are more complicated than this, partly in phonologically predictable ways).

This definition of dialect features assumes that the person who assumes something to be a dialect feature knows enough about a standard or reference variety in order to recognise that the two varieties are different. For linguists investigating dialects, we may expect that such knowledge is at a high level, but the extent to which this works for 'lay' speakers is in and of itself an interesting and complex point, which is worthy of study. The extent to which speakers of non-standard dialects are familiar with a standard variety has changed considerably over time, and this might be expected to affect how dialect features have been represented in dialect writing in different time periods. In the same way, it is likely the case that authors' knowledge of non-standard dialects that are not their own, but which they nonetheless aim to represent in writing (as in some of the cases of 'literary dialect' considered by Hodson, this volume, among others), has increased over time, or at least that it varies from author to author. It could be that speakers of a particular dialect might define (some of) the dialect features that they are aware of in terms of differences with other (perhaps neighbouring or nearby) non-standard dialects – so, for example, something may be a salient dialect feature of Liverpool English because it is different from South Lancashire English, or Manchester English (see in this regard the discussion of the salience of differences between the dialects of Geordie and Mackem, spoken in the neighbouring cities of Newcastle upon Tyne and Sunderland, in Beal 2000). To keep things manageable, I assume here that writers are aware of differences between the varieties that they are representing and Standard/Reference English.

Some basic assumptions that are necessary for the existence of phonologically relevant respellings in dialect writing and for how we should interpret them are thus: (i) that writers are aware of what they are doing; (ii) that writers and readers know the Standard English spellings of words, so that any divergence from this will be recognised and will mark out a form as 'dialect'; (iii) that writers and readers furthermore know the segmental principles of English orthography, in terms of the mappings that are possible for grapheme-to-phonological-entity (for example, that a tense high rounded vowel can be represented in English in several different ways, such as <u…e> as in *chute*, <oo> *boot*, <ew> *blew*, <ue> *true*, <ioux> *Sioux*, <ough> *through*), and can use them in creative ways; and (iv) that writers and readers know about the phonological differences that exist between the reference variety and the dialect that is being represented. I have just considered how complex point (iv) is, and point (iii) really invites considerable reflection, too. Even if we set aside the immense complexity of English orthography and the vast range of options that exist in it for spelling phonological features, the full picture is that writers and readers of dialect writing need to understand English orthography-to-phonology mappings in the light of both the phonology of Standard/Reference English *and* the dialect that is being represented (which are never exactly the same and are often considerably different), and be able to compare the two in order to recognise analogues between them. I will need to set many of these complexities aside here.

A short example of dialect writing that Hodson (2014) reports, found on a sign from the Lake District, will allow us to explore some of these points. She writes that 'the respelling is aimed at showing how Cumbrian English differs from RP' and reproduces the sign as in (1).

(1) TEK CARE
LAMBS
ONT ROAD

There are two respellings here: *tek* is used instead of *take*, and *ont* is used instead of *on the*. The first of these is relatively straightforward to interpret. The writer of the sign has recognised that the phonology of the Cumbrian corresponds to Reference English /teɪk/ (with a diphthong, or at least a long, tense monophthong) and that the two are different, and has adopted a spelling to represent this. The spelling unambiguously represents the fact that the writer's dialect has a short/lax vowel in this word (something like /tɛk/) – although <Cek> is not at all common in English spelling (with 'C' standing for 'any consonant'), <e> can only represent a long/tense/diphthongal vowel if the <k> represents a consonant in an onset, as in *eureka*, or if it is part of a split digraph (<e…e>), as in *eke*. The sequence <CeC#> is not unusual as a representation of /ɛ/ in English (as in *step*, *net*, *yes*) and there is one model for <Cek>: *trek*.

The second respelling is clearly intended to represent Definite Article Reduction (DAR), which is a highly salient difference between many dialects from the North of England (in which the definite article can be realised in fully vowelless forms, such as [t], [ʔ] and [θ] – see, for example, Jones 2002), and other dialects, including Standard/Reference English (where the definite article is typically realised as [ðə], or perhaps as [ð], but only through extreme vowel reduction). The form *ont* represents DAR quite clearly, including the absence of any vowel in the definite article, although it is not clear whether the writer intended to represent [t] or [ʔ] (or indeed whether they could differentiate between them) because <t> could obviously represent [t], but <t> is also the letter that most commonly corresponds to the segment that is involved in *t*-glottalling in those varieties of English that feature it, so the <t> in *but* and *butter* could be seen as a way to represent a [ʔ] if a speaker pronounces them as [bʊʔ]/[bʌʔ] and [bʊʔə]/[bʌʔə]. A further complicating factor here, however, as Jones (2007: 61) writes, is that DAR 'has a long tradition of orthographic representation in literature and the media, most commonly as <t'>'. It is by no means the case that each act of dialect writing involves a completely novel invention of an orthography for the variety represented – it surely does sometimes, but in the majority of cases it does not. As Beal (2000) notes, certain dialectal spelling conventions can 'become tokens of a regional identity', and traditions of dialect writing can develop in areas which can lead to the development of established orthographic conventions for the spelling of dialect features, such as the use of <oo> to spell the fact the words such as *town*, *down*, *about* have a monophthong in English from the north-east of England, which is different from the diphthong found in reference varieties (giving *toon*, *doon* and *aboot*). Since Agha (2003), this kind of codification of particular dialect features as part of a fixed repertoire of features that speakers are highly aware of is often called 'enregisterment' (as discussed in several other chapters of this book, especially that by Cooper). It seems to me that this notion of enregisterment has something important to tell us about which features may get written in a piece of dialect writing – it can offer clear 'dialect spellings', such as the case just mentioned where <oo> (rather than, for example, <u…e>, <ew> or <ue>) is used for cases of [uː] which correspond to [aʊ] in many other varieties – but I suspect that many dialect features never become enregistered but may still be spelt, at least on occasion, in dialect writing (as long as writers can be aware of them at all). It can surely be the case that certain dialect spellings are handed down from writer to writer, but others (perhaps in the same text) may well be invented (or reinvented anew) as the writer writes.

As Agha uses the term enregisterment, it refers to a 'linguistic repertoire differentiable within a language as a socially recognised register' (2006: 231; see also Asprey, this volume). This raises another limitation of the notion which we need to explore here in order to get to grips with my main point of interest – one which, in fact, somewhat challenges the very notion of 'dialect writing'. It is clearly the case that much of what happens in the kinds of texts that are under discussion in this book is indeed done with reference to the differences that exist between the variety that is being represented and a standard or reference variety (as argued thus far in this chapter), but there can be a competing impetus behind the production of such texts: the idea that the variety being represented can or should be treated as an independent system in its own right – as a 'language' rather than as a 'dialect' (which is 'within' an overarching language, such as English). This impetus can be seen at its starkest in, for example, the representations of Scots in sections of such works as *Trainspotting* (Welsh 1993), and in the 'translations into Scots' that are regularly brought out by such publishers as Itchy Coo (such as Robertson's 2008 translation of *Winnie the Pooh* and Fitt's 2017 translation of *Harry Potter*). There is a case to be made (and a movement making it) that Scots should be seen as a separate language from English, but there is no standard Scots (although there are some established Scots spelling traditions), and the kind of Scots texts just mentioned are at least in part intended to be readable by those who unambiguously identify as speaking English. But yet also, there is an impetus to understand at least some such texts as being produced in a coherent system (a 'written language') which is distinct from that of English, not inherently 'leaning on' Standard English orthography and dialect. Many pieces of locally produced humorous dialect literature (of the type labelled 'CHLDL' in Honeybone and Watson 2013 – a term considered further here in Section 10.3) pretend to be phrase books, of the type that are typically produced for learners of different languages. This is intended as a joke – not a serious claim to 'languagehood' on the part of the dialect represented – but it is not entirely absurd to argue that robust and distinct dialects from the North of England have as much right as contemporary Scots does to be seen as separate languages from English (googling 'Geordie is a language' and 'Scouse is a language', for example, brings up some positive results). There are some lengthy published texts produced in contemporary Northern dialects, some following the lead of *Trainspotting*, and there are semi-serious translations in such dialects, such as Shaw and Williams' (1967) version of *The Gospels in Scouse*. I investigate an example of each of these genres in Section 10.4. Many complex issues arise here, but for our purposes, we need to acknowledge that the conception along these lines that a writer has of the variety that they are representing (or perhaps, the conception that a writer wants to promulgate of the variety) might affect how they represent it – should it been seen as very clearly 'a dialect of English' or should it be seen as a linguistic system in its own right? In the discussion of orthographies devised for Scots (see, for example, Bann and Corbett 2015: 93), these issues are discussed in terms of whether a writer takes a 'minimalist' or a 'maximalist' approach – the question is: should a writer stay as close to Standard English as possible (in order to allow for the greatest possible comprehensibility of the text), or should they emphasise the difference between the text (and the form of language that it represents) and Standard English? The same issues resonate in considering which features get represented in dialect writing, and more generally how phonological dialect writing might be done: if a text is intended for a readership of dialect speakers, a 'maximalist' approach to representing dialect features (and to the way in which the features are represented) may be felt appropriate by a writer.

To return to the short text in (1), there is more to say. It is very unlikely that the ɛ~eɪ correspondence and the presence of DAR are the only phonologically relevant differences between the writer's phonology and that of Reference English. If a speaker has those two features, it is highly likely that they would not have the RefE diphthongs in *care* and *road* (/kɛə/ and /rəʊd/). It is more likely that the writer would have long general Northern monophthongs (/kɛː/ and /roːd/), which could be spelt either as something like *kehr*, *rohd*, which might aim to represent vowel length, or as something like *kare* and *rode*, which would equally work as spellings for the RefE forms (as eye dialect), but could serve to direct attention to the word as different from their RefE correspondents, relying on the knowledge of the reader to fill in the details. It is therefore worth considering why the writer did *not* respell *care* and *road*. It is possible that they are not aware of the differences (that is, that the dialect features in question are not salient to the writer), or if they are aware of the differences, that they do not think them salient enough to warrant writing. This is another factor that might constrain which dialect features get represented in dialect writing: they need to be salient enough to writers to be available for respelling.

The point just made about *kare* and *rode* is worth pursuing. It may be difficult for a dialect writer to respell words to represent dialect phonology straightforwardly, because the mappings that are possible for grapheme-to-phonological-entity in English are established on the basis of RefE phonology, and many dialect features involve phonological segments that are not in RefE. This need not mean that such dialect features are unspellable, however. It could be enough to simply respell a word (in whatever way is possible) in order to draw attention to it. This means that forms which are eye dialect for Standard English need not be eye dialect for other dialects, so, for example, Liverpool English has a front/central GOOSE vowel (around /ʉː/), but there is no grapheme in Standard English to clearly spell a high central rounded long vowel. A respelling like *skewl* for *school* is eye dialect in RefE: as discussed above, <ew> is one of the spellings available to represent the tense high rounded vowel that occurs in RefE, so *skewl* works as well as *school* to represent /skuːl/, but when it is used in LE (as in Shaw 1966, a text discussed below), it may be thought to be a phonologically motivated respelling of a dialect feature – the simple fact that the word is respelt draws attention to it, which flags up the fact that it has a different phonological form from that of RefE (/skʉːl/).[2] Equally, even when the phonological entities involved in a difference between a dialect and RefE *are* describable in terms of segments that are all present in RefE, there may not be an unambiguous way to spell some phonological form. For example, every grapheme used widely to spell /ʊ/ in RefE (<oo> *book*, <u> *put*, <o> *wolf*) is also used to spell /ʌ/ (*blood*, *cup*, *love*), but a writer in the North of England may want to represent the absence of the FOOT–STRUT split (that is, that STRUT has the same vowel as in FOOT, unlike in RefE accents). This can still be done. If *strut* is spelt *strutt*, even though the respelling works perfectly well as eye dialect in RefE, in dialect writing it could function to signal the phonological difference between the dialect and RefE.

A final point to make about (1) is that it is quite minimalist in its difference from Standard English. One of the tasks in understanding dialect writing is to understand why certain decisions that could be taken to differentiate a text from Standard/Reference English may *not* be taken. As well as the fact that the two dialect features just mentioned are not represented, *lambs* keeps its Standard English 'silent b' – this maintains a relationship with Standard English and implies that the writer intends the text to be seen as representing a variety of English, not of a separate system (that is, it really is 'dialect writing' in the strict sense). The write *could* have written the text as in (2).

(2) TEK KEHR
LAMZ
ONT ROHD

The text in (2) is heading towards a maximalist approach to dialect spelling, including an eye dialect respelling for *lambs*. As mentioned above, eye dialect spellings are often viewed negatively as it is assumed that they are intended to show (or unintentionally emphasise a perception of) speakers' illiteracy or lack of education. It strikes me that this need not be the case in dialect writing, and that eye dialect need not contribute negatively to a dialect writing text. Eye dialect spellings often provide a phonologically 'better', more phonemic spelling, and can thus show a writer's phonologically sophisticated awareness, but more importantly (and more relevantly for readers), it can help to differentiate a text from Standard English, potentially reinforcing the perception that the variety being represented is an independent linguistic system that is fully distinct from Standard English.

To sum up this section, there are quite a few factors which can constrain the way in which dialect phonology can get represented in dialect writing and (relatedly, but more broadly) the way in which respellings are used in dialect writing. These factors include those set out in items (i) to (viii), below. The first four of these relate to issues that have been discussed above and the second four have not yet been much discussed in this chapter, but also clearly play a role.

(i) The extent to which a dialect feature is *salient* might influence the likelihood with which it might be represented in dialect writing through respelling – we might expect more salient features to be more likely to be represented. Salience is a complex notion, and I discuss it a little further in Section 10.4, but it seems clear that there are multiple types of salience: different types of phonological feature can have different degrees of salience to speakers, and the extent to which a feature is localised to a particular place and/or dialect can affect its degree of salience.

(ii) Related to (i), it might be that *how observant a writer is* might affect the extent to which they are able to represent phonological dialect features in writing (some might notice only the most salient features, and some might notice more). There is good evidence that there are individual differences in terms of speakers' ability to perceive phonological distinctions (see, for example, Hall-Lew *et al.*, to appear), and we might expect that those writers with keener perceptual abilities might be more likely to represent a wide number of dialect features. Differences in this regard might well also be influenced by the extent to which a writer has had some linguistic training and is aware of the kind of thing that might count as a dialect feature.

(iii) Also related to (i), but not exactly the same point, is the question of whether particular dialect features have become enregistered or not. We would expect that those phonological features that have become enregistered would be more likely to be represented in dialect writing through respelling. It is quite probable that particularly salient features are the most likely to become enregistered, but we cannot assume that this is always the case, because there may be other factors (including some of those discussed in this list of eight) which militate against certain salient features being written (or which maintain perhaps archaic features in an enregistered tradition). Also, there is a feedback loop at play here: the features which are most commonly written in dialect writing are probably those features which are likely to become enregistered, and those features which are enregistered are probably those features which are likely to be written. Teasing the two points apart (and teasing apart both points' relationship to the differential salience of features) is likely to be an intricate undertaking.

(iv) The position that a writer chooses to take on the maximalist~minimalist orthographic axis will affect the extent to which respellings are used in a text. If a writer wants to minimise the differences between their text and Standard English (to encourage readers of many varieties to engage with it), they will likely minimise the use of eye dialect and may choose to only represent particularly salient and/or enregistered dialect features, while at the same time minimising the 'non-Englishness' of the spellings adopted (for example, spelling /tɛk/ as *tek* as in (1) is entirely effective, as discussed above, but it would fit in better with the regularities and expectations of English orthography to spell it *teck*, because /ɛk#/ sequences are most commonly spelt <eck#>, as in *deck*, *neck*, *speck*). If, on the other hand, a writer wants to emphasise the differences between the variety represented and Standard/Reference English (in order, perhaps, to make a claim that it deserves to be seen as a clearly distinct variety, perhaps even as a separate language), a writer will likely maximise the differences, which could lead to a large number of respellings, of both the 'eye dialect' and 'phonologically motivated' kind. Related to this is the extent to which a writer takes the task of representing a variety seriously – as is well recognised (see, for example, Clark, this volume, and Hodson, this volume), much dialect writing is intended to be at least in part comic, and sometimes this involves laughing at the variety represented and its speakers. If written with this kind of attitude, there may be no impetus to represent the variety accurately: some of the representations discussed by Hodson do indeed simply rely on an inventory of 'generic rustic features' to mark off a character as speaking something that is non-standard, with no attention paid to whether the features actually form part of the dialect that is being represented or not. However, many dialect writing texts are written with an entirely different intention – perhaps as an expression of pride or solidarity, or as an expression of identity, or perhaps simply because it is fun to use dialect writing. Much of the humour in dialect writing is of the 'laughing with', rather than 'laughing at', type, and many of these latter kinds of impetus may lead to a writer making a concerted attempt to represent dialect features accurately. All of these considerations could affect the extent to which dialect features might be represented in a text.

(v) All of the discussion thus far in this section has focused on the intentions, abilities and knowledge of the writer of a text. This may be all that needs to be considered for unpublished texts, like certain ego-documents of the type discussed by Beal (this volume) and tweets of the type discussed by Nini *et al.* (this volume), but if we want to understand all kinds of dialect writing, we also need to recognise that many kinds of text are the product of more than one person. Published texts undergo editing, and the editorial process can involve making considerable changes to texts. If an editor has different intentions, abilities or knowledge from the writer of a text, this could have a considerable impact on which features get represented in texts, on the extent to which respellings are used, and on the consistency with which this is done (see also Maguire, this volume). The issues here are quite obvious when we think about them, but we do need to think about them in addressing the points considered in this chapter. It may be that a writer of a text is a speaker of the dialect represented, but that an editor is not, and so an editor may make changes to the way features are represented because they don't understand what a writer intended. I consider a case of this in Section 10.3 below. A final point in this regard is that dialect writing can be characterised by variation – that is, a writer may sometimes spell a dialect feature and sometimes not, or they may respell one word in more than one way. As Honeybone and Watson (2013) show, the degree of variability can be constrained by phonological or dialectology factors, but, also, Escott (2016) has argued that the very fact that there can be this variability in dialect writing is meaningful, as it reflects what happens in speech (as studied in sociophonetics, for example) and this might have both the effect of linking dialect writing more closely to spoken language than is the case for writing in Standard English, and might flag it up as 'subversive' (see also Clark, this volume, on aspects of subversiveness in dialect writing). An editor might be tempted to remove such variation, missing these points, so it may only show up in unedited or lightly edited texts.

(vi) Related to (v), but also all the other points just discussed, the type of text that any piece of dialect writing is may well play a role in the issues discussed in this section. One aspect of this interacts with the differentiation of texts along the literary-dialect~dialect-literature axis, but it might be that there are different expectations of different text-types – it may even be that traditions of expectation in terms of the spelling conventions and inventories of features might emerge for specific types of text (this is a similar point to that made in (iii), about enregisterment, but it is not quite the same as assuming that there might be one set of features that are available to writers who are writing in one dialect).

(vii) A small point, but nonetheless one which is separate and can affect the way in which words are spelled in dialect literature, is that in texts which are primarily intended to be humorous, one quite common feature is what Honeybone and Watson (2013) call 'forced lexical reanalysis'. This involves a punning misparsing of the words of a phrase so that they are respelled as other existing words (or pseudo-words); one of the examples that Honeybone and Watson reproduce is the respelling *Chuck Doubt* for *chucked out*. Clark (this volume) discusses a number of cases of this kind of thing, including the phrase *shoes daz much*, which is a representation of 'it's used as much'. Such respellings may be eye-dialect-like in that they could represent the pronunciation of most or even all dialects of English, so the first word in this example is a realisation of the string [ɪtsjuːzd], with the last consonant removed as it is represented in the onset of the following syllable (where it could be after phrasal resyllabification), and with the elision of the pronoun, which leaves from the first word (the contraction *it's*) just the sibilant of the auxiliary, which is represented as having coalesced with the following palatal approximant, giving the string [ʃuːz]. All of these phenomena (resyllabification, elision and coalescence) are common in dialects of English, including RefE, so they are not dialect features, and it is very likely that the first word is written as *shoes* because it is funny, if somewhat forced, to point out that it can be homophonous with the plural of *shoe*. If a writer is aiming to use this kind of humour, it will have an impact on how much respelling occurs in a piece of dialect writing (some use it a lot, for example, Robinson and Wiltshire's (1970) *Krek Waiter's Peak Bristle*, as is clear from their title, which is a respelling of '(the) correct way to speak Bristol').

(viii) A final point, but one which has a big impact on the extent to which dialect features might get represented in dialect writing, is that writers are constrained by what is orthographically possible, in both general and English-specific ways. In terms of general constraints, an alphabetic orthography cannot represent a number of phonological phenomena, such as intonation or voice quality, even though such things can provide salient dialect features. In terms of English-specific constraints, writers are largely limited by the set of mappings that are possible for grapheme-to-phonological-entity which are fundamentally established on the basis of RefE phonology, so, for example, the rhotic is realised as [ʁ] in some far north-eastern varieties (the ‘Northumbrian burr’), but English orthography has no way of representing uvular fricatives as they do not occur in reference varieties. In this connection, it is fair to note, however, that English is a particularly good language for phonological dialect writing because its spelling system is ripe for respelling. English has a ‘deep orthography’ – it is ‘irregular’, which means that there are a lot of graphemes which can be reused in dialect respelling (for example, Carney 1994 lists fourteen different main graphemes that are used in English to spell the FACE vowel, and fifteen for the FLEECE vowel; see also Cook 2016, Roca 2016 and Ryan 2016 for phonologically informed considerations of the English spelling system, illustrating how complex – and hence ripe for reuse – its elements are). There are thus many resources that writers can use for eye dialect or for the representation of dialect features. We should also recognise that writers are not completely limited to Standard English spelling conventions: the non-standard glottal stop realisation of /t/ is often represented using <’>, as in *bu’er* for *butter* (see, for example, Darnton 1993). However, the fact that certain features would require specific acts of orthographic invention in order to represent them can be expected to constrain what types of phonological dialect features get represented in dialect writing. Certain phonological dialect features simply may not be representable in dialect writing, no matter how salient they are.

There are several different types of constraint in the above list of eight. Some are linguistic in the narrow sense, some are orthographic, and some are due to very different kinds of factor. I do not claim that this is an exhaustive list of factors that are relevant to understanding the patterns that occur in the kinds of respellings that are found in dialect writing, nor that we fully understand how all of them work. By setting them out in this way, however, I hope to contribute to our understanding of the envelope of possibilities in phonological representation and respelling in dialect writing. As I set out at the start of this chapter, my own prime interest in understanding these things is in order to be able to figure out what might count as a phonological dialect feature, and which dialect features might get to be salient, but I recognise that we need to understand all of the factors mentioned in this section before we can hope to do that. Earlier in this section, I devoted around 2,000 words to discussing issues that arose on the basis of two respellings in the five-word dialect writing text in (1). This strikes me as the right level of detail. Understanding one dialect (re)spelling can take a large amount of analysis in order to work through the possible intentions of and constraints on a writer, and the phonological, orthographic and dialectological issues involved, and as I have argued above, we also need to analyse why dialect features are sometimes *not* respelt in dialect writing. All of this shows that dialect writing is a fantastically complicated thing. It is therefore certainly well worth asking *which phonological features get represented in dialect writing?* But it is difficult to do so. I make a start in the next section. I am cautious about trying because I am aware that each respelling mentioned should really have as much attention as was given to each in this section. That would not be possible in one chapter, so I do not attempt it in many cases, but the issues discussed here should always be in the background.

10.3. Dialect Writing in Liverpool English

The texts considered below (in Section 10.4) all feature representation of Liverpool English. This variety is well-recognised in Britain, always featuring prominently in lists of 'accents in Britain' and their alleged characteristics that are compiled on the basis of perceptions (see such work as Montgomery 2007; Coupland and Bishop 2007). It is tightly centred on the city of Liverpool and the neighbouring urban areas which together make up the Liverpool City Region and the county of Merseyside. The popular name for the dialect is 'Scouse' (see Crowley, this volume, for further discussion of the variety and of the name 'Scouse').

Some of the dialect writing that exists in LE is well known (even to some extent beyond the circles of those who are interested in dialect) throughout Britain. The volumes of the *Lern Yerself Scouse* series, the first of which was published in 1966, form some of the first volumes published in the genre of 'Contemporary Humorous Localised Dialect Literature' (CHLDL), which Honeybone and Watson (2013) describe. I discuss them further in Section 10.3.1 (and then I report on an investigation of the respellings found in one in Section 10.4.1). Crowley (this volume) shows, however, that the traditions of dialect writing in LE are much more extensive than this (and start before 1966). I also consider one of the recent texts that Crowley describes as part of a wave of dialect writing that involved the 'recent appearance of a number of "Scouse" novels' in Sections 10.3.3 and 10.4.3. There is, of course, even more LE dialect writing that Crowley can consider. In Sections 10.3.2 and 10.4.2, I discuss one text which was written in 1990 and published in 2015: a translation of *Alice's Adventures in Wonderland*.

The full extent of the corpus of LE dialect writing is not (and cannot ever be fully) known, because it includes a no doubt vast amount of ephemeral writing on the internet, and other ego-documents, and also sometimes brief appearances of literary dialect in who-knows-how-many novels. One example of the latter is Katie Flynn's (1994) *The Girl from Penny Lane*. Katie Flynn is a pseudonym for Judy Turner, who was born and grew up in Norwich. The volume includes passages such as that in (3)

(3) Kitty nodded earnestly and the movement caught the young lady's eye. She swung round, looking properly at Kitty for the first time.
'Oh! I'm sorry, I didn't see you there – are you being served or did I push in ahead of you?'
'S'orlright,' Kitty said. 'I ain't a customer, I's brung work in.'

The character Kitty is from Burlington Street in Liverpool, and so her two utterances are LE dialect writing. The first, *S'orlright*, is likely simply intended as eye dialect, spelling the same kind of elision of *it* that was seen in the discussion of point (vii) above, and <orl> is as good a representation of [ɔːl] (which is both the LE and RefE pronunciation of the first syllable of *alright*) as is <al>, although the context of use in this case implies that it could be read as implying that LE is rhotic, which it very definitely is not. It could be that this respelling is used here because the writer is using a set of generic non-standard features, as discussed in point (iv) and by several other chapters in this volume (especially by Hodson), and this feature is part of this set because certain non-standard dialects do retain rhoticity. This kind of thing certainly is the case in the second utterance: *I's brung work in* could not be LE.[3] The first person singular present form for *have* in LE is *have* (or *'ave*, as *h*-dropping can occur), which would be contracted with the pronoun to *I've*. The form *I's* is clearly intended as a contraction with *has*. This implies a levelled present tense for the verb *has*, which is likely attested in some traditional dialect in England, but is clearly used here because the writer is using generic non-standard dialect features that are available for use in direct speech in literary dialect. In texts like this it does not really matter if the respellings are linguistically motived by dialect features in the variety that is being represented (hence the suspicion that the *orlright* spelling may not simply be eye dialect) – the only important thing for the writer is that the respelling marks out a character as speaking non-standard

English. I do not consider such 'generic', non-phonologically motivated dialect spellings further. I focus on extracts from three pieces of LE dialect writing which are all fundamentally aiming to accurately represent LE dialect features. I introduce the texts in the next subsections, in chronological order of publication.

10.3.1. Lern Yerself Scouse

The best-known volumes of LE dialect writing are the *Lern Yerself Scouse* (*LYS*) books. This is a series of short volumes which began publication in 1966, with a volume which has the full title *Lern Yerself Scouse: How to Talk Proper in Liverpool.* The five volumes that make up this series are classic examples of a genre of dialect writing that Honeybone and Watson (2013) call 'Contemporary Humorous Localised Dialect Literature' (CHLDL). Texts of this sort are intended to be comic, have been published since the mid to late twentieth century (and are typically kept in print), and are 'localised', by which is meant that they are published by regionally based publishers and are fundamentally intended for locally restricted distribution, often only being available where the dialect in question is spoken. They are typically sold in bookshops in the area concerned, but are also often available in museums, various other kinds of shops and local tourist information centres.

Crowley (2012, this volume) sees the first volume of *LYS* as a founding text in 'the Scouse industry', which is related to the enregisterment of the dialect. It is certainly well known in Liverpool. Crowley gives further details about the volume and its origins, and about its main author, Frank Shaw, who was born in Tralee, Ireland, but was raised in Liverpool, and who knew the dialect intimately (he died in 1971). Fritz Spiegl, who edited and published the *LYS* series, claims in the introduction to the 'millennium reprint' of the volume in question here that they were the first in a modern wave of such texts (and that it was 'flattered by numerous imitations from other regions').[4] In any case, *LYS* is resolutely local, being published by the Scouse Press, which is based in Liverpool. It is still in print.

Most of *LYS* takes the form of a pseudo-phrase book, of the sort produced for those who need to learn phrases of a foreign language. It gives phrases written in 'Scouse' (i.e. LE) followed by a 'translation' into Standard English. This sets up LE as a separate language from English, worthy of separate treatment, but this point should not be taken too far as the volume is intended as a piece of humour and much of the comedy derives from the fact that the LE forms include taboo-breaking and/or scatological language, whereas the 'English' translations are extremely formal, as in the examples given in (4), from page 18 of *LYS*.

(4) Boogeroff.
No. Please depart.
Ere's yer at, wur's de urry?
It has been nice to meet you, but I now have pressing business to attend to.
T'sarrahwell.
Farewell!

It will be clear from this short extract that there is some forced lexical reanalysis in the text, but there is also a considerable amount of phonologically motived respelling of LE dialect features: *booger* ('bugger') draws attention to the lack of FOOT/STRUT split, *wur* ('where') draws attention to the absence of the NURSE/SQUARE contrast, *t'sarrah* ('tara' = 'goodbye') spells the affrication of plosives, *de* ('the') spells DH-stopping, and *ere, at* and *urry* ('here, hat, hurry') spell *h*-dropping.

The volume was edited by Spiegl, who was a native speaker of Austrian German, but who moved (permanently) to Liverpool in the late 1940s and became very familiar with the dialect. We do not know what the editing process involved, but the text is of a similar style to Shaw's other LE dialect writing (some of which was published elsewhere, such as *The Gospels in Scouse*, mentioned above), so we might assume that the editing process was not heavy-handed. *LYS* concludes with a translation into LE of selected verses from the Rubaiyat of Omar Khayyam by Stan Kelly (a pseudonym of Stanley Bootle), which is an independent piece of LE dialect writing.

Five volumes of *LYS* texts have been published in total, up until the end of the twentieth century. They form together the text that was investigated in Honeybone and Watson (2013), which gives some further background about the texts. This first *LYS* volume (from 1966) is the first LE dialect writing text that I investigate (an extract from) in Section 10.4. It is also the text that is analysed in Watson and Jensen (this volume).

10.3.2. A Scouse Interpretation of Alice in Wonderland

The second text that I investigate was written in 1990. A typewritten manuscript was produced by Marvin R. Sumner which includes a full text of *Alice's Adventures in Wonderland*, translated into LE. Sumner entitled the text *A Scouse Interpretation of Alice in Wonderland*. The manuscript came into my possession when I was asked to provide a commentary on it for the volume *Alice in a World of Wonderlands: The Translations of Lewis Carroll's Masterpiece* (Lindseth and Tannenbaum 2015), which is a volume that investigated all known translations of *Alice's Adventures in Wonderland*, in order to mark the 150th anniversary of the original publication of the text. The LE text had not at that point been published (apart from one short section which appeared in Lindseth and Tannenbaum 2015), but because of the attention that it received in the Carrollian community due to the Lindseth and Tannenbaum volume, a version of it (entitled *Alice's Adventchers in Wunderland*) was published in 2015 by Evertype, a publisher which specialises in publishing translations of *Alice in Wonderland*, among other things. The publisher is based in the United States, so this published version is not localised. It was edited before publication by the owner of Evertype, Michael Everson, and it offers a clear example of how the editing process can affect which dialect features get represented in a text, and how respelling is used in dialect writing.

Part of the original version (from 1990 – extracted from the part published in Lindseth and Tannenbaum 2015) is given in (5). This is the start of the passage which is briefly analysed in Honeybone (2015).

(5) *'Twinkel, twinkel, littul bat!*
'Ow I wunder wot yor at!

'Yunnow de song doyeray?'
'I've herd sumtin like it,' sed Alice.
It goezon, yernow,' de 'atter kontinyewed, 'in diss way:—

Up above de werld yew fly,
Like a tea-tray in de sky.
Twinkel, twinkel—'

'Ere de Dormowse shuk itzself an began singin innitz sleep 'Twinkel, twinkel, twinkel, twinkel—' an wenn on so long dat dey 'ad to pinch it to make it stop.

'Well, I'd 'ardly finished de ferst verse,' sed de 'atter, 'wenn de Kween bawlled out, "'E'z murdrin de time! Off wid 'iz 'ead!"'

''Ow dredfully savidge!' eksclaimed Alice.

'An ever since dat,' de 'atter wenn on inna mornful tone, ''E woan do a ting I ask! It's orlwayz sixa clok now.'

The published version of this passage, as edited by Everson, is given in (6).

(6) *'Twinkle, twinkle, little bat!*
Ow I wunder what you're at!

You know de song, do you?'
'I've eard sometin like it,' said Alice.
'It goes on, you know,' de Atter continued, 'in dis way:–

Up above de werld you fly,
Like a tea-tray in de sky.
Twinkle, twinkle –'

Ere de Dormouse shook itself an began singin in its sleep '*Twinkle, twinkle, twinkle, twinkle* –' an wenn on so long dat dey ad to pinch it to make it stop.

'Well, I'd ardly finished de ferst verse,' said de Atter, 'when de Queen bawled out, "E's murdrin de time! Off wid iz ead!"'

'Ow dreadfully savidge!' exclaimed Alice.

'An ever since dat,' de Atter wenn on in a mournful tone, 'E wo'n do a ting I ask! It's allus six o'clock now.'

The editor has clearly revised the text massively, to remove all eye-dialect and produce a minimalist version of the text, contrasting with the maximalist original. Several LE dialect features have been removed by the editor: *doyeray*, which represents 'do you, eh?', is rendered as *do you*, which misses the LE form; *herd* ('heard') which spells the absence of the NURSE/SQUARE contrast is rendered as *eard* which does not; and *orlwayz* which is clearly simply eye dialect for *always*[5] in the original is rendered as *allus*, which uses a dialect word ([ɒləs]) which is not found in LE – *allus* is found in Lancashire English, which is perhaps what has confused the editor, but it is not LE (for example, as Crowley, this volume, reports, Shaw 1952 states in his glossary of LE forms that *always* is to be pronounced as *alwiz* in LE, a fast-speech form of *always*).

The editing process has massively altered the original text, to a degree that makes it unrecognisable. Many of the characteristics of dialect writing identified above have been removed (eye dialect, variation, lexical reanalysis), and dialect features have been confused. What could be seen in the original as a spectacularly confident claim to being an independent linguistic system has been rendered a poor and apologetic version of a text which is highly dependent on the Standard English original. It is a great shame that the original text was not published as the author intended, and I recommend that anyone interested in LE dialect writing ignores the published version and considers the original. I analyse a section of the original version (from 1990) in what follows.

10.3.3. Stump

The third text that I investigate is *Stump* by Niall Griffiths, published in 2003. This is a novel, published by the national publisher Cape, and widely available in Britain (i.e. it is not localised). It won the Welsh Books Council Book of the Year Award and the Arts Council of Wales Book of the Year

Award. Griffiths was born and raised in Liverpool, so is closely familiar with the dialect. He later moved to Wales, and is now highly associated with Welsh literature (hence the Wales-based awards). The *Guardian* newspaper has reported that he has been called the 'Welsh Irvine Welsh' (2001), and indeed, while not derivative of *Trainspotting*, *Stump* is clearly influenced by it. It features a high proportion of dialect writing, and while there is humour (as in many novels), it is far from being a comic text (as *LYS* is). Crowley (this volume) discusses the context of the novel in further detail and an extract is given in (7). Some passages of the text may be describable as literary dialect, but others include non-standard features in the background text (that is, in sections that are not direct speech).

(7) – Fuckin useless mudderfucker *cunt* of a car … fuckin Tommy givin *this* pure piecer fuckin wank …

Alastair the passenger does not look up from the *Reader's Digest Book of the Road* he is studying balanced on his trackie'd knees.

– Yeh want Runcorn.

– I know I want Runcorn, Ally. I *know* me way out of the fuckin city.

– Runcorn, an then we can gerron to the M56 til … Hapsford or somewhere, wharrever the fuck it's called.

There are several phonologically motivated respellings here: for example, *fuckin* spells *g*-dropping (that is, (-ing) variation), *mudderfucker* spells DH-stopping, *gerron* spells T-to-R. An extract from *Stump* is the third text that I consider in the following section.

10.4. Which Features Are Represented in Liverpool English Dialect Writing?

My key goals in investigating dialect writing are to understand the use of respellings in such material generally, and – more specifically – to consider whether such material can show which dialect features are salient. Some previous work has shown that a quantitative investigation of dialect writing respellings can be insightful in terms of the latter question. Honeybone and Watson (2013) and Honeybone *et al.* (2017) show that it is not just which phonological dialect features are represented in respellings that is interesting, but also the *extent* to which they are represented. This work decided in advance which dialect features may be worth investigating and set out to see how commonly they were represented in a corpus of *LYS* texts, and found that the NURSE/SQUARE absence of contrast (when compared to RefE) was represented much more robustly than the FOOT/STRUT lack of contrast. These are phonologically very similar features which are both realised in a relatively small set of words, but Honeybone and Watson (2013) found, on counting both where each feature is respelled and where it is not, that the results are as in (8), which shows the extent to which words which are relevant to the two dialect features are respelled in the corpus of LE dialect writing that was investigated.

(8)

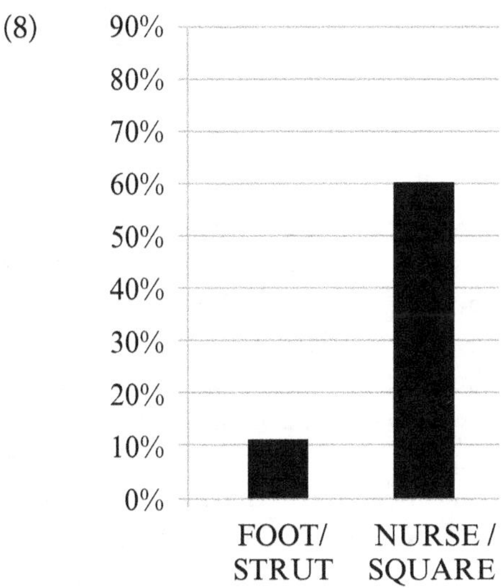

The interpretation of this in Honeybone and Watson (2013) is that the NURSE/SQUARE feature is much more localised than is FOOT/STRUT (because NURSE/SQUARE is shared with very few other dialects, while FOOT/STRUT is shared with all Northern dialects), so NURSE/SQUARE is more salient to speakers of LE.

Honeybone and Watson (2013) and Honeybone *et al.* (2017) show that localisedness is not all that there is to consider in this regard. Two other phonological dialect features (which can both affect /t/ in LE) pattern very differently. T-to-R (which we see spelled in (7)) is shared with a large number of Northern dialects, and Liverpool Lenition (which affects /t/ and other stops, and which we see spelled in (4)) is heavily localised to LE. Nonetheless, as shown in (9), which is extracted from Honeybone *et al.* (2017) to show only those words in which T-to-R is canonically allowed, forms which are respelled to show T-to-R (using <r>) are very common in the phonological environment that allows the phenomenon ([__#V]), whereas respellings to indicate *t*-lenition, which is very common in speech in the word-final environment (using, for example, <-ce>), are practically absent.

(9)

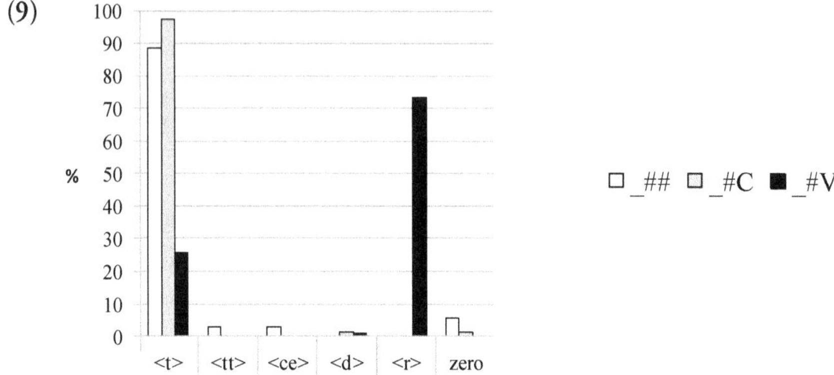

The interpretation of this in Honeybone *et al.* (2017) is that it is due to the fact that Liverpool Lenition and T-to-R are phonologically very different kinds of features. Lenition is a 'late' phonological process: it creates segments which don't exist in the lexicon (the result of lenition of /t/ does not neutralise with /s/), and it is exceptionless, whereas T-to-R is an 'early' phonological process: it involves segments which exist in the lexicon and it is distinctly tied to the lexicon as not all words that have the environment which allows T-to-R actually show the phenomenon. Phonological theory would predict that T-to-R should be more salient to speakers than lenition, and this seems to be borne out in the dialect writing respellings, indicating that Liverpool Lenition is (surprisingly, given its localisedness) not very salient.

Work like this points us towards answers to some questions that are of interest if we are trying to understand dialect writing from the perspective set out at the start of this section, but it does not answer all the questions that we will have. One crucial question is, indeed, which features get represented in LE dialect writing at all? One way of investigating this is considered in Watson and Jensen (this volume), who take an automated approach, offering a promising 'big-data'-type methodology. In this chapter, I take a more 'hand-crafted' approach, focusing on the precise details of small amounts of text. I considered extracts of around 1,000 words from the three texts mentioned in Sections 10.3.1, 10.3.2 and 10.3.3, and considered every case of respelling in them, allocating the respellings to a category which suggested itself. One category is 'eye dialect', and this includes all respellings which I judged to be not phonologically motivated in spelling a difference between LE and RefE. Other categories that I have used will hopefully make sense to those familiar with English phonological dialectology. This is a 'bottom-up' kind of methodology in a sense, but it is informed by my expectations in terms of the dialect features that might be represented, and these expectations are due to my decades-long investigation and appreciation of LE. It is a quantitative methodology, because I recorded each case of a spelling which can be fitted into one of the categories that I identified. I am well aware that there are issues with the replicability of this methodology (it depends on the contents of my own head in terms of my experiences and knowledge of the dialect, and in terms of my interpretation of the intention of each respelling). I think the results are robust, but I am also cautious about them. The recognition of a respelling is straightforward because British English spelling is heavily standardised, and any word (or group of words) which does not fit with this standard can be counted as a respelling. The differentiation of the respellings into eye dialect and phonologically motivated respellings, is more complex, however, and it is here that subjectivity can creep into the methodology.

As an example: the first sentence in *LYS* is *Ullo dur*. I analysed this as containing three respellings: 1 × *h*-dropping, 1 × DH-stopping, and 1 × the absence of contrast in SQUARE/NURSE. I report the proportion of all respellings from the three texts that each feature represents in the following sections. Several things need to be borne in mind while interpreting the results: they do not show how commonly a feature is spelt in relation to how commonly it *could* be spelt (that is, for example, cases of non-*h*-dropping are not counted), and also I do not attempt to break down the eye dialect respellings into categories in terms of which kind of phonological features are respelt (although I expect that this could be done, and that interesting generalisations would emerge). I simply give a percentage figure which shows how much of the total respellings in a text each feature represents. What the numbers *do* thus show is (i) which phonological dialect features have been represented in the extracts from the three texts considered, (ii) how much of an impact each individual feature contributes to the representation of LE in the extracts, and (iii) how maximalist each text can be considered to be.

10.4.1. Results: Lern Yerself Scouse

I only considered the passages which are intended to represent LE (ignoring the 'translations' into Standard English), and I considered the first 31 pages of *LYS*, which contained approximately 1,000 words. I found 292 respellings in total, which represents around 29 per cent of the words in the text. The set of features that I identified, and the proportion of the respellings that they make up, are given in Table 10.1. The numbers do not add up to 100 because a few other 'one-off' respellings also occur.

10.4.2. Results: A Scouse Interpretation of Alice in Wonderland

For this text, I began at the start of the passage which was discussed in Honeybone (2015), and considered just over 1,000 words, finishing at a suitable break in the text. I found 546 respellings in total, which represents

Table 10.1 Respellings in *Lern Yerself Scouse*

Respelling	%
EYE DIALECT	6
DH-stopping	29
h-dropping	15
SQUARE/NURSE	7
yer	7
-in	6
schwa = *-er*	6
me = *my*	5
T-to-R	3
ew = ʉː	2
C = CC	2
owl = *old*	2
a = *of*	1
an = *and*	1
T's-	0.5
yiz/*yews*	0.5
are = *our*	0.5
TH-stopping	0.5
STRUT	0.5
ewk = *ook*	0.5
wha	0.5

around 55 per cent of the words in the text. The set of features that I identified, and the proportion that they make up of the respellings in the passage, are given in Table 10.2. The numbers again do not add up to 100 because a few other 'one-off' respellings also occur.

10.4.3. Results: Stump

For this text, I considered the first 1,000 words of the chapter 'Car', an extract from which is given in (7). I found 109 respellings in total, which represents around 10 per cent of the words in the text. The set of features that I identified, and the proportion that they make up of the respellings in the extract, are given in Table 10.3. Again, the numbers do not add up to 100 because a few other 'one-off' respellings also occur.

10.4.4. Discussion

I hope that the nature of the features mentioned in the tables is clear. It would take considerably more space than is available in this chapter to discuss the phonology and dialectology of each feature, but most should be interpretable for those who are familiar with these things. A few points should be clear from Tables 10.1, 10.2 and 10.3:

Table 10.2 Respellings in *A Scouse Interpretation of Alice in Wonderland*

Respelling	%
EYE DIALECT	46
DH-stopping	19
h-dropping	9
-in	4
an = and	4
SQUARE/NURSE	4
T-to-R	2
TH-stopping	2
STRUT	2
ter	2
C = CC	2
won/ce = one	1
yer = you	1
dinnt	1

Table 10.3 Respellings in *Stump*

Respelling	%
EYE DIALECT	2
-in	46
schwa = *-er*	13
h-dropping	6
thee = the/they	6
T-to-R	4
an = and	3
DH-stopping	3
SQUARE/NURSE	2
me = my	2
ar = our	2
ahl = old	2
djer = did you	1
ad = I'd	1

- The extent to which respelling are used in a dialect writing text can vary considerably; in terms of the texts considered here, this varies from around 55 per cent to around 10 per cent
- The amount of eye dialect used in a text can vary considerably; in terms of the texts considered here, this varies from around 46 per cent of the respellings in a text to around 2 per cent
- The extent to which dialect features are represented in a text can also vary considerably; in terms of the texts considered here, this varies from

around from 29 per cent in *Alice*, to 27 per cent in *LYS*, to 10 per cent in *Stump* (these figures were obtained by subtracting the number of eye dialect respellings from the total number of respellings in a text and working out the percentage of the number remaining from the number of words in an extract)

- Different dialect features are represented to different extents in the texts; in large part this is doubtless due to the difference in terms of the token frequency of the features themselves, but it does give an idea of which dialect features make up the biggest part of the impression that a piece of dialect writing makes on a reader
- To consider the question of which dialect features are salient to speakers and which are not, we can say the following: the features represented here have some degree of salience; those dialect features that are not represented here may well have less salience to speakers, and it may be that those that are represented frequently, and in more than one text, are highly salient.

The full set of features that I noted in the texts is given in Table 10.4. This table also represents several of the points just made. The features are ranked in order of how frequently they are spelled in the three texts – this is also indicated by the numbers in the final column, which was obtained by a simple addition of the percentages with which they are represented in the texts. The percentages are reproduced in the second column, which also thus indicates how many texts each feature is found in. Table 10.4 is thus one way of answering the question *which phonological dialect features get* represented *in LE dialect writing?* The other piece of information given in Table 10.4 is which dialect features I judge to be quite highly localised to Liverpool (the localised features are given in bold and are marked with an asterisk). The decision about this is quite subjective, and might reasonably be queried, but I give it because it feeds into the issues discussed at the start of Section 10.4 – other factors relevant there (such as the degree of phonological salience) have not been indicated because it would take some considerable discussion of each feature to justify it.

Table 10.4 raises a large number of issues and invites a lot more interpretation. Unfortunately, that cannot be done in this chapter. Some of the localised features seem highly salient, and others do not, but it needs to be remembered that this could be due to different textual frequencies of the features, as well as the nature of the types of features that they represent – a full analysis would consider all this. We might also want to investigate which dialect features of LE are *not* represented in the texts. There is no full list of LE dialect features (and the list would need to consider only those features

Table 10.4 Summary of proportions of respellings in all three LE texts

-in	6 + 4 + 46	56
DH-stopping*	**29 + 19 + 3**	**51**
h-dropping	15 + 9 + 6	30
schwa = *-er*	6 + 13	19
SQUARE/NURSE*	**7 + 4 + 2**	**13**
T-to-R	3 + 2 + 4	9
an = and	1 + 4 + 3	8
yer	7 + 1	8
me = my	5 + 2	7
thee = the/they	6	6
ahl = old; owl = old	2 + 2	4
C = CC	2 + 2	4
ar = our; are = our	2 + 0.5	2.5
STRUT	0.5 + 2	2.5
TH-stopping*	**0.5 + 2**	**2.5**
ew* = ʉː	**2**	**2**
ter	2	2
a = of	1	1
ad = I'd	1	1
dint	1	1
djer = did you	1	1
won/ce = one	1	1
ewk = ook*	**0.5**	**0.5**
T's-*	**0.5**	**0.5**
wha*	**0.5**	**0.5**
yiz/yews*	**0.5**	**0.5**

which are in principle spellable), but some LE features that spring to mind but are not represented in the texts are: the BATH vowel, velar-nasal-plus and *r*-tapping. It may, of course, be that other dialect writing texts (or other sections of the three texts considered here) might include representations of these features, but this question can and should, at least, be considered.

10.5. Conclusions and Questions

This chapter has considered a range of issues that arise when we consider the nature of the respellings that are found in dialect writing. Some of the arguments made in the above concern the very possibility of spelling phonological dialect features and the constraints that affect writers when they compose dialect writing. Others are specifically aimed towards answering questions concerning my key points of interest, which connect to issues related to the phonological salience of dialect features, and the basic question of what can count as a dialect feature. What I am fundamentally interested in is: *what does it* take *and* mean *for a phonological feature to be represented in dialect writing?* I hope that I have got some way towards answering this question in this chapter, but I am well aware that in doing so I have raised many more questions, which I leave unanswered. For a phonologist who is interested in non-standard varieties of spoken English, there is a vast amount still to understand in the patterning of respellings in non-standard written English.

Notes

1. Some of the material discussed here was first presented at the *Seventh Northern Englishes Workshop* at the University of Edinburgh in 2016. I thank the audience there for discussion, and I also thank Tony Crowley, Warren Maguire and Kevin Watson for discussion of the full chapter.
2. This kind of spelling could also be, especially among the young, an insightful attempt to spell GOOSE-fronting, which is now rapidly spreading through many varieties of English (consider Macleod 2018, who discussed a case where an adult used the spelling *skool*, but an adolescent used *skewl*).
3. How do I know this? Consultation with two LE-native-speaker linguists (Tony Crowley and Kevin Watson) confirmed my suspicion.
4. This is a controversial claim because Stanley Baxter had produced *Parliamo Glasgow* earlier (for example, a record with that title was released in 1963). Baxter's work was not 'localised', however, as it was made available nationally (and it may be more 'laughing at' than 'laughing with' the variety depicted), so it was not exactly like *LYS*, but the fundamental idea was already in the public realm.
5. This is clearly not representing rhoticity, given the broader context of the text and its general accuracy at representing LE. When compared to *the Girl from Penny Lane*, this shows how one spelling (<orl>) may represent different intentions in different texts.

References

Agha, Asif (2003) The social life of cultural value. *Language and Communication* 23, 213–73.

Agha, Asif (2006) *Language and Social Relations*. Cambridge: Cambridge University Press.

Bann, Jennifer and John Corbett (2015) *Spelling Scots: The Orthography of Literary Scots, 1700–2000*. Edinburgh: Edinburgh University Press.

Beal, Joan (2000) From Geordie Ridley to Viz: popular literature in Tyneside English. *Language and Literature* 9:4, 343–59.

Carney, Edward (1994) *A Survey of English Spelling*. London and New York: Routledge.

Cook, Vivian (2016) Background to the English writing system. In Vivian Cook and Des Ryan (eds), *The Routledge Handbook of the English Writing System*, pp. 5–23. Abingdon: Routledge.

Coupland, Nikolas and Hywel Bishop (2007) Ideologised values for British accents. *Journal of Sociolinguistics* 11:1, 74–93.

Crowley, Tony (2012) *Scouse: A Social and Cultural History*. Liverpool: Liverpool University Press.

Darnton, John (1993) 'The English are talking funny again'. *New York Times*. http://www.nytimes.com/1993/12/21/world/the-english-are-talking-funny-again.html.

Escott, Hugh (2016) Dialect representation in Yorkshire texts and socio-cultural accounts of literacy and orthography. Talk presented at the Seventh Northern Englishes Workshop, University of Edinburgh.

Fitt, Matthew (2017) *Harry Potter and the Philosopher's Stane* (Translation of *Harry Potter and the Philosopher's Stone* into Scots). Edinburgh: Itchy Coo.

Flynn, Katie (1994) *The Girl from Penny Lane*. London: Heinemann.

Guardian (2001) Niall Griffiths's Top 10 Welsh books. 7 February. https://www.theguardian.com/books/2001/feb/07/bestbooks.fiction.

Hall-Lew, Lauren, Patrick Honeybone and James Kirby (to appear) Individuals, communities, and sound change: a systematic review. To appear in *Glossa*.

Hodson, Jane (2014) *Dialect in Film and Literature*. Basingstoke: Palgrave Macmillan.

Honeybone, Patrick (2015) Analysin de werdz ov de Scouse Alice: translating Standard English into Scouse. With back-translation and notes. In Jon Lindseth and Alan Tannenbaum (eds), *Alice in a World of Wonderlands: The Translations of Lewis Carroll's Masterpiece*. New Castle, Delaware: Oak Knoll Press, vol. 1, 661–4; vol. 2, 602–5.

Honeybone, Patrick and Kevin Watson (2013) Salience and the sociolinguistics of Scouse spelling: exploring the phonology of the Contemporary Humorous Localised Dialect Literature of Liverpool. *English World-Wide* 34:3, 305–40.

Honeybone, Patrick, Kevin Watson and Sarah van Eyndhoven (2017) Lenition and T-to-R are differently salient: the representation of competing realisations of /t/ in Liverpool English dialect literature. In Sylvie Hancil and Joan Beal (eds), *Perspectives on Northern Englishes*, vol. 96, 83–108. Berlin, Boston: De Gruyter Mouton.

Jones, Mark (2002) The origin of Definite Article Reduction in northern English dialects: evidence from dialect allomorphy. *English Language and Linguistics* 6, 325–45.

Jones, Mark (2007) Glottals and grammar: definite article reduction and morpheme boundaries. *Leeds Working Papers in Linguistics* 12, 61–77.

Lindseth, Jon and Alan Tannenbaum (eds) (2015) *Alice in a World of Wonderlands: The Translations of Lewis Carroll's Masterpiece*. New Castle, DE: Oak Knoll Press.

Macleod, Nicola (2018) Talk at the University of Edinburgh.

Montgomery, Chris (2007) Northern English dialects: a perceptual approach. Unpublished PhD thesis, University of Sheffield.

Preston, Dennis (1982) Ritin fowklower daun rong: folklorists' failure in phonology. *Journal of American Folklore* 95, 304–26.

Preston, Dennis (1985) The L'il Abner syndrome: written representations of speech. *American Speech* 60, 328–36.

Robertson, James (2008) *Winnie-the-Pooh in Scots* (Translation of *Winnie the Pooh* into Scots). Edinburgh: Itchy Coo.

Robinson, Dirk (Derek) and Vic Wiltshire (1970) *Krek Waiter's Peak Bristle: A Guide to What the Natives Say and Mean in the Heart of the Wess Vinglun*. Bristol: The Abson Press.

Roca, Iggy (2016) Phonology and English spelling. In Vivian Cook and Des

Ryan (eds), *The Routledge Handbook of the English Writing System*, pp. 65–91. Abingdon: Routledge.

Ryan, Des (2016) Linguists' descriptions of the English writing system. In Vivian Cook and Des Ryan (eds), *The Routledge Handbook of the English Writing System*, pp. 41–64. Abingdon: Routledge.

Shaw, Frank (1952) *The Scab: A One Act Play Set in Liverpool during the General Strike, 1926. With a Note on the Liverpool Way of Talking*. Typescript, Liverpool Record Office.

Shaw, Frank and Dick Williams (1967) *The Gospels in Scouse*. Liverpool: Gear Press.

Shaw, Frank, with Fritz Spiegl and Stan Kelly (1966) *Lern Yerself Scouse: How to Talk Proper in Liverpool, A Teach-Yourself Phrase Book By Frank Shaw. Edited with Notes and Translations by Fritz Spiegl and a Scouse Pome by Stan Kelly*. Liverpool: Scouse Press.

Shorrocks, Graham (1996) Non-standard dialect literature and popular culture. In Juhani Klemola, Merja Kyto and Matti Rissanen (eds), *Speech Past and Present: Studies in English Dialectology in Memory of Ossi Ihalainen*, pp. 385–411. University of Bamberg Studies in English Linguistics. Frankfurt am Main: Peter Lang.

Sumner, Marvin R. (1990) *A Scouse Interpretation of Alice in Wonderland* (Translation of *Alice's Adventures in Wonderland* into Scouse). Typescript.

Sumner, Marvin R. (2015) *Alice's Adventchers in Wunderland* (Translation of *Alice's Adventures in Wonderland* into Scouse, ed. by Michael Everson). Portlaoise: Evertype.

11

Phonological Analysis of Early-Nineteenth-Century Tyneside Dialect Literature: Thomas Wilson's *The Pitman's Pay*

Warren Maguire

11.1. Introduction

Linguistic documentation of the phonology of Tyneside English (TE) is, like other urban British dialects, relatively recent. Strictly linguistic records of the phonology of north-east English dialects began in the late nineteenth century with Ellis (1889) and Wright (1905), though these are fragmentary, difficult to interpret and, in the case of Wright's data, not assignable to a precise location.[1] The amount of data specifically from the Tyneside area is small. Twentieth-century sources for traditional north-east English dialects are much more copious, especially those documented in Orton (1933), in the *Orton Corpus* from the 1930s (Rydland 1998), and the dialects covered in the *Survey of English Dialects* (SED; Orton and Dieth 1962–71), though again most locations surveyed lie outside the Tyneside area. Even this more copious twentieth-century data is limited in scope, however, with many words and patterns of phonological interest being rarely or never recorded (for the example of the word *heaven*, see Section 11.3). And by the time we get to the mid twentieth century, the dialects closest to Tyneside show a considerable degree of dialect levelling (Kerswill 2003; Watt and Milroy 1999), as exemplified by the low levels of endogenous developments of OE /ɑː/ at the SED locations detailed in Table 11.3. How recently this situation has developed is difficult to determine. For these reasons, and for a fuller history of the phonology of Tyneside English more generally, earlier data are required. Although Ellis (1889) and Wright (1905) represent the first *linguistic* descriptions of north-east dialects, there is a great deal of earlier data available, especially for Tyneside English, in the form of Dialect Literature (DL; see the introductory chapter in this volume), stretching right back to the end of the eighteenth century. If evidence from DL can be used for historical phonological analysis, this has the potential to extend our knowledge of the phonology of Tyneside English back by about 100 years, to a time before the rapid urban expansion in the mid nineteenth century, and to provide both a window into its Early Modern past and a baseline for understanding later changes in the dialect. However, there are potential problems with using DL (and other forms of dialect writing) as linguistic evidence, including issues of artificiality, imprecision, stereotyping, spelling traditions and editorial interference. All of these have the potential to reduce the usefulness of DL for understanding the phonological history of English dialects. This chapter takes the stance that the only way to determine the usefulness of DL as linguistic evidence is to analysis it and to compare the results to what we know about the history of the language and later records of it.

The piece of DL analysed in this chapter is Thomas Wilson's *The Pitman's Pay* (TPP), a long poem from the early nineteenth century written for the most part in the Tyneside dialect by a native speaker of the variety. TPP has a number of characteristics which make it particularly suitable for analysis, including its early date, its length, the working-class, local background of its author, its publication as an author's edition, its copious use of non-standard orthography and its straight-forward metre and rhyme scheme. It will be seen from the analysis in this chapter that TPP is extremely suitable for linguistic analysis and has much to tell of the phonology of late-eighteenth- and early-nineteenth-century Tyneside English.

The rest of this chapter is structured as follows. In Section 11.2, I describe *The Pitman's Pay* and summarise the life of its author, Thomas Wilson. In Section 11.3, I give two case studies on this piece of Tyneside DL, the first an analysis of the evidence for the pronunciation of the word *heaven* in the poem, the second a detailed exploration of the evidence from the spellings and rhymes in *The Pitman's Pay* for the pronunciation of the FACE vowel[2] in early-nineteenth-century Tyneside English. In Section 11.4, I summarise what a close analysis of *The Pitman's Pay* can tell us, and what this reveals about the usefulness of DL for historical phonological analysis. In this chapter, I demonstrate that the combination of Wilson's regular rhyme scheme and his consistent non-standard spellings, and a comparison of those with what we know about earlier and later stages of the language, allow us to reconstruct the phonology of his early-nineteenth-century dialect in rich detail, thus extending our knowledge of the phonology of Tyneside English back considerably. This chapter thus demonstrates that nineteenth-century DL can be an important linguistic resource for understanding the phonological history of English dialects, and illustrates the kinds of techniques we need to employ to do justice to such an analysis. It will be seen that we have much to learn about the earlier history of dialects in Britain such as Tyneside English through careful analysis of literature of this sort.

11.2. Tyneside Dialect Literature and Thomas Wilson's *The Pitman's Pay*

Tyneside has a rich and copious tradition of DL, stretching right back to the end of the eighteenth century (for an overview, see Harker 1972; Hermeston 2009; Beal 2000). This tradition consists of poems, songs, prose stories and 'translations' of Standard English works, much of which is written in non-standard orthography designed to represent aspects of the phonology and morphology of the dialect. Some of the most well-known examples of Tyneside DL have been gathered together in collections, especially *Allan's Tyneside Songs* (e.g. Allan 1972), where the editorial hand may be apparent not only in the selection of materials, but also in their presentation and content, with not insignificant changes in orthography and subject matter being made (see Harker 1972: xxv–xxvi), often obscuring the original intent of the authors of this local literature. As a result, any analysis of Tyneside DL should, where possible, be made of the original or author's editions of the work.

One of the apparent aims of *Allan's Tyneside Songs* was to standardise the divergent spelling practices of the authors included in the volume. This, together with a general trend towards the establishment of specific orthographic practices, means that as the Tyneside DL tradition developed, the relationship between the written and spoken word may well have begun to diverge (see Brunner 1925 and Shorrocks 1996: 393 for discussion of this issue). Examples of this trend can be seen in the mid-twentieth-century *Larn Yersel' Geordie* (Dobson 1969, with continued editions up to the present day), a humorous presentation of the Tyneside dialect in the CHLDL tradition (Honeybone and Watson 2013). This booklet includes archaic features of north-east English dialects including <yeu> for [jʊ] from northern Middle English /øː/ in *byeuts* 'boots' (p. 31) and <or> for [ɔʁ] in *weor* 'where' (p. 16) which are long extinct in the dialect (*boots* and *where* being pronounced [buːts] and [weɐ] in conservative Tyneside English in the second half of the twentieth century). This means that earlier examples of Tyneside DL not only have the advantage of representing an older state of affairs in the dialect, but are also less likely to contain fixed spelling practices that do not necessarily reflect current usage. Thomas Wilson, as one of the earliest and most important writers of Tyneside dialect, was more likely to be the originator of later spelling practices rather than a writer who adopted the spelling conventions of others. Ellis (1889: 639) makes precisely this point, when he states that '[t]he classic work in the se.Nb. [southeast Northumbrian] or Pitman's dialect is Thomas Wilson's *Pitman's Pay* … It has set the norm for spelling, which, however, is rather confusing to a Southerner'.

11.2.1. Thomas Wilson

Thomas Wilson was born in 1773 in Low Fell, Gateshead, to working-class parents.[3] When he was eight years old, he began to work in the local pits as a 'trapper boy',[4] where he spent up to eighteen hours a day and, as a result, he received very little formal education as a child. By the age of nineteen, Wilson had become a 'hewer' in the mines, but he had also received a considerable amount of education by attending evening classes with a local teacher and through independent learning. This education led to employment as a teacher in Low Fell at the age of nineteen, followed by his appointment as schoolmaster. After 1799, he moved to Newcastle to work as a clerk, ultimately becoming a partner in a counting-house in 1805. Having married in 1810, Wilson returned some time after to Low Fell, where he was elected as a councillor on the new Gateshead Town Council in 1835, and he remained an alderman until his retirement in 1853. By the time of his death in 1858, he was a respected philanthropist and vernacular poet.

Although Wilson did not begin to publish his dialect poems until 1824 (see Allan 1972: 261), his date of birth puts him among the earliest of the Tyneside dialect poets and songsters (for example, Thomas Thompson was also born in 1773, John Shield in 1768, Henry Robson in 1774 and John Selkirk in 1781). Certainly his dialect was learned in the last quarter of the eighteenth century and, given that Wilson himself states in the 1843 edition of his works that TPP depicted life 'some five-and-forty years ago' (Wilson 1843: vi), we can assume that the dialect of the TPP comes from the same period.

11.2.2. The Pitman's Pay

The Pitman's Pay illustrates in rich detail the professional and domestic life of Tyneside miners and their families as they socialise and reminisce on 'Pay Night' (see further Hermeston's chapter in this volume). It was first published in 1826 (Part 1), 1828 (Part 2) and 1830 (Part 3) in *Mitchell's Magazine* (Wilson 1843: xiv; see also Allan 1972: 260). Wilson (1843: xiv) tells us that it was immediately reprinted by a Mr George Watson of Gateshead, but he notes that 'the reprint was an incorrect edition, and has been out of print for some time'. However, Wilson published a definitive edition of his works, including TPP and a preface written by himself, in 1843. Further editions appeared through the nineteenth century, culminating in the 1872 edition, published after Wilson's death, which reproduced the contents of the 1843 version faithfully, but with the addition of a further six of his poems.

Although I have not been able to trace copies of the original published versions of TPP, we can assume that the 1843 version of the poem is produced as the author intended it. This is important for the analysis of TPP, as it is for the analysis of other works of dialect literature, since it removes concerns we might have about editorial interference, including changes to the original spellings.

The Pitman's Pay consists of 1376 lines (9200 words) in 344 stanzas of four lines each, and is divided into three parts, labelled A, B and C in this chapter (A has 103 stanzas, B has 107 and C has 134).[5] Stanzas 1–8, 10–40, 67, the first half of 68, 86, the first three lines of 87, 88, 95–6, 104–13 and 339–43 are in Standard English orthography (241 lines in all, or 17.5 per cent of TPP), these sections making up most of the authorial frame of the poem (termed in this chapter the 'non-dialect' part of TPP).[6] The rest of the poem, termed here the 'dialect' part of TPP, consists almost entirely of the speech of the poem's protagonists, and is written in an adapted spelling designed to reflect features of the dialect. In the terminology of Beal (2006), we can call most of this 'semiphonetic spelling', though 'semiphonemic spelling' may be more appropriate in this case. Approximately one-third of the words in the dialect part of TPP deviate from Standard English orthography in some way.

The TPP is in strict iambic tetrametre (or at least it can be interpreted as such given Wilson's willingness to stress words which would normally not be stressed, e.g. A.51.203 *And íf I's tíll the éfternúin* 'And if I'm till the afternoon'), though there are occasional cases of (what should probably be interpreted as) line-initial trochaic substitutions (e.g. B.180.718 *Móny a wéary, wárkin' byén* 'Many a weary, warking bone') and fairly frequent weak endings (A.52.206 *As shé gets á'ways móney plénty* 'As she gets always money plenty').

The rhyme scheme for each stanza is ABAB, with weak endings rhyming in their entirety as expected. The rhymes in TPP are extremely consistent given certain assumptions about the phonology of early-nineteenth-century Tyneside English based on etymology and later records;[7] of the 568 rhyming pairs in the dialect part of the poem, only ten are not readily interpretable as being exact rhymes. Of these ten, five are wrenched rhymes, for example, *free–slavery* (B.169.673/675), three are probably partial rhymes (e.g. *on–son*, B.151.601/3), one is a rhyme not justified by the etymology (*here–bear* (n.), B.164.654/6, explicable due to confusion with the verb *bear*), and one is a non-rhyme (*fand–need* 'found-need', C.275.1097). Although there are a few instances where Wilson's rhymes involve pronunciations which are clearly of non-local origin (e.g. *best–breast*, B.129.513/5, suggesting /ɛ/ in both words when we would expect /ɛ/ in *best* and /iː/ in *breast* traditionally), most rhymes are interpretable as involving dialect pronunciations only (cf. Robert Burns's well-known rhyme *storm–warm* in *Tam o'Shanter*, as discussed in Smith

2007). These aspects of TPP mean that its rhymes are extremely important from a dialectological perspective, as discussed further in the examples analysed in Section 11.3.

11.3. Case Studies

In this section, two case studies involving phonological and phonetic analysis of spellings in TPP are presented. The first, in focusing on the spelling of a single word (*heaven*), illustrates the methods that can be used to analyse DL and the results that can be attained. The second case study analyses the spellings and rhymes involving words of the FACE lexical set, which has a complex history of change in the dialect. The analysis shows that despite this complexity, TPP can be used to reconstruct a detailed history of the development of the vowels in this set of words.

11.3.1. Evidence for the Pronunciation of heaven *in* The Pitman's Pay

In my analysis of the word *heaven* in TPP, I examine all the relevant evidence for the pronunciation of this word, and compare that evidence with what we know about its earlier history and with pronunciations of it and related words as recorded in later dialect sources.

The word *heaven* has an interesting phonological history in English. It derives from OE *heofon*, which became [ˈhɛvən] in early ME. Given that the short [ɛ] is in a penultimate open syllable, it was a possible candidate for the important early ME change Open Syllable Lengthening (OSL), whereby short vowels in penultimate open syllables lengthened (Bermúdez-Otero 1998). In the case of [ɛ], this would have given [ˈhɛːvən], resulting in Modern English [ˈhiːvən] due to the raising of [ɛː] in the Great Vowel Shift (GVS) and the MEAT–MEET merger (Harris 1985: 231–41; Lass 2000: 91–3). But OSL was a variable change, especially in words which remained disyllabic, so that not infrequently lengthening is not evidenced (as is the case with Modern English [ˈhɛvən]). Given the variable nature of OSL, we should expect that such words might have developed differently in different dialects of English. Unfortunately the word *heaven* was not included in the SED questionnaire, so our knowledge of its pronunciation in many modern dialects is limited. As far as north-east English dialects are concerned, there is some data for its pronunciation in the late nineteenth and early twentieth centuries, which I return to below.

Details of the tokens of *heaven* in TPP are summarised in Table 11.1. There are six tokens of *heaven* in TPP, including one in the non-dialect part of the poem (greyed out in Table 11.1), and one token of *heavenly*. The metre in line 1339 requires *heaven* to have two syllables, and this must also be the case for the line-final tokens of the word (as indicated by the feminine

Table 11.1 Data for *heaven* in *TPP*

Spelling	Rhyme	Line	Text
heaven	*forgiven*	A.17.68	*To díe in péace, and gó to héaven.*
heeven	*believin'* (believing)	A.99.396	*The cáre o' mé will wín thee héeven.*
heeven	*conceivin'* (conceiving)	B.176.704	*Aw thínk he mún gan stríte to héeven.*
heevenly		B.175.700	*Then slíde him thróugh the héevenly gátes.*
heeven	*leevin'* (living)	B.202.808	*There'll nyén ax hów we gát te héeven.*
heeven	*leevin'* (living)	C.309.1236	*Te myék a wáy streight úp te Héeven.*
heeven		C.335.1339	*We túik wi' thánks what Héeven sént,*

rhymes with *-ing* words). The metre of line 700 suggests that *heavenly* has two syllables, unless it contains an unusual instance (for TPP) of an anapest. There is no way of telling from TPP whether the second syllable of *heaven* is [ən] or [n̩]. Given this disyllabic pronunciation and the presence of <v> in all tokens, there is no indication of /v/-deletion in the word in TPP (as there is, for example, in one token of *devil* <de'il>, line 1306). Likewise, there is no indication of /h/-dropping in this (or any other /h/-initial) word in TPP, which is not unexpected given that the dialect of Tyneside has retained initial /h/, even though locations further south in County Durham have at least a degree of /h/-dropping (Anderson 1987: 140, 144).

Turning to the stressed vowel in *heaven*, and setting aside for now the token from the non-dialect part of TPP, all of the evidence points to it being an [iː]-type vowel.[8] Firstly, all tokens are spelt with <ee>, which of course is frequently employed to represent [iː] in Standard English spelling and which is used to represent what can only be [iː] (or the like) in words such as *feet* and *cheese* (lines 215 and 216). Secondly, all of the rhymes involving *heaven* in the dialect part of the poem require the first vowel in the word to be [iː], most obviously the rhymes with *believing* and *conceiving*, but also the two rhymes with *living*, which is also spelt with <ee> and which is recorded in later surveys with [iː] (cf. Rydland 1998: 172). This pronunciation of *living* with [iː] is a result of (specifically northern) OSL of the original short [ɪ] (OE *lifian*) to [eː], also found in Scots (Aitken and Macafee 2002: 13–14), followed by GVS raising of the vowel to [iː].

Although the evidence for [iː] in *heaven* in TPP is unambiguous, this does not match the pronunciation of the word recorded in most later sources for dialects of the region. As noted, the mid-twentieth-century SED unfortunately does not record any data for this word, but earlier sources from across north-east England do give pronunciations of *heaven*. Apart from a few cases with [ɛ], which probably represent recent borrowings from Standard or supra-local English, all but one of these has the vowel [ɪ]. Thus we get [ɪ] recorded in the *Orton Corpus* (late 1920s and 1930s) in Allendale,

Belford, Coanwood, Coxhoe, Cullercoats, Glanton, Matfen, Newbiggin, Newbrough, Newburn, Ovingham, Stanhope and Wooler (Rydland 1998), and in the late nineteenth century in middle-east, south-east, south-west and south Northumberland (Wright 1905) and in south-east Northumberland, South Shields, Wark-on-Tyne and Warkworth (Ellis 1889). In one case only ('(County) Durham') is *heaven* recorded with [iː] (Wright 1905, specifically [īvn], with /h/-dropping), though Ellis also records an [iː]-type vowel in *heaven* in Laithkirk, just south of the Durham–Yorkshire border in Teesdale. When we look at words with a similar phonological history, however, there is much more evidence for [iː] in later sources. These words are *devil* (OE *deofol*), *eleven* (OE *endleofon*) and *seven* (OE *seofon*), the first and last of which are represented by <deevil>/<de'il> and <seeven> (rhymed with <relievin'>) in TPP.[9] In nineteenth-century sources (Ellis 1889; Wright 1905), an [iː]-type vowel is commonly recorded in all three of these words across much of Northumberland and Durham, especially in the Pennines, but also sometimes elsewhere, including in *devil* in south-east Northumberland next to Tyneside. However, [ɪ] is the most commonly recorded vowel in these words in most of Northumberland and the Tyneside area. In the early twentieth century (Rydland 1998), an [iː]-type vowel is not infrequently recorded across Northumberland, including in some cases in locations in and around Tyneside, though [ɪ] predominates in this area and beyond. By the time we get to the SED in the 1950s, [iː] in these words is largely restricted to far north Northumberland and the Pennines (especially in County Durham), though it turns up sporadically elsewhere (but never in the locations around Tyneside); otherwise [ɪ] and, occasionally, [ɛ] are recorded. Thus the later evidence suggests that [iː] is a likely development of the stressed vowel in OE *heofon*, but that [iː] in words of this type has been subject to replacement by [ɪ] in traditional north-east English dialects, with [iː] pronunciations retreating away from the Tyneside area and into the Pennines and other peripheral areas of the region. It is unsurprising, then, that twentieth-century records of [iː] in *heaven* are absent, while it is equally unsurprising that TPP had [iː] in this word.

The evidence for [iː] in *heaven* in the dialect part of TPP also does not appear to match the pronunciation of this word in the non-dialect part of the poem. This token is not respelt with <ee>, and the word is rhymed with *forgiven* (also not respelt). Assuming this is a true rhyme, this suggests that *heaven* had the vowel [ɪ] in the non-dialectal part of the poem. This matches the pronunciation of *heaven* recorded in most later sources, one which appears to have replaced pronunciations with [iː]. Wilson's use of this pronunciation in the non-dialectal part of the poem suggests that for him [ɪ] was a more standard form, and this may indicate the origin of this pronunciation in north-east dialects more generally, which has spread at the expense of original [iː].

This investigation of a single word demonstrates how to analyse DL for phonological information, and the kinds of results we can get from doing so. It shows that a careful analysis of DL, taking full account of all the relevant data and comparing it to earlier stages of the language and later data, is a very worthwhile task for understanding the historical phonology of the dialects under investigation. Thus TPP gives us a window into an older past of TE that is not available from later sources.

11.3.2. The FACE *Vowel in* The Pitman's Pay

The second case study is a detailed examination of the spellings and rhymes involving words of the FACE lexical set (Wells 1982: 141–2) in TPP. The pronunciation of the vowel in this set of words is one of the most distinctive features of the Tyneside dialect at the end of the twentieth and start of the twenty-first centuries. In conservative forms of TE, as spoken by older working-class males, the vowel in this lexical set is [ɪə] (Wells 1982: 375; Watt and Milroy 1999: 27–8, 32, 34–5; Beal *et al.* 2012: 26, 30), though this exists alongside and is being replaced by general Northern English [eː]~[ɛː] and a middle-class variant [eɪ]. Other than a small number of words with different vowels in traditional Tyneside English (e.g. [ɛɪ]~[æɪ], identical to the PRICE vowel, in *eight*, *straight* and *weight*, and [ɛ]~[a] in *make* and *take*), all words in the FACE lexical set have the same vowel, making TE, in this respect at least, structurally very similar to RP English (which has [eɪ] in FACE). This represents an important change, in both varieties, from ME, which had two main vowel phonemes in words in the FACE lexical set, in addition to a number of smaller subsets from other sources. These vowels were:

(1) /aː/, typically represented in spelling in modern Standard English by <a_(e)> (as in *face*, *name*, *table*), which mostly derives from the ME Open Syllable Lengthening of short /a/ (Lass 1992: 47–8);
(2) /ai/, typically represented in spelling in modern Standard English by <ai> and <ay> (as in *brain*, *day*, *nail*), which mostly derives from diphthongs of a similar sort in early ME and French (Lass 1992: 49–52).

Additional origins of the FACE vowel include ME /ex/ (as in *eight*, *straight* and *weight*, which, as mentioned previously, have a different vowel in traditional TE) and ME /ɛː/ when it failed to rise to /iː/ (as in *break* and *great*; see Labov 1994: 304–6), both of which may also have different vowels, for example, [ɪ] and [iː], in traditional TE.

Concentrating on the two chief inputs to the FACE lexical set, ME /a:/ and /ai/, the modern situation in RP, TE, and indeed most current varieties of English, arose as a result of the merger of these two vowels (Wells 1982: 192–3 calls this the 'FACE Merger'). In the ancestor of RP, this merger is dated to the sixteenth and seventeenth centuries after a period of vacillation between competing systems (Lass 2000: 91–4). A similar merger took place in Scots dialects as well, at least in non-peripheral dialects, beginning in the sixteenth century (with some early precursors), and it has continued to spread to peripheral dialects to the present day (Johnston 1997a: 76–7; Aitken and Macafee 2002: 143–6). In other dialects of English and Scots, the distinction between ME /a:/ and /ai/ survived into the twentieth century, and such a distinction was characteristic of many traditional Northern English dialects, including at least some from the north-east (see, for example, Anderson 1987: 57, 60–1, 68–9, based on data from the SED). Typically the opposition was between [ɪə] for ME /a:/ and [e:]~[eə] for ME /ai/ (Anderson 1987: 57).

This of course raises the question as to what happened to this opposition in traditional TE as recorded in the second half of the twentieth century, where [ɪə]~[e:] was found equally in FACE words from ME /a:/ and from ME /ai/.[10] A closer examination of the SED data for locations close to Tyneside (Nb8 Heddon-on-the-Wall and Du1 Washington) reveals that for the most part the vowels in words which had ME /a:/ and /ai/ were the same in the 1950s too, in the phonetic range [e:]~[eə]~[ɪə].[11] In both locations, a small number of /a:/ words were recorded with [jɛ], a sequence not found in the /ai/ words, evidencing the last remnants of the distinction between ME /a:/ and /ai/ in the Tyneside area. Table 11.2 summarises the patterns found in these two dialects.

Thus the FACE Merger was almost complete even in the conservative traditional dialects around Tyneside in the 1950s, and the general FACE variation between [e:], [eə] and [ɪə] in these dialects does not represent a continuation of the distinction between ME /a:/ and /ai/ as it does in other Northern English dialects. Instead [jɛ] is the last vestige of a distinct vowel for ME /a:/. This is confirmed by examination of the vowel which developed

Table 11.2 FACE vowels in the SED dialects recorded at Nb8 (Heddon-on-the-Wall) and Du1 (Washington)

Location	ME	e:	eə	ɪə	jɛ
Nb8 (Heddon)	a:	8	12	24	8
	ai	2	10	9	0
Du1 (Washington)	a:	2	6	34	8
	ai	0	2	10	0

Table 11.3 The reflexes of OE /ɑ:/ in the SED dialects recorded at Nb8 (Heddon-on-the-Wall) and Du1 (Washington)

Location	ɪə	eə	e:	jɛ	GOAT, etc.
Nb8 (Heddon)	2	0	0	7	36
Du1 (Washington)	0	0	0	5	27

from OE /ɑ:/ (in non-final position) in the dialect in words such as *bone*, *both*, *home*, *loaf*, *most*, *stone*, *toad* and *whole*. As was noted previously, OE /ɑ:/ became /a:/ in northern ME, the same vowel which resulted from Open Syllable Lengthening (as in *name*) and as was found in French loans such as *face* (Lass 1992: 46–8). In southern ME, this vowel raised and rounded to /ɔ:/ (ultimately giving rise to the typical GOAT vowel, or a vowel which subsequently developed from it, e.g. [ʌ] in *none*, [wʌ] in *one*, in these words in Standard English and most other dialects of English today). We should expect this vowel to develop in the same way as /a:/ in words like *name* in traditional Northern English dialects, and, where ME /a:/ is distinguished from ME /ai/, for the development of /a:/ in *bone*, *home* and *whole* to match the development of /a:/ in *face*, *name* and *table* rather than the development of /ai/ in *brain* and *nail*. Table 11.3 shows the development of these OE /ɑ:/ words in Nb8 (Heddon) and Du1 (Washington), which can be compared with the developments of /a:/ from other sources and with /ai/ in Table 11.2.

The most striking thing about the figures in Table 11.3 is the preponderance of GOAT (etc.) vowels for OE /ɑ:/ in these dialects. This can only be the result of massive levelling (Watt and Milroy 1999; Kerswill 2003) of these traditional north-east English dialects already by the mid twentieth century, such that the endogenous development of ME /a:/ in these words has been replaced by non-northern (including Standard English) GOAT (etc.) vowels. This change is even more apparent in conservative TE today, given the complete absence of any mention of a vowel other than GOAT (etc.) in these OE /ɑ:/ words in more recent accounts (e.g. Wells 1982; Watt and Milroy 1999; Beal *et al.* 2012). The common pronunciation of *home* as [(h)jɛm] and the very occasional pronunciations of *both*, *most* and *whole* with [jɛ] that can still be heard on Tyneside today are the last traces of this traditional northern pattern in the dialect. Other than that, the main development in these words in the two dialects in the SED is [jɛ], exactly the same as is found, at least as a relic, in words with ME /a:/ from other sources (Table 11.2). The almost complete absence of [e:]~[eə]~[ɪə] in the OE /ɑ:/ words shows that this vowel is not the original development of ME /a:/, but instead represents a spread, as a result of levelling, of the vowel which developed for ME /ai/ to all words in the FACE lexical set, just as the GOAT (etc.) vowel had spread to become the majority realisation of the /ɑː/ words. [jɛ] remained, in the 1950s, as a relic of the development of ME /aː/, from whatever source, and as the last traces of the distinction between this vowel and ME /ai/, and had essentially disappeared by the second half of the twentieth century.

The major take-away from this exploration of the reflexes of ME /aː/ and /ai/ in twentieth-century TE is that although the dialect appears to have undergone the FACE merger, this is unexpected in the wider context of traditional Northern English dialects, which mostly retain the distinction. This change in TE was not the result of endogenous developments, but instead reflects the significant effects of dialect levelling on the FACE and GOAT lexical sets, a change that was almost complete by the mid twentieth century. If we want to understand how ME /aː/ and /ai/ developed in the dialect, and how the levelling process affected them, we need data from a period substantially earlier than the SED materials from the 1950s. Given its early date and the considerable number of FACE words in the poem (as a result of its length), TPP is a substantial source of information, both in terms of spellings and of rhymes, for the pronunciation of these vowels in early-nineteenth-century TE, and examining the evidence for their pronunciation in the dialect part of the poem provides a significant exploration of the usefulness of the text for historical phonology.

The usual range of FACE spellings is present in TPP, including <ai> (*tail*), <ay> (*pay*), <ey> (*obey*) and <a_(e)> (*nation, place*). <eigh> (*eight*) also occurs, but it rhymes with PRICE words (e.g. *quite*), as also evidenced in later linguistic descriptions (as noted above). <aigh> in *straight* is absent, since it is replaced with <eigh> or <i_(e)>, indicating the same identity with PRICE, as expected. In addition, a non-standard spelling <ye> commonly occurs in FACE words, for example in <fyece> *face*, <myed> *made* and <nyem> *name*. Furthermore, spellings associated with the FACE lexical set are found for some other words for well-known historical-phonological reasons (e.g. <byens> *bones*, <maister> *master*, <nyen> *none*, <waiter> water). Conversely, spellings indicative of other vowels are found in some FACE words, again with transparent historical-phonological explanations and close parallels in other Northern and Scots dialects (e.g. <brick> *break*, <compleen> *complain*, <greet> *great*). For my analysis of rhymes involving the FACE vowel in TPP, all spellings characteristic of the FACE lexical set and suggestive of a vowel derived from northern ME /aː/ and /ai/ were included, regardless of etymological vowel. In addition, rhymes involving the <e> spelling of words in the DRESS lexical are also included. The analysis of the relevant rhymes is summarised in Figure 11.1.

Unfortunately there are very few rhymes involving <ai>, though even with the limited data we have, words with this spelling are never rhymed

<ai>	<ay>	<a_(e)>	<ye>	<e>	
2	1	4	0	0	<ai>
	33	0	0	0	<ay>
		9	1	2	<a_(e)>
			18	23	<ye>
				26	<e>

Figure 11.1 FACE rhymes in *The Pitman's Pay*

with (FACE) words spelt with <ye> or (DRESS) words spelt with <e>. Since <ay> is only found in morpheme-final position, it is no surprise that words with it rhyme only with words with the same spelling, the single (expected) exception being *paid*, rhymed with *stayed* <stay'd>. <ye>, on the other hand, rhymes not only with itself, but also commonly with words in the DRESS lexical set (spelt with <e>). This spelling, found in words such as <fyece> *face*, <myed> *made* and <nyem> *name*, must unambiguously represent [jɛ] (or some similar phonetic form, such as [ĭɛ], though see further below), given the spelling itself and the frequent rhymes with <e> in DRESS (likely to represent [ɛ], as it still does today). And, indeed, this matches one of the pronunciations recorded by the SED for ME /a:/, as discussed above.[12] The last FACE spelling, <a_(e)>, is not common, but can rhyme with all the other non-final spellings (four times with <ai>, once with <ye> and twice with <e>). These rhymes reveal interesting patterns of variation that I explore further below, but to understand them better, I first explore the use of the spellings involved, specifically the etymological classes that they represent.

In the following analysis of spellings, I consider three sets of words: (1) FACE words which had ME /a:/, almost all of which are spelt with <a_(e)> in Standard English (the 'MATE' set); (2) FACE words which had ME /ai/, which are all spelt with <ai> in Standard English (the 'BAIT' set); (3) words which had OE /ɑ:/, mostly in the GOAT lexical set in Standard English, or with vowels historically derived from the same source (the 'STONE' set). In all cases, only vowels in non-morpheme-final position are considered. The results of this analysis are as follows.

- There are 173 MATE tokens, 103 of which have non-standard spellings:
    - one is spelt with <ya> (*able*);

- two are spelt with <y> only (*pate* and *laced*); the glossary in TPP gives these as <pyet> and <lyec'd>, so these look like typesetting errors in the text rather than genuine spellings;
- the remaining 100 non-standard spellings have <ye> (57.3 per cent);
- otherwise MATE tokens are spelt with <a_(e)>, i.e. the same as their spelling in Standard English.

- There are 58 BAIT tokens, 20 (34.5 per cent) of which are spelt with <ye> (otherwise they are spelt with <ai>, as in Standard English):
  - the <ye> spellings of BAIT are confined to three lexemes: *again*, *fail* and *tailor*.
- There are 102 STONE tokens, of which four (all <claes> *clothes*) probably represent a vowel before a morpheme boundary (cf. <frae> for *from* and <hae> for *have*), while another six (in *hindmost* and *whin-stone*) occur in unstressed position and likely represent [ə] in the dialect, and thus no respelling was felt necessary; excluding these cases we have:
  - 78 tokens (90.7 per cent) spelt with <ye> (e.g. <byens> *bones*, <hyem> *home*);
  - only eight tokens (9.3 per cent) retaining the Standard English spelling (e.g. *boats*, *load*, *rope*).

The absence of <ai> spellings (almost always associated with ME /ai/) in the MATE set is striking, suggesting that it is not a possible spelling for words which had ME /aː/. The one token in this set which has an <ai> spelling in Standard English (*waist*) is spelt <wyest> (rhymed with *dressed* <drest>) in TPP. Concerning the FACE lexical set, Wells (1982: 194) warns us that '[t]oday's spelling does not always reflect the historical situation accurately', and he specifically mentions the word *waist*, which had /aː/ in ME, and which Thomas Wilson accurately treats as a MATE word in TPP, despite its Standard English spelling. Including *pate* and *laced* in the count, 59.0 per cent of MATE words are spelt with <ye>, and the only word spelt with <ya> is likely intended to mean the same (though perhaps influenced by Standard English orthography), given that it is rhymed with *table* <tyeble>. I return to the substantial number of MATE words spelt <a_(e)> below.

Although the levels of <ye> spellings for the BAIT group appears high (at 34.5 per cent), especially since <ai> is never used for MATE words and <ye> is otherwise indicative of ME /aː/, only three BAIT lexical items are spelt this way (and only this way): *again* (<agyen>), *fail* (<fyel>) and *tailor* (<tyelyer>). Although these words had ME /ai/ in the ancestor of Standard English, this is not the case for all dialects descended from OE, especially those in far northern England and in lowland Scotland. In the case of *fail* and *tailor*, they derive from Anglo-Norman *faillir* and *taillour*, with [ʎ] ('L-mouillé') in northern ME and Older Scots, which in effect swallowed the second element of the /ai/ diphthong and gave /a:/ by compensatory lengthening of the nucleus (Aitken and Macafee 2002: 51–2). The original [ʎ] is reflected in the <ly> spelling used by Wilson in *tailor*, surviving in intervocalic position (this type of pronunciation is also recorded in the SED question IV.8.10 in Northumberland and north Durham in the term *long-legged-tailor* for 'daddy-long-legs'). In the case of <agyen> for *again*, there is also evidence that the Northern English and Scots pronunciation of this word derives from an earlier form with /a:/. Aitken and Macafee (2002: 142) suggest that Northern forms of this word derive from OE *ongēan* (which, by a commonly occurring shift in the diphthong peak after palatals, gave /a:/ in ME) rather than *ongegn* (which gave ME /ai/). This explains why *again* is widely attested with reflexes of /a:/, not /ai/, in Northern dialects which otherwise keep the reflexes of these two source vowels distinct (see, for example, the pronunciations given for this word in a wide range of English dialects in Wright 1905, especially the preponderance of [ɪə] and [ɪa] forms, instead of or alongside [e:] forms, recorded in northern counties). In other words, the apparently exceptional <ye> spellings in these three BAIT words in TPP are not exceptions at all, because these three words are not BAIT words in the traditional north-east English dialects. They derive from forms with ME /a:/, and the <ye> spelling in TPP reflects the endogenous development of this in nineteenth-century TE. Strikingly, Wilson gets the etymology of these words right (as indicated in the spellings he uses), regardless of the fact that the Standard English orthography hides their origin, as it does the origin of *waist*.

Not surprisingly, given that it is never used in the spelling of MATE words, <ai> is not used in STONE words (which also had northern Middle English /a:/) in TPP. Instead STONE groups with MATE, as the etymological vowel would lead us to expect, in having a high proportion of <ye> spellings (and associated rhymes, e.g. *bone–then*, *home–dame*, *oak–check*). The eight tokens, from five lexemes, that retain their Standard English spelling include *boats* and *road*, which appear to have been borrowed early by Northern English and Scots dialects from dialects south of the Ribble–Humber Line (Wakelin 1972: 102–3), since they are almost always recorded with a back, rounded vowel development even in the North and in Scotland (see, for example, the entry for these words in Wright 1905). Two of the other tokens (*backbone* and *homely*) are compound or derived forms, which perhaps helps to explain why they have not retained the traditional vowel of the base form. The remaining two lexemes, *load* (three tokens) and *rope* (one token), were not infrequently recorded with front-vowel developments in the North in later studies (again, see the entries for these words in Wright 1905), and thus are likely to represent the beginnings of the levelling of the vowel (in the direction of the GOAT vowel) in this group of words that is so evident in later data for TE (as discussed above), though *rope* may also constitute an example of the aversion to [jɛ] after /r/ so evident in the MATE set, as is discussed further below.

We are left with the MATE words with <a_(e)>, i.e. those which Wilson did not respell, a not insignificant 40.5 per cent of tokens (n = 70) in the group. Why did Wilson not respell those words when he was so careful with his spellings otherwise? It could be that he just failed to respell in some cases (there being, after all, no requirement to respell every word when writing a piece of DL). But a closer look at the data shows that there is more to it than that. The small number of relevant rhymes reveal that although <a_(e)> words could be rhymed with either <ye> or <ai> (see Figure 11.1), in relative terms this is much more likely for <ai> (four of the seven <ai> rhymes are with <a_(e)>, compared to only one of the forty-two rhymes involving <ye> and only two of the fifty-one rhymes involving <e>). When the words which are not respelled are examined, other patterns are revealed. Among them are the three words (one token each) *change*, *dangers* and *strange*. These words have complicated phonological histories with a range of variants in ME, including both /aː/ and /ai/ (Kökeritz 1953: 184; Dobson 1957: 555–8; Minkova 2014: 255). In fact, most of the dialect forms of *change*, *danger* and *stranger* in Wright (1905) suggest ME /ai/ or a realignment, based on Standard English patterns, to the reflex of /ai/,[13] so these words are not typical MATE words, and may in fact be better placed in BAIT for many dialects. There is also a range of phonological factors affecting which spelling is used. Table 11.4 sets out a number of factors which appear to affect the choice of spellings of MATE words in TPP, giving the percentage of tokens spelt with <a_(e)> and with <ye> (the other spelling of MATE words) which match the factors given in the first column.

Table 11.4 Factors affecting spelling choice of MATE words in TPP[c]

Factor	<a_(e)> (n = 70)	<ye> (n = 100)
Non-final stressed syllable (e.g. *patent*)	48.6%	10.0%[a]
Onset /Cl/ or /(C)r/ (e.g. *place, race, trade*)[b]	34.3%	0.0%
Neighbouring palatal consonant (e.g. *age, shape*)	20.0%	0.0%
Following voiced fricative (e.g. *save*)	17.1%	2.0%

Notes

a. Note that six of the ten tokens are inflected forms (e.g. *making*), which may pattern with the uninflected monosyllabic forms of these words, so that the real figure for this cell may be 4.0%.

b. Initial /l/ on its own does not appear to prohibit <ye> spellings (e.g. *laces* <lyeces>, *lame* <lyem>, *late* <lyet>).

c. The percentage figures for each column may add up to over 100% because individual tokens can contain more than one factor (e.g. *nature*).

These differences between the two spelling types are all highly significant (χ^2), as is the overall difference between them. In terms of all of the factors combined, only seven <a_(e)> tokens (10.0 per cent) are left which don't match any of them. For <ye>, only twelve tokens match any of the factors, reducing to six (6.0 per cent) if we exclude inflected bisyllabic forms, as noted. It is clear that the two spelling types represent real phonological differences, as these intricate patterns could not be produced by random chance. The prohibition on [jɛ] after palatals, /r/ (also found in *rope*, as noted above) and clusters of a consonant + /l/ is probably related to the widespread English change 'Early Yod Dropping' (Wells 1982: 206–7), whereby [j] was lost in sequences of a palatal consonant + /j/, and in /rj/ and /Clj/ (in words like *sure*, *rude* and *blue*; cf. words like *lewd*, which are more likely to retain /j/, though it may be lost here too).[14] This change, as well as a preference for [eː] rather than [jɛ] for ME /aː/ in non-final syllables and before palatal consonants and voiced fricatives, is also evident for other dialects in Northumberland, as recorded in Rydland (1998). The low occurrence of [jɛ] before voiced fricatives is particularly interesting, since it appears to be part of a wider set of changes related to the 'Scottish Vowel Length Rule' (SVLR; Aitken 1981), which is also known to be present, in limited form, in Northumberland and north Durham (Glauser 1988; Milroy 1995). In morpheme-final position (e.g. in *no* (adj.), *sloe, so, toe, two, who* and *woe*), ME /aː/ is traditionally represented by /eː/ in north Northumberland and by /iː/ elsewhere in the north-east, rather than by /jɛ/ (or other local equivalents of this vowel). Similarly, ME /aː/ before /r/ (e.g. in *bare* and *hare*) is represented by [eə] in all dialects rather than by [jɛ] (etc.). When we add to this the dispreferment of [jɛ] before voiced fricatives evident in TPP (and later sources), we have a situation whereby [jɛ] is the reflex of ME /aː/ in SVLR short environments, with other vowels occurring in SVLR long environments (though the distinction is not absolute, and of course these other vowels can occur in SVLR short environments, e.g. [eː] as a reflex of ME /ai/ in words like *bait*). A similar pattern exists for northern ME /øː/ (from earlier /oː/ as a result of 'Northern Fronting'; see Rydland 1998 for examples), with different developments before /r/ and morpheme boundaries, and a dispreferment of the usual [jʊ]~[jɵ] development before voiced fricatives (a similar situation also pertains in Scots; see Johnston 1997b: 465–6 for details). When we add to this the well-known SVLR conditioning of the PRICE vowel in north-east English dialects (Glauser 1988; Milroy 1995), it is clear that the 'Scottish' Vowel Length Rule has played an important role in the historical phonology of north-east English dialects, and TPP provides key early indications of it.

All of the evidence, the lack of respelling, the rhymes, the phonological conditioning, and data from later sources, suggests that for the most part

<a_(e)> spellings in TPP do not represent [jɛ] but instead reflect the spread of the reflex of ME /ai/ (probably [eː] at this time going by the evidence in early data sources such as Ellis 1889, Wright 1905 and Rydland 1998, often changing to [eə]~[ɪə] by the mid twentieth century, as evidence in the SED) into the FACE lexical set more generally. It is clear that [eː] was viewed in this change as the default FACE vowel, whereas [jɛ] was considered to be a marked, local variant, given the ultimate displacement of [jɛ] by [eː] ([eə], [ɪə]). It is not surprising, then, that Wilson did not respell those MATE words which had the vowel typical of the BAIT lexical set, because that vowel ([eː] rather than [jɛ]) would have been the default reading of these spellings from a Standard English point of view. It was only when his dialect departed from expected phonological norms (e.g. in having [jɛ] in some FACE words) that he needed to indicate this in his spellings in TPP.

In summary, then, this analysis of the FACE lexical set in TPP reveals the following patterns:

(1) A couple of minor lexical subsets aside, non-final FACE vowels are spelt in two ways in TPP: <ai> and <je>;

(2) <ai> is only used for ME /ai/, never for ME /aː/, despite the fact that the etymology of some words is obscured by the Standard English spelling (*waist*) and by differences in southern and northern ME (*again*, *fail*, *tailor*);

(3) The <je> spelling is also usual for GOAT words which had OE /ɑː/ (northern ME /aː/);

(4) That is, Wilson is exact in his use of <je> for ME /aː/ and of <ai> for ME /ai/ in TPP;

(5) The rhymes of <je> with words in the DRESS lexical set and the dispreferment of this spelling after /r/ and /Cl/ clusters points to it representing [jɛ], as is also evidenced in later sources; the phonetics of the vowel represented by <ai> in TPP cannot be determined on internal evidence alone, but later sources suggest it was [eː] (changing to [eə]~[ɪə] by the mid twentieth century);

(6) Wilson retains a not insubstantial number of <a_(e)> spellings of MATE words in TPP, but these spellings are not random, and instead are conditioned by phonological environment, including complex patterning along SVLR lines; it is likely that they represent the beginnings of the spread of the default FACE vowel [eː] into the MATE set (i.e. the 'FACE Merger'), a process which is far advanced in the Tyneside dialects recorded in the SED in the 1950s and which was complete in late-twentieth-century TE, and thus they required no respelling to indicate divergence in the dialect from the Standard English pattern;

(7) The FACE Merger had an exogenous motivation in TE, it being characteristic of Standard and supra-local varieties of English, but its application to TE proceeded, at least initially, by specific phonological environments.

Given all of 1–7 above, it is clear that Thomas Wilson's spellings of the FACE vowel are far from random. In fact, they very accurately encode complex phonological patterns reflecting the history of the language and ongoing change. In so doing, they provide us with a detailed and otherwise unavailable picture of the phonology of the FACE lexical set in early-nineteenth-century TE, and an early snapshot of a change that ultimately obscured all traces of the long-standing distinction between ME /aː/ and /ai/ in the dialect. This review of all of the data relevant to the FACE vowel in TPP shows not only the value of the poem for the historical phonology of north-east English dialects, but also the importance of a systematic analysis of patterns in dialect literature for evaluating their use as linguistic evidence. In the case of TPP at least, such an analysis pays rich rewards.

11.4. Conclusions

The analysis in this chapter of the phonology of *heaven* and of the FACE lexical set in TPP was conducted not only in order to find out more about the history of these features in the dialect, but also to determine how valuable TPP (and potentially other instances of DL) is as linguistic evidence, and to illustrate how this kind of data can be analysed. The analysis revealed that Thomas Wilson was extremely consistent and accurate in his orthographic representations and in his rhymes and metre, so that a coherent picture emerges as to why the features under analysis are represented in the way that they are. Both features have undergone complex changes in the dialect, and Wilson captures this complexity in his representation of the dialect in TPP. None of this is by accident, and it speaks of his deep knowledge of the dialect and his ability to capture essential aspects of it in his writing. As a result, we have a good picture of the phonology of the word *heaven* in late-eighteenth- and early-nineteenth-century Tyneside English, and have a much better understanding of the development of the FACE lexical set in the dialect than is available from later sources.

Of course, there are things we cannot tell about the dialect from this kind of source. The phonetics of many features remain unknown, though we can guess at them from what we know of earlier stages of the language, from later data and from the spellings used by Wilson. For example, it is likely that the speakers of the dialect represented in TPP pronounced /r/ as a uvular fricative, the famous 'Northumbrian Burr' (Wells 1982: 368–70), but there is no direct indication in TPP that Tyneside English was characterised by this feature in Wilson's time. But all kinds of data are deficient in some way, and when we can rely only on written records rather than audio-recordings it is inevitable that many aspects of a dialect will remain unknowable. What is more remarkable is how much information on the phonology of late-eighteenth- and early-nineteenth-century Tyneside English there is in TPP. The analysis in this chapter suggests that DL can be an important source of information on the earlier phonologies of English dialects, though doubtless the extent to which this is true will vary for different authors and different sources. Thomas Wilson was extremely good at capturing the phonological subtleties of his dialect, and although the same may not be the case for every instance of DL, he is unlikely to have been unique in this respect. There is much to learn about the history of the English dialects that were documented in the poems, songs and stories of the eighteenth and nineteenth centuries, long before linguists began to record them.

Notes

1. In addition, much of Wright's data for north-east England is copied (but in a broader phonetic transcription) from Ellis's survey, so it has no independent value.
2. Throughout this chapter I make use of John Wells's 'lexical sets' (identified by use of small caps, e.g. FACE), as described in Wells (1982).
3. This brief biography of Thomas Wilson draws on details of his life given in the 1872 edition of TPP and Allan (1972: 258–63).
4. According to Wilson (1843: xxxii), a trapper boy was responsible for the door in a mine, in order to allow the circulation of air.
5. Examples from TPP in this chapter are identified by Part, Stanza and Line, so that C.314.1254 means that the example is from the third part, 314th stanza and 1254th line of the poem.
6. Line 11 includes a quote, in Scots, from Robert Burns' *Auld Lang Syne*.
7. Thus, for example, the pair *now-knew* (C.301.1202/4) is readily interpetable as an exact rhyme, given the traditional pronunciations of *now* [nuː] and *knew* [njuː] (Rydland 1998).
8. The precise realisation of this vowel is of course uncertain, but [iː] is the usual non-final realisation of the high front unrounded long vowel recorded in later surveys in Tyneside and Northumberland.
9. The <de'il> form of *devil*, also found in Scots, likely represents the pronunciation [diːl], as recorded in some later sources, with loss of [v]. This is probably a development of earlier [ˈdiːvəl] (as indicated in the <deevil> spelling and as recorded in some later sources). *eleven* does not occur in TPP.
10. ME /aː/ from Open Syllable Lengthening did not occur in morpheme-final position, so that the vowel did not contrast with ME /ai/ in this environment in many dialects of the language. However, in northern ME and Older Scots /aː/ was found in final position, developing there from OE /ɑː/, for example in *no* (adj.), *sloe, so, toe, two, who, woe.* In the traditional dialects of north-east England, this vowel developed in two ways, to an [eː] vowel in north

Northumberland, and to an [iː] vowel in the rest of Northumberland, Tyneside and in County Durham. Since these words do not belong to the FACE lexical set in Standard English, they have never had the FACE vowel in TE, either traditionally (where they had [iː]) or as the result of levelling in contact with non-local varieties (which gives rise to pronunciations of the these words with the GOAT vowel, typically [øː]~[oː] in conservative TE). As a result, I do not discuss the development of the FACE vowel in morpheme-final position in the dialect in detail in this chapter, as it peripheral to the main discussion.

11. The phonetic distinctions made in the SED were even finer than these (including transcriptions such as [ẹːᵊ], [ẹˑə], [ɪ̣ə], etc.), but I have collapsed these statistically insignificant differences into these broader categories for the purposes of this analysis.
12. Beal (2000: 350) suggests that <ye> in nineteenth-century Tyneside dialect literature represents the sound found in conservative TE speech in the second half of the twentieth century, [ɪə] (see the discussion at the start of this section). The evidence presented here (the spellings and rhymes from TPP, and the phonetic evidence from the SED) suggests that this is not the case, and that modern TE [ɪə] is a relatively recent (though already old-fashioned) development replacing [jɛ] as the vowel in part of the FACE lexical set.
13. E.g. Northern English dialects which preserve a distinction between ME /aː/ and /ai/ typically have [eː] in these words rather than [ɪə].
14. This cannot just have been a loss of /j/ in TE, however, since these words rarely rhyme with words in the DRESS lexical set. Instead it appears that the aversion to these clusters involving /j/ led to the replacement of [jɛ] by the vowel typical of the BAIT set.

References

Aitken, A. J. (1981), 'The Scottish vowel-length rule', in Michael Benskins and Michael Samuels (eds), *So Meny People, Longages and Tonges: Philological Essays in Scots and Medieval English Presented to Angus McIntosh*, Edinburgh: Edinburgh University Press, pp. 131–57.

Aitken, A. J. and Caroline Macafee (2002), *The Older Scots Vowels*, Edinburgh: Scottish Text Society.

Allan, Thomas (1972), *Allan's Tyneside Songs*, ed. by David Harker (editions 1–6 published 1862–91), Newcastle upon Tyne: Frank Graham.

Anderson, Peter (1987), *A Structural Atlas of the English Dialects*, North Ryde, NSW: Croom Helm.

Beal, Joan (2000), 'From George Ridley to Viz: popular literature in Tyneside English', *Language and Literature* 9(4), 343–59.

Beal, Joan (2006), 'Dialect representations in texts', in *The Encyclopedia of Language and Linguistics*, Amsterdam and London: Elsevier, pp. 531–7.

Beal, Joan, Lourdes Burbano-Elizondo and Carmen Llamas (2012), *Urban North-eastern English: Tyneside to Teesside*, Edinburgh: Edinburgh University Press.

Bermúdez-Otero, Ricardo (1998), 'Prosodic optimization: the Middle English length adjustment', *English Language and Linguistics* 2(2), 169–97.

Brunner, Karl (1925), 'Die Schreibtradition der Dialektschriftsteller von Lancashire', *Englische Studien* 60, 158–79.

Dobson, Eric (1957), *English Pronunciation 1500–1700*, Oxford: Clarendon Press.

Dobson, Scott (1969), *Larn Yersel' Geordie*, Newcastle upon Tyne: Frank Graham.

Ellis, Alexander (1889), *On Early English Pronunciation, Part V: The Existing Phonology of English Dialects Compared with That of West Saxon*, New York: Greenwood Press.

Glauser, Beat (1988), 'Aitken's Context in Northumberland, Cumberland and Durham: a computer assisted analysis of material from the Survey of English Dialects (SED)', in Alan R. Thomas (ed.), *Methods in Dialectology: Proceedings of the 6th International Conference Held at the University College of North Wales*, Cleveland: Multilingual Matters Ltd, pp. 611–24.

Harker, David (1972), 'Thomas Allan and the "Tyneside Song"', in Thomas Allan, *Allan's Tyneside Songs*, ed. by David Harker, Newcastle upon Tyne: Frank Graham, vii–xxviii.

Harris, John (1985), *Phonological Variation and Change: Studies in Hiberno-English*, Cambridge: Cambridge University Press.

Hermeston, Rodney (2009), 'Linguistic identity in nineteenth-century Tyneside dialect songs', unpublished PhD thesis, University of Leeds.

Honeybone, Patrick and Kevin Watson (2013), 'Salience and the sociolinguistics of Scouse spelling: exploring the phonology of the Contemporary Humorous Localised Dialect Literature of Liverpool', *English world-wide* 34(3), 305–40.

Johnston, Paul (1997a), 'Older Scots phonology and its regional variation', in Charles Jones (ed.), *The Edinburgh History of the Scots Language*, Edinburgh: Edinburgh University Press, pp. 47–111.

Johnston, Paul (1997b), 'Regional variation', in Charles Jones (ed.), *The Edinburgh History of the Scots Language*, Edinburgh: Edinburgh University Press, pp. 433–513.

Kerswill, Paul (2003), 'Dialect levelling and geographical diffusion in British English', in David Britain and Jenny Cheshire (eds), *Social Dialectology: In Honour of Peter Trudgill*, Amsterdam and Philadelphia: John Benjamins, pp. 223–43.

Kökeritz, Helge (1953), *Shakespeare's Pronunciation*, New Haven, CT: Yale University Press.

Labov, William (1994), *Principles of Linguistic Change, Vol. 1: Internal Factors*, Oxford and Cambridge, MA: Blackwell Publishers.

Lass, Roger (1992), 'Phonology and morphology', in Norman Blake (ed.), *The Cambridge History of the English Language, Vol. 2: 1066–1476*, Cambridge: Cambridge University Press, pp. 23–155.

Lass, Roger (2000), 'Phonology and morphology', in Roger Lass (ed.), *The Cambridge History of the English Language, Vol. 3: 1476–1776*, Cambridge: Cambridge University Press, pp. 56–186.

Milroy, James (1995), 'Investigating the Scottish Vowel Length Rule in a Northumbrian dialect', *Newcastle and Durham Working Papers in Linguistics* 3, 187–96.

Minkova, Donka (2014), *A Historical Phonology of English*, Edinburgh: Edinburgh University Press.

Orton, Harold (1933), *The Phonology of a South Durham Dialect: Descriptive, Historical and Comparative*, London: Kegan Paul, Trench, Trübner and Co.

Orton, Harold and Eugen Dieth (eds) (1962–71), *Survey of English Dialects (B): The Basic Material*, Leeds: Arnold and Son.

Rydland, Kurt (1998), *The Orton Corpus: A Dictionary of Northumbrian Pronunciation, 1928–1939*, Oslo: Novus Press.

Shorrocks, Graham (1996), 'Non-standard dialect literature and popular culture', in Juhani Klemola, Merja Kytö and Matti Rissanen (eds), *Speech Past and Present*, Frankfurt am Main: Peter Lang, pp. 385–411.

Smith, Jeremy (2007), 'Copia verborum: the linguistic choices of Robert Burns', *The Review of English Studies* 58, 73–88.

Wakelin, Martyn (1972), *English Dialects: An Introduction*, London: Athlone Press.

Watt, Dominic and Lesley Milroy (1999), 'Patterns of variation and change in three Newcastle vowels: is this dialect levelling?', in Paul Foulkes and Gerard Docherty (eds), *Urban Voices: Accent Studies in the British Isles*, London: Arnold, pp. 25–47.

Wells, John (1982), *Accents of English*, Cambridge: Cambridge University Press.

Wilson, Thomas ([1843] 1872), *The Pitman's Pay and Other Poems*, London: George Routledge and Sons.

Wright, Joseph (1905), *The English Dialect Grammar*, Oxford, London, Edinburgh, Glasgow, New York and Toronto: Henry Frowde.

12

The Graphical Representation of Phonological Dialect Features of the North of England on Social Media

Andrea Nini, George Bailey, Diansheng Guo and Jack Grieve

12.1. Introduction

This chapter focuses on social media and considers whether and how the graphological reflection of dialect writing is affecting these new forms of communication. By foregrounding the importance of the ways in which speakers construct and project personae (Eckert 2012), third-wave theoretical approaches to the study of linguistic variation would predict that users can break orthographic conventions in order to encode their dialect and linguistic identity on social media (see Beal, this volume, for a similar idea relevant to ego-documents from the eighteenth and nineteenth centuries). However, the extent to which users of social media use spelling resources to convey dialectal identities and to what purposes is not immediately obvious and one of the objectives of this chapter is to shed light on this phenomenon both quantitatively and qualitatively.

Recent research on dialect variation using social media data has so far provided evidence that spelling variants that reflect phonological dialect features are found in social media posts, such as tweets. This is an important finding because it opens the possibility of analysing the dialect of a region using naturally occurring social media posts as opposed to using interviews or questionnaires.

In addition, if users do adopt dialectal spelling variants in their social media communications, it is not clear whether their geographical patterning would match their respective phonetic forms. The question of the extent to which social media like Twitter can be used to answer questions about language variation and change is still an open one, even though the evidence so far is particularly promising. The other objective of this study is therefore to attempt to derive dialect patterns from social media data on the basis of the frequency with which dialectal spelling is used and estimate the degree of match of these dialect patterns with established knowledge of their phonetic equivalents gathered using survey methods. For these reasons, the analysis will focus on a subset of features of the dialects of the North of England that can potentially be expressed using spelling variation.

In this study, using a corpus of 183 million geocoded tweets totalling 1.8 billion words, we explore how phonological features of the dialects of the North of England such as HAPPY-laxing (e.g. *happy* > 'happeh'; *funny* > 'funneh') and the retention of [uː] in MOUTH are realised graphically by social media users. We adopt a quantitative methodology, similar in principle (but different in detail) to the chapters in this volume by Cooper and by Watson and Jensen. We present results that show that the geographical distribution of these features as found on Twitter is similar to those attested in other studies carried out with other more conventional methods. Furthermore, our research reveals how and how often these dialect features are used in written online communication, adding to our understanding of the relationship between language and the projection of identity.

In the following sections, we provide firstly an overview of previous dialectological studies that have used social media data and, secondly, a brief description of Northern English dialectology with an outline of the specific features under consideration in this study.

12.2. Social Media Data for Dialectology

Data for corpus and computational linguistics has been collected using the Internet for more than a decade and, despite theoretical issues concerning representativeness, has so far led to interesting and useful results for various corpus linguistics endeavours (Kilgarriff and Grefenstette 2003). Among all the types of Internet data, though, the one type that started a revolution is social media data, which is responsible for the emergence of the new field of *computational sociolinguistics* (Nguyen *et al.* 2016). Social media data offers several advantages to a sociolinguist or dialectologist compared to survey data sets, such as, above all, the substantially large size and the fact that it is 'observer paradox' free. Conversely, however, social media data comes with the problem of biased sampling and with its 'bad language' (Eisenstein 2013) in terms of its adherence to standard variety, which is, however, not necessarily a drawback, as many studies on the emergence and spread of innovations based on social media data have demonstrated. The drawbacks of using social media data are, however, small compared to its benefits: this type of data allowed research of unprecedented scale that could finally tackle some research questions or tasks that would otherwise be impossible, such as identifying neologisms as they occur (Kerremans *et al.* 2012) or studying how words emerge and become popular (Grieve *et al.* 2017).

Dialectology is probably the branch of linguistics that can benefit the most from social media data such as Twitter data because of its availability with geocoded information. Users of social media can choose to add the GPS coordinates of the place they sent their message from and thus corpora of geocoded tweets can be used to directly observe dialectal variation almost in real time. Dialectological studies using Twitter data have already been carried out and, because of the ease with which it is possible to extract lexical items, geocoded Twitter data has been mostly explored in terms of lexical variation (Eisenstein *et al.* 2012; Gonçalves and Sánchez 2014; Kulkarni *et al.* 2016; Shoemark *et al.* 2017).

Despite the latest achievements of the studies that use geocoded Twitter data, Eisenstein (2018) stresses that important limitations in terms of representativeness can be a danger, since arguably the population of users of Twitter is not necessarily a random sample of the general population of a country. Studies carried out in the UK indeed confirm that the population of Twitter users is not generally representative of the UK population as a whole. For example, Longley *et al.* (2015) inferred demographic information for each user in a corpus of four million geotagged tweets sent in London using their usernames and concluded that the population of Twitter users is biased towards men and younger adults compared to 2011 Census data. Results about ethnicity indicate that all ethnic groups beside White are underrepresented, although the confidence over these results is unclear. Additional evidence comes from Mellon and Prosser (2017), who carried out a study using the 2015 British Election Study survey and concluded that, compared to a random and representative sample of eligible British voters, users of Twitter are younger (mean age of thirty-four compared to forty-eight), more likely to be men, more likely to have A-levels or a degree and more liberal in terms of political views than non-users.

In addition to these biases of Twitter users in general, there seems to exist an additional bias in the population of users who use geocoded posts. Pavalanathan and Eisenstein (2015) studied the possible bias in geotagged US Twitter data and uncovered that geolocation is preferred by younger people and women. Interestingly, they find that the users who choose to geotag their tweets are also the ones that are more likely to use non-standard regional words.

Although the evidence therefore points to a substantial disparity between the population of Twitter users and geocoded Twitter users compared to the population of a country as a whole, this by itself does not mean that dialectological work carried out on Twitter is necessarily invalid, and, in spite of the representativeness shortcomings, so far research has managed to successfully replicate dialect studies carried out with more conventional methods (Cook *et al.* 2014; Doyle 2014; Eisenstein 2015; Jones 2015; Huang *et al.* 2016; Rahimi *et al.* 2017). Recently, Grieve *et al.* (2019) performed a comparison of 139 dialect maps from the BBC Voices survey to the equivalent maps generated using Twitter data and found a high degree of alignment, which further validates the use of Twitter for dialectology.

An area that has so far showed promising advances is the study of graphological reflections of dialectal phonetic variation, with a few studies so far showing that graphological representations are consistent with the same variation present in speech. The act of encoding phonological features in orthographic forms long pre-dates the advent of social media platforms and has been widely documented, for example, in nineteenth-century poetry or in 'dialect literature' (see Asprey, Braber and Maguire this volume, for example). As highlighted by the other chapters in this volume, one of the defining features of dialect writing is not simply the use of specific lexical items but also the creative way in which writers flout orthographic norms in order to reflect their spoken accent.

Parallels can be drawn between this traditional style of dialect writing and the contemporary stylistic practices of users on social media platforms such as Twitter. The open nature of Twitter data makes it a fruitful area of linguistic research, and there has been a number of existing studies that have explored the relationship between phonological features in speech production and the way they are reflected orthographically on social media. Analysing a corpus of over 100 million geotagged tweets, Eisenstein (2015) compares the variable use of *g-dropping* (e.g. <walkin> for *walking*) and *t/d-deletion* (e.g. <jus> for *just*) on Twitter with their pattern of variation in speech, finding similarities in the way they are conditioned between these two mediums. Specifically, the widely established 'nominal–verbal continuum' that sees verbs favour [ɪn] and nouns [ɪŋ] (Labov 1989) is reflected in the orthographic variation, as is the phonological conditioning of *t/d-deletion* in which deletion is favoured before consonant-initial words but inhibited pre-vocalically (e.g. Guy 1991; Tagliamonte and Temple 2005; Tanner *et al.* 2017). Although the grammatical conditioning of *g-dropping* was not replicated in UK Twitter data by Bailey (2016), non-standard <in> and <in'> spellings were found to occur at higher frequencies in northern England and Scotland, reflecting the same regional patterning that has been reported for the phonological alternation (Labov 2001: 90).

In a separate line of work, Tatman (2016) investigated how sociophonetic features of New York City English – such as /ɹ/-deletion (e.g. <beah> for *beer*) and certain vocalic differences (e.g. <woyld> for *wild* and <nawt>

for *not*) – are encoded on Twitter in impersonations of this dialect, arguing that the salience of these features modulates the extent to which they are employed in the projection of dialect on Twitter.

Despite these recent advances in our understanding of how phonetically motivated spelling is utilised by users of social media, the extent to which varieties of Northern English are reflected in this way remains an unexplored avenue of research.

12.3. The North of England

Broadly speaking, the 'linguistic north' of England may be defined as the region where the vowels in FOOT and STRUT and in TRAP and BATH are pronounced the same (see the Introduction to this volume); these are two well-known and highly salient features that characterise the linguistic north/south divide in England. The isoglosses for these two vocalic features run approximately from the River Severn to the Wash, and as such they include the Midlands regions and the dialects spoken therein; in this chapter we focus primarily on those varieties spoken in the north-west (e.g. Manchester, Merseyside, Lancashire), the north-east (e.g. Tyneside and Wearside) and Yorkshire, excluding Birmingham and Black Country varieties spoken in the Midlands.

There is a long history of dialectology in the North of England (for overviews, see Wakelin 1977; Wells 1982; Beal 2004; Hughes *et al.* 2012). Additionally, contemporary variationist linguistics has often placed the lens of inquiry on Northern dialects such as those spoken in Manchester (Drummond 2012; Baranowski and Turton 2015; Baranowski 2017), Liverpool (Honeybone 2007; Watson 2007; Cardoso 2015), Tyneside (Milroy *et al.* 1994; Watt 2002; Beal *et al.* 2012) and Yorkshire (Petyt 1985; Tagliamonte 2004).

Dialectal variation in the North of England is a fruitful area of research given the extreme linguistic diversity we find here; it is said that differences between dialects are 'sharper in the north than in any other part of England' (Wells 1982: 351), and this statement has been echoed by Beal (2004: 120), who claims that more features differentiate Northern dialects from each other than are common to all of them. For example, even within the north-east alone there are significant differences between the Newcastle and Sunderland varieties despite their close proximity to each other (Beal 2000; Beal *et al.* 2012). Trudgill (1999) also notes how traditional dialect speakers can still be found in the North of England, particularly in rural areas and more endocentric, geographically peripheral communities. The wealth of linguistic diversity in the North could in part stem from geography and its role in inhibiting contact-induced levelling (cf. southern areas such as the Fens that are conducive to dialect contact, as explored by Britain 2002) and, on a related note, how its distance from London more generally inhibits the influence of the standard on the more traditional varieties spoken in the North. In the Old English period, regional norms in the written language had already begun to develop from different scribal centres across the country, laying the foundation for later regional diversity (see Beal 2004 for a brief overview of the history and development of Northern English). In this chapter, we show that variation in written English is still present, at least in the case of phonetically motivated orthography on social media.

12.3.1. Northern Dialect Features

In selecting variable phonological features to be included in this study, there are two important pre-requisites to be considered in addition to regional stratification: (1) they must be perceptually and socially salient enough to be used orthographically as an index of local dialects, and (2) they must plausibly be encoded in orthographic representations. As such, we cannot investigate Northern features such as the presence of dark /l/ variants (Carter 2002; Turton 2017) or post-nasal [ɡ]-presence in words such as *sing* or *wrong* (Wells 1982: 365); both features have relatively low social profiles (see Bailey 2019) and it is not clear how either could be reflected transparently in the orthographic representation.

Eleven features have been selected for analysis, covering both consonantal and vocalic variation; all of these features have been said to occur in the North of England, with a subset of these features occurring exclusively in the North and many others said to occur more frequently in these dialects relative to the other regions of England. The features are listed below, alongside descriptions and examples of their phonetic and orthographic realisation.

(1) **T-to-R**: In some Northern varieties, a final /t/ in a monosyllabic word can be realised as [ɹ] if followed by a vowel-initial word, for example, *get off* [gɛɹɒf]; this is typically associated with Liverpool English (Watson 2007; Buchstaller *et al.* 2013; Honeybone *et al.* 2017), but is also present in other Northern dialects such as Tyneside English (Watt and Milroy 1999). However, there have been reports suggesting that this feature is stigmatised and receding over time (Foulkes and Docherty 2007), and that its occurrence is restricted to highly frequent collocations (Clark and Watson 2011). For example, *get off, lot of* → *geroff, lorra*

(2) **HAPPY-laxing**: The HAPPY lexical set refers to the word-final unstressed /i/ vowel, which in most varieties is realised as either tense [i] or lax [ɪ]; in Manchester English, however, a super-lax variant [ɛ]

is also possible (Ramsammy and Turton 2012; Hughes *et al.* 2012). This is highly salient and encoded in stereotypes of supporters of the football club Manchester City, for example, *citeh*; Braber (this volume) shows evidence of a productive graphical representation of this feature in dialect writing literature of the East Midlands. Although it is also a productive process in speech, it remains to be seen whether or not the orthographic form is restricted to this lexical item as a sociocultural symbol on social media. For example, *happy* → *happeh*

(3) **LETTER-backing**: Like happY-laxing, lettER-backing is another vocalic feature exclusive to Manchester English, targeting word-final unstressed /ə/. Ramsammy and Turton (2012) find that the phonetic quality of this vowel is approaching [ʌ] rather than [ɒ], but this is nevertheless perceived and stereotyped as the latter, and therefore will likely be reflected orthographically by replacement of <er> with <oh>. This is likely to be enregistered most strongly in the word Manchester itself, as is typically the case with place-names. For example, *Manchester* → *Manchestoh*

(4) **AW to UW**: The retention of [uː] in mouth is one of the defining features of Tyneside English spoken in the north-east (Hughes *et al.* 2012: 155) as well as of Scots (Johnston 1997; McColl Millar 2007). It is claimed to be particularly frequent in specific lexical items that enact local identity such as *toon* (*town*) and *broon* (*brown*), referring to Newcastle United Football Club and Newcastle Brown Ale, respectively (Beal *et al.* 2012: 35). As with happY-laxing and lettER-backing, it is possible that the orthographic representation of this feature may be lexically restricted. For example, *down* → *doon*

(5) **FOOT–STRUT**: The lack of distinction between vowel in the foot and strut lexical sets, in which both have /ʊ/, is associated with all dialects in the North and, to a lesser extent, the Midlands. Alongside the bath–trap split, it is described as the most important characteristic differentiating Northern and Southern dialects (Wells 1982), although there is recent evidence to suggest that the /ʌ/ vowel in strut is spreading northwards (MacKenzie *et al.* 2014). In addition to this, Trudgill (1986) notes an apparent discrepancy in the relative social salience of these two features, stating that although Northerners are stereotyped by Southerners as lacking both the bath–trap and foot–strut oppositions, Northerners themselves only comment on the Southern [ɑː] vowel in bath. This is an important point to consider given the aforementioned issue of salience and the likelihood of these features being represented orthographically. For example, *love*, *London* → *luv*/*lav*, *Landan*

(6) **G-dropping**: The variable realisation of unstressed *-ing* as either alveolar [ɪn] or velar [ɪŋ] is widely studied in sociolinguistics and has been attested throughout the British Isles. Although this feature is not restricted to Northern dialects in the same way as the features discussed thus far, it has nevertheless been argued that [ɪn] occurs more frequently in the North of England and Scotland (Moore *et al.* 1935; Houston 1985; Watts 2005), so much so that Levon and Fox (2014: 201) describe it as a regional (rather than social) variable in the British Isles. A third possible variant, [ɪŋg], *is* unique to the north-west and West Midlands, but is unlikely to be reflected orthographically given the existing presence of <g> in the standard spelling. For example, *walking → walkin, walkin'*

(7) **TH-stopping**: Word-initial dental fricatives /θ, ð/ can sometimes be realised as alveolar stops [t, d], for example, *think* [tɪŋk]. Although this is more strongly associated with the performance of ethnic rather than regional identity and has strong ties to Multicultural London English (see Drummond 2018), it has at least been attested in Northern varieties such as Liverpool English (Watson 2007) and Manchester English (Drummond 2018). For example, *think, this → tink, dis*

(8) **TH-fronting**: Not to be confused with the aforementioned process of stopping, the dental fricatives /θ, ð/ can also undergo fronting to labiodental position, i.e. [f, v]. This process has been described as one of the fastest-spreading sound changes in British English (Trudgill 1999), but is possibly less frequent in the North given that it originated and subsequently diffused from London and the south-east (Williams and Kerswill 1999). It has been attested in Manchester English, where it is described as an 'urban youth norm' (Baranowski and Turton 2015: 303). For example, *think, with → fink, wiv*

(9) **H-dropping**: Deletion of word-initial /h/, for example, *house* [aʊs], has been reported in dialects of British English for hundreds of years and is described as 'the single most powerful pronunciation shibboleth in England' (Wells 1982: 254); it is especially found in function words. As such, it is not necessarily a Northern feature but it has been attested in Manchester English (Baranowski and Turton 2015) where it has been claimed to be frequent in conversational speech (Hughes *et al.* 2012: 116). For example, *happens, have → appens, av(e)*

(10) **Consonant reduction**: Rather than being a single phonological process, we use the term consonant reduction to refer to a group of pronunciation variants that are characteristic of conversational speech; there is no reason to believe these are geographically restricted, but they are often found in traditional dialect poetry from regions such as

Lancashire. For example, *doesn't, didn't, isn't, with* → *dunt, dint, int, wi*

(11) **Vowel reduction**: As above, but for the general process of vocalic reduction instead. Again, these are characteristic of conversational speech where unstressed vowels are often reduced and centralised to a more [ə]-like quality. For example, *your, you, I've, our, my* → *yer, ye/ya, av, ar(e), mi/ma*

12.4. Data

The corpus used in this study was collected at the University of South Carolina using the Twitter API and consists of 183 million geocoded tweets. The corpus contains a total of 1.8 billion words written by almost two million users in the United Kingdom for the year 2014.[1] Using the longitude and latitude of each geocoded tweet the corpus was divided into sub-corpora, grouping together all tweets from the same postcode area. There are in total 124 postcode areas in the United Kingdom and the data for these areas varied widely, from 54,000 tweets in the Outer Hebrides to 5.5 million in Manchester, which is the largest area because London is subdivided into smaller areas. We decided not to alter the corpus in any way, as for example by filtering it for retweets or for tweets sent by bots as done in some previous studies. This decision was taken to guarantee that the sample analysed is a representative data set that replicates what a typical user would encounter in the real world, while the size of the data set allows for the geographical signal to be captured despite the noise that might be created by these factors.

12.5. Methodology

To find the eleven features considered for this study we compiled a list of words belonging to each category ordered by frequency, with measures taken from the SUBTLEX-UK corpus of television subtitles and operationalised using the Zipf scale (van Heuven *et al.* 2014). For each of these words we replaced the standard spelling with predicted spellings for its dialectal variants. We then filtered these lists in two ways, firstly by frequency and secondly by word search feasibility. We kept all words for each category with Zipf[3] ≥5, since the most frequent types account for the majority of the tokens in the corpus, as per Zipf's law.[2] After this frequency filtering, we manually scrutinised the word lists and eliminated words that could be problematic when searched automatically. For example, the 'AW to UW' word *now* would be spelled in its dialectal form as *noo* but searching for this form would be problematic as there would be considerable noise coming from standard *no* with an elongated vowel representation. The descriptive statistics of the features in terms of their problematic words are reported in Table 12.1.

Table 12.1 List of features including the number of words per feature and the percentage of these words that were judged to be problematic with examples

	Number of words (≥ 5 zipf)	% of problematic words	Example of problematic words
T-to-R	6	0	-
HAPPY-laxing	60	0	-
LETTER-backing	2	0	-
AW to UW	25	20	*now* → *noo*
FOOT–STRUT	8	12.5	*done* → *dan*
G-dropping	40	2.5	*being* → *bein*
TH-stopping	54	22	*than* → *dan*
TH-fronting	54	74	*than* → *van*
H-dropping	44	41	*his* → *is*
Consonant reduction	6	33	*wasn't* → *want*
Vowel reduction	12	25	*I* → *a*
Average	28.27	20.91	

Despite problems with certain categories, such as TH-fronting or H-dropping, the majority of the spelling replacements were not highly problematic in terms of being confused with other existing standard or non-standard words of English.

Each word that was judged not to be problematic was then searched in the corpus and the relative frequency of each word was calculated by normalising the number of occurrences of the non-standard variant by the sum of the occurrences of the non-standard variant plus the standard variant. The formula to calculate the relative frequency was therefore as follows, where $rf_{w,a}$ is the relative frequency of the word *w* in the area *a*, $f_{n,a}$ is the number of times the non-standard variant of the word occurs in the area *a* and $f_{s,a}$ is the number of times the corresponding standard variant occurs in the area *a*.

$$rf_{w,a} = \frac{f_{n,a}}{f_{s,a} + f_{n,a}}$$

The overall relative frequency of the feature across all words for each area, $rf_{f,a}$, was calculated as follows:

$$rf_{f,a} = \frac{\sum f_{n,a}}{\sum(f_{s,a} + f_{n,a})}$$

Each array of frequencies was then mapped to represent the geographical distribution of both the single words and the features. Using this method, all the words belonging to a feature contribute equally to the calculation of the overall relative frequency of the feature. A full list of the words that were searched for in the corpus can be found in the appendix.

12.6. Results

The analysis resulted in various findings, some of which confirm previously established patterns of phonetic variations while others are harder to interpret. This section outlines the results for each feature, leaving the interpretation of the general patterns to the discussion section. A general trend that can be noticed across the maps is that the relative frequencies of the non-standard variants and of the features are relatively small. Despite this limitation, for most of them clear geographical patterns can be detected and this suggests that the geographical signal contained in these frequencies is also relatively strong.

The results for the T-to-R feature are consistent with the expectations given by what is known from previous studies carried out using conventional methods. Figure 12.1 shows that overall the non-standard spellings of these T-to-R words are mostly in the North of England (top left map), with some forms more common in Tyneside (*gerra*, *gerrup*), as in the examples below:[3]

(1) Some people walk so stupid that it actually annoys me. **Gerra** grip ya idiots
(2) Time to **gerrup** and work out before the derby.

Alternatively, other words are more common in the north-west (*gerroff*, *lorra*):

(3) pub quiz is tomorrow night. Come & have a **lorra lorra** laughs and get your thinking caps on
(4) so much for revising ya liar **gerroff** twitter

Similarly, the results of the analysis of HAPPY-laxing confirm that this phenomenon is reflected in spelling in areas which are known to have the phonetic equivalent. In addition, both the quantitative results and the manual exploration of the tweets, such as the examples below, suggest that the graphological variation is somewhat productive. Figure 12.2 shows that not only *citeh* but also *babeh*, *funneh*, or *happeh* are relatively more frequent in the North and even more in the north-west.

(5) Don't care if it's pre-season, I'd like to see the red men smash **Citeh** tonight!
(6) oh yes so **happeh** to be eating chicken nugs
(7) Sorry we won't be having one of these tomorrow happy valentines **babeh**

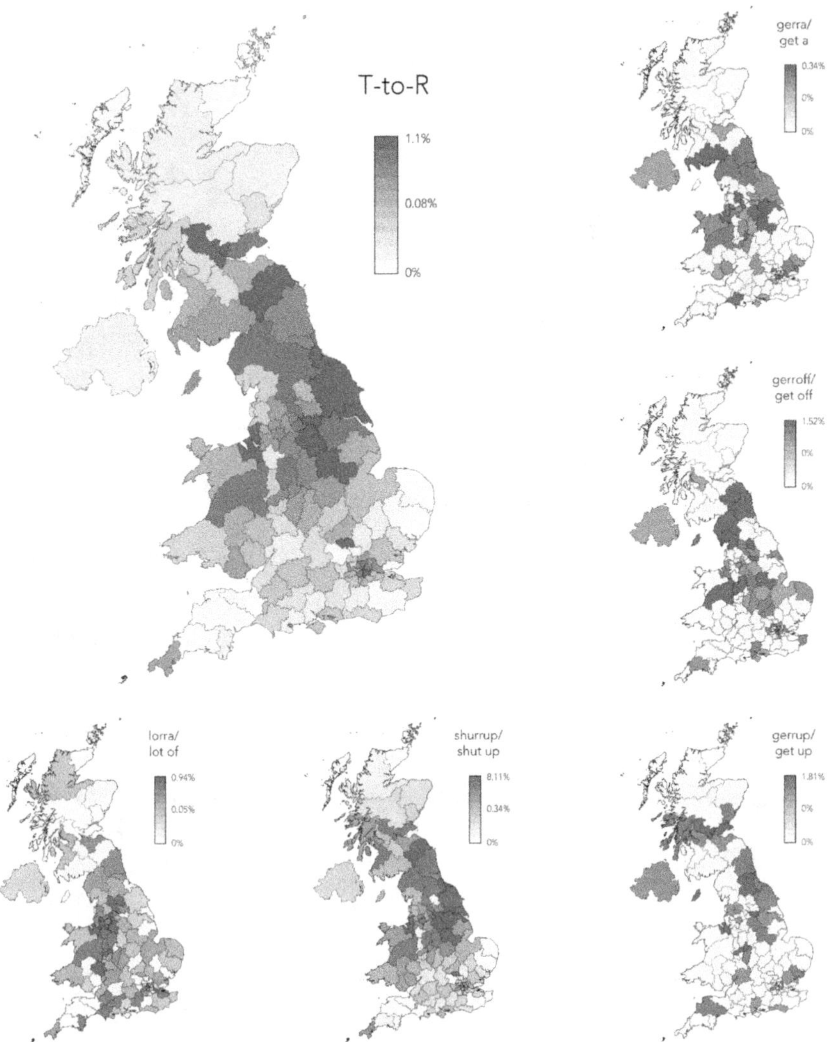

Figure 12.1 Maps for the T-to-R feature and for a sample of its words (*gerra*, *gerroff*, *gerrup*, *lorra*, *shurrup*)

Although the two words considered for LETTER-backing, *manchestah* and *manchestoh*, are clearly geographically marked, the maps for this feature in Figure 12.3 reveal that there is no uniform or clear spatial pattern in their use, a result probably due to the very low frequency of this feature. A qualitative exploration of a random sample of the tweets, however, suggests that there was no error in the analysis and that Twitter users do adopt these spellings to refer to Manchester:

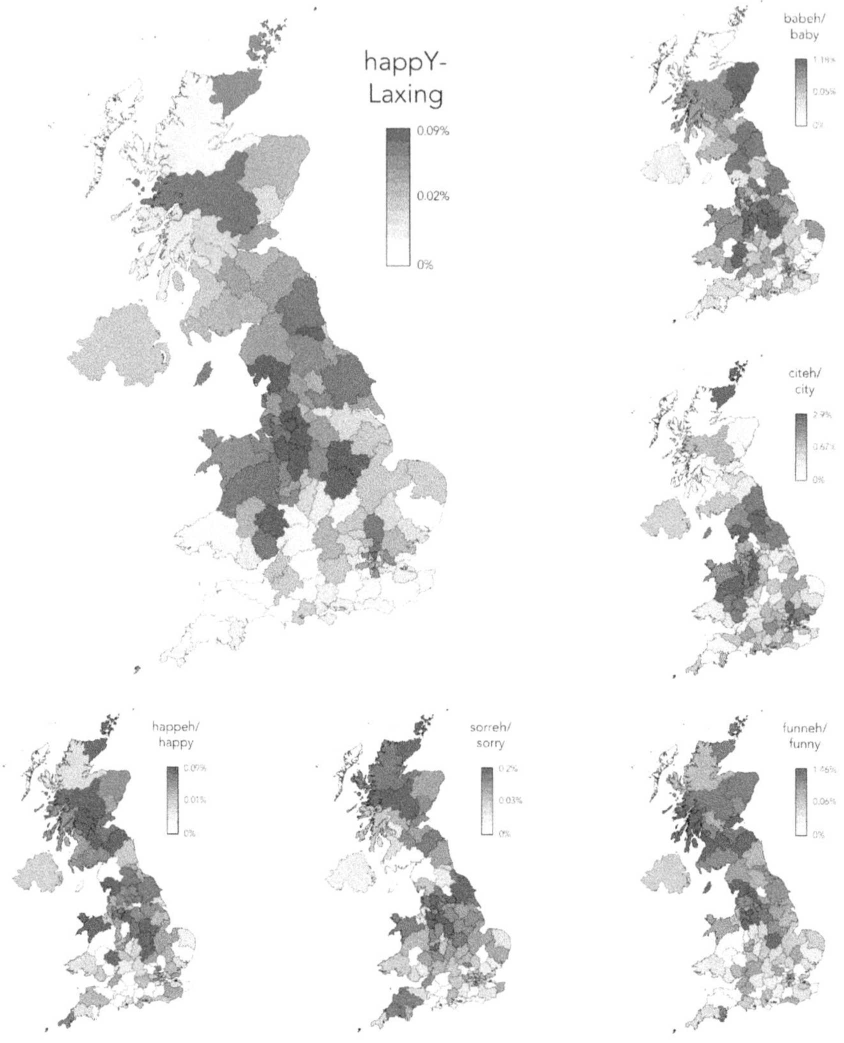

Figure 12.2 Maps for the HAPPY-laxing feature and for a sample of its words (*babeh*, *citeh*, *funneh*, *happeh*, *sorreh*)

(8) that's why I'm on the vip list from Miami too **Manchestoh**
(9) he's the biggest FOOL in **Manchestah**
(10) tour tickets booked for **MANCHESTAH**. I'm a happy man!

The sparseness of the frequency of this feature could be attributed to the fact that it is a stereotypical form that can be used by all speakers, regardless of dialect, in order to imitate a Mancunian accent.

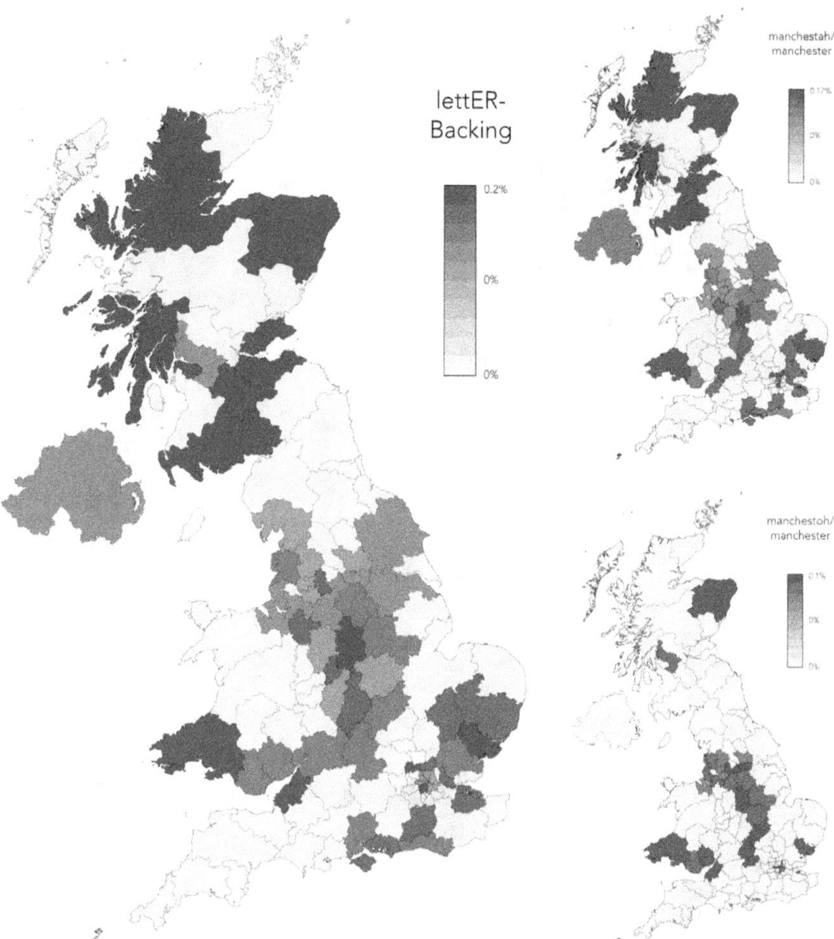

Figure 12.3 Maps for the LETTER-backing feature and for all of its words (*manchestah*, *manchestoh*)

For the retention of [uː] in MOUTH, the maps resulting from the Twitter corpus analysis represented in Figure 12.4 indicate that its equivalent graphological phenomenon is distributed similarly to the phonological variation, if not even more extensively. In addition to the expected focus in Tyneside, the words considered are also used very much in Scotland and, to a lesser extent, other parts of the United Kingdom.

As predicted, some words are more widely adopted even outside of the area of origin of the phonetic variation, due to their general popularity as cultural stereotypes of this region (e.g. *broon*, *toon*). When the feature is used

Figure 12.4 Maps for the 'AW to UW' feature and for a selection of its words (*aboot*, *ootside*, *doon*, *toon*, *broon*)

in these popular forms, it is very likely that the Twitter users are consciously portraying a Northern identity, as in the following examples:

(11) I miss you too and the **doon toon** bantaaa
(12) How dare the **toon** lose another match
(13) Can't believe they ran out of **broon** ale last night

However, certain users do not restrict themselves to the most popular forms but extend the variation to other, less common forms, such as *without, house, now* and even *council*:

(14) my mum trying to read **withoot** her glasses is hilarious
(15) Finally got internet workin again in ma **hoose noo** to watch some game of thrones
(16) Was going to go for a nap but as always **cooncil** are cutting the grass

The non-standard spellings that represent presence or absence of the FOOT–STRUT split are mapped in Figure 12.5, revealing a somewhat inconsistent geographic distribution on Twitter.

The distribution of *landan* is particularly interesting, deserving specific mention. This non-standard spelling likely represents lowering of the Southern STRUT vowel, but its regional patterning in Figure 12.5 actually suggests that it is used most frequently outside of London and the south-east of England. This is likely to be another case – discussed earlier in the context of LETTER-backing in *manchestoh* – in which speakers outside of a dialect region are using these variants in an imitative manner to stereotype speakers from that region. It is also not surprising to find this kind of dialectal imitation registered most strongly in place-names. It is also interesting to note that in this Twitter corpus the collocation *landan town/taan/tarn* is particularly frequent, exemplified in (17), and that this non-standard spelling commonly co-occurs with other features stereotypical of Estuary English, as in (18).

(17) just touched down in **landan** town
(18) apparently I sound like I'm from **saaaaahf landan** when drinking

It is not easy to interpret the meaning of these results for dialectology because of the confounding factor of users portraying a particular identity or stereotype. However, it is possible that the patterns we observe indicate that Twitter users are more likely to focus on a lowering of this vowel (orthographically represented as <a>), therefore suggesting that this is the most salient dimension along which FOOT–STRUT words differ.

The analysis of the G-dropping feature presented in Figure 12.6 shows a remarkable degree of consistency with respect to the clear Northern trend of g-dropping, thus indicating that this feature is commonly adopted in spelling in the north of the UK. As such, there are strong parallels between the regional patterning of the phonetic feature and its orthographic reflection on Twitter, corroborating the aforementioned claim that this feature is primarily associated with region, rather than social status, in the case of British English.

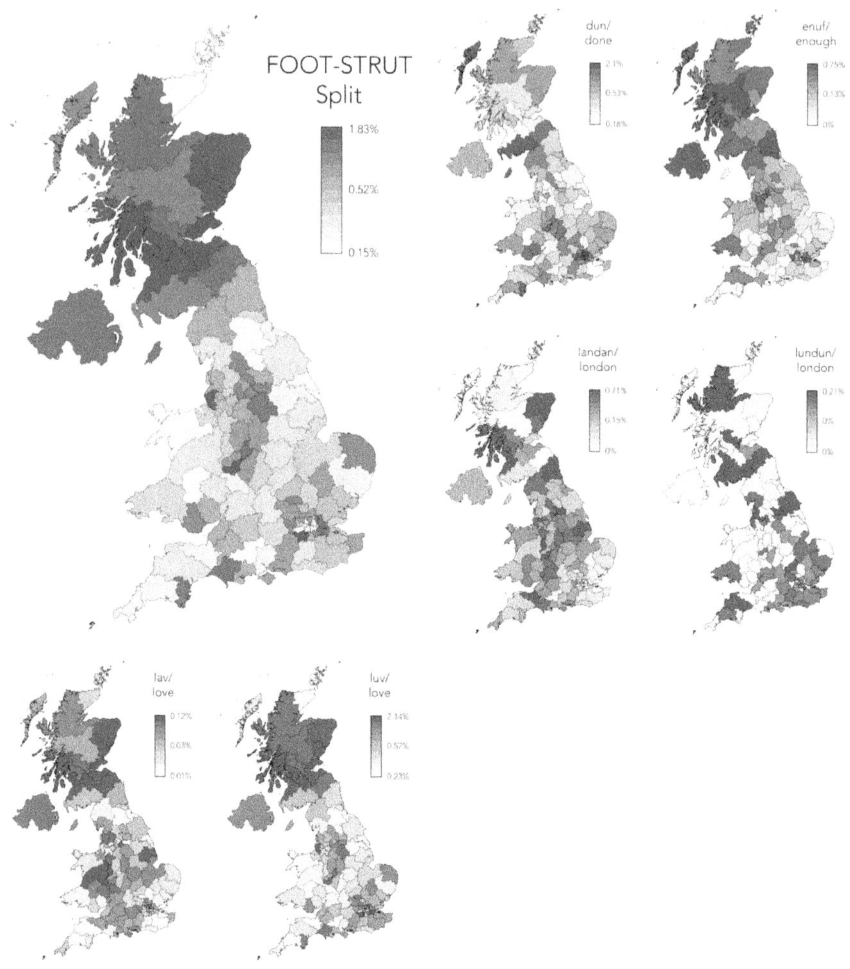

Figure 12.5 Maps for a sample of FOOT-STRUT words (*dun*, *enuf*, *landan*, *lundun*, *lav*, *luv*)

An interesting picture also emerges for TH-fronting and TH-stopping, mapped in Figure 12.7 and Figure 12.8, respectively. Both of these features have strong ties to the South of England, specifically London, but their phonetically motivated spelling variants show a different geographic distribution on Twitter. While TH-fronting has clearly diffused throughout most of the UK, showing no clear regional pattern, TH-stopping is somewhat more restricted to London and its surrounding area. This is particularly evident in the case of *ting* and *dem*, which are arguably the most salient examples of this sociophonetic phenomenon.

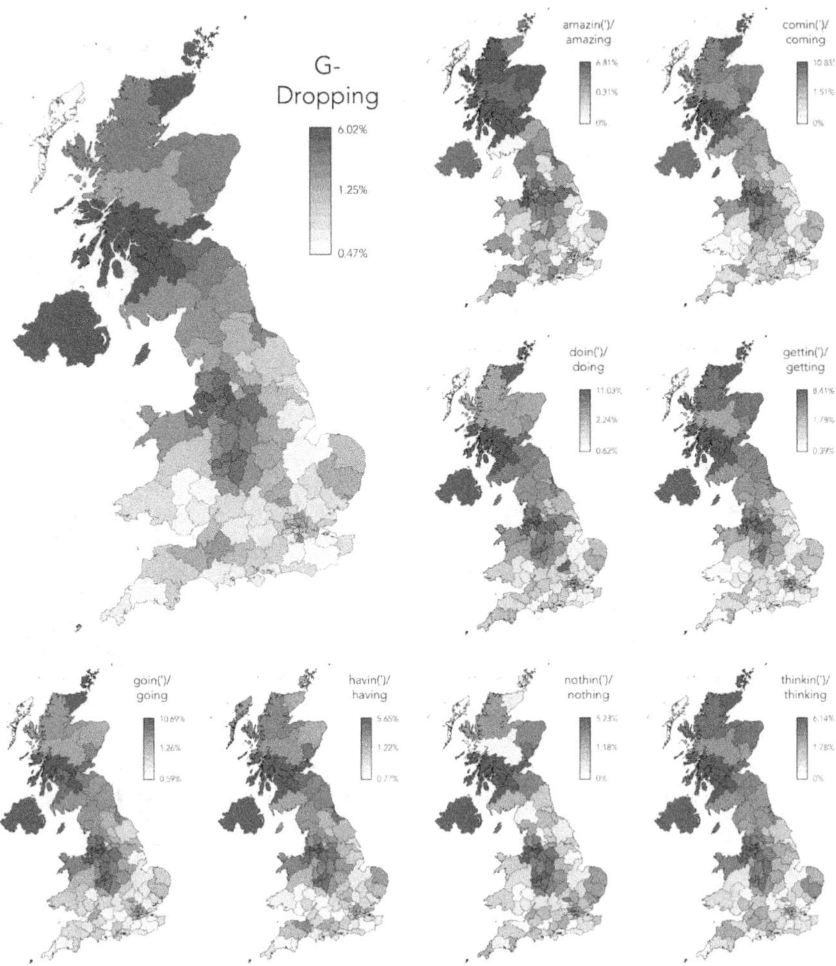

Figure 12.6 Maps for the G-dropping feature and for a sample of its words (*amazin*/*amazin'*, *comin*/*comin'*, *doin*/*doin'*, *gettin*/*gettin'*, *goin*/*goin'*, *havin*/*havin'*, *nothin*/*nothin'*, *thinkin*/*thinkin'*)

The graphical representation of H-dropping seems also to be widespread across the UK on Twitter, despite being overall more common in the North (top left of Figure 12.9). Although other studies have found that H-dropping in content words is more typical of the North while H-dropping in function words is common everywhere, our results largely found the reverse of this pattern, with H-dropping in function words, such as *have* or *here*, seemingly more frequent in the North and particularly in Scotland.

The top left map in Figure 12.10 confirms that, even in social media writing, consonant reduction on Twitter seems to be more common in the

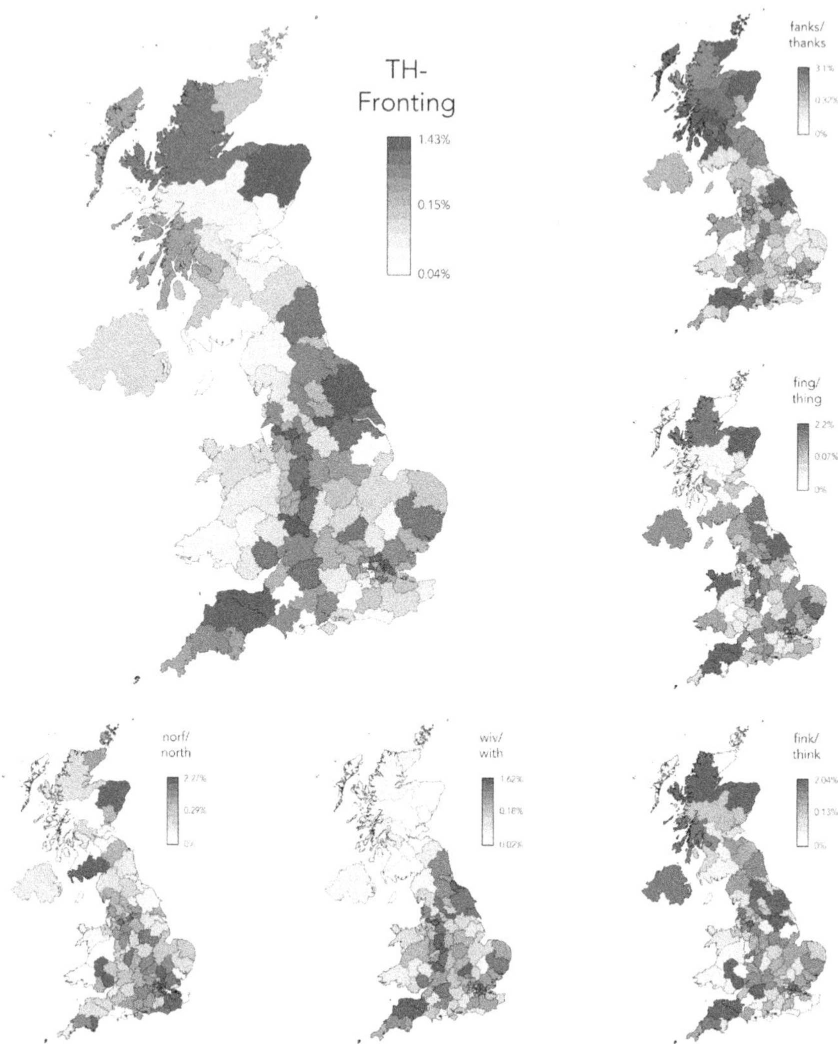

Figure 12.7 Maps for the TH-fronting feature and for a sample of its words (*fanks*, *fing*, *fink*, *norf*, *wiv*)

North of England and in Scotland. The morphosyntactic function of this phonetic feature also has an effect on the regional distribution, with the contracted forms of auxiliaries (*dint*, *dunt* and *int*) largely patterning together in the North of England while the abbreviation of the preposition (*wi*/*wi'*) is more frequent in Scotland. Examples from the data reveal that these reduced variants commonly co-occur with other non-standard spellings: note the rep-

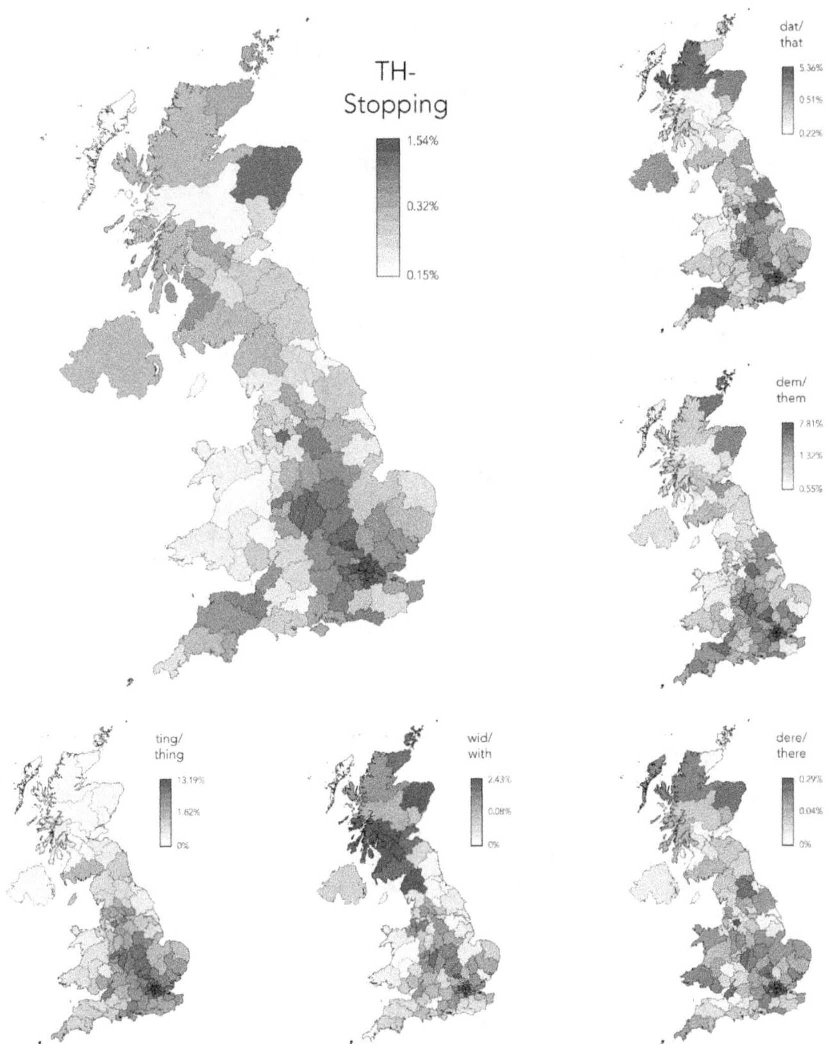

Figure 12.8 Maps for the TH-stopping feature and for a sample of its words (*dat*, *dem*, *dere*, *ting*, *wid*)

resentation of *right* as <reyt> in (19), reflecting the [ɛɪ] realisation typical of varieties spoken in Yorkshire, as well as the presence of TH-fronting (*bovva*) and vocalic reduction (*sez*) in (20).

(19) Get so use to people calling me by my last name; then when I get called by my first name it **dunt** sound reyt!

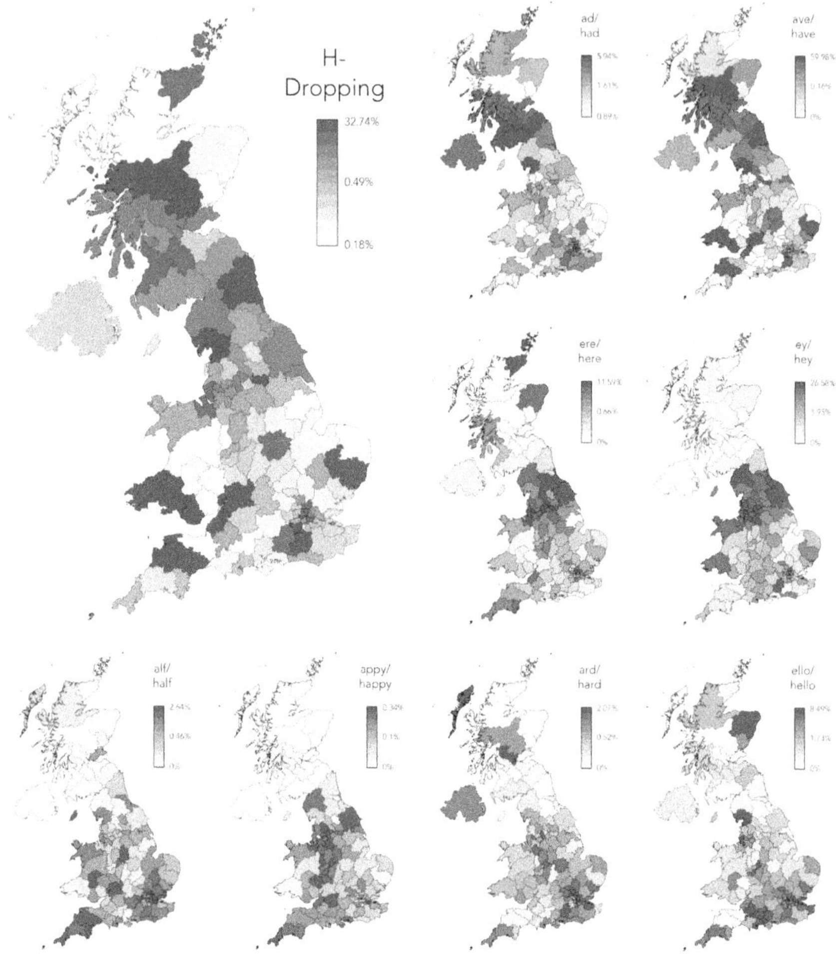

Figure 12.9 Maps for the H-dropping feature and for a sample of its words (*ad, ave, ere, ey, alf, appy, ard, ello*)

(20) **dunt** bovva me but mum sez I'll have no jacket left!
(21) Always have the urge ti start singing along **wi** ma music when am on public transport

The variants for vowel reduction altogether show a Northern pattern, being favoured particularly in Scotland and in the north-west of England, as can be seen in the maps in Figure 12.11. This feature is particularly interesting since the justification of its use cannot even be found in its length, which is often equal to its standard counterpart. In other words, Twitter users are not using these reduced variants because they are quicker to type or because

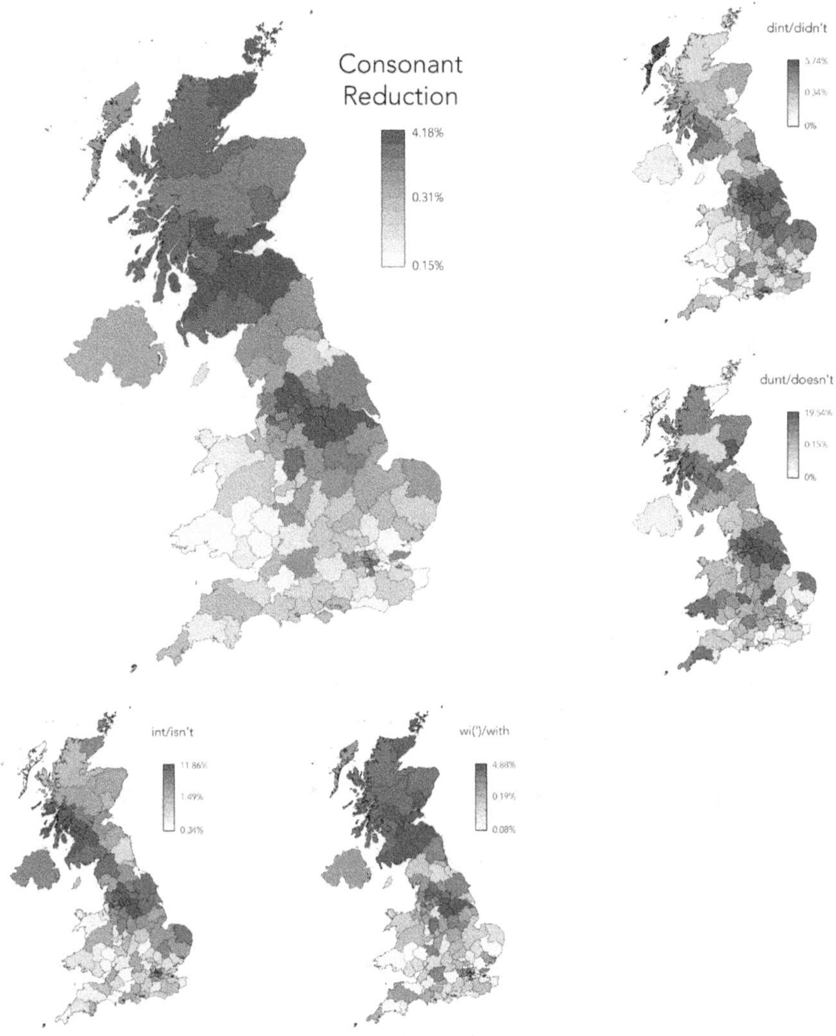

Figure 12.10 Maps for the consonant reduction feature and for all of its words (*dint, dunt, int, wi/wi'*)

of character restrictions in tweets, but rather because they wish to convey a particular identity or stance. For example, consider:

(22) Some ppl are just so rude sort **yerself** out
(23) i guess that means **am** buying **yer** pints all night
(24) think i've got food poisoning from **ma** chippy tea

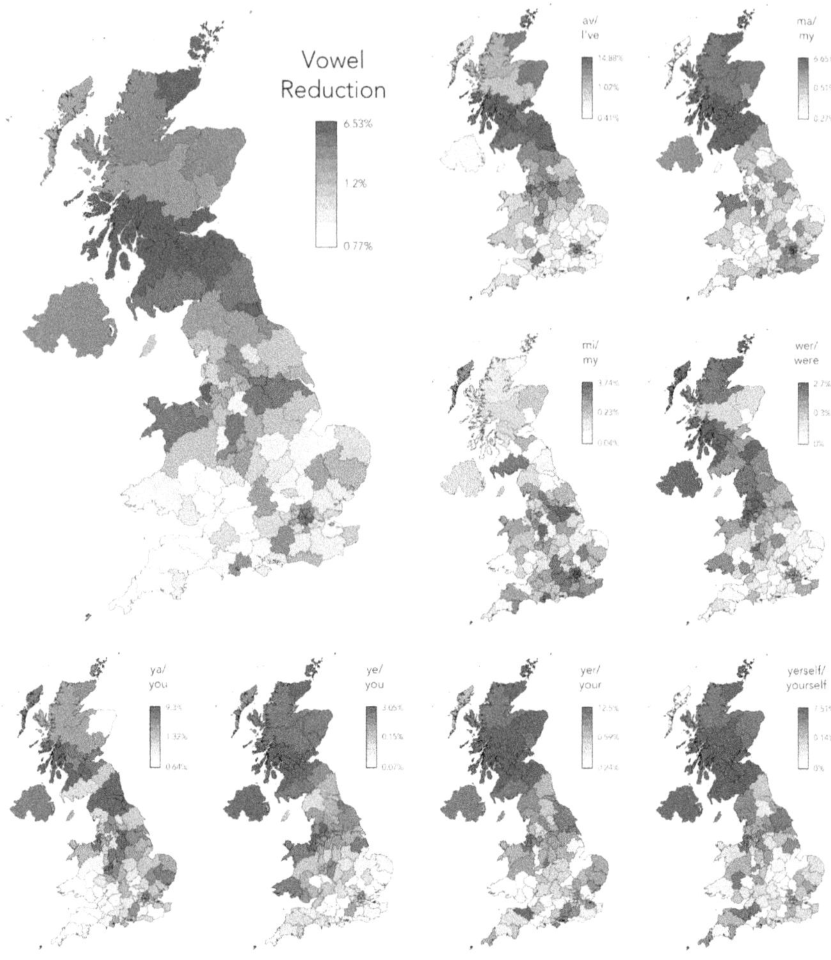

Figure 12.11 Maps for the vowel reduction feature and for a sample of its words (*av*, *ma*, *mi*, *wer*, *ya*, *ye*, *yer*, *yerself*)

12.7. Discussion

In this chapter we have shown that despite being a written medium of communication, Twitter can be used as a rich source of natural language data for contemporary studies of phonological dialectal variation, and the results presented here have a number of implications both for theoretical and methodological issues in this field of study.

As discussed above, third-wave approaches to language variation and change foreground the importance of indexicality and the active way in which speakers employ socially meaningful variants in acts of identity construction and stance-taking. While there is a sizeable body of work adopting this line of inquiry in the domain of speech production (e.g. Labov 1963; Eckert 2000; Zhang 2005; Pharao *et al.* 2014), there is comparatively little consideration of how these same forces are at play in other modalities, such as orthographic variation in written forms on social media. Our results present strong evidence that users of social media often employ creative non-standard spellings that reflect the phonetic realisation of the same words in their own spoken dialect, at least in the case of Northern English. For many of the Northern features under study, the regional distribution of these non-standard forms matches well with the regional distribution of their phonetic equivalents. This suggests that in a large majority of cases we are indeed seeing phonetically motivated orthography and a clear relationship between how dialect is projected across both speech and writing.

These results also lend insight into the relative salience of different dialectal features, which is an important concept in contemporary approaches to language variation and change but is difficult to operationalise and – as a result – often poorly defined (Auer *et al.* 1998; see also discussion in Jaeger and Weatherholtz 2016). Although, as discussed earlier, the third-wave variationist approach emphasises the active role of speakers in using particular variants, it remains the case that many dialectal features are used in a relatively subconscious manner as a natural consequence of speakers' own linguistic systems. However, the use of orthographic equivalents on Twitter presents an interesting contrast in that most of the features explored in this study require a much more deliberate action. These considerations imply that most of the words and features we observed are subject to a high level of indexicality in the speech community and can therefore be considered *stereotypes* (Labov 1978). To the extent that the non-standard spellings found are made with full awareness of their social meanings, this study shows that the process of dialect *enregisterment* (Agha 2005) that has been attested in literary and artistic contexts, especially by authors in this volume (e.g. see Beal, Clark and Cooper), is also used with similar purposes by the speech community in social media.

In turn, we can gain insight into the social salience of a dialectal feature by looking closely at the extent to which it is registered orthographically on Twitter. In other words, which features do people tend to focus on when attempting to construct and project a particular dialectal identity through writing? Of course, it is important to note that in some cases this is confounded by the correspondence – or lack thereof – between sound and spelling in English, and how certain features are simply not possible to reflect through graphemic replacement or substitution. However, it nevertheless provides an interesting and novel approach to the study of social and linguistic salience in the context of non-standard dialectal features. The relevance of salience is arguably most notable in cases of mismatch between the regional patterns of graphemic and phonetic variation. As shown in the results in Section 12.6, this occurs most frequently with place-names when users perform a kind of dialect imitation. In other words, quantitative and qualitative analysis of the data suggests that when certain sociophonetic features can be registered in place-names, they tend to be used not by speakers of those dialects but by other speakers drawing on such features in stereotypes of that variety. Although this is problematic if the primary goal is to use these methods of analysis to replace conventional methods in dialectology, which would rely on the assumption that a person's graphemic forms reflect their phonetic forms, it provides yet more insight into the features that are socially salient in stereotypes of certain dialects. These findings therefore also provide new evidence for the understanding of salience and the influencing or constraining factors of phonetic dialect writing (see Honeybone, this volume).

Another important point to highlight is the way in which these phonetically motivated orthographic forms often co-occur with other non-standard spellings, as seen in many of the examples given in Section 12.6. Although this calls for a more nuanced approach to the covariation between different dialectal features, the fact that these spelling variants do not occur as isolated examples suggests that they are indeed used as part of a wider linguistic style tailored to a user's own dialectal identity.

Finally, from a methodological point of view, it is very important to note that, as in previous sociolinguistic or dialect studies using Twitter, the effects found in this research are largely consistent with previous findings. This confirmation is particularly important because geocoded Twitter data has at least two major limitations. Firstly, the population of geocoded Twitter users is not a representative sample of the population of the UK, as discussed above. Secondly, although a geocoded tweet contains exact information of the location from which it was sent, it does not contain information of the dialect background or area of origin of the person who is writing it. For these reasons, social media data should always be treated carefully, as these representativeness biases are well known. However, despite these problems, the results presented in this chapter contribute to suggesting that, if a very large data set has been collected, the geographical signal underlying dialect patterns can be still detected in social media data of this kind even through the noise generated by these two confounding factors.

12.8. Conclusions

In conclusion, the present chapter offered an analysis of a large corpus of geocoded tweets for graphological variation reflecting dialectal phonetic variation of features found in the dialects of the North of England. The results of the analysis provide a new angle on both the study of the dialects of the North and on wider issues related to methods in dialectology. The findings of this analysis reveal that users of social media adopt spelling variants that reflect their dialects and, more specifically, to represent their identity in social media. This phenomenon is therefore consistent with third-wave sociolinguistics considerations that stress the importance of identity performance. Moreover, these results suggest that the analysis of social media like Twitter, especially if they are geocoded, can not only offer a lot of useful real data in much less time than a survey would take, but that they can also offer an altogether new perspective. As the qualitative and quantitative analysis revealed, naturally occurring corpus data, which is not affected by the observer paradox, can uncover how these variants can either have a stereotyped function within a speech community or be used to portray an identity. This new approach to the study of dialectology and sociolinguistics not only can lead to interesting new findings but can lead to new fundamental questions on the nature of linguistic variation altogether.

Appendix 12.1 List of forms searched in the corpus:

T-to-R	*lorra, gerra, gerrout, gerroff, gerrup, shurrup*
HAPPY-laxing	*vereh, realleh, onleh, aneh, maneh, moneeh, actualleh, evereh, famileh, countreh, loveleh, sorreh, probableh, absoluteleh, happeh, parteh, readeh, pretteh, alreadeh, storeh, citeh, everybodeh, exactleh, properteh, obviousleh, certainleh, earleh, easeh, babeh, definiteleh, somebodeh, historeh, centureh, companeh, bodeh, economeh, ladeh, completeleh, finalleh, worreh, communiteh, quickleh, hopefulleh, nearleh, nobodeh, particularleh, opportuniteh, funneh, anybodeh, luckeh, yesterdaeh, secretareh, basicalleh, clearleh, energeh, especialleh, plenteh, qualiteh, buseh, slightleh*
LETTER-backing	*manchestah, manchestoh*
AW to UW	*aboot, oot, doon, aroond, hoose, roond, foond, withoot, sooth, ootside, hoors, toon, groond, hoor, soond, cooncil, soonds, amoont, thoosands, broon*
FOOT-STRUT	*dun, enuf, enaf, lundun, landan, luv, lav*
G-dropping	*goin|goin', somethin|somethin', bein|bein', doin|doin', lookin|lookin', comin|comin', gettin|gettin', nothin|nothin', havin|havin', tryin|tryin', makin|makin', sayin|sayin', workin|workin', mornin|mornin', talkin|talkin', takin|takin', amazin|amazin', playin|playin', thinkin|thinkin', livin|livin', feelin|feelin', interestin|interestin', runnin|runnin', buildin|buildin', usin|usin', durin|durin', movin|movin', waitin|waitin', evenin|evenin', givin|givin', seein|seein', watchin|watchin', puttin|puttin', hopin|hopin', happenin|happenin', startin|startin', meetin|meetin', sellin|sellin', sittin|sittin', spendin|spendin'*

Appendix 12.1 (*cont.*)

TH-stopping	*dat, dis, dey, wid, dere, tink, dem, deir, dese, someting, oder, ting, tings, tought, anoder, anyting, everyting, togeder, widout, wheder, monts, sout, tinking, nort, moder, wort, fader, widin, furder, eider, tird, demselves, deat, healt, oders, weader, aldough, nordern, mont, tousands, broder, eart*
TH-fronting	*wiv, fink, somefing, fing, fings, anyfing, everyfing, nofing, togever, wivout, fanks, finking, norf, furver*
H-dropping	*ave, ere, ad, ome, ouse, elp, aving, ello, ard, appy, ope, alf, appened, ey, eard, appen, uge, istory, imself, ealth, appens, opefully, ospital, oping, uman, appening*
consonant reduction	*dunt, dint, int, wi|wi'*
vowel reduction	*yer, yerself, ye, ya, av, ar, mi, ma, wer*

Notes

1. No data was collected in two days in June and four days October for technical reasons.
2. The Zipf scale ranges from 1 to 7 and a value ≥ 4 indicates that the word is a high-frequency word. A value of 5 roughly corresponds to 100 occurrences per million words.
3. The Twitter examples in this book chapter were slightly altered to protect the anonymity of the users. A few words in the tweets were replaced with synonymous ones so that the tweets cannot be easily traced back to their users.

References

Agha, Asif (2005) Voice, footing, enregisterment, *Journal of Linguistic Anthropology*, 15(1), 1–5.

Auer, Peter, Barden, Birgit and Grosskopf, Beate (1998) Subjective and objective parameters determining 'salience' in long-term dialect accommodation, *Journal of Sociolinguistics*, 2(2), 163–87.

Bailey, George (2016) Regional variation in 140 characters: Mapping geospatial tweets, in *Workshop on Using Twitter for Linguistic Research*, University of Kent.

Bailey, George (2019) Emerging from below the social radar: Incipient evaluation in the North West of England, *Journal of Sociolinguistics*, 23(1), 3–28.

Baranowski, Maciej (2017) Class matters: The sociolinguistics of GOOSE and GOAT in Manchester English, *Language Variation and Change*, 29, 301–39.

Baranowski, Maciej and Turton, Danielle (2015) Manchester English, in *Researching Northern English*, Hickey, Raymond (ed.), Amsterdam, John Benjamins, pp. 293–316.

Beal, Joan C. (2000) From Geordie Ridley to Viz: Popular literature in Tyneside English, *Language and Literature*, 9(4), 343–59.

Beal, Joan C. (2004) English dialects in the North of England: Phonology, in *A Handbook of Varieties of English, Vol. 1: Phonology*, Schneider, Edgar W., Burridge, Kate, Kortmann, Bernd, Mesthrie, Rajend and Upton, Clive (eds), Berlin, Mouton de Gruyter, pp. 113–33.

Beal, Joan C., Burbano-Elizondo, Lourdes and Llamas, Carmen (2012) *Urban North-Eastern English: Tyneside to Teesside*, Edinburgh, Edinburgh University Press.

Britain, David (2002) Diffusion, levelling, simplification and reallocation in past tense BE in the English Fens, *Journal of Sociolinguistics*, 16(1), 16–43.

Buchstaller, Isabelle, Corrigan, Karen P., Holmberg, Anders, Honeybone, Patrick and Maguire, Warren (2013) T-to-R and the Northern Subject Rule: Questionnaire-based spatial, social and structural linguistics, *English Language and Linguistics*, 17(1), 85–128.

Cardoso, Amanda (2015) Variation in nasal–obstruent clusters and its influence on PRICE and MOUTH in Scouse, *English Language and Linguistics*, 19(3), 505–32.

Carter, Paul (2002) Structured variation in British English liquids, University of York.

Clark, Lynn and Watson, Kevin (2011) Testing claims of a usage-based phonology with Liverpool English t-to-r, *English Language and Linguistics*, 15(3), 523–47.

Cook, Paul, Han, Bo and Baldwin, Timothy (2014) Statistical methods for identifying local dialectal terms from GPS-tagged documents, *Dictionaries: Journal of the Dictionary Society of North America*, 35, 248–71.

Doyle, Gabriel (2014) Mapping dialectal variation by querying social media, in *Proceedings of the 14th Conference of the European Chapter of the Association for Computational Linguistics*, Wintner, Shuly, Goldwater, Sharon and Riezler, Stefan (eds), Gothenburg, Sweden, pp. 98–106.

Drummond, Rob (2012) Aspects of identity in a second language: ING variation in the speech of Polish migrants living in Manchester, UK, *Language Variation and Change*, 24(1), 107–33.

Drummond, Rob (2018) Maybe it's a grime [t]ing: TH-stopping among urban British youth, *Language in Society*, 47(2), 171–96.

Eckert, Penelope (2000) *Linguistic Variation as Social Practice*, Oxford, Blackwell.

Eckert, Penelope (2012) Three waves of variation study: The emergence of meaning in the study of sociolinguistic variation, *Annual Review of Anthropology*, Annual Reviews, 41(1), 87–100.

Eisenstein, Jacob (2013) What to do about bad language on the internet, in *Proceedings of the 2013 Conference of the North American Chapter of the Association for Computational Linguistics: Human Language Technologies*, Stroudsburg, Pennsylvania, pp. 359–69.

Eisenstein, Jacob (2015) Systematic patterning in phonologically-motivated orthographic variation, *Journal of Sociolinguistics*, 19(2), 161–88.

Eisenstein, Jacob (2018) Identifying regional dialects in online social media. In Charles Boberg, John Nerbonne & Dominic Watt (eds.), *The Handbook of Dialectology*, 368–83. Hoboken, NJ: Wiley-Blackwell.

Eisenstein, Jacob, O'Connor, Brendan, Smith, Noah A. and Xing, Eric P. (2012) Mapping the geographical diffusion of new words, *arXiv*, 1210.5268, 1–13.

Foulkes, Paul and Docherty, Gerard (2007) Phonological variation in England, in *Language in the British Isles*, Britain, David (ed.), Cambridge, Cambridge University Press, pp. 52–74.

Gonçalves, Bruno and Sánchez, David (2014) Crowdsourcing dialect characterization through Twitter, *PLoS ONE* 9(11): e112074, 10.

Grieve, Jack, Montgomery, Chris, Nini, Andrea, Murakami, Akira and Guo, Diansheng (2019) Mapping lexical dialect variation in British English using Twitter, *Frontiers in Artificial Intelligence*, 2, 11. https://doi.org/10.3389/frai.2019.00011.

Grieve, Jack, Nini, Andrea and Guo, Diansheng (2017) Analyzing lexical emergence in Modern American English online, *English Language and Linguistics*, 21(1), 99–127.

Guy, Gregory R. (1991) Explanation in variable phonology: An exponential model of morphological constraints, *Language Variation and Change*, 3(1), 1–22.

Heuven, Walter J. B. van, Mandera, Pawel, Keuleers, Emmanuel and Brysbaert, Marc (2014) SUBTLEX-UK: A new and improved word frequency database for British English, *Quarterly Journal of Experimental Psychology*, 67(6), 1176–90.

Honeybone, Patrick (2007) New-dialect formation in nineteenth century Liverpool: A brief history of Scouse, in *The Mersey Sound: Liverpool's Language, People and Places*, Grant, A. and Grey, C. (eds), Liverpool, Open House Press, pp. 106–40.

Honeybone, Patrick, Watson, Kevin and van Eyndhoven, Sarah (2017) Lenition and T-to-R are differently salient: The representation of competing realisations of /t/ in Liverpool English dialect literature, in *Perspectives on Northern Englishes*, Beal, Joan C. and Hancil, Sylvie (eds), Berlin, Mouton de Gruyter, pp. 83–108.

Houston, Ann Celeste (1985) Continuity and change in English morphology: The variable (ING), University of Pennsylvania.

Huang, Yuan, Guo, Diansheng, Kasakoff, Alice and Grieve, Jack (2016) Understanding U.S. regional linguistic variation with Twitter data analysis, *Computers, Environment and Urban Systems*, 59, 244–55.

Hughes, Arthur, Trudgill, Peter and Watt, Dominic (2012) *English Accents and Dialects*, London, Routledge.

Jaeger, T. Florian and Weatherholtz, Kodi (2016) What the heck is salience? How predictive language processing contributes to sociolinguistic perception, *Frontiers in Psychology*, 7, 1–5.

Johnston, Paul (1997) Regional variation, in *The Edinburgh History of the Scots Language*, Jones, Charles (ed.), Edinburgh, Edinburgh University Press, pp. 433–513.

Jones, Taylor (2015) Toward a description of African American Vernacular English dialect regions using 'Black Twitter', *American Speech*, 90(4), 403–40.

Kerremans, D., Stegmayr, S. and Schmid, H. (2012) The NeoCrawler: Identifying and retrieving neologisms from the Internet and monitoring ongoing change, in *Current Methods in Historical Semantics*, Allan, K. and Robinson, J. A. (eds), Berlin, de Gruyter Mouton, pp. 59–96.

Kilgarriff, Adam and Grefenstette, Gregory (2003) Introduction to the special issue on web as corpus, *Computational Linguistics*, 29(3), 1–15.

Kulkarni, Vivek, Perozzi, Bryan and Skiena, Steven (2016) Freshman or fresher? Quantifying the geographic variation of internet language, in *Proceedings of the Tenth International AAAI Conference on Web and Social Media (ICWSM 2016)*, Strohmaier, Markus and Gummadi, Krishna P. (eds), Palo Alto, CA, The AAAI Press, pp. 615–18.

Labov, William (1963) The social motivation of a sound change, *Word*, 19, 273–309.

Labov, William (1978) *Sociolinguistic Patterns*, Oxford, Blackwell.

Labov, William (1989) The child as linguistic historian, *Language Variation and Change*, 1, 85–97.

Labov, William (2001) *Principles of Linguistic Change, Vol. 2: Social Factors*, Malden, MA; Oxford, Blackwell Publishers.

Levon, Erez and Fox, Sue (2014) Social salience and the sociolinguistic monitor: A case study of ING and TH-fronting in Britain, *Journal of English Linguistics*, 42(3), 185–217.

Longley, Paul A., Adnan, Muhammad and Lansley, Guy (2015) The geotemporal demographics of Twitter usage, *Environment and Planning A*, 47, 465–84.

McColl Millar, Robert (2007) *Northern and Insular Scots*, Edinburgh, Edinburgh University Press.

MacKenzie, Laurel, Bailey, George and Turton, Danielle (2014) Crowdsourcing dialectology in the undergraduate classroom, in *Methods in Dialectology XV*, University of Groningen.

Mellon, Jonathan and Prosser, Christopher (2017) Twitter and Facebook are not representative of the general population: Political attitudes and demographics of British social media users, *Research and Politics*, 4(3), 1–9.

Milroy, James, Milroy, Lesley, Hartley, Sue and Walshaw, David (1994) Glottal stops and Tyneside glottalization: Competing patterns of variation and change in British English, *Language Variation and Change*, 6, 327–57.

Moore, Samuel, Meech, Sanford B. and Whitehall, Harold (1935) *Middle English Dialect Characteristics and Dialect Boundaries*, Ann Arbor, University of Michigan Language and Literature Series.

Nguyen, Dong, Doğruöz, A. Seza, Rosé, Carolyn P. and De Jong, Franciska (2016) Computational sociolinguistics: A survey, *Computational Linguistics*, 42(3), 537–93.

Pavalanathan, Umashanthi and Eisenstein, Jacob (2015) Confounds and Consequences in Geotagged Twitter Data, in *Proceedings of the 2015 Conference on Empirical Methods in Natural Language Processing*, Lisbon, Portugal, pp. 2138–48.

Petyt, Keith M. (1985) *Dialect and Accent in Industrial West Yorkshire*, Amsterdam, John Benjamins.

Pharao, Nicolai, Maegaard, Marie, Møller, Janus Spindler and Kristiansen, Tore (2014) Indexical meanings of [s+] among Copenhagen youth: Social perception of a phonetic variant in different prosodic contexts, *Language in Society*, 43(1), 1–31.

Rahimi, Afshin, Cohn, Trevor and Baldwin, Timothy (2017) A neural model for user geolocation and lexical dialectology, *arXiv*, (1704.04008).

Ramsammy, Michael and Turton, Danielle (2012) Higher or lower? An investigation of the unstressed vowel system in Mancunian English, in *Manchester and Salford New Researchers Forum in Linguistics*, Manchester.

Shoemark, Philippa, Kirby, James and Goldwater, Sharon (2017) Topic and audience effects on distinctively Scottish vocabulary usage in Twitter data, in *Proceedings of the Workshop on Stylistic Variation*, Copenhagen, Denmark, pp. 59–68.

Tagliamonte, Sali (2004) Somethi[ŋ]'s goi[n] on! Variable (ing) at Ground Zero, in *Language Variation in Europe: Papers from the Second International Conference on Language Variation in Europe (ICLaVE 2)*, Gunnarson, Britt-Louise *et al.* (eds), Uppsala, Uppsala University, pp. 390–403.

Tagliamonte, Sali and Temple, Rosalind (2005) New perspectives on an ol' variable: (t,d) in British English, *Language Variation and Change*, 17(3), 281–302.
Tanner, James, Sonderegger, Morgan and Wagner, Michael (2017) Production planning and coronal stop deletion in spontaneous speech, *Laboratory Phonology: Journal of the Association for Laboratory Phonology*, 8(1), 1–39.
Tatman, Rachael (2016) 'I'm a spawts guay': Comparing the use of sociophonetic variables in speech and Twitter, *University of Pennsylvania Working Papers in Linguistics: Selected Papers from NWAV 44*, 22, pp. 160–70.
Trudgill, Peter (1986) *Dialects in Contact*, Oxford, Blackwell.
Trudgill, Peter (1999) *The Dialects of England*, Oxford, Blackwell.
Turton, Danielle (2017) Categorical or gradient? An ultrasound investigation of /l/-darkening and vocalization in varieties of English, *Laboratory Phonology: Journal of the Association for Laboratory Phonology*, 8(1), 1–31.
Wakelin, Martyn (1977) *English Dialects: An Introduction*, London, Athlone Press.
Watson, Kevin (2007) Liverpool English, *Journal of the International Phonetic Association*, 37, 351–60.
Watt, Dominic (2002) 'I don't speak with a Geordie accent, I speak, like, the Northern accent': Contact-induced levelling in the Tyneside vowel system, *Journal of Sociolinguistics*, 6(1), 44–63.
Watt, Dominic and Milroy, Lesley (1999) Variation in three Tyneside vowels: Is this dialect levelling?, in *Urban Voices: Accent Studies in the British Isles*, Foulkes, Paul and Docherty, Gerard (eds), London, Arnold, pp. 25–46.
Watts, Emma (2005) Mobility-induced dialect contact: A sociolinguistic investigation of speech variation in Wilmslow, Cheshire, University of Essex.
Wells, John C. (1982) *Accents of English, Vol. 2: The British Isles*, Cambridge, Cambridge University Press.
Williams, Ann and Kerswill, Paul (1999) Dialect levelling: Change and continuity in Milton Keynes, Reading and Hull, in *Urban Voices: Accent Studies in the British Isles*, Foulkes, Paul and Docherty, Gerard (eds), London, Arnold, pp. 141–62.
Zhang, Qing (2005) A Chinese yuppie in Beijing: Phonological variation and the construction of a new professional identity, *Language in Society*, 34(3), 431–66.

13

The Bolton/Worktown Corpus: A Case of Accidental Dialectology?

Ivor Timmis

13.1. Introduction

As this volume shows, there are many ways in which dialect can be represented, including dialect literature, literary dialect and the often jocular dialect 'phrase books' to be found in tourist information offices (labelled 'CHLDL' in Honeybone and Maguire, this volume, and elsewhere). In this chapter, I consider a different type: an extended representation of a dialect written by non-specialists which seems to have been produced as a by-product of an ethnographic study rather than for specific linguistic, literary or entertainment purposes. It is in part rather like the kind of written representation produced by folklorists that is discussed by Preston (1982, 1985), but I adopt a very different approach to it from that proposed in Preston. The case in question is the representation of late-1930s Bolton dialect to be found scattered among the Worktown papers of the Mass Observation archive. This fragmentary representation of the dialect arose from an ethnographic and sociological study of the Lancashire industrial town, Bolton, between 1937 and 1940. To assess the value of the dialect representation in this small and perhaps unique corpus of some 20,000 words extracted from the Worktown papers, it is essential to examine the motivation for the study as a whole, and its aims and methods. Accordingly, the chapter begins with a discussion of the genesis of the Worktown project and its approach to participant observation research. A number of extracts from the dialect data are then analysed to provide a picture of the kind of dialect features the observers were able to capture. The discussion which follows the analysis focuses on the challenges of this kind of approach, its strengths and limitations, and how we might account for the kind of representation achieved.

13.2. Background: Mass-Observation in Bolton

Mass Observation (henceforward, M-O) was a sociological and ethnographic movement established in 1937 by Tom Harrisson (an anthropologist), Charles Madge (a sociologist) and Humphrey Jennings (a documentary film-maker). The movement arose from a belief that the English working classes were poorly understood, a view colourfully expressed by Harrisson (1961, cited in Jeffery 1999: 20) in a retrospective comment on the Worktown project: 'The wilds of Lancashire or the mysteries of the East End of London were as little explored as the cannibal interior of the New Hebrides or the head hunter hinterland of Borneo.' There was a need, argued Madge and Harrisson (1937: 10), for an 'anthropology of ourselves', and a need in particular for a deeper knowledge of the English working classes: 'How little we know of our next door neighbour and his habits. Of conditions of life and thought in another class or district our ignorance is complete. The anthropology of ourselves is still only a dream.'

Among 'the wilds of Lancashire', Harrisson chose the Lancashire industrial town, Bolton, which was code-named 'Worktown' in M-O circles, as the location for a particularly detailed study of the working class, the majority of whom were employed in the cotton mills or their ancillary industries in the late 1930s. Harrisson (1970: 6) saw the Worktown project as a wide-ranging participant observation study in which every detail counted and nowhere was off-limits: 'We sought to fully penetrate the society we were studying, to live in it as effective members of it and to percolate into every corner of every day and every night of industrial life.'

It is notable that Harrisson does not specify a research aim for this percolation into every corner of every day and every night of industrial life. In a sense, as Willcock (1943: 447), one of the Worktown observation team, notes, there was something proudly non-academic about M-O: 'It has always been M-O's policy to avoid the closed circle of academic aloofness and to interest the people they are studying in both the collection of facts and their final correlation and interpretation.' As we see below, the amateur (in the strict sense of the word) representation of Bolton dialect which arose from the Worktown study may have been one of the ways in which they sought to break free of the 'closed circle of academic aloofness'.

The foci for participant observation emerged somewhat piecemeal during the Worktown project and included, among many other things, pub life, sport, local politics, shopping, the war, religion and local ceremonies. The Worktown papers are organised in topic boxes on the lines above. What is crucial for my purposes, since I am specifically concerned with the representation of Bolton dialect, is that language is *not* treated as a topic for specific study apart from a short section which focuses explicitly on swearing. There is no rationale for why the spoken data was collected (except in the case of surveys on specific issues such as the war situation), no analysis of it and very little metalinguistic comment about it. For this reason, we could take the uncharitable view that the language data was merely a random by-product of the somewhat indiscriminate approach to research for which, as Jeffery (1999) points out, Harrisson was criticised: gather data first, find a use for it after. More charitably we could see it as a by-product of what researchers now call 'thick description', i.e. the attempt to give a rich and detailed description of everyday life in a community, a descriptive process in which there is an obvious role for language. Similarly, the record of language could be seen as being motivated by the ethnographic nature of the research. The potential value of spoken data is stressed by Moerman (1988: 8, cited in Meyer and Schareika 2009: 4) and the phrase 'the droppings of talk' seems peculiarly apt for the Worktown data:

> Ethnography's central and sacred data are what one native says or does to another, or to the ethnographer. The objects we record, examine, consider, and write about occur in the course of social interaction. Whether observing a meeting, conducting an interview, or just sitting and chatting around the campfire, our primary data are things said as part of socially organised scenes. We collect the droppings of talk.

The 'overheards 'and 'indirects' (see below) in the Worktown papers could also be seen as what Meyer and Schareika (2009: 1) term 'participant audition', which they define as 'an ethnographic way of data collection that consists in the recording of verbal interaction in situations that are not directed by the researcher'. However, while the language data which accrued in the Worktown project may have been motivated by the kind of ethnographic concerns outlined above, it was never, to the best of my knowledge, analysed or discussed in ethnographic terms, unless we include the short section on swearing mentioned above.

While, as noted above, language is not specified or catalogued as a research topic for the project, there are numerous written records of spoken data in the form, for example, of incidental comments, snippets of conversations, short complete exchanges, monologues and street survey responses. This data, however, has to be retrieved from the 400,000 pages of the archive, which is no easy task given that the spoken data is dispersed among all the other records. As Timmis (2010, 2015, 2017) points out, there are three basic categories of spoken data in the Worktown papers. The terms used by the observers to describe these categories were 'overheards', 'directs' and 'indirects', though it should be noted that some of the spoken data in the papers is not labelled at all:

- overheards, i.e. conversations overheard by observers surreptitiously eavesdropping in the pub, at work, around sports fields etc.;
- indirects, i.e. when an observer was a participant in a conversation with local people with the opportunity to 'steer' the conversation to specific topics;
- directs, i.e. when an observer asked a question, and noted down the answer, as part of a street survey on topics such as the war situation, voting intentions or particular political figures.

As we shall see, for the purposes of this study, the 'overheards' are of most value as these yield the clearest attempts to capture spontaneous speech in general, and the dialect in particular.

13.3. Compiling the Worktown Dialect Corpus

Compiling the dialect corpus from the scattered spoken data in the Worktown papers was a three-stage process. The first step was to identify and collate the spoken data in the archive, which involved manual retrieval of the relevant data as the material cannot be electronically searched to identify direct speech. There is a wide variety of documents and observational records in the Worktown papers, ranging from the serious to the apparently frivolous. A flavour of these records is given in Timmis (2017: 18):

> the printed documents are as diverse as church sermons, newspaper articles, tea-shop menus, fairground adverts, political manifestos and wrestling programmes, to name but a few. The observational records include, among many other things, descriptions of sports events, ceremonies, drinking habits and the layout of pubs.

The second step was to exert some quality control on the emerging corpus by excluding spoken data which looked more like a summary or a cleaned-up version of what was said, rather than a detailed attempt to record exactly what the observer heard. The culmination of the second step was the Bolton/Worktown corpus which includes around 80,000 words of spoken data which survived the filtering process. The third step, which I initially took some time ago, but revisited for the purposes of this chapter, was to create a sub-corpus containing only data where the observers appeared to have made a clear attempt to capture the *dialect*. The data in the Bolton Worktown Dialect Corpus (BWDC), then, has in effect been subjected to a double filtering process. This filtering process, however, cannot be a totally reliable or objective process, no matter how diligently it is carried out. The question which drives the filtering process amounts, in essence, to: 'Is the data *plausible* as natural interaction?'. Deciding from the written record what constitutes plausible spoken data, and what does not, is necessarily somewhat subjective, especially at a distance of eighty years. There is no clear dividing line between plausible and implausible written records of spoken data, as I discovered when, rather optimistically and somewhat naively, I initially tried to approach the task of identifying plausible data with objective criteria such as, 'to be included in the corpus, the utterance must have at least two features typical of spoken language'. It quickly became clear that 'all-or-nothing' criteria could not be applied to the plausibility of data. I came to the view that there is a continuum of verisimilitude and that intuition cannot be factored out of decisions about where to place data on this continuum. In my defence, however, I can claim informed intuition on the following grounds: I have communed with the Worktown data for many years (Timmis 2010, 2014, 2015, 2017); I was born and brought up in Bolton; I have referred to Shorrocks' two-volume, comprehensive *A Grammar of the Dialect of the Bolton Area* (1999) to check intuitions; and I have been a student of spoken language for many years (for example, Timmis 2013, 2017). The qualifications for the task which I claim, however, do not make my judgement infallible and, as I present extracts from the data exactly as I found them, readers can judge for themselves the degree of verisimilitude.

As well as factors specific to the Worktown material, we need to consider factors which apply to assessing how far any record of spoken data, including present-day data, can be seen as an authentic record of what was said. In the absence of video or audio recording, for example, data is stripped of its physical and psychological context and also of its prosodic features, so it is only ever a partial record. In the case of historical data, these difficulties are compounded since it is particularly difficult to mentally reconstruct the context in which the words were originally spoken as there are highly likely to be unfamiliar elements in the contexts, references to people, places, events and institutions, for example, which were common knowledge at the time but which have now faded into obscurity. It is one thing to be familiar with Bolton pubs (as I happen to be), for example, but it is quite another to understand the culture and surroundings of the 1930s all-male Vault room in the pub, with its spittoons and sawdust on the floor. In view of the difficulties, outlined above, of describing records of spoken data, especially historical data, as 'authentic', I prefer the term 'verisimilitude' to the term 'authenticity' as it conveys a sense of likeness to reality rather than proof of reality.

13.4. The Verisimilitude of the Data

To assess the degree of verisimilitude of the data, we will necessarily be interested in who recorded the data and how they did it. There is little explicit information about the methods used to capture the spoken data, but there is some relevant background which throws some light on who recorded the data and how. There has long been a view that much of the Worktown project was carried out by middle-class observers who had no connection with Bolton, and it is true that some of the observers certainly fall into this category, examples of which are future notable politicians, such as Richard Crossman and Tom Driberg, a future editor of *The Times*, Woodrow Wyatt, and the eminent artist, Julian Trevelyan. It has been argued by Hinton (2013), however, that the focus on such luminaries has drawn attention away from the longer-term and ultimately more important contribution of a core of local members of the team. Significantly for our purposes, among the latter was Harry Gordon, a local unemployed fitter, who acted as adviser to outside observers on the local dialect (Hinton 2013), though it is not clear what form this advice took.

We can get some idea of who was involved in the gathering of spoken data by the observers' initials which are often, but unfortunately not consistently, written on the observation reports. A significant amount of the dialect data was certainly recorded by Peter Jackson, a local man who came to M-O via a contact in the local Workers' Educational Association, as did three or four other local observers. However, by way of contrast to Jackson, Tom Harrisson, born in Argentina and educated at Harrow and Cambridge, also contributed significantly to the dialect data. While at first sight Harrisson, as an outsider, seems less qualified than Jackson for the task of transcribing dialect, it should be noted that he had spent some time in Bolton even before the Worktown project (Hinton 2013) and famously sought minute detail in everything he did. It can also be argued that much work in dialectology has long been successfully carried out by scholars who are not native speakers either of the dialect they are studying or the language to which the dialect belongs. The backgrounds of all the observers involved in the representation of dialect, as far as this can be ascertained, are briefly summarised in Table 13.1.

Table 13.1 The observers

Observer	Background
Peter Jackson	Bolton; student from the Workers' Educational Association
Tom Harrisson	Harrow- and Cambridge-educated; project leader; anthropologist
Eric Letchworth	Bolton; unemployed shop assistant
Leslie Taylor	Bolton; unemployed shop assistant
John Summerfield	London; novelist
Peter Howarth	Blackpool; Oxford-educated
Joe Wilcock	Lancashire; working class
Bill Naughton	Lorry driver; in Bolton from the age of 13
Walter Hood	Ex-miner from Durham

However, whatever their commitment to detail, neither Harrisson, nor Jackson, nor any of the other observers were professional dialectologists working to a linguistic brief. The danger of not working to a brief, as Shorrocks (1999: 120) observes, is that 'the dialectologist who relies entirely on focused listening may simply be noting those forms that he is predisposed to collect'. Observers seem to have developed their individual style of recording speech by trial and error, and by discussing techniques with other observers. In addition, while Harrisson did not provide any pre-training to observers on any aspect of the observation task, he did give helpful feedback to new recruits on their initial efforts (Hinton 2013). The observers, then, were essentially 'accidental and incidental dialectologists' who, given that they were not equipped with recording technology of any kind, faced the significant challenge of transcribing dialect 'live'. The main source of information for how the observers approached this challenge is Ferraby (1944), but the information is both sparse and at a rather general level. According to Ferraby (1944), observers could be divided into three main groups depending on the degree to which their focus was on language or content. I have adapted Ferraby's tripartite categorisation below, based on my own experience of reading the transcriptions in the Worktown Papers. The categories are not watertight, but I think they are helpful in understanding why the data is the way it is.

Category 1: those who only sought to capture the sense of what they heard. A typical example of this is given below, but note that even here, the exclamative *why* is included, which does not contribute to propositional content. There is also a representation of the weak form of *been* (*bin*).

Extract 1 (BWC): The Life of a Councillor
[Enoch Bates – ex-Labour Councillor] I wouldn't be a councillor again if my time had to come again. I've had to burn the candle at both ends – I got time off work but it meant me doing my firm's work at home, such as keeping accounts till well after midnight 5 nights a week. I could have had a better time of it but I wouldn't buy my friends – that to me is bribery, why I would have bin to a lot more social functions but I did not wish to sell my services for financial gain or climb the social ladder like Alderman Demaine.

Category 2: those who were inconsistent in their approach to transcription, sometimes choosing to represent features of natural speech and the dialect, and sometimes not. A typical example of this kind of transcription is given below, with numerous swear-words and the non-standard *there's thousands* interspersed with words such as *coming* which could easily have been respelt (e.g. as *comin'*) to represent how the word was probably pronounced.

Extract 2 (BWC): Anger at the Unemployment Office
What's the bloody use of coming here when there's thousands signing on here. I said I'm bloody fed up of coming here for buggar all. He said, 'Have you been up yonder [vacancies]'. I said which bloody end? That? There's only bloody jobs selling ice creams. He told me you're only a kid and ought to be glad to draw your money regular! I said I'll swop your bloody job for 6 months – you sign a paper and send it up to London and keep it, doing a bloody sight better than you can.

Category 3: those who aimed to represent natural speech and the dialect as closely as they could, as in this short extract produced by a spectator at a bowls match, speculating on how he would use his unemployment benefit to generate ten shillings a week by gambling.

Extract 3 (BWDC): Gambling on Bowls
Ah wish ah wer ot dole, ah'd tak 10 bob a wik, theau con bet thi' bloody life o'that. Ah'd tak ten bob's wuth on 'eer. Ah know wor ah'm talking abeaut.

It is the work of these last observers which is analysed in detail below, but first it is important to discuss the nature of the transcription challenge when aiming for a close representation of speech: with only conventional orthography, rather than phonetic or phonemic symbols, at their disposal, how did the observers seek to represent the dialect? This is not to say that orthographic transcription is inherently inappropriate for the task, as Kortmann and Wagner (2005: 10) remark in relation to their work with the Freiburg English Dialect Corpus (FRED), 'since our explicit focus was on morphosyntactic variability, for all relevant features of dialect grammar we expect to investigate …, a phonetic and phonemic transcription would not only have been unnecessary, but even counterproductive in some cases'.

However, in this case, I am concerned with their representation of phonology as well as morphosyntax, and in the question of how far a variety of observers could be consistent in such a transcription of the dialect. As it turns out, the similarity in the way different observers transcribed dialect data suggests strongly that there *was* a shared system, at least among some of them, whether tacit or explicit. This system may well have originally been based on examples of representations from dialect literature. Judging by the number of popular nineteenth- and early-twentieth-century Lancashire dialect writers referred to by Salveson (1993), for example, Samuel Laycock and Benjamin Brierley, there would have been no shortage of dialect representation to call on. To take a concrete example of this possibility, in Box 19 (D) of the Worktown Papers, there is a transcription of a play in local dialect performed by a Methodist Sunday School in December 1937, and transcribed by a local observer, Peter Jackson. The similarities in convention between this extended transcription and dialect transcriptions in the Worktown papers, in which Jackson played a large part, are very close indeed. The local version of the MOUTH vowel (Wells 1982), for example, is most frequently rendered by Jackson as 'eau' as it is in the play. This convention is also used by a number of other observers. For comparison purposes, a short extract from the dialect play and a short dialogue from the Worktown papers are included below.

Extract 4 (Dialect Play): The Knocker
UpWell dost see t'knocker-up us bin knockin' ta 'ard an mi mother's getton 'eart trouble, so mi fayther said 'ee 'a t' knock sawfter! Ah think 'ee mun 'a' put a spunge o' 'is stick this mornin' becos ah nar yard 'im! An as fer them theer lairums, well, wi carn't afford one eaut o' wot wi geton wi warkin' 'ere! Why mi fayther said 'ee 'a' t' pawn 'is watch ta pay 5 knocker-up wi</EXT>

Extract 5 (BWDC): Boxing Talk
1 S1: Well, Chris, what dun think abeaut t'big feight what's gooin t'appen.
2 S2: Ah durnt know, Sam, but ah think there's a bit of feeshin going on.
3 S1: Ah'll tell thi wot, if yon mon its Louis gradely, its aw o'er bar sheautin.
4 S2: Aye, if Farr licks yon mon, Sam, ee'll owd championship a bit un then e'll chuck it.
5 S1: Aye, ah think so, becos he's beaunt get wed.
6 S1: Chris, if ee'll tak my advice ee'll let wimmin a be!
7 S3: Ah think theau art a woman 'ater, Sam Algar.
8 S1: Ah went o't' 'oly 'arbour last neet

Conspicuous examples of similarities between the two texts are as follows. The first number given is the dialogue number, the second is the line number (i.e. 1.2 = dialogue 1, line 2):

- Weak form of pronoun *I* = *ah* 1.2; 2.2; 2.3; 2.5; 2.7; 2.8
- Weak form of *because* = *becos* 1.3; 2.5
- Enclitics = *o'*; *t'*
- /h/-Dropping, e.g. *ee* 1.2; 1.4; 2.4; 2.6; 2.8
- /n/ for /ŋ/ = *knockin'*; *mornin'*; *gooin'*; *feeshin'* 1.1; 1.2; 1.4; 2.1; 2.2; 2.3
- Schwa = *us*; *un*
- *wot* 1.4; 2.3
- Dialect /ɛ:/ for Standard English (SE) /au/ 1.3 *eaut*; 2.1 *abeaut*; 2.3 *sheautin*; 2.5 *beaunt*; 2.7 *theau*

The data in the BWDC, as exemplified above and in further extracts below, indicate that on the occasions when the observers chose to represent the dialect they had at least a rudimentary tool for the task and could achieve a good degree of verisimilitude in their representation of the dialect.

13.5. Dialect Representation in the BWDC

I now examine two data extracts from the BWDC. The extracts were chosen as they include a range of the grammatical, lexical and phonological feature of the dialect which the observers sought to represent.

> *Extract 6 (BWDC): Criticism of Church Architecture*
> I durn't caw that a church, it's like Dobson's factory, its aw done for cheapness, it shows that folk are not interested the same, I mean them as as the brass, there's nown o' them us live reaund here neaw, thean made there brass and gone weer they con spend it, I durn't blame em in a way … Look at yon Parish Church (Bolton) that's made to last, it'll be standin when this is comin deawn, bricks no good!, this concrete sort onyway.

This extract contains a number of phonological, grammatical and lexical features which Shorrocks (1999) shows to be features of the Bolton dialect. Where possible, I have given further references to where the same feature is discussed by other scholars in a wider Northern or historical context.

Analysis of Extract 6 – phonology (NB: the number in brackets is the line number from the extract above):

- *l*-vocalisation (Johnson and Britain 2007), e.g. *aw* and *caw* in line 1
  Shorrocks (1999: 383) notes that, compared with SE, word final /l/ is missing in a large number of words in the dialect. Among the word-final examples he gives are *caw* and *aw* for SE *call* and *all.* By far the most common instance of *l*-vocalisation in the BWDC is *aw* with fifty-five instances. There are six instances of *baw* ('ball') and one each of *faw* ('fall') and *foo* ('fool'). The number of instances of *baw* can be accounted for by the fact that so much data was gathered around sports grounds.
- /ɛː/, e.g. *reaund* (3), *neaw* (3), *deawn* (5), corresponding to SE /aʊ/
  The sound /ɛː/, with over 250 examples in the dialect corpus (*c.* 1 per 100 words), is one of the most conspicuous elements of the local dialect (Shorrocks 1999: 281–2), though we have to keep in mind the obvious caveat that the frequency of the sound is dictated by the frequency of the words in which it appears. Further examples of /ɛː/ from the BWDC include: *eauw* ('how'); *eauwt* ('out'); *peaund* ('pound'); *meauth* ('mouth').
- /ɪə/ for SE /eə/ (Shorrocks 1999: 286)
  While there is only one instance of *weer* for *where* in the DC, there are fourteen instances of *theer* for *there.* (When I was at primary school in

Bolton in the 1960s, we still used to celebrate scoring a goal with a raucous cry of 'theer!'.)

- /ɒ/ for SE /æ/ (Shorrocks 1999: 235)
  The most common example of this dialect pronunciation in the BWDC is *mon* with thirty-five instances (there are sixty-two examples of *man*). The next most frequent example is *con* with twenty-four examples. Other examples include *ond.*
- /h/-Dropping (Shorrocks 1999: 401; Baranowski and Turton 2015)
  Absence of /h/ in initial position is ubiquitous in the dialect corpus. Shorrocks (1999: 401) remarks that the glottal fricative is not a phoneme of the dialect. *He*, for example, is consistently rendered by the observers as *ee* or *e*. There are also one or two instances of hypercorrection, i.e. the inclusion by speakers of /h/ when it would not be used in SE. A local man, for example, describes Hitler as a 'hinsect'.
- /n/ for SE /ŋ/ (Shorrocks 1999: 377; Kul 2017)
  This feature is represented orthographically by either simply omitting the <g> or replacing it with an apostrophe. It is another ubiquitous feature in the DC. Examples include: *standin*; *comin*; *suppin*; *takin*; *meetin*; *mornin*; *courtin*; *screamin*; and *stranglin.*
- /au/ or /oː/ for SE /ʌ/ (Shorrocks 1999: 281–2)
  Following Shorrocks (1999), *nown* would actually be produced as / nɛːn/, so if the observers were consistent in their transcription, and the speakers were consistent in their pronunciation, then / nɛːn/ would be rendered as *neaun.*

Analysis of Extract 6 – grammar:

- them **us** live (Shorrocks 1999; Poussa 1991)
  Us in this utterance is a represention of the weak form ([əz]) of the dialect relativiser *as*. Shorrocks (1999: 98) remarks that *as* is the chief relative pronoun in the dialect, and it may have both human and non-human antecedents. It is not quite so common in the BWDC as in Shorrocks' (1999) data, though there are thirty-two instances, and it is more common in the BWDC than in the BWC as a whole, as in the following examples:
  - 'im as sent that wood a'll win this bloody game. T'other mon knows bloody little abeaut bowling
  - It makes a living for them as buys a shop
- **thean** made there brass
  Here the observer is representing cliticisation to the dialect third person plural of *have* (*an*) to the weak form of *they* (/ðɪ/) (see Shorrocks 1999: 170). There are four instances of *thi an* and five instances of *wi an* in the

BWDC. *Thi* is commonly used to represent weak forms of *they*, *thee* and *thy*. Similarly *tha* is used to represent weak forms of *thou*.

- I **durn't** blame **em** in a way
  In this utterance, *durn't* is the first person singular negative of *to do* (Shorrocks 1999: 177). There are twenty-seven such instances in the BWDC. *em* represents the weak form of the demonstrative pronoun *them*. There are twenty such instances in the BWDC and thirty-four of *um* used in the same way.

Extract 7 (below) is given both to illustrate further features which the observers attempted to represent and to show how a degree of consistency was achieved in transcription. We can see the following consistencies in transcription: /ɛ:/, e.g. *peaund*; /ɪə/, e.g. *theer*; /h/-Dropping, e.g. *'ire*; /n/ for /ŋ/, e.g. *buildin'*.

> *Extract 7 (BWDC): Pride in the Sports Ground*
> Wi gie five hundred peaunds for this greaund awf Manchester collieries abeaut twenty-faar yar un ah reckon we did a good deal when we bowt it! Wi corn't sell it for buildin' on, so wi should " t'sell it um back if we' parted it. But that's not likely! Theau sees this bowwlin green? Well, there's 28 on neauw. That's its limit. Thi con bowwl theer fer tuppence. Anybody con come on un bowwl, an sometimes we get parties us u'll 'ire it for t'afthernoon, like. Members, same as me, generally pay 10 bob a year, un wi con bowwl when we want. Wi pay another tanner fer a keigh [key] for t'bowl-'eause, so wi' con gerrin when we want: dost see. Theau sees this chap cumin? Well, its owd Worthington; 'ee were t'president fer yars.

In addition to features discussed in relation to Extract 6, the transcriber of Extract 7 has attempted to render a number of other dialect pronunciation features, as exemplified below.

- Dialect /ɔ:/ for SE /ɒ/ (Shorrocks 1999: 199)
  There are twenty-six instances of dialect *awf* for SE *off* in the BWDC, but no other examples of this pronunciation difference.
- Dialect /a:/ for SE /ɔ:/ (Shorrocks 1999: 192)
  There are three instances of *faar* rather than SE *four*. This is the only instance of this pronunciation difference in the BWDC.
- T-to-R Rule, e.g. *gerrin* (line 7) (Shorrocks 1999: 394; Wells 1982; Hughes *et al.* 1979)
  The T-to-R Rule (Wells 1982) is a feature which involves replacement of /t/ with /r/, as immortalised by the TV star, Cilla Black. The feature also co-occurs in the BWDC with the verbs *get*, *put*, *let*, *shut* and *bet*,

with the conjunction *but*, the negative particle *not* and the interrogative *what*.

- Enclitics (Shorrocks 1999: 23; Barras 2015; Buchstaller and Corrigan 2015; Jones 2002)
  Examples of 't' as a cliticised form of the definite article ('Definite Article Reduction'; Jones 2002) are legion in the BWDC. Cliticised 't' is also used to represent the infinitive marker *to* as in the sentence *Tha owt t'ave more bloody sense*. The definite article can also be seen cliticised as *th*, as in *th'booze* or *th'licence*. *Thou* is cliticised in the form *th'art* (thou art).

Analysis of Extract 7 – grammar:

- *Gie* (line 1)
  This is described by Shorrocks (1999) as a possible preterite from of *give*, though not a particularly common one.
- *Theau sees* (line 3)
  Shorrocks (1999: 110; Buchstaller and Corrigan 2015; Anderwald 2009) describes 's' as the usual second person inflection in the present tense. Timmis (2017) remarks that in the Worktown data, second person 's' inflection is most common in the form *tha knows*.</BL>

In the BWDC there are a number of examples of 's' as a first person inflection when local people were asked to describe their daily routines. This accords with Shorrocks' (1999: 116) observation that first person 's' is commonly used when people are 'describing habitual behaviour, or their more permanent tastes and opinions'.

- *There's 28 on neauw* (line 4) (*Shorrocks* 1999; Buchstaller and Corrigan 2015; Tagliamonte 1998)
  Variable concord with existential *there* is certainly not unique to Bolton dialect, but it is frequent and commented on by Shorrocks (1999). Indeed, Timmis (2017) shows that with plural noun phrase complements, *there's* is significantly more frequent than *there are*.

The single-utterance extract below, unlike the extracts above, was chosen because it illustrates two specific features which I wanted to discuss: right dislocation (e.g. Melchers 1983; Durham 2011; Timmis 2017) and end-weight apposition (Timmis 2017). These two features are important, I argue below, because they illustrate potential advantages of the unorthodox approach to data collection of these incidental and accidental dialectologists.

Extract 8 (BWDC): Old Eric

Ee's a bloody seet wuss nar, owd Eric, the bloody grabbing free ale bugger.

Table 13.2 The frequency of right dislocation in five corpora

Corpus	Reference	Frequency (normalised per 100,000 words)
The Longman Spoken and Written English corpus (four-million word spoken component)	Cullen and Kuo (2007)	20
London–Lund Corpus (170,000 words of spoken extracts)	Aijmer (1989)	30
CANCODE mini-corpus (30,000 words)	McCarthy and Carter (1997))	37
York Corpus (1.5 million words) Durham (2011)	Durham (2011)	42
Bolton Worktown Corpus	Timmis (2015)	142

As the example above shows, right dislcoation involves the inclusion of an element in the post-clause slot (*owd Eric*) which is co-referential with an element in the preceding clause, usually the subject (*ee*). Table 13.2 shows that the structure is far more frequent in the BWDC than studies show in other corpora.

Extract 8 also illustrates a feature that I have never seen described in grammars, which Timmis (2017: 77–8) terms end-weight apposition. In this feature, the appositional element (*the bloody grabbing free ale bugger*) adds referential information about the subject of the previous clause (*ee*), unlike right dislocation which only adds co-terminous elements. There are some twenty examples of this structure in the BWC as a whole.

13.6. Discussion

We have seen that the observers were able to represent quite an impressive range of phonological and grammatical features of Bolton dialect. Having compared their representation with the patterns described in Shorrocks (1999), I have been able to attribute a high degree of verisimilitude to some of the work of these accidental dialectologists. As noted earlier, the Worktown Study was never intended to provide a representative picture of Bolton dialect. The picture emerged opportunistically and piecemeal, so there is a strong possibility that certain features may be inaccurately represented, while other features may be under- or over-represented. I consider the issues of accuracy and representativeness below.

13.6.1. Representation: Tools and Challenges

Capturing details of phonetics and phonology armed only with orthography is clearly a challenge (see also Honeybone, this volume), which, as we have seen in the extracts above, the observers made an admirable attempt to meet. A number of the observers achieved a high degree of consistency across their own transcriptions, and there is often a high degree of consistency between observers. There are occasions, however, where the observers clearly struggled to represent aspects of the dialect orthographically. The word *fight*, for example, is rendered on one occasion as *feight*, which is an admirable attempt to render the distinctive Bolton dipthong /ɛɪ/, though without knowing the dialect it would be hard to interpret. Schwa, which is such a common sound, is also difficult to render orthographically. From a grammatical point of view, representation is somewhat easier as orthography is generally up to the task unless one counts weak forms and contractions as being integral to certain structures.

In seeking to account for the nature of this amateur representation of a dialect, I do not believe that we can turn to folk linguistics and perceptual dialectology as explanatory concepts as these are largely concerned with overt perceptions of dialect by lay people often supported by explicit comment. In the case of the BWDC, we have to infer the reasons why the dialect is represented as it is, and I would suggest that the notion of salience is a promising avenue. Salience is defined by Llamas *et al.* (2016: 1–2) as

> that property of a spoken form which causes listeners to respond to the form in such a way as to indicate that it encodes information about the (presumed) social characteristics and/or geographical origins of the speaker, alongside the linguistic functions that the form simultaneously fulfils.

I noted above, for example, that /n/ for /ŋ/ was often represented, but only in 25 per cent of the instances where it could have occurred. This could be because it was not a salient feature for the observers: as a general feature of colloquial English, it may even have been part of their own speech.

13.6.2. Representativeness

A further aspect we need to consider is, for want of a better phrase, the representativeness of their representation. To exemplify this, I consider three syntactic features: right dislocation, end-weight apposition and *beaunt.*

I would suggest that right dislocation and end-weight apposition, as vehicles for forthright evaluation, appealed to Harrisson, the team leader, as iconic representations of a community whose vigour and straightforwardness he appreciated (Harrisson 1973). We can also turn to the notion of enregisterment as defined by Agha (2003: 231, cited in Beal and Cooper 2015: 2) as 'a linguistic repertoire differentiable within a language as a socially recognised register [which has come to index] speaker status linked to a specific scheme of cultural values'. This notion of enregisterment might account for how even the local observers came to see certain features as salient. In relation to the structures we considered to be potentially over-represented – right dislocation and end-weight apposition – it may have been their role as vehicles for strong emotive comment that made them salient for the observers. By way of contrast, a possible reason for the apparent under-representation of *beaunt* is that it is phonologically and semantically similar to SE *bound to* and has not been enregistered.

13.7. Conclusion

In conclusion, I would argue that the unorthodox work of these accidental dialectologists has provided something of real value in capturing aspects of the dialect with sufficient consistency and clarity for us to make a plausible reconstruction of a wide range of aspects of the dialect at that time. There are unique aspects of the data in the BWC which result from the fact that the researchers were not bound by the research ethics we take for granted nowadays: they eavesdropped on conversations, for example, listened to conversations in public toilets, and engineered conversations, while operating incognito, for the sake of gathering data. They recorded the words of people who do not feature in modern corpora, for example, drunks and prostitutes. All this was done without the consent of those whose words they recorded and without reference to the research ethics of any institution. We are privy, then, to unguarded, emotive language to a far greater extent than is normally the case. This revealed structures such as end-weight apposition rarely described elsewhere.

The BWC has given us, then, some insights into the dialect at a specific stage in its history and much food for thought about the theme of this book: the representation of Northern dialects. We get a glimpse of features of the dialect which are obsolescent, for example, *beaunt*, but we also see that non-standard features of spoken English such as right dislocation were very much alive and well, and were often recorded as a result of the nature of the data that was gathered. The BWC encourages, then, reflection on stability and change in spoken language, and on the role of communicative context on grammatical choice.

There is much, too, for the social historian as we gain insights into a variety of aspects of the lives of the Bolton working class at that time, for example, their drinking habits, their behaviour at football matches, and idiosyncratic customs such as the Westhoughton 'kayed' festival (which involved cutting the head off a cow). We also learn something about their attitudes to the great events of the day such as the Munich crisis, the outbreak of war and the fall of France. An aspect of the data which particularly fascinated me was the evidence it gives, through oral surveys, of the attitudes of the Bolton working class to prominent people of the day such as Chamberlain, Churchill and Eden, often expressed in colourful terms. It is this combination of linguistic and historical data which points to the potential of the BWC for interdisciplinary research.

The BWC, I have argued, is a rich and unique source for both the linguist and social historian. However, it has to be conceded that the observers' rather unsystematic approach to the task of gathering data, and the absence of useful demographic data, set limits on its value. The data is tantalising: it offers unexpected glimpses of the past and provides rare linguistic and historical evidence, but the data is rarely systematic or sufficient enough to provide a comprehensive picture of any given element. Nevertheless, the observers in late-1930s Bolton showed that gifted and committed amateurs have something to offer dialectology. We have a remarkable piece of accidental dialectology thanks to the original and unorthodox work of M-O in Bolton. I am not sure we will ever see its like again.

References

Agha, Asif (2003), 'The social life of cultural value', *Language and Communication* 23: 231–73.

Anderwald, Louise (2009), *The Morphology of English Dialects*, Cambridge: Cambridge University Press.

Baranowski, Maciej and Danielle Turton (2015), 'Manchester English', in R. Hickey (ed.), *Researching Northern English*, Amsterdam: John Benjamins, pp. 293–316.

Barras, William (2015), 'Lancashire', in R. Hickey (ed.), *Researching Northern English*, Amsterdam: John Benjamins, pp. 271–93.

Beal, Joan and Paul Cooper (2015), 'The enregisterment of Northern English', in R. Hickey (ed.), *Researching Northern English*, Amsterdam: John Benjamins, pp. 27–50.

Buchstaller, Isabelle and Karen Corrigan (2015), 'Morphosyntactic features of Northern English', in Raymond Hickey (ed.), *Researching Northern English*, Amsterdam: John Benjamins, pp. 71–89.

Durham, M. (2011), 'Right dislocation in Northern England: frequency and use – perception meets reality', *English Worldwide* 32/3: 257–79.

Ferraby, John (1944), 'Recording and classifying verbatim information', *Field Report 2146*, Mass Observation Archive.

Harrisson, Tom (1970), *Living through the Blitz*, London: Collins.

Harrisson, Tom (1973), *The Pub and the People*, Welwyn Garden City: Seven Dials Press.

Hinton, James (2013), *The Mass Observers, a History, 1937–1949*, Oxford: Oxford University Press.

Hughes, Arthur, Peter Trudgill and Dominic Watt (1979), *English Accents and Dialects*, London: Routledge.

Jeffery, Tom (1999), 'Mass-Observation: a short history', *MOA Occasional Paper* 10, University of Sussex.

Johnson, Wyn and David Britain (2007), 'L Vocalisation as a natural phenomenon', *Language Sciences* 2/3: 294–315.

Jones, Mark (2002), 'The origin of Definite Article Reduction in northern English dialects: evidence from dialect allomorphy', *English Language and Linguistics* 6/2: 325–45.

Kortmann, Bernd and Susanne Wagner (2005), 'The FRED project and corpus', in Bernd Kortmann Tanja Herrmann, Lukas Pietsch and Susanne Wagner (eds), *A Comparative Grammar of British Dialects*, Berlin: Mouton de Gruyter, pp. 1–13.

Kul, Malgorzata (2017), 'Lancashire and RP: a comparison of processes of connected speech', *Socjolingwistyka* 31/4: 51–70.

Llamas, Carmen, Dominic Watt and Andrew MacFarlane (2016), 'Estimating the relative sociolinguistic salience of segmental variables in a dialect boundary zone', *Frontiers in Psychology* 7: 1163.

Madge, Charles and Tom Harrisson (1937), *Mass Observation*, London: Frederick Muller.

Melchers, Gunnel (1983), '"It's a sweet thing is tea-cake": a study of tag statements', in S. Jacobson (ed.), *Papers from the Second Scandinavian Symposium on Syntactic Variation*, Acta Universitatis Stockholmensis, pp. 57–66.

Meyer, Christian and Nikolaus Schareika (2009), 'Participant audition: audio-recording as ethnographic method', *Working Papers 101 of the Department of Anthropology and African Studies*, Johannes Gutenberg University of Mainz.

Moerman, Michael (1988), *Talking Culture: Ethnography and Conversation Analysis*, Philadelphia: University of Pennsylvania Press.

Poussa, Patricia (1991), 'Origins of the non-standard relativizers *what* and *as* in English', in P. Ureland, and G. Broderick (eds), *Language Contact in the British Isles: Proceedings of the Eighth International Symposium on Language Contact in Europe*, Douglas, Isle of Man, pp. 295–316.

Preston, Dennis (1982), 'Ritin fowklower daun rong: folklorists' failure in phonology', *Journal of American Folklore* 95: 304–26.

Preston, Dennis (1985), 'The L'il Abner syndrome: written representations of speech', *American Speech* 60: 328–36.

Salveson, Paul (1993), Region, class culture: Lancashire dialect literature 1746–1935, Unpublished PhD thesis, University of Salford.

Shorrocks, Graham (1999), *A Grammar of the Dialect of the Bolton Area, Part 1: Phonology; Part 2: Grammar*, Bamberg: Peter Lang.

Tagliamonte, Sali (1998), 'Was/were variation across the generations: a view from the city of York', *Journal of Language Variation and Change* 10/2: 153–91.

Timmis, Ivor (2010), '"Tails" of linguistic survival', *Applied Linguistics* 31/3: 325–45.

Timmis, Ivor (2013), 'Spoken language research: an applied linguistic challenge', in B. Tomlinson (ed.), *Applied Linguistics and Materials Development*, London: Bloomsbury, pp. 79–95.

Timmis, Ivor (2014), 'Evaluation: tails', in K. Aijmer and C. Ruehlemann (eds), *Corpus Pragmatics*, Cambridge: Cambridge University Press, pp. 304–27.

Timmis, Ivor (2015), 'Pronouns and identity: a case study from a working-class community, 1937–1940', *ICAME (International Computer Archive of Modern and Medieval English) Journal* 39: 111–35.
Timmis, Ivor (2017), *Historical Spoken Language Research*, London: Routledge.
Wells, John (1982), *Accents of English*, Cambridge: Cambridge University Press.
Willcock, Bob (1943), 'Mass observation', *American Journal of Sociology* 48: 4.

14

Automatic Analysis of Dialect Literature: Advantages and Challenges

Kevin Watson and Marie Møller Jensen

14.1. Introduction

As the chapters of this volume demonstrate, the investigation of dialect writing can be approached from a number of methodological perspectives. All levels of language can be investigated – we focus here exclusively on phonological issues, and thus on the kinds of respellings that occur in such texts. With a qualitative approach (Asprey, this volume; Braber, this volume), we might observe a particular spelling and closely analyse the surrounding context. With a quantitative approach, we might analyse the proportion of texts in a corpus which contain a particular non-standard spelling (Cooper, this volume), or we might identify all non-standard spellings in a text and calculate the proportion of them that a particular respelling accounts for (Honeybone, this volume). These approaches all involve focusing solely on the *non*-standard spellings, which is of course precisely what we often want to do. Another approach is to consider the standard spellings as well, by quantifying non-standard spellings not just when they do occur but also when they could occur but do not (Maguire, this volume; see also Honeybone and Watson 2013; Honeybone *et al.* 2017). This essentially treats dialect spellings as sociolinguistic variables, which can shed light on relative differences between the non-standard representations of different linguistic features.

As with the analysis of sociolinguistic variables in speech, taking this approach with dialect writing requires the identification of the relevant variable contexts and the labelling of the different variants. In speech research, great advances have been made in the use of automatic methods for identifying relevant tokens (for example, the Penn Forced Aligner, Yuan and Liberman 2008; LaBB-CAT, Fromont and Hay 2012), but in the analysis of spelling variants in dialect literature, manual identification and labelling is still the norm (but see Nini *et al.*, this volume, for a large-scale computationally driven analysis). Manual labelling increases the time needed to carry out the analysis, and limits the size of the datasets that can be considered.

In this chapter, we discuss a series of tools which can assist with automating the analysis of dialect writing. To do this, we:

(1) digitise a piece of dialect writing using optical character recognition software;
(2) identify and standardise the non-standard spellings in this text, using VARiant Detector (VARD, see http://ucrel.lancs.ac.uk/vard/about/; Baron and Rayson 2008);
(3) add phonological transcriptions to all words, from the CELEX database (Baayen *et al.* 1995);
(4) identify and quantify the non-standard spellings, using R, an open-source statistical programming language (R Core Team 2018).

The steps and tools we describe here are no panacea for taking a CHLDL text and instantly, automatically and completely accurately calculating which spelling changes are made and how often. If this is the ultimate goal (and we are not sure it is), then it is not yet possible (at least using the tools we describe here, and using the current skill sets of the authors!). As we will show, there are challenges to be addressed along the way, and at many points there are decisions to be made that a human is needed for. This is good, we think. The spelling strategies in dialect writing are so variable, and relevant contexts are so localised, as are many of the words, that we should probably not trust a computer to do all the work for us, at least if we want to trust the results (see, for example, the distinction in Honeybone, this volume, between automated and 'hand crafted' approaches). However, once we recognise these challenges, there are also advantages in using these tools, or tools like these, to automatically assist our analysis.

Our approach in this chapter is to provide enough information so that these tools and strategies can be tested on other dialect texts. Most of the tools we use are freely available, and those that aren't can be bought for a reasonably low cost, or have freely available alternatives. When we reach Step 4, where we use R to demonstrate how to identify and quantify the non-standard spellings, we provide and explain code examples to illustrate how a particular task can be done. There are in fact several ways to do the same kind of thing in R, so there will certainly be other ways of doing what we suggest. As well as the code examples in the chapter, we have provided a more detailed R script, with additional commentary and a sample datafile, so that interested readers can try it out. This code is available at https://github.com/nzilbb/autochldl.

We begin in Section 14.2 with further discussion of the methodological challenges for dialect spelling research, in order to provide further background for Steps 1–4 outlined above. In Section 14.3 we briefly describe the piece of dialect literature we use in this chapter, and the phonological features which characterise the variety being represented. As we will see, we focus almost entirely on a well-known piece of dialect writing representing the accent of Liverpool (UK). We originally intended to explore a piece of dialect literature representing the accent of Newcastle upon Tyne (UK) as well, but it turned out to be much more difficult using the same tools. This highlighted an unexpected challenge, to which we return later. In Sections 14.4, 14.5 and 14.6 we proceed through Steps 1–4 in turn, and in Section 14.7 we reflect on the challenges we have encountered and, given those, what we think are the advantages of using these tools to automate the analysis of dialect literature.[1]

14.2. Methodological Challenges for Dialect Spelling Research

Relevant methodologies and analytical techniques that could be used for the analysis of dialect literature can be found in various different places, including corpus linguistics and sociophonetics. The data itself sits somewhat in between the two fields: it is obviously written, not spoken, but the non-standard spellings render typical corpus linguistic tools less than ideally suited to its analysis, particularly if we are interested in the phonological features that are being signalled by any non-standard spellings. Cooper (2013) uses corpus linguistics tools to analyse Yorkshire dialect literature. Specifically, Cooper (2013: 96) uses alphabetised word lists to shed light on groupings of non-standard spellings (e.g. <abaht> and <abbut> as spellings of 'about'). This of course requires some manual decision-making. It can be difficult to automatically count the 'words' in a dialect literature corpus, because the spellings of the same word can be so variable. One way around this would be to annotate the non-standard spellings with their standardly spelled counterparts, in much the same way as part of speech annotations are often added to lexical items in corpus linguistics and other areas. However, part of speech tags can quite easily be automatically added to corpora in which the words are standardly spelled, but standard spellings cannot easily be automatically added to a text of non-standardly spelled words. This is a necessary and important early step in the automatically assisted analysis of dialect writing, to which we return later.

For analyses of dialect writing that address the accent features that are represented, we need to know how the words map onto their phonological representations. A typical approach in research on dialect writing is to manually tag each word for the phonological features it contains (see Honeybone, this volume; also Honeybone and Watson 2013). This approach is time-consuming, labour-intensive and considerably limits the size of the dataset that can be analysed. Over the years in sociophonetic research we have seen a considerable increase in the size of a typical dataset. For example, Labov *et al.* (1972) had a dataset of about 150 tokens and, more than four decades later, Sóskuthy and Hay (2017) used over 270,000 tokens. This has not been a straightforward linear increase over time, and we do not mean to imply that all recent work has or should have a very large dataset – different projects with different questions obviously require different methodologies and result in datasets of different types and sizes. And, of course, excellent work in sociophonetics is still done with smaller samples. Nevertheless, overall, there has been a noticeable increase in the size of a typical sociophonetic dataset. This increase has been facilitated by advances in technology. Tools such as the Penn Forced Aligner (Yuan and Liberman 2008) and its implementation, FAVE Align (Rosenfelder *et al.* 2014), along with LaBB-CAT (Language, Brain and Behaviour Corpus Analysis Tool; Fromont and Hay 2008, 2012), have meant that hundreds of hours of audio data can be analysed efficiently. FAVE and LaBB-CAT are different systems but speech analysis using them begins in a similar way: a user uploads an audio file and an orthographic transcript, and the system matches each word in the transcript with a dictionary entry which also contains a phonological transcription. A phonological transcription is added to each word, and can be used in an analysis (they are also used to time-align the audio signal to the transcript at the word/segment level).

In corpus sociophonetic work, the ability to automatically align the orthographic transcription, a computer-generated phonological transcription and the audio signal has been arguably the most important development in allowing researchers to upscale the size of a typical dataset. The connection between levels of representation is essentially the key principle for the automatic analysis of dialect spellings, too. For work which is concerned with grammatical and morphological features, knowing the phonemic structure of the word that a non-standard spelling is intended to represent is perhaps not so important, but there still needs to be a connection between the non-standard spelling and the standardly spelled counterpart of a word if common corpus linguistic techniques are to be used in the analysis. In this chapter we focus largely on how phonological features are represented in dialect writing, and for this the connection between the non-standard spelling and the underlying phonology of the intended word is very important. That is, to allow automatic analysis in the way we outline below, each word in a dialect literature corpus must have a corresponding phonological transcription. For this to be automated, as it is in much corpus sociophonetic work, the non-standard spellings must first be translated into standard orthography. Then, each word can be looked up in a dictionary which contains phonological codes, and the phonological transcription can be added to each word. This presents challenges. One difficulty is that phonological representations of words in dictionaries will likely be of a standard or reference variety, and so could be quite unlike the phonology of the variety being represented in dialect writing. And, of course, there will be words present in the dialect literature corpus which are not present in a dictionary at all, and phonological transcriptions for these words will need to be added manually. These are not problems specific to dialect literature – the issues arise for FAVE Align (which is trained on General American English) and LaBB-CAT (which usually takes its phonological codes from Received Pronunciation), too. We return to this issue in Section 14.4.3.

14.3. CHLDL Texts

The dialect literature we examine in this chapter represents the variety of English spoken in Liverpool, in the north-west of England. Liverpool English (LE), or *Scouse* as it is commonly known, is a well-recognised variety of English (Coupland and Bishop 2007; Leach *et al.* 2016). The features of LE have been mentioned elsewhere in this book (e.g. Honeybone, this volume), and many of the key features have been discussed elsewhere too (e.g. Watson 2007; Clark and Watson 2016; Watson and Clark 2017), so we will mention only the key characteristics briefly here. LE is in many ways a typical accent of Northern England. Like other accents of Northern English English, LE has the same vowel in FOOT as it has in STRUT, typically [ʊ], and a short vowel in BATH, [a], which has the vowel of TRAP rather than the vowel of PALM or START, as in much of the south of England. Also like some other Northern Englishes, Liverpool maintains [g] following [ŋ] in words like *thing* and *finger*, the so-called velar-nasal-plus (Bailey 2019a, 2019b), and [h] is typically dropped in both function words and content words, which is of course common not just in northern England but in many regional accents across the United Kingdom.

As well as these more or less commonly shared characteristics, LE has several accent features which are not very geographically widespread. In the vowel system, for example, START can be produced as [aː], further forward than is typical in some other Northern Englishes, and NURSE/SQUARE are typically merged to a front vowel in the open-mid/close-mid region, such as [ɛː] or [eː], (Watson 2007; Watson and Clark 2013). In the consonant system, Liverpool English traditionally has (th) and (dh) stopping, a feature thought to have been introduced into LE due to contact with Irish varieties in the 1850s as LE was developing (Honeybone 2007). (th) and (dh) stopping are often commented on as features that listeners strongly associate with Liverpool, although Watson and Clark (2017) show that stopping was perhaps not as common in older Liverpool English as first thought, and Watson and Clark (in prep) show that (th) fronting has now arrived in LE, as it has in many other varieties of British English. Perhaps the most regionally restricted feature of LE is plosive lenition, whereby plosives are realised as affricates or fricatives in certain non-initial positions (e.g. 'cat' [kaθ̠], 'walk' [wɔːχ], 'but' [bʊh]; see Honeybone 2001; Clark and Watson 2016).

Dialect writing representing Liverpool English has also been mentioned several times in this book (Honeybone, this volume; Crowley, this volume). Probably the most famous example of this, certainly in the context of the study of Liverpool dialect writing, but probably also in Liverpool at large, is the *Lern Yerself Scouse* book series. The first of these books (hereafter referred to as *LYS1*) was first published in 1966 (Shaw 1966; see Crowley, this volume, for some background to this text). It is an early example of what Honeybone and Watson (2013) call contemporary, localised, humorous dialect literature (CHLDL), but is also so well-known as to have become something of a cultural icon. The books have been referred to as 'the bible' for anyone who wants to learn how to speak with a Scouse accent (Martin 2016), suggesting that a lay perception of the books is that they contain appropriate representations of Liverpool English.

LYS1, along with the other *LYS* books, is designed as a foreign-language phrasebook, with examples written 'in Scouse' followed by Standard English 'translations'. As with much other CHLDL literature, the translations are not word-for-word, since there is often an attempt to be humorous. The first page of dialect spellings in *LYS1* (p. 17 of the book) is shown in Figure 14.1. We can see respellings which are probably linked to phonological variation (e.g. <ullo dur>, <ere>), but also words which have not been respelled that could have been (e.g. <wack>, <tatty>). There are also words which are respelled but which do not obviously represent phonological dialect features, so called 'eye dialect' forms (for example, <lite>).

In Honeybone and Watson (2013) *LYS1* is one of the texts in the CHLDL corpus that is used to understand the relationship between dialect spellings and sociolinguistic salience (and other types of salience). As noted above, Honeybone and Watson (2013) treat the spellings as sociolinguistic variables, identifying when a non-standard spelling was used, but also when one could have been used but was not. Honeybone and Watson (2013) preselected the following features to focus on: FOOT, STRUT, START, NURSE, SQUARE, (h), (t), (d), (k), (th), (dh). They used a manual process for coding the spellings. They write that the spellings in the dataset were

Forms of Address

Ullo dur!
Greetings; I am pleased to make your acquaintance.

Wack.
Sir.

Yis.
Yes.

Gisalite.
Could you oblige me with a match, please?

Ay-ay.
I say!

By subtle changes of inflexion this useful expression can be used for saying, "*Beware!*" or "*I thought as much!*" or even "*Watch your step, my friend!*" as for example, "*Ay-ay*" (*unspoken*: "*Dur's a queue ere*").

La.
I say, young man.
La: abbreviation of *lad*.

Ere, tatty-ead!
I say, young woman!

Figure 14.1 Learn Yerself Scouse volume 1, page 17

> manually annotated with two sets of tags. The first provided an identifying label for the variable and the second categorised the variable as being spelled standardly or non-standardly … [then] some were annotated further. For example … (th), (dh), (t), (d), and (k) were coded according to their word position (initial, medial, final). (2013: 321)

Figure 14.2 shows the summary results from Honeybone and Watson (2013: 332). The results show that there is a high degree of variation in the respellings. The most commonly spelled feature is (dh), but even that is not respelled 100 per cent of the time. There is also variation in how often different features are respelled, which Honeybone and Watson related to the sociolinguistic and phonological salience of the features concerned.

Honeybone and Watson (2013) had a systematic coding strategy, but the manual coding of all this data, in at least two (and in reality many more than two) rounds, was a lot of work. Despite that, the corpus is incompletely annotated, since the variables which were to be coded were chosen in advance and only those variables were coded. But, as Honeybone (this volume) notes, there are plenty of questions which remain unanswered. For example, are there other features which are respelled but were missed (e.g. is velar-nasal-plus ever signalled as a respelling?)? And to what extent is eye dialect used in the *LYS* series? These questions cannot be answered using the same corpus without a considerable amount of further work adding extra codes to the texts.

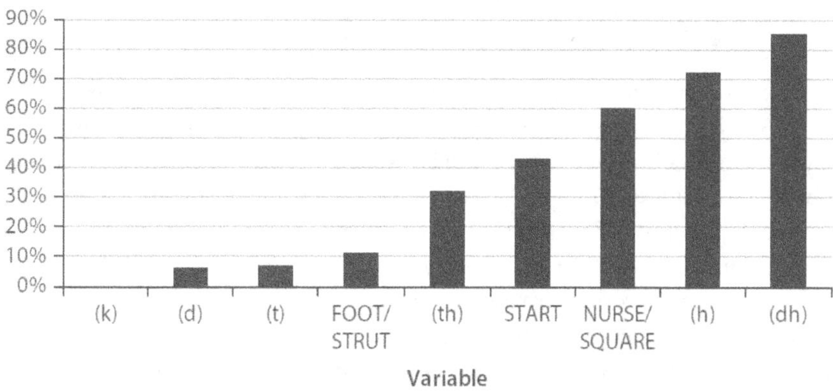

Figure 14.2 Summary results from Honeybone and Watson (2013: 332)

In the remainder of this chapter we explore whether we can arrive at a similar set of results to those in Figure 14.2, using automatically assisted methods. This will result in a more completely annotated corpus (of just one of the volumes of *LYS*, used as an example), which will be able to explore as yet unanswered questions.

14.4 Digitising and Annotating CHLDL Texts

14.4.1. Step 1: Digitising the Text

As *LYS1* is only available as a hard-copy publication, we first had to produce a computer-readable version. We did this, with the permission of the publisher, by scanning the book and saving it as a PDF, before using optical character recognition (OCR) software to produce a machine-readable copy. Many different OCR programs are available, and we used Abbyy Finereader (https://www.abbyy.com/). While not 100 per cent perfect, as we note below, the quality of the character recognition was very good. As mentioned above, and as shown in Figure 14.1, the format of *LYS1* as a foreign-language phrasebook means that it contains both writing which is meant to be 'in Scouse' and the Standard English 'translations'. Not all of the text that is 'in Scouse' is written with non-standard spelling, but the 'translations' are always written with Standard English orthography. Since we do not focus on the 'translations' themselves here, we manually removed this section of the text from the file. What was left was a text consisting of the 'in Scouse' part of *LYS1* (some of which is written with standard spelling, some of which is not).

14.4.2. Step 2: Spelling Standardisation with VARD

The next step was to standardise the non-standard spellings, not by correcting them so that the original spellings were lost, but by creating an additional layer of annotation. For this we used VARiant Detector (VARD, see http://ucrel.lancs.ac.uk/vard/about/), a Java-based tool which helps a user standardise spelling in texts (Baron and Rayson 2008). It was initially designed as a tool for historical texts (Alexander *et al.* 2015; Archer *et al.* 2015), but it has also been used for other text types (e.g. learner corpora (Rayson and Baron 2011) and SMS 'text message' communication (Tagg *et al.* 2012)). It has to the best of our knowledge not yet been used to investigate dialect writing. Essentially, VARD allows a user to load in a text containing non-standardly spelled words and annotate those words with standardised spellings. These annotations are stored as XML tags, so the non-standard and standardised words are stored alongside each other. When a text is loaded into VARD, it uses techniques from modern spell-checkers to identify words it believes to be variant spellings, by highlighting those words that are not present in its lexicon. An example of this, using the first couple of pages of *LYS1*, is shown in Figure 14.3. This is a good start – many of the words that are highlighted here are in fact spelling variants (e.g. <Ullo dur>), but it's not perfect, since some of the highlighted words are not respelled words (e.g. <wack>, which is absent from VARD's dictionary but is spelled standardly) and some non-highlighted words are in fact respelled (e.g. <ere> for standard *here*). An incorrectly highlighted word can be manually marked as a *non-variant*, while

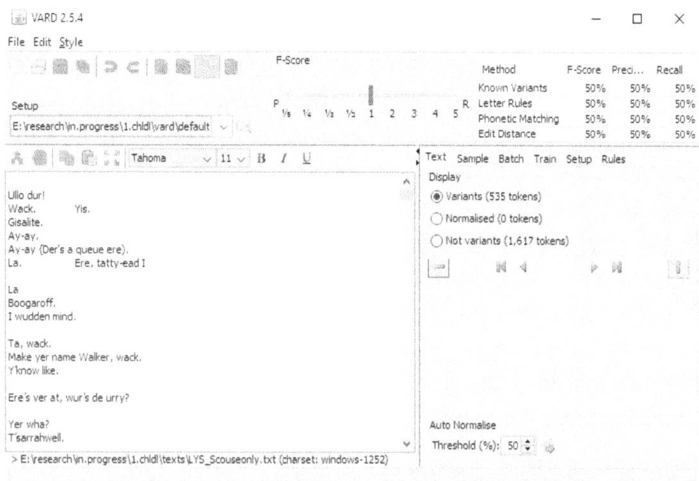

Figure 14.3 VARD; view file

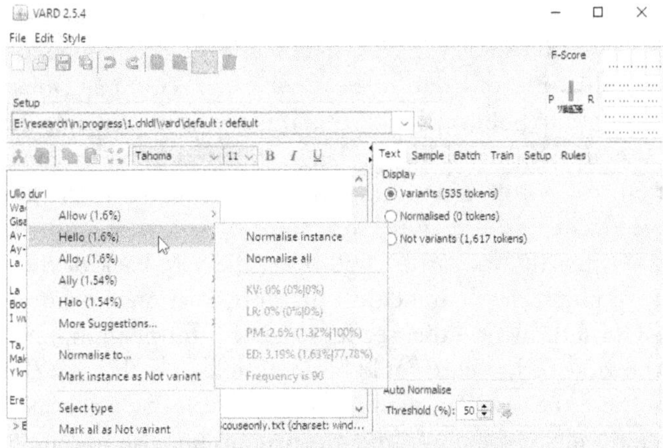

Figure 14.4 VARD; standardise variant spellings

an incorrectly unhighlighted word can be manually marked as a *variant*. In each case, the user can choose to change the status of one word at a time, or every instance of the word spelled in that particular way across the whole text.

For all words marked as a variant, a user can *normalise* the spelling. This means add the standard spelling alongside the non-standard form. For each word identified as a variant, the user is offered a list of standardly spelled options, ranked using a confidence score, and can choose from that list or can normalise to a different word. If the normalised word is not in the lexicon, it can be added, so that it will appear in the suggestion list in future. An example is shown in Figure 14.4, for the first word, spelled non-standardly as 'Ullo'. The user can select 'Hello' in the pop-out menu, and choose to 'Normalise all' to standardise the spellings of all instances of 'Ullo' in this text.

A portion of the completed file is shown in Figure 14.5. This shows the tagging labels that are used. The standardised spelling of the word is shown between > < (the first example in Figure 14.5 is 'Hello'). The original spelling is preceded by 'orig=' (the first example is 'orig=Ullo', because the first word in the text marked as a variant is 'Ullo'). Each normalised word is tagged in this way.

```
<?xml version="1.0" encoding="UTF-8"?>
<documents>
<normalised orig="Ullo" auto="false">Hello</normalised> <normalised
orig="dur" auto="false">there</normalised>!
<notvariant>Wack</notvariant>.  <normalised orig="Yis"
auto="false">Yes</normalised>.
```

Figure 14.5 VARD output .xml

Recall above we said that our original intention for this chapter was to examine *LYS1* and also a text from Newcastle English (popularly known as *Geordie*). This text was due to be *Larn Yersel' Geordie* (Dobson 1986, hereafter *LYG*), first published in 1969. This text is in principle designed in the same way as *LYS1*, as a foreign-language phrasebook. It consists of an introduction to Geordie pronunciation, then a few important phrases and then a few 'translation exercises', for example, an excerpt from the Book of Exodus written in Newcastle English. At the very back of the book is a vocabulary of phrases with Standard English translations (for more on *LYG* and other CHLDL in Geordie, see Jensen 2013, forthcoming). At first, we assumed the same techniques would be applicable to both texts. But in practice, this was not the case. The main reason for this is that a common practice in *LYG* is not only to use non-standard spellings but also to omit the spaces between words. An example is: 'Gizabroonjack' (*LYG*, p. 15). This would be 'translated' into Standard English spelling as 'give us a brown, jack'. The lack of spaces no doubt serves to highlight a difference from Standard English spelling, but it makes it very difficult for VARD, and presumably other techniques too, to automatically identify where the words are. Currently, VARD would treat this whole phrase as one single item, and not a sequence of words, as follows:

- <normalisation orig="Gizabroonjack"> give us a brown jack</normalisation>

This makes automatic detection of possible spelling variants more difficult, and it would make the automatic addition of phonological transcriptions impossible (see Section 14.4.3). Using the tools we present here, the user would essentially have to manually insert spaces where possible between the words in the original dialect literature, before VARD can attempt to make suggestions for possible standard spellings. This would be possible, but it is time-consuming, and unless done in a careful, recoverable and analysable way, it actually removes an aspect of authenticity from the original texts (assuming that the lack of spaces is a deliberate decision made by the author and thus is serving a stylistic purpose). There were a considerable number of these kinds of spellings in the *LYG* texts, and these present a challenge to the automatically assisted analysis of CHLDL. We are currently working on a solution to this problem, since the tools we describe here do not provide a suitable answer. For this chapter, we decided to progress with *LYS1*. As we will see, there are examples in *LYS1* of phrases with no spaces between words, but the number is smaller than *LYG* and so we were able to add in phonological annotations manually. This should obviously be taken into

	A	B	C
1	Filename	Normalised	Original
2	LYS_Scouseonly_wxml3.t	here	ere
3	LYS_Scouseonly_wxml3.t	a	a
4	LYS_Scouseonly_wxml3.t	queue	queue
5	LYS_Scouseonly_wxml3.t	Here	Ere
6	LYS_Scouseonly_wxml3.t	tatty-head	tatty-ead
7	LYS_Scouseonly_wxml3.t	La	La
8	LYS_Scouseonly_wxml3.t	I	I
9	LYS_Scouseonly_wxml3.t	La	La
10	LYS_Scouseonly_wxml3.t	bugger off	Boogaroff
11	LYS_Scouseonly_wxml3.t	wouldn't	wudden
12	LYS_Scouseonly_wxml3.t	I	I
13	LYS_Scouseonly_wxml3.t	mind	mind
14	LYS_Scouseonly_wxml3.t	wack	wack
15	LYS_Scouseonly_wxml3.t	Ta	Ta

Figure 14.6 .csv output from Python script

account when choosing the appropriate techniques for a particular type of dialect literature.

Turning back to the more successfully normalised *LYS1* text, the final step before we were able to add the phonological codes was to convert the .xml file into a different format. We needed to create a spreadsheet structure, with the original spelling in one column and the standardised spelling in a second column. This information was already encoded in the .xml file, so we used a Python script to restructure the .xml data into a comma-separated values (CSV) file, a sample of which is shown in Figure 14.6. The Python script is available at https://github.com/nzilbb/autochldl, and we thank Jonathan Dunn for writing it.

14.4.3. Step 3: Adding Phonological Transcriptions

Before we were able to search for the phonological features that are represented as respellings, we had to add phonological transcriptions of the words to our spreadsheet. We extracted these from CELEX (see https://catalog.ldc.upenn.edu/LDC96L14). CELEX is an electronic database which contains the following information for English, Dutch and German words: orthography, phonology, morphology, syntax and word frequency. CELEX information is stored as ASCII text files, rather than in a database system, so we performed a search (using R, see below) to match each standardised lexical item in our

LYS1 text, with the corresponding word in CELEX. When a match was found, the phonological transcription was added to our dataset. CELEX uses the DISC phonology coding system – an ASCII-based system which uses precisely one character for each phonological symbol (e.g. /t/ = 't', /s/ = 's', [ʊ] = 'U', [aɪ] = '2'). This is essentially exactly the same process that is followed for sociophonetic work using LaBB-CAT. For example, the Origins of Liverpool English corpus (OLIVE; see Watson and Clark 2017) uses CELEX to add phonological transcriptions to its words in precisely the same way.

Examining non-standard language varieties using a dictionary like CELEX, which has phonological codes for a standard variety (for example, Received Pronunciation), should be done with some caution because the phonological systems will likely not completely align. Sometimes it is helpful if words are given a phonological code from a standard variety. If we wanted to examine the possible respellings of FOOT and STRUT words, for example, we would need the phonological transcription to recognise that /ʊ/ and /ʌ/ are different vowels, even if, in LE, both lexical sets have /ʊ/. However, in cases where a non-standard variety has a phonological contrast which a standard variety lacks, adding phonological codes from the standard variety would lose the contrast available to speakers of the non-standard variety. Again, this is not a problem specific to dialect writing, and users of OLIVE, for example, must grapple with the same issues.

14.5. Step 4: Data Exploration and Cleaning

To identify spelling patterns in our dataset, we used R (R Core Team 2018). R is a statistical and graphical programming language which is an industry standard in data science. As well as the base system, there are many thousands of freely available packages which perform a very wide range of functions. R, and its packages, are open source, and are supported by a large community of users. For readers with some experience of computer programming, the R environment will feel familiar. For others, it will not feel familiar. It might even feel hostile. If so, relax! We think it is worth learning the basics, even if the learning curve feels steep, because once the basics are understood it is only a relatively short step to more complex tasks, and then a vast and ever-growing range of analytical tools become available, not just for statistical analysis, but also for data management and visualisation.

As a reminder, what we have done so far to get to this point is digitised the hard copy of a book, used an automatically assisted method of adding standard spellings to non-standardly spelled words and added DISC phonology codes using a look-up technique from CELEX. These steps resulted in a spreadsheet with three columns: the original spelling of a word, the standard spelling of that word and the phonological transcription of the word. There are many ways to get this, of course, other than by the steps we have set out (for example, by already having an electronic version of non-standard spelling, such as tweets, as in Nini *et al.*, this volume, or by using some other phonemic transcription method). But once this spreadsheet exists, via whatever steps, the strategies below should work.

In this section, we provide example code, to illustrate the commands that can be run in R. These are shown in the displayed sections. We also provide comments in the code, prefixed by #. Further notes are provided in the supplementary materials (https://github.com/nzilbb/autochldl).

Before we could begin to analyse the spellings, some cleaning of the data was required. To do this, we used several R packages. First, we loaded the *tidyverse* package (see https://www.tidyverse.org/). tidyverse is a suite of packages designed for data science, and it includes tools for the main tasks we will carry out in the remainder of this chapter: tools for the management of the data such as *dplyr* (Wickham *et al.* 2018) and *stringr* (Wickham 2018), and tools for the plotting of the data such as *ggplot2* (Wickham 2016). All of these tools, and others, are loaded into R when the user loads the *tidyverse* package. Then we loaded into R the spreadsheet which contains the data, by setting the working directory to the path of the folder which has the relevant file, and then reading in the file itself, and storing it as an object called *dat*. (Note that the tidyverse has a particular syntax, which is sometimes different from the syntax of non-tidyverse R. When we demonstrate R code below, we use the code we think is most transparent for a given task. Readers can consult the supplementary materials for further information.)

```
#if tidyverse is not installed, install it
install.packages("tidyverse")
#this loads tidyverse
library(tidyverse)
#this sets the working directory which contains your file
setwd("f:/chldl_data")
#this loads in the spreadsheet containing the data,
#and stores it in an object called dat
dat<-read.csv("chldl_withDISC.csv")
```

Now that the spreadsheet is in R, as an object called *dat*, we can explore it. We first checked that the columns had headings that we recognised.

```
#check column names
names(dat)
## [1] "original" "wordform" "phonemes"
```

Here we see the three columns that we were expecting. The *original* column is the original spelling found in *LYS1*, the *wordform* column is the same word in Standard English orthography, and the *phonemes* column is the phonological transcription of the standardised spelling, extracted from CELEX. Next we might want to know how many words there are, and perhaps what proportion of words are respelled. To approximately count the words, we counted the rows in the spreadsheet. This isn't exactly the number of words in the dataset, since although most of the rows contain a single word, a few contain more than one, as we will see below.

```
#get the length of the wordform column
length(dat$wordform)
## [1] 2078
```

There are approximately 2,078 words in the dataset. To identify the words that are respelled, we compared the contents of the *original* column and contents of the *wordform* column. Any difference would signal that a respelling of some sort has taken place. Since we might later want to be able to easily identify whether a word is non-standardly spelled, we will add a column called *non-standard* and label a row *TRUE* if the word is in fact spelled non-standardly.

```
#create a new column called 'nonstandard', compare the contents
#of the 'original' and 'wordform' columns. Create a new column.
#If the two columns are different (signalled by !=) add
#'TRUE' to the nonstandard column; if they are the same add
#'FALSE' to the non-standard column.
dat<-dat %>%
  mutate(nonstandard = original != wordform)
```

We then generated a table from the *non-standard* column, which shows that there are 639 words which are respelled (almost 31 per cent of the dataset). Interestingly, Honeybone (this volume) considered about 1,000 words of *LYS1*, and manually calculated that around 29 per cent of the words were respelled. This not only acts as a validation of the methods, but also indicates that the respellings are remarkably consistent throughout the volume.

```
#display a table of the nonstandard column
table(dat$nonstandard)
##
```

```
## FALSE TRUE
##  1439  639
```

We can look at the first six rows of the datafile using the *head()* command. This is another good way of making sure the structure of the data is as expected, and in this particular case it reveals that some further steps of data cleaning are necessary before we can begin to analyse the non-standard spellings.

```
#look at the first 6 rows of the data file
head(dat)
##    original          wordform phonemes nonstandard
## 1      ullo             hello   h@-'l5        TRUE
## 2       dur             there     'D8R        TRUE
## 3      wack              wack     'w{k       FALSE
## 4       yis               yes     'jEs        TRUE
## 5 gisalite give us a light     <NA>        TRUE
## 6 ay-ay                ay-ay     <NA>       FALSE
```

As noted above, the column *original* is the original spelling from *LYS1*. The column *wordform* is the standardised spelling. The *phonemes* column is the phonemic representation of the standard word, using DISC phonology codes. The *nonstandard* column, which we added above, identifies whether there is a difference between the *original* and *wordform* columns. There is an obvious problem with the rows which have 'NA' in the *phonemes* column. This means that these words do not have a phonological transcription, which is because it was not possible to automatically extract one from CELEX. Without a phonemic representation, it is much more difficult to find the appropriate variable context in which to look for spelling changes. In the examples shown above, the problem exists for two different reasons. For <ay-ay>, it was not possible to add the CELEX phonological codes because the word is not present in the CELEX dictionary, so no match with accompanying phonological symbols was found. This is common because these texts rely on local knowledge and local words. For <give us a light>, while the individual words are each in CELEX, the search cannot be done at the phrase level, and this item is treated as a phrase rather than a series of four lexical items. As explained above, this happens because of the way VARD treats variants ('gisalite' is treated as one word, even if it is corrected to 'give us a light'). Ideally, we would want to split these phrases into individual words, and then extract DISC codes. But this is not always straightforward. With 'gisalite', for example, 'gisa' would be standardly spelled as 'give us a', making 'gis' 'give us'. Exactly where to make the split between 'give' and 'us', or even whether a split can be sensibly made, is far from clear. To explore just how much of a problem this is, we first calculated how many words had missing phonology codes:

```
#display a table which counts how many items
#*do not* have phonological codes (i.e.
#no code = TRUE)
table(is.na(dat$phonemes))
##
## FALSE TRUE
##  1760  318
```

Some 318 words/phrases have no associated phonology codes. Some of these words are repeated – there are actually 255 unique words which do not have a phonological code. This must be rectified before we can proceed. First, we can look at the words which do not have associated phonological representation to understand the reasons for the problem (the code immediately below would show all of the words, but here we show just a sample).

```
dat %>% #take the dat datafile and then
  filter(is.na(phonemes))%>% #filter those words which do not
  #have a phonological code and then
  distinct(wordform)%>% #look at only the unique wordforms and then
  pull() #tell me what they are as a vector
## [1] "this avvy" "anfield"        "effin"    "got any"
## [5] "bevvy"     "droopydrawers" "fagends" "liverpool"
```

There are several reasons why these words do not have a phonological entry in CELEX. There is the problem of including a space as mentioned above, where the individual words would likely be in CELEX but the phrase is not (e.g. *got any* which is spelled non-standardly as <gorrany>). This is the cause of the problem in thirty-five unique instances. The other cause of the problem is the very frequent use of local place-names (e.g. <anfield>, <liverpool>) and dialect words (e.g. <bevvy> [alcoholic drink], <fagends> [end of a cigarette]). The nature of CHLDL spellings means that respelling strategies, particularly for localised words, will be highly unpredictable. Because of this, we decided to manually add phonology codes for each of these examples – the 255 unique words which were not automatically given a phonological transcription. The process was reasonably fast, and, as noted above, is necessary even in research on spoken language (i.e. in LaBB-CAT, words which cannot be given automatic phonological codes from CELEX must be manually added).

Once these missing phonological codes were added, we looked closely at the phonological transcriptions. We looked at the vowels and consonants in turn, to check the words had been given appropriate phonological codes. Here we look at the START vowel, as an example.

```
dat %>% #take the dat datafile and then
  filter(str_detect(phonemes, "#"))%>%
  #filter those words which
  #include the #START vowel
  #(which is #) and then
  distinct(wordform)%>% #look at only the unique wordforms and then
  pull() #tell me what they are as a vector
## [1]  la         ta         are         shawlies   tart
## [6]  jockeybar  father     barn        park       parly
## [11] bar        martin     half-a-pint clerk      spiceballs
## [16] sarneys    marred     parkie      clayballs  hardfaced
## [21] hardclock  arm        charlies    cargo      glassblower
## [26] arse       armholes   yard        droopy
                                         drawers    ask
## [31] scarper    cart       jars        barmaids   coalyard
## [36] marmalise  start      calm        nextdoor   halfdreaming
## [41] starting   hard       last        threlfalls guardian
## [46] discarded  bare-arsed heart       hartleys   youre
## [51] half
## 943 Levels: 'grotto' 1 a abnabs about across act ago airyated
alas ... zipper
```

Looking through these words, we noticed some problems with the phonological transcriptions. For example, included in this list are the words <nextdoor>, <spiceballs> and <youre>, which do not actually contain a START vowel. We extracted the phonological transcriptions of these words to take a closer look:

```
#show the contents of the phonemes column when the
#wordform column is equal to 'nextdoor'
dat$phonemes[dat$wordform=="nextdoor"]
## [1] "nEkst-d#"
#show the contents of the phonemes column when the
#wordform column is #equal to 'spiceballs'
```

```
dat$phonemes[dat$wordform=="spiceballs"]
## [1] "sp2s-b#lz"
#show the contents of the phonemes column when the wordform column
#is equal to 'youre'
dat$phonemes[dat$wordform=="youre"]
## [1] "j#"
```

These items are transcribed with the # vowel, which is the DISC phonology code for START, but here they should be transcribed with $, which is the DISC code for THOUGHT/FORCE. There are also a few other items, such as *tkisawy* and *bruwer* which appear to have been incorrectly recognised by the OCR software (as we noted above, the OCR process is not perfect). These needed to be fixed, and this was done manually, with code like the following:

```
#overwrite the phonemes column when the wordform column
#matches the text following ==
dat$phonemes[dat$wordform=="nextdoor"]<-"nEkst-d$"
dat$phonemes[dat$wordform=="spiceballs"]<-"sp2s-b$lz"
dat$phonemes[dat$wordform=="youre"]<-"j$"
dat$original[dat$original=="tkisawy"]<-"thisavvy"
dat$original[dat$original=="bruwer"]<-"bruvver"
```

We did this in the same way for the other words too – checking and making corrections to the transcriptions, as appropriate. We followed the same manual process for START as for other phonemes.

14.6. Finding Non-standard Spellings

With a dataset where all words have phonological codes, we were able to look for non-standard spellings containing particular phonemes. Essentially the strategy we used was to identify words with a particular phoneme, and then to pay attention to the *original* column and the *wordform* column. We counted the number of relevant graphemes across the two columns. If the number was the same, we assumed no respelling had taken place (involving that grapheme). If the number was different, we suspected a respelling had occurred. As we did this comparison several times, we wrote a short function in R to speed up the task. The function is:

```
getRespelledWords <- function(phon, ortho){
  dat %>%
    filter(str_detect(phonemes, phon) &
```

```
        str_count(wordform, ortho)!=str_count(original, ortho)) %>%
    distinct(original)%>%
    pull()
}
```

This code creates a function called *getRespelledWords*, which requires two additional pieces of information: a phoneme to focus on, and a grapheme to count. When provided with this information, the function looks at the dataset, examines a subset of the data which contains only words which have the phoneme given, and then compares the number of times the grapheme provided appears in the *wordform* column with the number of times it appears in the *original* column. When the grapheme appears a different number of times in the two columns, we are told which words the mismatch has occurred in. If exactly what is being done here is unclear, we hope it will become clearer with some examples. We begin by examining consonants, and then move onto vowels.

14.6.1. (h)

We begin with (h), so we told the *getRespelledWords* function to focus on words which have the /h/ phoneme, and then to count the number of <h> graphemes in the *original* and *wordform* columns.

```
getRespelledWords("h","h")
## [1] "ullo"     "ere"      "tatty-ead"   "at"        "urry"
## [6] "is"       "lugole"   "er"          "ee"        "atpegs"
## [11] "e"       "ooter"    "ed"          "berkened"  "unchback"
## [16] "ad"      "im"       "gammy-anded" "atchets"   "ippy"
## [21] "ouse"    "ackins"   "ay"          "enries"    "igh"
## [26] "cudda"   "eds"      "ave"         "ead"       "eee"
## [31] "ardfaced" "ardclock" "it"         "andbag"    "avent"
## [36] "armoles" "andler"   "ooever"      "avin"      "arry"
## [41] "ook"     "urry-up"  "musta"       "urdu"      "ill"
## [46] "ell"     "oo"       "ang"         "ey"        "ard"
## [51] "od"      "ookey"
```

We see all the words in which <h> is non-standardly spelled (which actually, here, means that <h> is missing). The function as written above returns only the word types, not tokens, so we do not know from this list how frequently these words are respelled. To do this, we calculated proportions of respellings for words containing <h>. We do this over several steps below. It is possible to do the same thing in fewer steps, but we take this approach for (we hope) greater clarity (in the supplementary materials to this chapter we provide a second function, which does the job of the code below). First we added a column to the datafile called *h_word* and coded for whether the word has /h/ in its phonology (yes = *h word*; no = *not h word*). Then we added a new column called *h_respelled* and coded for whether the number of <h> graphemes matched across the *original* and *wordform* columns (yes = *not respelled*; no = *respelled*). This is essentially what the *getRespelledWords* function does, but the way it is written above doesn't add columns.

```
#add a column called h_word, to label all words which
#contain the phoneme /h/
dat<-dat %>%
  mutate(h_word = str_detect(phonemes, "h"))

#rename FALSE to 'not h word' and rename TRUE to 'h word'.
#This isn't really #necessary, but it helps make the
#tables clearer, later
dat$h_word[dat$h_word==FALSE]<-"not h word"
dat$h_word[dat$h_word==TRUE]<-"h word"

#add a column called h_respelled, to label all instances
#where the /h/ #is spelled non-standardly

dat<-dat %>%
  mutate(h_respelled = str_count(wordform, "h")!=str_
  count(original, "h"))

#rename FALSE to 'not respelled' and rename TRUE to
#'respelled'. This isn't really #necessary, but it helps
#make the tables clearer, later
dat$h_respelled[dat$h_respelled==FALSE]<-"not respelled"
dat$h_respelled[dat$h_respelled==TRUE]<-"respelled"
```

Now we've got the columns, it is easy to look at the data in tabular form. We can count the data in columns and produce a table of the number of times each h_word is respelled.

```
dat %>% #take dat and then
  filter(h_word=="h word")%>% #filter to keep only words
  #that are h words
  count(h_respelled)%>% #count them
```

```
  mutate(prop = prop.table(n)*100) #work out percentages and
  #put them in a column called 'prop'
  #nb: a 'tibble, shown below, is a particular kind of table
  #in the tidyverse
## # A tibble: 2 x 3
##   h_respelled     n  prop
##   <chr>       <int> <dbl>
## 1 not respelled 20   15.0
## 2 respelled    113   85.0
```

It is clear that the representation of <h> dropping is very common in *LYS1*, with 85 per cent of the words being respelled. This is not surprising. /h/-dropping is easy to represent in writing, and indeed we know it is commonly represented in dialect literature, not just in LE but a great many different varieties. It is of course a very well-known marker of low-status speech. Wells (1982: 254), for example, describes /h/-dropping as 'the single most powerful pronunciation shibboleth in England'. It was the second most frequently respelled feature identified in Honeybone and Watson (2013).

14.6.2. (dh)

(dh) was the phonological characteristic which was most commonly found to be respelled in Honeybone and Watson (2013). Like /h/-dropping, (dh)-stopping is quite straightforward to spell, which, along with its local salience, likely contributes to its frequent representation in dialect writing. To examine (dh), we passed the phoneme 'D', which is the DISC phonology code for /ð/, and the orthography 'th' to the *getRespelledWords* function.

```
getRespelledWords("D","th")
##  [1] "dur"         "der's"     "de"    "der"     "wid"
##  [6] "darrell"     "dale"      "dee"   "dem"     "farder"
## [11] "dephil"      "dey"       "dis"   "dese"    "dere"
## [16] "kick-de-can" "bayden"    "dat"   "bruvver" "deyre"
## [21] "den"         "anudder"   "dats"
```

Here we see a considerable number of cases where <th> is spelled as <d> (e.g. <de> for *the*, <dem> for *them*), and the occasional other spelling (e.g. <bruvver> for *brother*). While there is not a large number of different word types here (recall that *getRespelledWords* just shows the unique words), when we look at the tokens, we see that (dh)-respelling is very frequent indeed.

The code below might seem long and complicated, particularly if you are not used to looking at such things. But, essentially, all we have done is replaced all the cases of 'h' with 'dh' or 'th', and replaced the phoneme in the second line of code with 'D'. All of the other code remains the same. This is part of the advantage of working with the spelling data in this way. Once there is an annotated corpus, and once there is a bit of R code which works for one particular spelling feature, it will likely work for other features with just a few tweaks. This means getting started on the analysis can take time, but the analysis becomes more efficient as it progresses.

```
#add a column called dh_word, to label all words which contain
#the phoneme /D/
dat<-dat %>%
  mutate(dh_word = str_detect(phonemes, "D"))

dat$dh_word[dat$dh_word==FALSE]<-"not dh word"
dat$dh_word[dat$dh_word==TRUE]<-"dh word"

#add a column called dh_respelled, to label all instances where
#the /D/ is spelled non-standardly

dat<-dat %>%
  mutate(dh_respelled = str_count(wordform, "th")!=str_
count(original, "th"))

dat$dh_respelled[dat$dh_respelled==FALSE]<-"not respelled"
dat$dh_respelled[dat$dh_respelled==TRUE]<-"respelled"

dat %>%
  filter(dh_word=="dh word")%>%
  count(dh_respelled)%>%
  mutate(prop = prop.table(n)*100)
## # A tibble: 2 x 3
##   dh_respelled      n  prop
##   <chr>         <int> <dbl>
##   1 not respelled  17  7.14
##   2 respelled     221 92.9
```

We see, unsurprisingly given the results in Honeybone and Watson (2013), that the respelling of (dh) is a very common feature indeed – almost 93 per cent of tokens are respelled.

14.6.3. (ing)

So far we have examined two features that were included in Honeybone and Watson (2013), and we have replicated those patterns with the automatically assisted coding. We now turn to (ing), which Honeybone and Watson (2013) did not examine as it was not coded in their dataset. To examine (ing) we passed the phoneme 'N', which is the DISC phonology code for /ŋ/, and the grapheme 'ng' to the *getRespelledWords* function.

```
getRespelledWords("N","ng")
##  [1] "crackin"     "stepdashin" "lettin"      "janglin" "rantan"
##  [6] "livin"       "carryin"    "carryin-out" "chuckin" "bayden"
## [11] "playin"      "saggin"     "skippin"     "shapin"  "spittin"
## [16] "blowin"      "runnin"     "hoppin"      "avin"    "lookin"
## [21] "earwiggin"   "werkin"     "sweatin"     "lampin"  "keepin"
## [26] "everythink"  "standin"    "puddn"       "mornin"  "weedin"
```

There are quite a few different words which have (ing) respelled. The vast majority of respellings seem to be signalling the use of the alveolar [n] rather than the velar [ŋ], except one: <everythink>. There are no spellings which apparently represent the velar-nasal-plus, [ŋg]. Indeed, all of the words returned here have /ŋ/ in <ing> sequences; there are no examples of tokens in which the velar-nasal-plus but not the alveolar [n] would be possible (e.g. words like *wrong* [ɹɒŋg] and *thing* [θɪŋg]). We can tweak the code used so far to examine the frequencies of these respellings.

```
#add a column called ing_word, to label all words which contain
#the phoneme /N/
dat<-dat %>%
  mutate(ing_word = str_detect(phonemes, "N"))

dat$ing_word[dat$ing_word==FALSE]<-"not ing word"
dat$ing_word[dat$ing_word==TRUE]<-"ing word"

#add a column called ing_respelled, to label all instances where
#the /N/ is spelled non-standardly

dat<-dat %>%
  mutate(ing_respelled = str_count(wordform, "ng")!=str_
count(original, "ng"))
```

```
dat$ing_respelled[dat$ing_respelled==FALSE]<-"not respelled"
dat$ing_respelled[dat$ing_respelled==TRUE]<-"respelled"

dat %>%
  filter(ing_word=="ing word")%>%
  count(ing_respelled)%>%
  mutate(prop = prop.table(n)*100)
## # A tibble: 2 x 3
##   ing_respelled     n  prop
##   <chr>         <int> <dbl>
## 1 not respelled    27  42.2
## 2 respelled        37  57.8
```

(ing) words are spelled non-standardly almost 58 per cent of the time, which is not as often as (dh) or (h), but is still a considerable proportion of the dataset. The spelling <in>, signalling the alveolar realisation of (ing), is not specific to Liverpool but is common across the United Kingdom and in other Englishes across the world too. Like /h/-dropping, it is used more often by lower-status speakers and more often in informal styles, and it is also easy to represent in orthography, so it is likely this strategy is used to signal a casual style rather than a regional feature of Liverpool English.

14.6.4. (k) and (t)

The final consonants we consider are (k) and (t). These are both somewhat trickier than the variables considered so far. We examine /k/ first. For words that include a phonological /k/, we can examine the phonemes column, as before. For the spelling, though, we have to be aware that there are different ways of spelling the /k/ phoneme (e.g. <k>, <ck>, <q>). When counting the graphemes in the *original* and *wordform* columns, we need to include any spelling variants. There are several ways to do this, and we use a simple one below. We basically provide a sequence of graphemes (and store it in a vector object called k_list), and loop through the function taking one grapheme at a time. The function returns three sets of results – one for the comparison of each grapheme.

```
k_list<-c("k","c","q")
for(i in k_list) {
  print(getRespelledWords("k",i))
  }
## [1] "skewl" "skea" "skwur"
## [1] "skewl" "skea"
## [1] "skwur"
```

All of the words that are returned are respelled words which have /k/ in their phonology, and the grapheme representing /k/ is indeed respelled in each case, usually because <k> is used instead of one of the other ways that is typical in Standard English (e.g. <sk> for 'school', <sk> for 'square'). While there are accent features being represented in these spellings, they are not features related to the /k/ (they are actually indicative of vowel features, which we address below). All of these /k/ respellings are eye dialect forms.

We now turn to /t/. We passed the phoneme /t/ and the grapheme <t> to *getRespelledWords*, and explored the output.

```
getRespelledWords("t","t")
##  [1] "wudden"     "wha"      "don"      "wanna"   "worrell"
##  [6] "darrell"    "iddle"    "purra"    "gorran"  "gorra"
## [11] "lassnight"  "gorrup"   "gorrany"  "dat"     "wen"
## [16] "less"       "cudden"   "gerrup"   "wouldn"  "butt"
## [21] "norra"      "dats"
```

This is good, but not perfect, since the function has returned <dat> and <dats>. It is quite right to return these words, given what the function was told to do – find words with a phonological /t/ in them, then count the <t> graphemes, and if they don't match across the *original* and *wordform* columns, tell us what the word is. The words <dat> and <dats>, respellings of *that* and *that's*, are returned because there is an extra <t> in the standardly spelled words compared to the original CHLDL spellings. But of course this is because of the respelling of (dh), not because of the respelling of (t). We are developing a more nuanced new function which allows for these types of issue, but for now we'll fix this problem manually.

```
#add a column called t_word, to label all words which contain the
#phoneme /t/
dat<-dat %>%
  mutate(t_word = str_detect(phonemes, "t"))

dat$t_word[dat$t_word==FALSE]<-"not t word"
dat$t_word[dat$t_word==TRUE]<-"t word"

#add a column called t_respelled, to label all instances where
#the /t/ is spelled non-standardly

dat<-dat %>%
  mutate(t_respelled = str_count(wordform, "t")!=str_
count(original, "t"))
```

```
dat$t_respelled[dat$t_respelled==FALSE]<-"not respelled"
dat$t_respelled[dat$t_respelled==TRUE]<-"respelled"

#change the t_respelled column to 'not respelled' for the words
#dat and dats
dat$t_respelled[dat$original=="dat"]<-"not respelled"
dat$t_respelled[dat$original=="dats"]<-"not respelled"

#check the final list of unique words in which /t/ is respelled
unique(dat$original[dat$t_word=="t
word"&dat$t_respelled=="respelled"])
##  [1] "wudden"    "wha"     "don"      "wanna"   "worrell"
##  [6] "darrell"   "iddle"   "purra"    "gorran"  "gorra"
## [11] "lassnight" "gorrup"  "gorrany"  "wen"     "less"
## [16] "cudden"    "gerrup"  "wouldn"   "butt"    "norra"
#calculate proportions
dat %>%
  filter(t_word=="t word")%>%
  count(t_respelled)%>%
  mutate(prop = prop.table(n)*100)
## # A tibble: 2 x 3
##   t_respelled       n  prop
##   <chr>         <int> <dbl>
## 1 not respelled   311  88.9
## 2 respelled        39  11.1
```

We see that /t/ is respelled only 11 per cent of the time – more than /k/, but much less often than the variables examined so far. Even in these few examples, we see evidence of the observation in Honeybone *et al.* (2017) that so-called T-to-R, where /t/ is realised as an approximant or tapped /r/, is the most common type of respelling in the *LYS* texts (e.g. <worrell> *what will*, <darrell> *that will*, <gorrany> *got any*). Other realisations of /t/ (e.g. as [θ] or [h]) are not respelled as frequently.

14.6.5. NURSE

NURSE, like many other vowel variables, and even some consonant variables, is spelled in Standard English with a number of different graphemes (e.g. <ir> *bird*, <ear> *learn*, <or> *word*, <er> *her*, <ur> *hurt*, plus less commonly <eur> *entrepreneur* and <our> *courteous*). As we did with /k/ we can supply a vector of graphemes and loop through them, examining each one in turn.

```
nurse_list<-c("ir","ear","or", "er","ur", "eur","our")
for(i in nurse_list) {
  print(getRespelledWords("3",i))
  }
##  [1] "berkened" "gerl"     "derty"        "shert"
##  [5] "berdcage" "shert-button"
##  character(0)
##  [1] "werd"   "wert"    "clockwerk"    "werkin"    "werld"    "werms"
##  [1] "werd"     "berkened" "gerl"         "derty"
##  [5] "wert"     "shert"    "ergent"       "clockwerk"
##  [9] "berdcage" "werkin"   "shert-button" "werld"
## [13] "werms"
##  [1] "ergent"
## character(0)
## character(0)
```

The results from each iteration of nurse_list begin with ##[1] or, if no results are found, with ##character(0). The first iteration of nurse_list examines <ir> spellings. The results from that comparison begin with *berkened* ('Birkenhead', a town in the nearby Metropolitan Borough of Wirral). Words in this first list are being returned because the standard NURSE spelling is <ir> but something else is being used. Below that list we see 'character(0)', which means no results are found for NURSE words standardly spelled with <ear>. The next list, comparing <or> spellings, begins with <werd> (*word*) and ends with <werms> (*worms*). The other lists follow this. It is worth pointing out that spelling *word* as <werd>, for example, might be considered an eye dialect spelling in the dialect literature of other varieties of English, since one permissible Standard English grapheme for that vowel is being substituted for another. Here, however, it clearly seems to be marking a regional phonological feature. Quantification of the tokens shows that NURSE is respelled quite frequently, 57 per cent of the time.

```
dat %>%
  filter(nurse_word=="nurse word")%>%
  count(nurse_respelled)%>%
  mutate(prop = prop.table(n)*100)
## # A tibble: 2 x 3
##   nurse_respelled   n  prop
##   <chr>         <int> <dbl>
## 1 not respelled    12  42.9
## 2 respelled        16  57.1
```

14.6.6. Summary: Non-standard Spellings in Lern Yerself Scouse (Vol. 1)

Honeybone and Watson (2013) show that non-standard spellings are used along the following cline: (dh) > (h) > NURSE/SQUARE > START > (th) > FOOT/STRUT > (t) > (d) > (k) (see Figure 14.2). They use phonological and sociolinguistic criteria to explain these, pointing out that features which are related to phonological contrast (e.g. the merger of NURSE and SQUARE), and features which are restricted to a smaller geographical region, are more likely to take on social meaning and to be represented in dialect literature, once the restrictions of English spelling are taken into account. For comparison with Honeybone and Watson's summary data in Figure 14.2, we plot the relative differences of non-standard spellings by variable, in Figure 14.7, using the automatically assisted coding we have presented in this chapter.

As expected, the results are very similar. But there are two differences. One is the inclusion of (ing), which was not discussed by Honeybone and Watson (2013). (ing) is one of five features to be represented with non-standard spelling more than 50 per cent of the time. The others are: NURSE, SQUARE and (h) which are involved in phonological contrast and, in the case of (h), a well-known sociolinguistic marker in Liverpool and elsewhere, and also (dh), which is not involved in phonological contrast but which is geographically localised, and which has much opportunity for respelling since it occurs in very high-frequency words such as *the* and *that*. It is perhaps unsurprising that (ing) occurs in this group since, as we noted above, while it is not geographically localised it is, like (h), a well-known sociolinguistic marker.

The other difference is the representation of START, which Honeybone and Watson (2013) show is respelled over 40 per cent of the time, but our automatically assisted analysis shows it is never respelled in *LYS1*. It is,

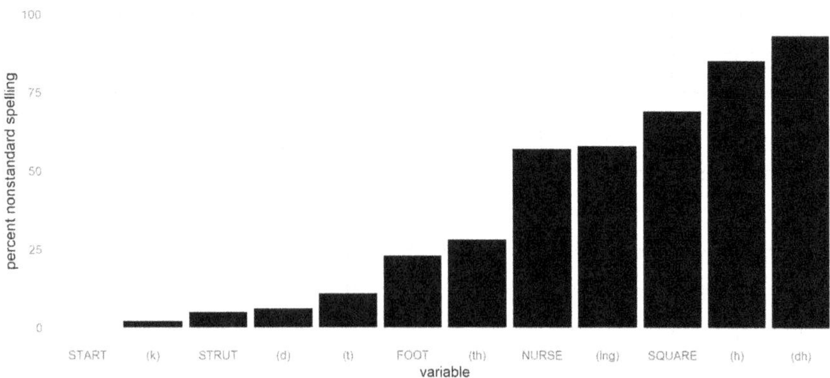

Figure 14.7 Non-standard spellings by variable in *LYS1*

though, respelled in other texts in the *LYS* series (e.g. <she caahn aahf jangle> *she can't half jangle* ['jangle' = talk]; Minard 1972). This difference illustrates the fact that different authors of dialect literature texts will likely have different spelling strategies, even when representing the same dialect.

14.6.7. What Respellings Haven't Been Coded Yet?

As we noted above, Honeybone and Watson (2013) chose some key features they believed to be likely to be respelled in the CHLDL texts, and they coded for them in a corpus. It was what might be termed in corpus linguistics a 'corpus-based' approach. In this chapter we have taken what would be described in corpus linguistic methodologies as a 'corpus-driven' approach, where the analysis has been from the 'bottom up', beginning with a simple comparison of all the standard vs non-standardly spelled words. We have shown how the bottom-up approach, with a fully tagged corpus, allows us to include other features, like (ing), which was respelled reasonably commonly. But of course we don't just have to look at commonly respelled features, we can look at every respelling, to see what emerges. We turn to this now, in our final look at the data for this chapter.

We have coded several features in our dataset from *LYS1* (all those coded for in Honeybone and Watson 2013 plus (ing)), and we can explore any words which are respelled but which haven't yet been identified as belonging to one of the features we have discussed so far. There are 170 words which have some non-standard spelling but which have not yet been coded as such. Thirty-four of these words occur only once. These are:

```
##  [1] "beroo"   "broo"     "cemetry" "closit"     "comeedjun"
##  [6] "fera"    "gisalite" "inter"   "isavvy"     "jeesez"
## [11] "lissen"  "meladdo"  "nuggit"  "o"          "oringe"
## [16] "outa"    "packeta"  "pinta"   "pox-docter" "prestin"
## [21] "quare"   "sarann"   "talint"  "thisavvy"   "togo"
## [26] "treesa"  "ut"       "whereup" "wus"        "ya"
## [31] "yerl"    "yews"     "yis"      "yknow"
```

Some of these words are probably eye dialect forms (e.g. <broo> *brew*, <lissen> *listen*, <oringe> *orange*), while others are eye dialect forms which still indicate a regional form (e.g. <yews> signals the plural of the second person pronoun *you*, and <yis> is perhaps an attempt to signal a pronunciation of the word *yes* with [ɪ], which is a possible form in Liverpool). We also find spellings which indicate reduced or connected speech forms (e.g. <comeedjun> *comedian*, <cemetry> *cemetary*). The words which occur more than once are shown in Figure 14.8.

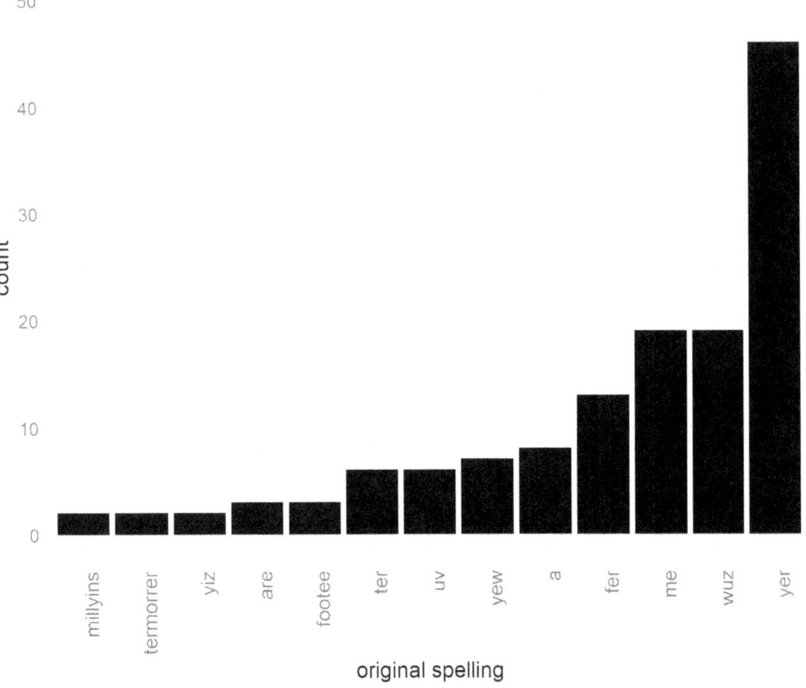

Figure 14.8 Spellings not yet coded which occur more than once

The words are: <millyins> *millions*, <termorrer> *tomorrow*, <yiz> *you* or *youse*, <are> *our*, <footee> *footy*, <ter> *to*, <uv> *of*, <yew> *you*, <a> *of*, <fer> *for*, <me> *my*, <wuz> *was*, <yer> *you* or *your*.

The most common word here is <yer>, which is used for *you* and *your* (<Fill yer boots> p. 69, <I'll snitch on yer> p. 45). This may be an eye dialect form, although it likely implies some sort of phonetic reduction. <wuz> and <uv> are also similar examples, marking *was* and *of*, possibly also with phonetic reduction, which is common in many varieties of English. We also see *of* respelled as <a> (<Yer standin dur like one a Lewises> p. 73). One interesting result is the use of <yiz> to mark what appears to be singular *you* (<O Jeez, another day before yiz, Jack> p. 76). A form such as [jɪz] or [juːz] for singular *you* is not common in LE speech, but it is not unattested in Northern English (see, for example, *See yuz, son!* in the extract from *The Bacons* cited in Honeybone and Maguire, this volume). Constraints of space mean we cannot discuss each of these examples in any detail, but the important point is that these spellings can be identified, even though they only occur a few times. The methodological steps we have taken here help us drill down into the small, but still interesting, details of dialect writing.

14.7. Advantages and Challenges

In this chapter we have outlined a set of steps which can be taken to assist in the automatic analysis of dialect literature. These steps involve the digitisation of the material, the standardisation of the spellings, the addition of phonological transcriptions to the words, and the detection and quantification of spelling variants. The task has presented several challenges. We saw, for example, that is was difficult to tag non-standard words in VARD if there were no spaces between the words. This is not an insurmountable problem, since spaces could be added manually to non-standard spellings, if necessary. But that adds another layer of manual annotation, and, we suggested, would remove a layer of authenticity to the text, unless it was done in a recoverable way. The other manual steps presented another challenge. Organising the data in the corpus takes time, and even during the R analysis there are many steps which must be done by hand.

The main advantage of this set of methods is that it makes the research reproducible and transparent. Following these steps, any other research could take the same text and arrive at the same analysis. Another advantage, which facilitates future research, is that the corpus is fully tagged – or further tags can be automatically generated – so there is no need to identify variables of interest before the analysis starts (we acknowledge that such an approach is likely to be of interest too, of course). Also, because of the automated tagging, it is possible to examine all the respellings, even finding low-frequency respellings which may be interesting but which might have been missed before.

As we said at the outset of this chapter, we do not have a magic button. There are always manual decisions to be made, even if to act as a validation technique for the automated results. Human intervention is still very much an important part of the approach we outline here, and that is a good thing, we think. But the automatically assisted coding of non-standard spellings, and the automatically assisted extraction of spelling forms, each done in a transparent and reproducible way, could offer us a way of comparing larger corpora of dialect literature, across historical and contemporary varieties of English and other languages.

Note

1. We would like to thank Alistair Baron (for writing VARD and answering our questions so efficiently), Jonathan Dunn (for writing the Python code we mention below), members of the Socio- discussion group of the NZILBB, and in particular James Brand (for very useful discussion of our R code), the editors of this volume (for their excellent feedback), and the University of Canterbury, NZ, and The British Academy, UK (grant: VF1\102877) for funding a period of research leave for the first author which facilitated the work on

which this chapter is based. Those mentioned may not necessarily agree with what we've done in this chapter (and possibly everyone has suggestions for how our R code can be improved – we welcome suggestions from all!). All errors remain ours.

References

Alexander, Marc, Fraser Dallachy, Scott Piao, Alistair Baron and Paul Rayson. 2015. Metaphor, popular science, and semantic tagging: Distant reading with the historical thesaurus of English. *Digital Scholarship in the Humanities* 30(suppl. 1), i16–i27. doi:10.1093/llc/fqv045.

Archer, Dawn, Merja Kytö, Alistair Baron and Paul Rayson. 2015. Guidelines for normalising Early Modern English corpora: Decisions and justifications. *ICAME Journal* 39(1), 5–24. doi:10.1515/icame-2015-0001.

Baayen, R., H. R. Piepenbrock and L. Gulikers. 1995. CELEX2 LDC96L14. Web download. Linguistic Data Consortium.

Bailey, George. 2019a. Emerging from below the social radar: Incipient evaluation in the North West of England. *Journal of Sociolinguistics* 23(1), 3–28. doi:10.1111/josl.12307.

Bailey, George. 2019b. Ki(Ng) in the north: Effects of duration, boundary, and pause on post-nasal [g]-presence. *Laboratory Phonology: Journal of the Association for Laboratory Phonology* 10(1), 3. doi:10.5334/labphon.115.

Baron, Alistair and Paul Rayson. 2008. VARD 2: A tool for dealing with spelling variation in historical corpora. *Proceedings of the Postgraduate Conference in Corpus Linguistics.*

Clark, Lynn and Kevin Watson. 2016. Phonological leveling, diffusion, and divergence: /t/ lenition in Liverpool and its hinterland. *Language Variation and Change* 28(1), 31–62. doi:10.1017/S0954394515000204.

Cooper, Paul. 2013. Enregisterment in historical contexts: A framework. PhD thesis, University of Sheffield.

Coupland, Nikolas and Hywel Bishop. 2007. Ideologised values for British accents. *Journal of Sociolinguistics* 11(1), 74–93. doi:10.1111/j.1467-9841.2007.00311.x.

Dobson, Scott. 1986. *Larn Yersel' Geordie.* Norton: Butler Publishing.

Fromont, Robert and Jennifer Hay. 2008. ONZE Miner: The development of a browser-based research tool. *Corpora* 3(2), 173–93. doi:10.3366/E1749503208000142.

Fromont, Robert and Jennifer Hay. 2012. LaBB-CAT: An annotation store. In *Proceedings of the Australasian Language Technology Association Workshop 2012*, 113–17. Dunedin, New Zealand.

Honeybone, Patrick. 2001. Lenition inhibition in Liverpool English. *English Language & Linguistics* 5(2), 213–49. doi:10.1017/S1360674301000223.

Honeybone, Patrick. 2007. New-dialect formation in nineteenth century Liverpool: A brief history of Scouse. In *The Mersey Sound: Liverpool's Language, People and Places*, 106–40. Liverpool: Open House Press.

Honeybone, Patrick and Kevin Watson. 2013. Salience and the sociolinguistics of Scouse spelling: Exploring the phonology of the Contemporary Humorous Localised Dialect Literature of Liverpool. *English World-Wide* 34(3), 305–40. doi:10.1075/eww.34.3.03hon.

Honeybone, Patrick, Kevin Watson and Sarah van Eyndhoven. 2017. Lenition and T-to-R are differently salient: The representation of competing realisations of /t/ in Liverpool English dialect literature. In Sylvie Hancil and Joan Beal (eds), *Perspectives on Northern Englishes*, vol. 96, 83–108. Berlin, Boston: De Gruyter Mouton. doi:10.1515/9783110450903-005.

Jensen, Marie M. 2013. Salience in language change: A socio-cognitive study of Tyneside English. PhD thesis, Northumbria University.

Jensen, Marie M. (forthcoming) 'Geordie style': The enregisterment of stylized Geordie. *English World-Wide.*

Labov, William, Malcah Yaeger and Richard Steiner. 1972. A quantitative study of sound change in progress: Volume 1. Report on National Science Foundation Contract NSF-GS-3287, University of Pennsylvania.

Leach, Hannah, Kevin Watson and Ksenia Gnevsheva. 2016. Perceptual dialectology in northern England: Accent recognition, geographical proximity and cultural prominence. *Journal of Sociolinguistics* 20(2), 192–211. doi:10.1111/josl.12178.

Martin, Daniel. 2016. Well in: How Lady Gaga could teach herself Cilla Black's Scouse. *The Guardian.*

Minard, Brian. 1972. *Lern Yerself Scouse, Vol. 3: Wersia Sensa Yuma?* Liverpool: Scouse Press.

Rayson, Paul and Alistair Baron. 2011. Automatic error tagging of spelling mistakes in learner corpora. In *A Taste for Corpora: In honour of Sylviane Granger*. Studies in Corpus Linguistics 45. Amsterdam: John Benjamins.

Rosenfelder, Ingrid, Josef Fruehwald, Keelan Evanini, Scott Seyfarth, Kyle Gorman, Hilary Prichard and Jiahong Yuan. 2014. FAVE (Forced Alignment and Vowel Extraction) program suite v1.2.2. doi:10.5281/zenodo.22281.

Shaw, Frank. 1966. *Lern Yerself Scouse*. Liverpool: Scouse Press.

Sóskuthy, Márton and Jennifer Hay. 2017. Changing word usage predicts changing word durations in New Zealand English. *Cognition* 166, 298–313. doi:10.1016/j.cognition.2017.05.032.

Tagg, Caroline, Alistair Baron and Paul Rayson. 2012. 'I didn't spel that wrong did i. Oops': Analysis and normalisation of SMS spelling variation. *Lingvisticæ Investigationes* 35(2), 367–88. doi:10.1075/li.35.2.12tag.

Team, R Core. 2018. R: A language and environment for statistical computing. R Foundation for Statistical Computing.

Watson, Kevin. 2007. Liverpool English. *Journal of the International Phonetic Association* 37(3), 351–60. doi:10.1017/S0025100307003180.

Watson, Kevin and Lynn Clark. 2013. How salient is the NURSE~SQUARE merger? *English Language & Linguistics* 17(2), 297–323. doi:10.1017/S136067431300004X.

Watson, Kevin and Lynn Clark. 2017. The origins of Liverpool English. In Raymond Hickey (ed.), *Listening to the Past: Audio Records of Accents of English*, 114–41. Cambridge: Cambridge University Press. doi:10.1017/9781107279865.007.

Watson, Kevin and Lynn Clark. (Th) fronting and stopping in Liverpool and its hinterland. In prep.

Wells, John. 1982. *Accents of English*, 3 vols. Cambridge: Cambridge University Press.

Wickham, Hadley. 2016. *Ggplot2: Elegant Graphics for Data Analysis.* New York: Springer-Verlag.

Wickham, Hadley. 2018. Stringr: Simple, Consistent Wrappers for Common String Operations.

Wickham, Hadley, Romain François, Lionel Henry and Kirill Müller. 2018. Dplyr: A Grammar of Data Manipulation.

Yuan, Jiahong and Mark Liberman. 2008. Speaker identification on the SCOTUS corpus. *Journal of the Acoustical Society of America* 123(5), 3878. doi:10.1121/1.2935783.

Index

EU representative:
Easy Access System Europe
Mustamäe tee 50, 10621 Tallinn, Estonia
Gpsr.requests@easproject.com

www.ingramcontent.com/pod-product-compliance
Lightning Source LLC
Chambersburg PA
CBHW051803230426
43672CB00012B/2616

* 9 7 8 1 4 7 4 4 4 2 5 9 6 *